ESSENTIAL TOOL FOR ACCOUNTANTS
MICROSOFT EXCEL™

JEFFERSON HASKINS CPA

Published by:
Jefferson Haskins Inc.
433 Clinton Ave.
Oak Park, Illinois 60302
Jefferson.haskins1950@gmail.com

ESSENTIAL TOOL FOR ACCOUNTANTS
MICROSOFT EXCEL™

International Standard Book Number (ISBN) 978-0-9711220-3-1
Library of Congress Catalog Card Number: 2011903399

ACKNOWLEDGMENTS

I would like to thank my clients and many students who insisted that I put to paper the topics I have evangelized over the past years.

Special thanks to Vernice, for her support, understanding, and patience while I wrote this book. Also thanks to Vanessa, Jennifer, Andrew, Markita, Briana, Autumn, Mark, Emiliano, Tyshawn (AJ), and Mark Lilly Sr. for giving up some of their time with me so that I could finish the book. I'll make it up to you this summer.

ABOUT THE AUTHOR

Jefferson Haskins is a Certified Public Accountant and president of the consulting firm "Jefferson Haskins Inc." (Jefferson.haskins1950@gmail.com). He has a BS in Accounting from University of Illinois at Chicago and a MS in Accounting from Roosevelt University in Chicago, IL. For many years, Jeff was Assistant Professor of Accounting at Roosevelt University where he taught Accounting, Auditing, Taxes, and Information Systems. He is a collector of everything "Apple" and is proud of his collection of Apple PCs and Macintosh SE for which he wrote general purpose accounting software.

TABLE OF CONTENTS

PART 1 - LEARN THE MECHANICS OF MICROSOFT EXCEL™

CHAPTER 1
INTRODUCTION TO MICROSOFT EXCEL™

Whether you work in a big, medium, or small organization as an accountant, you will be a lot more productive if you master the tools provided in Microsoft Excel™. Microsoft Excel is a spreadsheet product that is included in the Microsoft Office Suite of Products. It is a powerful tool for solving and presenting complex financial problems. Microsoft Excel consists of four (4) objects which we will manipulate to solve financial problems: (1) Application Object (i.e. the Microsoft Excel Program), (2) Workbook Object, (3) Worksheet Object, and (4) Range Object. When you open Microsoft Excel, your screen should look like Figure 1.1.

Figure 1.1

Each time you open Microsoft Excel you create a new Workbook which has a default name of "Book1" until you save it with a more descriptive name. The Workbook has three Worksheets by default. Don't worry, you can add more if you like. On each Worksheet are cells (an intersection of a column and a row). A single cell or a group of adjacent cells is called a range. Cells are important because that is where we enter data in our Microsoft Excel Worksheet. We refer to the active cell (it is the cell with the dark border) using the column heading first, then the Row heading. In Figure 1.1 the active cell is referred to as A1 (Column A and Row 1). Some advanced users use a different notation which we will discuss later. To summarize, when you open Microsoft Excel you are creating

1

four objects which you will use to manipulate and solve financial problems.

MICROSOFT EXCEL 2010 INTERFACE

Look closely at Figure 1.1. If you have used an earlier version of Microsoft Excel (this book is about Microsoft Excel 2010) you will not recognize the user interface (the user interface is the means by which user tells Microsoft Excel what she wants to do). In versions 2003 and earlier the interface consisted of Menus and Toolbars. There was a major redesign of Microsoft Excel in 2007. Now the interface consists of a Ribbon organized around "TABS". Each TAB has a number of "GROUPS" of similar or related activities, and each GROUP has a number of command buttons which are selected to perform the desired activity.

When you open Microsoft Excel the "HOME" tab is selected by default. In order to get anything done you have to be able to navigate to the command button necessary to perform the desired action. So knowing your way around the RIBBON is very important. You have to know which TAB on the RIBBON contains the GROUP and command button you need to perform the desired activity on the Worksheet. On the HOME tab you will find seven GROUPS. (1) The "Clipboard" group has command buttons to paste copied ranges to your worksheet. (2) The "FONT" group allows you to change the Font type and size. (3) The "Alignment" group allows you to align the position of data in the cells as either: left, right, center, top, middle, or bottom. (4) The "Number" group is where you change the format (look) of numbers; General, Accounting, and number of decimal places. (5) The "Styles" group lets you perform the following activities: Conditional formatting, Format as Table, Change Cell types. (6) The "Cells" group is where you insert, delete, and format cells. And (7) the "Editing" group is where you perform the activities: AutoSum, Sort and Filter, and Find and Sort. There are seven TABs on the RIBBON when Microsoft Excel opens, more can be added to perform specialized tasks.

The INSERT tab has groups that let you insert objects into your worksheet. See Figure 1.2.

Figure 1.2

The PAGE LAYOUT tab has groups that let you change the look or layout of your worksheet. See Figure 1.3.

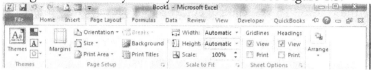

Figure 1.3

The FORMULAS tab has groups that let you manipulate Formulas and also gives you access to Microsoft Excel's many built in Functions. See Figure 1.4.

Figure 1.4

OK do you see a trend here? The DATA tab has groups that let you do things to Data. See Figure 1.5.

Figure 1.5

The REVIEW tab is where you check spelling, add comments, protect the Worksheet and Workbook, and share the Workbook with others. See Figure 1.6.

Figure 1.6

And the final tab is VIEW. This is where you manipulate the view of your Worksheets and also access the Macro capability of Microsoft Excel. See Figure 1.7.

Figure 1.7

3

I know we have not yet discussed most of the items on the RIBBON. So navigate to each tab and try out some of the features so you can get comfortable with the new interface.

BUILDING YOUR FIRST WORKSHEET

OK, be patient. I know you want to now jump in and start creating a spreadsheet. We need to discuss a few more housekeeping details. First, you will want to create a different workbook for each unique subject that you want to track. For example, you would need to create a separate workbook for customers, a separate workbook for products, and a separate workbook for sales. And you would want to use a different worksheet in the workbook for subsets of information. For example, if you are using Microsoft Excel to track financial data, you would want a separate worksheet for each year.

Microsoft Excel is a good tool for creating budgets. Let's create our first spreadsheet and prepare a yearly budget. You should be able to tell by looking at a worksheet the task that you are trying to accomplish. Click in cell A1. Cell A1 is now the "Active Cell". You can always tell the active cell because it is the cell surrounded with a heavy black outline and its contents appear in the formula bar. Type the name of your organization in cell A1 and in cell A2 type "Yearly Budget".

FORMATTING THE WORKSHEET

Now we are going to use Microsoft Excel formatting features to make the titles look pretty. Don't worry that the titles are bigger than the cells holding them. We will fix that problem a little later. After typing in "Your Organization" in cell A1, start typing "Yearly Budget" in cell A2 but before you can finish, Microsoft Excel puts "Your Organization" in that cell. This obviously is not what is intended. What happened? Microsoft Excel has a feature called *"AutoComplete"*. After typing in a few characters of the data that you want to enter, Microsoft Excel checks to see if the new data matches data already in a cell in that column and completes the entry for you. This is very useful and speeds up data entry in a list if it contains multiple instances of the same data. Other times it's aggravating. See Figure 1.8. To fix hit the delete key and type in "Yearly Budget.

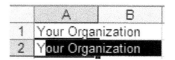

Figure 1.8 **AutoComplete** Yearly Budget

In cell B4 type the month "January". We want an Expense column for each month of the year to spread across our worksheet. There are two ways to do this. One way is to tab to cell C4 and type in February and then tab to cell D4 and type in March, continuing this process until we have typed in all of the months. A quicker way is to use Microsoft Excel's built in *"Series"* function. Microsoft Excel has a number of built-in series (numbers, days, months) that can automatically be placed in adjacent cells. After typing "January" in cell B4, position the cursor on the lower right border of the cell. Notice as you hover over this area (this is called the **fill-handle**) that the cursor changes to a **"+"** sign. Drag the fill handle to the right and the desired months will be placed in the adjacent cells.

Our worksheet needs work. Let's make it look a little more appealing. We need to increase the width of column A so that data does not overflow. Also we need to fix the heading appearance. The easiest way to increase the width of a column is to place the cursor on the right border of the column heading and drag until you achieve desired width. Another method is to select the "Format" command button in the "Cells" Group on the "Home" tab. Select Column Width from menu and set the desired width. See Figure 1.9. Yet another way to change column width is to use the "Auto-Fit feature. Double-click the right border of the column heading and column will automatically re-size to fit it contents.

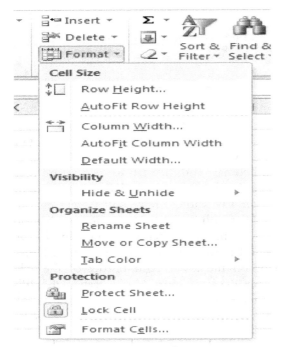

Figure 1.9 set Column Width

Next let's work on the month labels. I like my labels centered in the cell and bold. Click into cell B4, hold down the Shift Key and use the right arrow key and move right until all months are selected. We want to format all of the month labels at the same time. On the HOME tab find the Alignment Group and click the icon for center alignment. Next click the Bold "B" icon on the Font Group to make the text in the month labels bold. Microsoft Excel has a Shortcut Key that allows you to make contents of a cell bold by using the keyboard. The following shortcut key makes your selection bold: CTRL+B. When you see a combination written this way it means to hold down the CTRL key while at the same time typing the next key, "B" in this case. Microsoft Excel has many shortcut keys and we will discuss the more popular ones later. See Figure 1.10. I like my titles to be bold and centered across the affected columns in the worksheet. The effect "centered across affected columns" is called Merge and Center. Select columns A through G and select the Merge and Center Cells icon on the Alignment Group. See Figure 1.10.

Figure 1.10

We are making progress, but I don't like the way the expense numbers are formatted. I want them in the accounting format. Select all of the expense numbers and then on the Numbers Group, (Home tab), click the Comma Style icon. Now the worksheet looks like Figure 1.12. I love it when a plan comes together.

	A	B	C	D	E	F	G
1				Your Organization			
2				Yearly Budget			
3							
4		January	February	March	April	May	June
5	Expenses						
6	Salary	12670	13937	15330.7	16863.77	18550.15	20405.16
7	Payroll Taxes	1267	1393.7	1533.07	1686.377	1855.015	2040.516
8	Office Supplies	200	220	242	266.2	292.82	322.102
9	Postage	50	55	60.5	66.55	73.205	80.5255
10	Insurance	100	110	121	133.1	146.41	161.051
11	Telephone	1023	1125.3	1237.83	1361.613	1497.774	1647.552
12	Rent	2000	2200	2420	2662	2928.2	3221.02
13	Total	17310	19041	20945.1	23039.61	25343.57	27877.93
14							

General $ % .00 .00 Number

Comma Style Icon

Figure 1.11

SAVING THE WORKSHEET

Oops it 5:00 P.M. and we have to leave work for the day. We need to save our work so that we can start on it tomorrow morning. To save a workbook, you have to click the "File Tab" and choose "Save" or "Save As". Both options asks "Where do you want to save the current workbook?" and if this is the first time saving, you are also asked for a name. Make the name descriptive of the content in the workbook. Subsequent saves to the same location can be accomplished by using the shortcut key CTRL+S. See Figure 1.13.

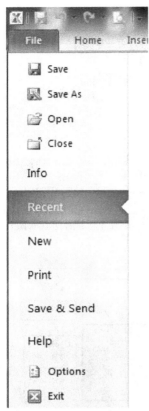

Figure 1.13 Save the Workbook

It is tomorrow and we are back at work. We have the employee name and salary on a separate piece of paper. We think we may be changing salary levels sometime during the year. Would it be neat if we could put this information in our workbook and somehow link it to the Budget Worksheet? And could we be flexible enough so that if we changed the salary levels the change would automatically be reflected in the Budget? The answer is yes to both questions. But how do we do this? Answer to first question requires us to select another worksheet in our workbook. Remember that the default workbook is opened with three (3) worksheets and we need to be able to navigate between worksheets. Notice the bottom of your currently active worksheet (it is the one you see on your screen). There are three "tabs" numbered Sheet1, Sheet2, and Sheet3. To move to and make another worksheet active just click its "tab". See Figure 1.14. While at Figure 1.14 notice the navigation arrows to the left of Sheet1. Click the left most arrow or the right most arrow to navigate to the first and last sheet in the Workbook, respectively. Click the inner most arrows to navigate to the sheet on the left or right of present sheet.

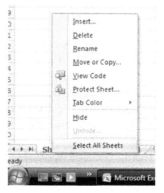

Figure 1.14 Worksheet Tabs

NAMING WORKSHEET TABS

Click on Sheet2 and enter employee name and salary data. See Figure 1.17. Now we have information on two different worksheets, Sheet1 and Sheet2. The question is "will we remember what information is on what sheet three hours from now?" Yes we will because we can rename the tabs. Right click the tab for Sheet1 and on the floating menu select "Rename". The Sheet1 tab text color changes to white on a black background. Type "Budget" and hit enter key. Sheet1 has been renamed to Budget. Do the same to Sheet2 and change name to "Salary". We could also rename a tab by double-clicking it. See Figure 1.15

Figure 1.15 Change name on Tabs

LINKING CELLS FROM DIFFERENT WORKSHEETS

Ok let's answer the second question about flexibility. We can link the information on the salary worksheet to the salary cell on our budget worksheet. Select the Budget worksheet (click its tab) and then click cell B6 (cell holding salary expense data). Type the equal (=) sign in cell B6. Next select the salary worksheet (click its tab). Notice that the total salary is 12,670. Click cell B10 and hit enter key. Notice that you are now back at the BUDGET Worksheet and the salary is 12,670. Look at the formula bar at the top of the BUDGET Worksheet for cell B6. If we already know the cell on the source worksheet for our link we can just type it into the target cell. Type equal sign (=) then name of the source worksheet, next type the exclamation mark (!), follow up with the source cell. In our example we would type "=Salary!B10" in cell B6 of the BUDGET worksheet. The Salary worksheet is the source and the BUDGET worksheet is the target. If source cell is in another workbook use same procedure or if typing precede Worksheet name by Workbook name enclosed in square brackets ([ ]). If source Workbook name has spaces you must also enclose the square brackets and Worksheet name in single quotation marks ('). See Figure 1.16.

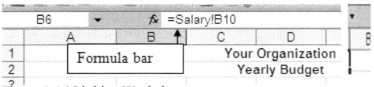

Figure 1.16 Linking Worksheets

Let demonstrate the flexibility concept. Give TJefferson a raise from 1,500 to 1,600. Total salary increases from 12,670 to 12,770. See cell B10 in Figure 1.17. As cell B6 on the BUDGET Worksheet is linked to cell B10 on the Salary Worksheet, salary in cell B6 is automatically updated anytime cell B10 on the Salary Worksheet changes. Now salary expense on our BUDGET worksheet is 12,770. See Figure 1.18 and compare to Figure 1.12.

B14	▾	fx				
	A	B		A	B
2		Salary	2		Salary
3	JD HAWKINS	1200	3	JD HAWKINS	1200
4	LEROBERTS	670	4	LEROBERTS	670
5	GWASHINGTON	1300	5	GWASHINGTON	1300
6	TJEFFERSON	1500	6	TJEFFERSON	1600
7	JADAMS	2300	7	JADAMS	2300
8	BCLINTON	4500	8	BCLINTON	4500
9	BOBAMA	1200	9	BOBAMA	1200
10		12670	10		12770
11			11		

Figure 1.17

	A	B	C	D	E	F	G
1			Your Organization				
2			Yearly Budget				
3							
4		January	February	March	April	May	June
5	Expenses						
6	Salary	12.770.00	14.047.00	15.451.70	16.996.87	18.696.56	20.566.21
7	Payroll Taxes	1.267.00	1.393.70	1.533.07	1.686.38	1.855.01	2.040.52
8	Office Supplies	200.00	220.00	242.00	266.20	292.82	322.10
9	Postage	50.00	55.00	60.50	66.55	73.21	80.53
10	Insurance	100.00	110.00	121.00	133.10	146.41	161.05
11	Telephone	1.023.00	1.125.30	1.237.83	1.361.61	1.497.77	1.647.55
12	Rent	2.000.00	2.200.00	2.420.00	2.662.00	2.928.20	3.221.02
13	Total	17.410.00	19.151.00	21.066.10	23.172.71	25.489.98	28.038.98
14							

Figure 1.18

GETTING HELP WITH MICROSOFT EXCEL

When it comes to Microsoft Excel I have decent skills. But often I need to perform an action in Microsoft Excel and I have no clue as to how to accomplish the desired action. That is when I turn to Microsoft Excel's Help feature. Beginning with version 2003, Microsoft is big on providing help on-line, i.e. you have to be connected to the internet to get the most out of the Help feature. Need help? Hit the F1 key and see your options for help. Microsoft Excel's Help feature provides information on the most popular requests or you can type your question in the Search box. See Figure 1.19.

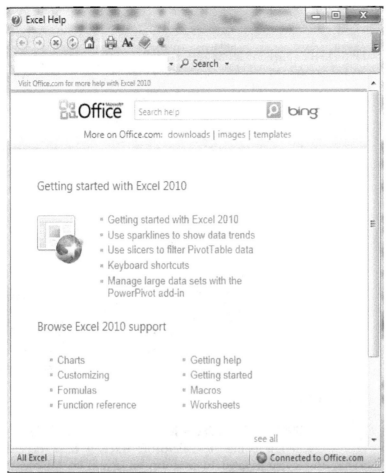

Figure 1.19

CREATE NEW WORKSHEET

Remember that when you start Microsoft Excel you are given three worksheets as a default. If you want to add a new worksheet at the end of existing worksheets, click the "Insert Worksheet" tab at the bottom of the screen (immediately following the last worksheet).

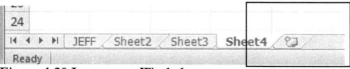

Figure 1.20 Insert new Worksheet

There is an alternative way to insert a new "Worksheet"; right-click a worksheet tab and select "Insert" from the floating menu.

HIDE / UNHIDE WORKSHEET

To hide a worksheet navigate to the "Home" tab, Cells group, and select the Format icon. Select the menu item "Hide & Unhide" and you are presented with choices to (1) Hide /Unhide Rows, (2) Hide/Unhide Columns, and (3) Hide/Unhide Sheet.

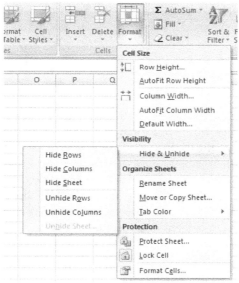

Figure   1.21

Hide/Unhide Worksheet

FORMAT: NUMBERS, LABELS, FONTS, TEXT STYLES, SUB AND SUPERSCRIPTS

All kinds of formatting activities can be accomplished by navigating to the "HOME" tab, "FONT" group or "NUMBERS" group. Can also access Format Cells dialog box by right-clicking a cell containing content and choosing "Format Cells" from the floating menu.

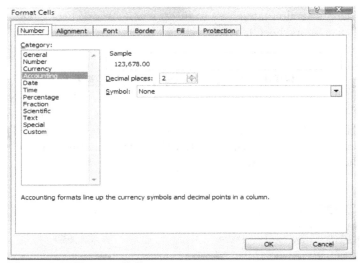

Figure 1.22 Format Cells

Determine what you want to format and click the appropriate tab. If you want to format numbers click the "Number" tab. If you want to change alignment of data in a cell, click the "Alignment tab. If you want to change Font, Border, Fill, and Protection, there are tabs to be clicked to make the desired changes. Be aware that using the DELETE key to remove content from a cell does not also delete the formatting from that cell. To remove formatting from a cell you must go to the HOME tab, EDITING group, and select the "Clear icon" and then the menu item "Clear Formats".

CHANGE SIZE OF ROWS OR COLUMNS

Look at Figure 1.21 which is a picture of the "HOME" tab, "CELLS" group, "FORMAT" icon. Notice the menu items to be selected to change column width or row height. You can also use the mouse and drag rows down (do this from the left margin of the worksheet) to increase size. Also you can increase width of column with mouse. In the column heading select and drag to the desired width.

INSERT / DELETE ROWS, COLUMNS, OR CELLS

To insert a new row into your worksheet click the cell where you want to insert a row and then on the HOME tab, CELLS group, click the "Insert icon" and choose the menu item "Insert Sheet Row". A new row will be inserted above the active cell. Use same procedure to add a new column.

Choose the menu item "Insert Sheet Columns" and a new column is inserted to the left of the active cell. Inserting a new cell requires the same procedure. Select the menu item "Insert Cells" and you will be presented with the "Insert Dialog Box". The dialog box asks you where to shift cells: (1) Shift cells right, (2) Shift cells down, (3) Entire row, and (4) Entire column.

Click the cell you want to delete to make it the active cell and then navigate to the HOME tab, CELLS group and click the "Delete icon". Choose the menu item "Delete Cells" and you will then see the "Delete Dialog Box". Choose one of the following options to tell Microsoft Excel where to shift cells: (1) Shift cells left, (2) Shift cells up, (3) Entire row, or (4) Entire column. The shortcut-key "CTRL+ - (CTRL key minus sign combination) will also delete a cell. Menu items to delete rows, columns, and worksheets are also found under the "Delete icon".

CONDITIONAL FORMATTING

What if you want data in a column or row to look different if a certain criteria is met. Look at our first spreadsheet in Figure 1.17. Suppose we feel it is important to highlight any salary that is greater than $2,300. Microsoft Excel has a feature called "Conditional Formatting" that makes it easy to draw attention to data that meets a certain criteria.

Figure 1.23 Conditional Formatting

Highlight Cells Rules is where we set the criteria that data in cell must meet in order to look different from other cells in a range. To apply conditional formatting you must first select a range of cells.

Let's apply conditional formatting to the column holding salary amounts and highlight any salary greater than $2,300. Highlight the column range holding salary data and then click "Conditional Formatting icon (Home tab, Styles group), and then pick the menu item "Greater Than". There will appear a dialog box where you will set criteria conditions. See Figure 1.24.

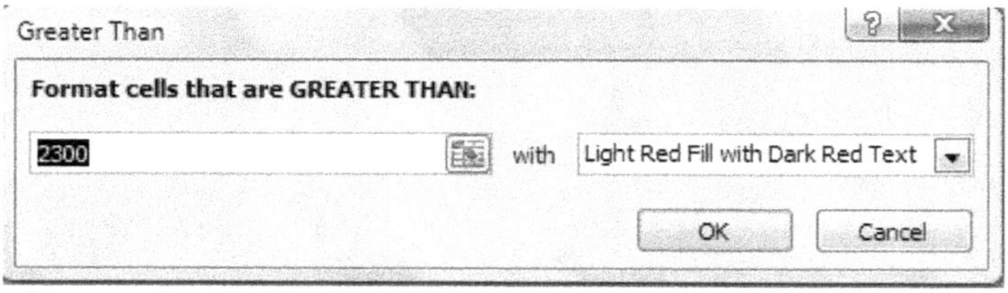

Figure 1.24 Conditional Formatting

Pick the cell to change format and indicate how this cell will appear different.

A	B
	Salary
JD HAWKINS	1200
LEROBERTS	670
GWASHINGTON	1300
TJEFFERSON	1600
JADAMS	2300
BCLINTON	4500
BOBAMA	1200
	12770

Figure 1.25 Conditional Formatting

Notice that data meeting the conditional formatting criteria is highlighted in green.

ADD COMMENTS TO CELLS

If you have a bad memory and cannot recall why data is in a specific cell or you want to give to another user information about a particular piece of data that is not apparent from looking at the spreadsheet, then you need to add a comment to the desired cell. Select the cell where you want to add a comment and then go to the REVIEW tab, COMMENTS group and select the NEW COMMENT icon. Another way to add comments is to right-click a cell and then select the "insert comment" command from the floating menu. Now when you hover over that cell the comment will be displayed.

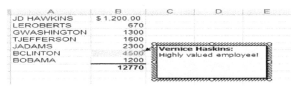

Figure 1.26 Add Comments to Cell

ZOOM IN OR OUT

This next feature comes in handy when I am demonstrating a problem using Microsoft Excel. Students who sit in the back of the classroom (the good students, RIGHT!) will sometimes complain, "I can't see the blackboard, please

17

make the spreadsheet bigger". I can make the spreadsheet display bigger by using the Microsoft Excel ZOOM feature which is located in the status bar at the bottom of the worksheet. Or you can find the ZOOM feature on the VIEW tab, ZOOM group on the RIBBON.

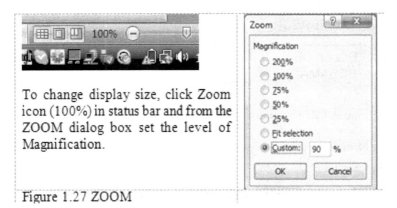

To change display size, click Zoom icon (100%) in status bar and from the ZOOM dialog box set the level of Magnification.

Figure 1.27 ZOOM

MODIFY THE QUICK ACCESS TOOLBAR

Sitting above the ribbon over the "File Tab" is the QUICK ACCESS TOOLBAR. There you will find command buttons to perform often used activities. Thus you do not have to drill down through the RIBBON tabs to find the command button icon needed to perform some activity. I keep icons there for frequently used Microsoft Excel features. I always have a SAVE icon and PRINT PREVIEW icon on my Quick Access Toolbar. The good news is that Microsoft Excel allows you to modify the toolbar, adding and deleting command buttons to make it work the way you want. To modify the Quick Access Toolbar, click on the down arrow just to the right of the toolbar.

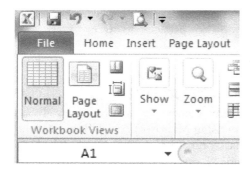

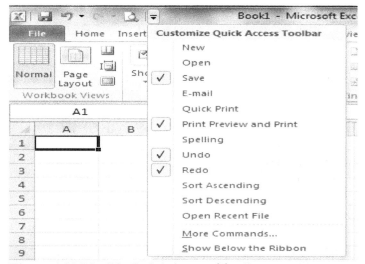

Figure 1.28 Modify Quick Access Toolbar

Command buttons that already appear on the Toolbar are checked. To add more buttons select the menu item "More Commands". While we are here notice that this is also where we can "Minimize" the RIBBON and change the location of the Quick Access Toolbar. From the Microsoft Excel Options dialog box change the Quick Access Toolbar to fit your needs. See Figure 1.29.

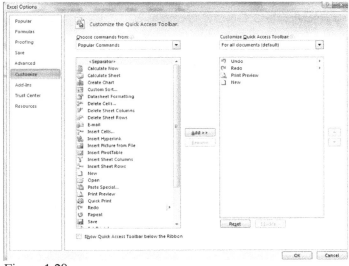

Figure 1.29

19

SELECT NON-CONTIGUOUS CELLS

To select noncontiguous cells click into the first cell you want to select and then hold down the CTRL key while you click the second cell. You then can perform any action at the same time on all of the cells in the selected group.

ENTERING DATA INTO WORKSHEET

The easiest way to get data into your worksheet is to click in a cell and start typing. We have already discussed how to get data into your worksheet by using the LINKING feature. To specify that cell input is text, you must precede data with a single quote mark (**'**). Following table shows what happens when you use the keyboard to enter data.

TYPE IN CELL AND THEN	SELECTED CELL
Hit ENTER Key	Selects cell below in same column
Hit TAB Key	Selects cell to the right in the same row
Hit SHIFT+ENTER Key	Selects cell above in same column
Hit SHIFT+TAB Key	Selects cell to the left in same row

CREATING DROP DOWN LIST IN A CELL

To save typing time you can create a drop-down list and pick for input an item that already appears in a column. Right-click the cell in the column where you want to enter data and select the menu item "Pick From Drop-down List". From the resulting list click on the item desired and Microsoft Excel will put it in the selected cell. See Figure 1.30.

	Postage	50.00
0	Insurance	100.00
1	Telephone	1,023.00
2	Rent	2,000.00
3		
4	Total	17,410.00
5	Expenses	
5	Insurance	
6	Office Supplies	
7	Payroll Taxes	
8	Postage	
9	Rent	
	Salary	

Figure 1.30

USE THE KEYBOARD AND SHORTCUT KEYS TO ENTER DATA

I like using Shortcut keys because they work the same across the many versions of Microsoft Excel. Following table lists the more popular shortcut keys.

Action Performed	Shortcut key
Center text in a row of table and text box	CTRL+E
Copy cell or range	CTRL+C
Cut data from cell or range	CTRL+X
Find data in Worksheet	CTRL+F
Go to a specific cell	CTRL+G
Go to end of Worksheet, last occupied cell	CTRL+END
Go to first cell in Worksheet	CTRL+HOME
Go to a specific cell	F5
Help	F1
Insert a function into Worksheet	SHIFT+F3
Hyperlink	CTRL+K
Open new Workbook	CTRL+N
Open new file	CTRL+O
Paste contents from clipboard	CTRL+V
Print Worksheet	CTRL+P
Replace contents of a cell	CTRL+H
Save a Workbook	CTRL+S
Select All Cells in a	CTRL+A

21

Worksheet	
Spell check	F7
Undo last action	CTRL+Z
Redo last action	CTRL+Y

FIND AND REPLACE DATA IN CELLS

Revisit our first spreadsheet. I want to find expense category "Rent" and replace with "Prepaid Rent". Hit the CTRL+F key combination and Microsoft Excel gives you a dialog box where you enter what you want to find. After finding desired data, click the "Replace" tab to get the dialog box for replacing data in a cell. On the "Find" tab hit the "Find All" command button to see the find results. You will be told the exact location of the data that you seek in the following format: Workbook name, Worksheet name, cell (row and column), the value in that cell, and the number of instances found. See the Find and Replace dialog box on the right side of Figure 1.31.

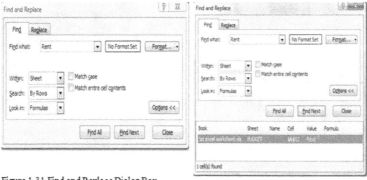

Figure 1.31 Find and Replace Dialog Box

Ok click the "Replace" Tab and a dialog box appears so that you can enter the required criteria. See Figure 1.32. Next hit "Replace" or "Replace All" to complete desired operation.

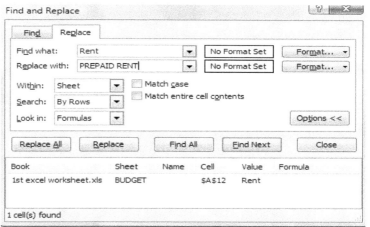

Figure 1.32

MOVE CELLS TO ANOTHER LOCATION

You can move contents of a cell or of a range from one location to another in Microsoft Excel. Click into the cell or select the range you want to copy. Now you have a decision to make: (1) Do you want to copy contents to another location while leaving source content in present location or (2) Do you want to move contents to a new location removing content from its present location. The answer determines whether you use Microsoft Excel's "Copy" feature or Microsoft Excel's "Cut" feature. If the answer is (1) then use Copy feature and if answer is (2) use the Cut feature. Both features are found on the HOME tab, CLIPBOARD group. These features must be used with the "Paste" feature found in the same location.

Let's discuss the Copy feature first. To copy content from one location to another (having two sets of the same content on the same worksheet) click the "Copy icon" on the HOME tab, CLIPBOARD group and then click the destination cell. Next click the "Paste icon" which is located in the same place on the RIBBON to paste the copied content to the new location. Notice the "SMART TAG" at the new location. The Smart Tag gives you options of how you want to paste the contents to the new location. See Figure 1.33. If you are in a hurry use the shortcut keys CTRL+C to copy the content and CTRL+V to paste the content.

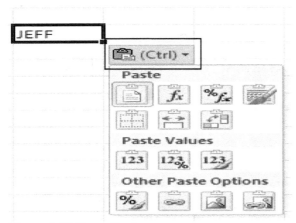

Figure 1.33 Paste Options

If you just want to move content from one location to another use the Microsoft Excel "Cut feature". Click the cell or range to cut and then click into the destination cell. Click Paste to place copied content into new location. I forgot to tell you earlier that with both the Copy and Cut feature you can skip the Paste feature by just hitting the Enter key after applying the copy or cut feature. After hitting the Enter key content will be pasted to the new location. Again if you are in a hurry use the shortcut keys CTRL+X to cut and CTRL−V to paste.

NAVIGATION AROUND A LARGE SPREADSHEET

How much of your worksheet you see at one time on your screen depends on the size of your computer's monitor. On my notebook computer I can see columns A through R and rows 1 through 32. The size of a worksheet in Microsoft Excel 2010 is 1,048,576 rows and 16,384 columns. So you see you will not be able to look at all of your data in the worksheet at one time. We need a way to navigate through a large worksheet and a way to have what is important on the screen at one time. On the right edge and the bottom left edge of your worksheet is a "SCROLL BAR". The SCROLL BAR on the right edge lets you scroll from the top of the worksheet to the last row containing data. The bottom SCROLL BAR lets you scroll (move) from the Column A to at least Column R on my computer.

Use the shortcut key F5 to navigate to any specific cell on the worksheet. Hit the F5 key and enter the destination cell reference in the "GO Dialog Box". The CTRL+G shortcut key combination will also display the "Go To" dialog box.

Figure 1.34 F5 key to go to specific cell

Another way to quickly navigate around large worksheets is to use the PAGEUP key and the PAGEDOWN key in lieu of the SCROLL BARS. Also if you hit the HOME key it will take you to Column A of the current row.

FREEZE PANES

If you want to freeze (make static) a column label or Row heading use the Microsoft Excel FREEZE PANES feature. This feature is found on the VIEW tab, WINDOW group. After you freeze a column or row it will stay on the screen as you scroll right or down the worksheet. Of course when done using this feature you can UNFREEZE the worksheet (click the Freeze Panes icon and select Unfreeze option). In order for this feature to work properly (freeze the desired column and row), the Active Cell must be one row below the freeze area and one column to the right of the desired freeze area.

25

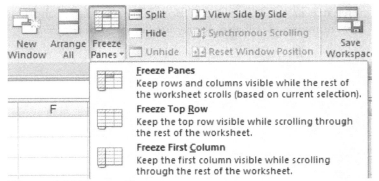

Figure 1.35 Freeze Panes

USE THE DATA FORM

Data can be entered directly into the Worksheet or you can use the "Data Form". In previous versions of Microsoft Excel the Data Form was easy to find. In Microsoft Excel 2010 it is hidden away in the Quick Access Toolbar (QAT). Thus we must modify the QAT before we can use the Data Form. Here are the steps:

1. Click the arrow next to the Quick Access Toolbar. Click "More Commands". In the "Choose Commands From" box, click "All Commands". In the resulting list box select "Form" button and then click "Add". Now Data Form icon appears on the QAT.

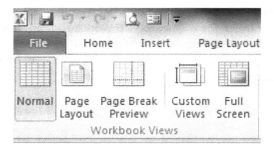

2. To use a Data Form you first have to enter field names (column names) into a row.

3. Enter data in one row below. This tells Microsoft Excel that this is a data row rather than a row containing labels.

4. Select the first two rows

5. Click on the" Form" icon on the QAT, to display the Data Form.

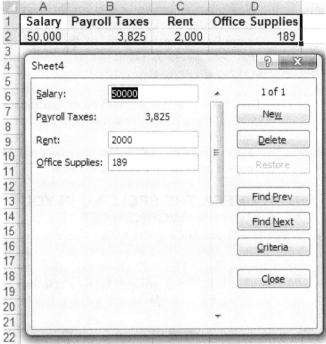

Figure 1.36

6. The caption of the data form in this example is "Sheet4". That tells you that you are entering data on "Sheet4".

7. There is a text box for each column that has a label. Text boxes for the first row containing data (i.e., not a row containing labels) is already filled-in when you deploy the data table. Navigate between text boxes by using the TAB key. If you press ENTER key that is equivalent to pressing NEW button before you are finished recording data.

8. Notice that there is no text box to fill-in for Payroll. That is because Payroll is a calculated value based on

the following formula: =A1*.0765. The Data form omits the text box for calculated items, so you don't accidentally enter a value that overrides calculated amount.

9. If the text boxes contain the data you want, click the "New" button and enter data for the next row. When you click the "New" button, data from Data Form is inserted into the next row of the Worksheet and a new Data Form is displayed to collect data for the next row.

10. The "Find Prev" and "Find Next" buttons allow you to scroll from row to row on the Worksheet to locate a specific piece of data. This comes in handy if you want to find a record (remember that a row represents a record in a table) to edit or to delete.

CHECK THE SPELLING IN YOUR WORKSHEET

If you are not a good speller don't worry. Microsoft Excel has a feature to find misspelled words and helps you correct misspellings. The spell-check feature is found on the REVIEW TAB, Proofing group. Or, after selecting a cell, use the shortcut key F7 to display spelling dialog box.

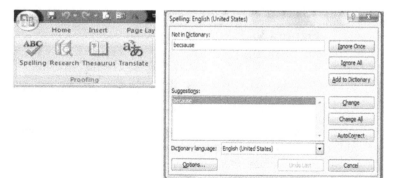

Figure 1.37

ADD A GRAPHIC TO THE WORKSHEET

Pictures can be placed on the Worksheet to make it look more pleasing or a graphic can be inserted to better explain something in the Worksheet. On the INSERT TAB select the picture icon to add a graphic to your worksheet.

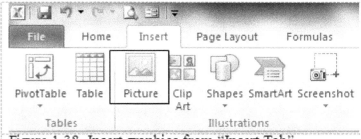
Figure 1.38. Insert graphics from "Insert Tab"

SUMMARY

Microsoft Excel has a new interface. Menus and ToolBars have been replaced by the Ribbon. Provided on the RIBBON are tools to change the appearance of Worksheets. There are several formats available to save workbooks. To help you remember why a particular value is in a cell, use the comment feature. The Quick Access Toolbar (QAT) can be modified to gain access to frequently used features. There are a number of ways to get data into a Worksheet. Especially popular is the use of shortcut keys. The data form speeds up entering data into a Worksheet.

CHAPTER 2
MICROSOFT EXCEL™ FORMULAS AND FUNCTIONS

Microsoft Excel is a great tool for keeping lists of things that are important to you. However, we usually want more functionality from Microsoft Excel. We want to answer questions about the list. For example, if we have a list of salesmen and their annual sales we can ask and get answered several questions. Questions that can be answered are: (1) what are total sales for the year, (2) what are average sales for the year, (3) which salesman had the most sales, (4) which salesman has the least amount of sales, and (5) a host of statistical questions. The list by itself is just data. Answers to questions about data are called information. In my opinion, the great use of Microsoft Excel is to perform calculations on data so that we can answer questions. In this chapter we discuss how to use formulas and Microsoft Excel's built-in functions to perform calculations on data. In later chapters we discuss how to use "Visual Basic For Applications" to create your own functions.

You must begin a formula with the equal sign (no spaces are allowed before the equal sign). A formula usually consists of a combination of the following: (1) mathematical operators (+,-,*, /, ^), (2) cell references, (3) numbers, (4) text, or (5) worksheet functions (SUM, AVERAGE, MAX, MIN, COUNT, ROUND, or SQRT.). The maximum number of characters allowed in a formula is 8,192.

As you enter a formula in a cell, it shows the results of the calculation. The actual formula appears in the Formula Bar. To edit a formula in a cell, click the cell and press the F2 key. You can also click into the Formula Bar to edit a formula.

CALCULATION OF FORMULA

By default, formulas are calculated immediately after they are entered into a cell. If you change the contents of a cell that is used in a formula, the formula immediately gets recalculated. This can slow down things if you have a lot of formulas relying on the same cells. You can change from automatic calculation to manual calculation and gain control over when formulas are calculated. To change from automatic to manual calculation, click the "File Tab", next click Microsoft Excel Options and then click the Formulas

Category. Under Workbook Calculation choose the "Manual option".

Now you are in control of when formulas are recalculated. To recalculate formulas that changed since the last calculation in all open Workbooks, press the F9 key. For recalculation only in the Active Worksheet, press the SHIFT+F9 keys. And to recalculate formulas in all open Workbooks, regardless of whether they have changed since last calculation, press the CTRL+ALT+F9 keys.

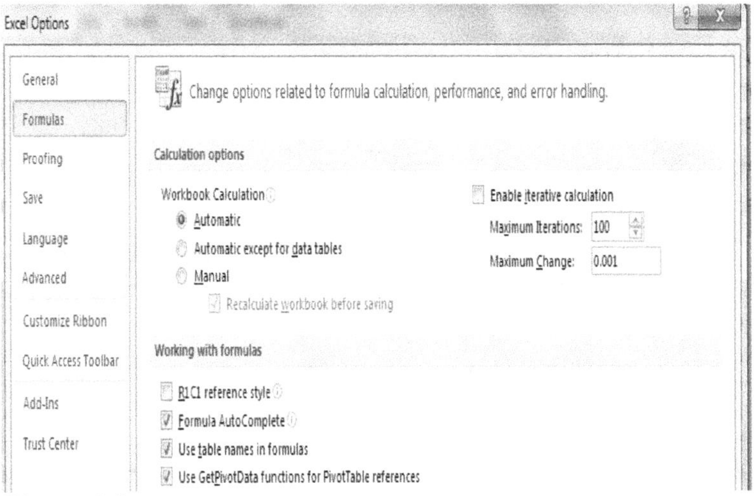

Figure 2.1

MATHEMATICAL OPERATORS

Most formulas use one or more mathematical operators. If a formula has more than one operator you need to know the order in which they will calculate. The following table shows operator precedence (which mathematical operator calculates first).

RANK	OPERATOR	ACTION
1	-	Negation
2	%	Percent
3	^ (Caret)	Exponentiation
4	* , /	Multiplication, Division
5	+ , -	Addition, Subtraction
6	&	Text Concatenation
7	=, <>, <=, >=, >, <, >	Comparison

If you have a complex formula you can change precedence order by using parentheses.

USING OPERATORS IN FORMULAS

Following are examples of the most commonly used operators. If you want to add two numbers together use the plus (+) operator. Add the number in cell B2 to the number in cell B3.

B4	▼	f_x =B2+B3	
	A	B	
1	Month	Rent	
2	January	1,240.00	
3	February	1,400.00	
4		2,640.00	

Figure 2.2 Addition

In figure 2.2, notice that the results of the formula are in the cell where the formula is located and the actual formula is displayed in the formula bar.

B4	▼	f_x =B3-B2	
	A	B	
1	Month	Rent	
2	January	1,240.00	
3	February	1,400.00	
4		160.00	

Figure 2.3 Subtraction

If you want to subtract two numbers use the minus sign (-). Subtract the number in cell B2 from the number in cell B3.

B4	▼	f_x =B2*B3	
	A	B	
1	Month	Rent	
2	January	1,240.00	
3	February	1,400.00	
4		1,736,000.00	

Figure 2.4 Multiplication

If you want to multiply two numbers use the asterisk sign (*) and use the forward slash (/) to divide one number by another. Multiply the number in cell B2 by the number in cell B3. Next divide the number in cell A1 by the number in cell A2.

A3	▼	*fx* =A1/A2

	A	B	(
1	100		
2	5		
3	20		

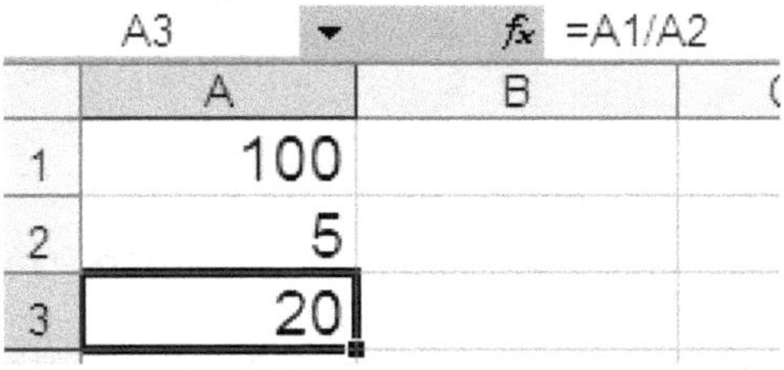

Figure 2.5 Division

To raise one number to a power use the exponentiation – **caret sign (^)**. Raise the number in cell A1 by the number in cell A2.

A3	▼	*fx* =A1^A2

	A	B	C
1	2		
2	5		
3	32		

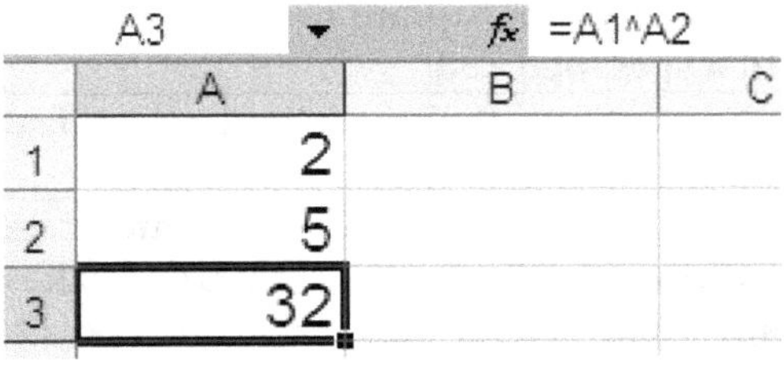

Figure 2.6 Exponentiation

I don't know how useful the following operator is in formulas. Think hard to see if you can come up with a use for the text concatenation operator.

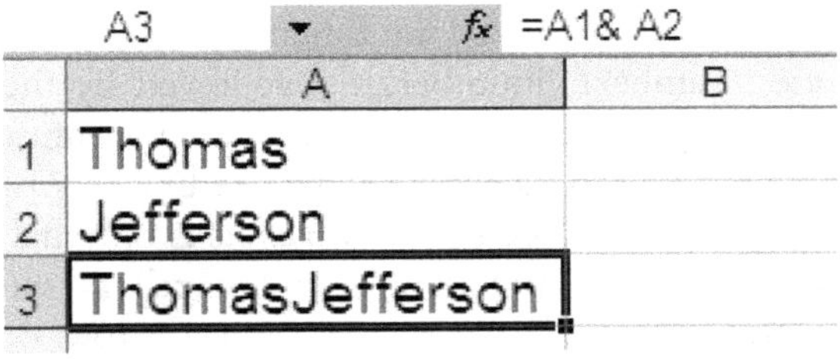

A3	▼	*fx* =A1& A2

	A	B
1	Thomas	
2	Jefferson	
3	ThomasJefferson	

Figure 2.7 Text concatenation

MICROSOFT EXCEL'S BUILT-IN FUNCTIONS

In addition to the many formulas you can create from scratch, Microsoft Excel comes prepackaged with predefined formulas (Worksheet Functions) that you can use to perform calculations on data. Following is a table of the most used functions. Functions, just like formulas, must begin with the equal sign.

FUNCTION	WHAT IT DOES
SUM	Adds numbers in specified cells
AVERAGE	Calculates average of numbers in specified cells
COUNT	Counts the number of items in specified cells
MAX	Finds the largest value in specified cells
MIN	Finds smallest value in specified cells
ROUND	Rounds a number in a specified cell
SQRT	Calculates the square root of a number in a specified cell
NOW ( )	Shows time the workbook was last opened
LOGICAL IF	Conditional formula. Evaluates an expression and if TRUE takes specified action, and if FALSE takes a different action

SUM FUNCTION

In my spreadsheets the most commonly used Microsoft Excel function is SUM. Type the equal sign, SUM function, and the beginning parentheses and Microsoft Excel gives you the required arguments for the function. In this case the arguments are "number1, [number2].... followed by the closing parentheses. **Arguments** are required items you must supply to the function. In this example the square brackets [ ] indicate that the argument enclosed in the brackets is optional. The usual placement of this function is in the cell at the bottom of a column of numbers or adjacent to a row of numbers.

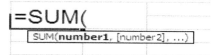

Figure 2.8 SUM Function

If the numbers you want to sum are in contiguous cells (i.e. adjacent to each other) the function is written as **"=SUM(B6:B12)".** Microsoft Excel interprets this to mean add up the numbers found in cells B6 through B12. If the numbers you want to add are in non-contiguous cells write the formula as "=SUM(B13,D13,F13)" which means sum the numbers found in cells B13, D13, and F13.

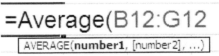

B13	▼	f_x =SUM(B6:B12)
	A	B	C
1			Your (
2			Yea
3			
4		January	February
5	Expenses		
6	Salary	12,770.00	14,047.00
7	Payroll Taxes	1,267.00	1,393.70
8	Office Supplies	200.00	220.00
9	Postage	50.00	55.00
10	Insurance	100.00	110.00
11	Telephone	1,023.00	1,125.30
12	Rent	2,000.00	2,200.00
13	Total	17,410.00	19,151.00

Figure 2.9 |

Summing non-contiguous cells

AVERAGE FUNCTION

What if you want to know the average Rent expense for the months of January to June in your budget? The AVERAGE FUNCTION can answer that question. In this example Rent expense is found in cells B12 to G12. And the average is found with the function "=AVERAGE(B12:G12). The beginning cell and the ending cell are separated by the colon sign (:). If you want to average numbers located in non-contiguous cells write the function as follows: "=AVERAGE(number1,number2...)".

=Average(B12:G12

AVERAGE(**number1**, [number2], ...)

Figure 2.10

COUNT FUNCTION

Use the COUNT FUNCTION to determine the number of cells in a range that contain numbers. The first argument "value1" is usually a range of cells. Argument "value2" usually contains some criteria used in the count.

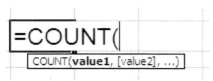

Figure 2.11

MAX AND MIN FUNCTIONS

Accountants sometimes have to separate mixed costs into their fixed and variable components. One of the ways to make the separation is to use the HIGH-LOW method and the formula for a straight line. We will discuss the details of this method in a later chapter. Now I want to use it just to demonstrate how the MAX and MIN functions can be useful.

	F28	▼	f_x =C20-(G26*B20)				
	A	B	C	D	E	F	G
1							
2							
3		(000)	Annual				
4	Store	SQ Feet	Sales				
5	1	1.7	3.7				
6	2	1.6	3.9				
7	3	2.8	6.7				
8	4	5.6	9.5				
9	5	1.3	3.4				
10	6	2.2	5.6				
11	7	1.3	3.7				
12	8	1.1	2.7				
13	9	3.2	5.5				
14	10	1.5	2.9				
15	11	5.2	10.7				
16	12	4.6	7.6				
17	13	5.8	11.8				
18	14	3	4.1				
19							
20	High	5.8	11.8				
21	Low	1.1	2.7				
22							
23				V = change in y / change in x			
24				$=(y_2 - y_1) / (x_2 - x_2)$			
25							
26				$=(11.8 - 2.7) / (5.8 - 1.1) =$			1.93617
27							
28				$Y_2 - VX_2$		0.570213	

Figure 2.12

In this example we have a spreadsheet that holds square feet and annual sales for 14 stores. What we need to know is which store has the highest number of square feet and which store has the fewest number of square feet. Using the MAX function we can calculate the store with the highest square feet as "=MAX(B5:B18)" (which is store number 13 with 5.8 square feet). To find the store with the fewest number of square feet use the MIN function; "=MIN(B5:B18)". Store number 8 has the fewest square feet of 1.1. To get MAX value in a contiguous range of cells, write the argument as shown above B5:B18. For non-contiguous cells write arguments as B1, B5, B17, ect.

Figure 2.13

ROUND FUNCTION

My students are always interested in the ROUND Function. This past semester one of my students asked me if she was going to get a grade of "A" for the Advanced Cost Accounting course she had just completed. Her average for the midterm and final was 89.975. To earn an "A" a student's average had to be at least 90. What grade do you think I gave her?

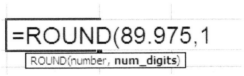

Figure 2.14

The required arguments are: (1) the number to be rounded "number" and (2) how many digits to round: "num_digits", 1 in this case so that the number 9 is rounded up.

SQUARE ROOT FUNCTION (SQRT)

On the following spreadsheet I was working on a what-if problem to evaluate the purchase of an asset. It required calculation of a variance and the standard deviation based on that variance. Don't worry about the statistics now. I will cover statistical functions later in the book. Looking at the worksheet you can see that the Standard Deviation is the square root of the variance. The variance can be found in cell D9. In cell D12 I used the SQRT function to calculate the standard deviation.

	A	B	C	D	E	F	G	H
1								
2			Asset X					
3	X_i	$P(X_i)$		Variance				
4	Return	Probability	$X_iP(X_i)$	$[X_i\text{-}E(X)^2P(X_i)]$				
5	8%	0.10	0.008	0.0001225				
6	9%	0.20	0.018	0.000125				
7	11%	0.30	0.033	7.5E-06				
8	14%	0.40	0.056	0.00025				
9	Expected Rate of Return		11.50%	0.000505				
10	= E(X)							
11		Standard Deviation						
12		=Square Root of Var.	0.022472205			=SQRT(D9)		
13		Coefficient Variation tells us the percentage of						
14		variation of our sample. It equals Standard Deviation / Expected Rate of Return						
15		Coefficient Variation = .014177447/.107		=		19.54%		

There are a number of Microsoft Excel features employed on this worksheet that I would like to discuss since we have it handy. All of the features we will be discussing can be found in the "Format Cells" group on the Home tab of the RIBBON. In rows 1 and 2 the text is bold and I used the merge and center feature. Cells C9, D9, and F15 are surrounded by a heavy black border (See the Border Tab of the Format Cells dialog box). And the fancy column labels in A3, B3, C4, and D4 use the Superscript and Subscript features found on the Font tab of the Format Cells dialog box.

NOW FUNCTION

The NOW function shows the date and time data was entered into the worksheet and shows the last time the workbook was opened. It changes each time you save the workbook, it updates to the present time when the workbook is reopened. The Now Function, unlike other functions, does not have any arguments. To apply the NOW function, type the equal sign, followed by the function name and an open and a close parentheses.

=NOW(

NOW()

Figure 2.16

01/03/10 20:16

Date and Military time (24 Hour Clock)

LOGICAL IF FUNCTION

The LOGICAL IF Function is a conditional formula that performs different actions depending on whether a logical test evaluates to TRUE or to FALSE. It is great for displaying messages when certain conditions are met. The syntax for this function is "=IF(logical test, True, False)". The first argument is a logical test to be evaluated by Microsoft Excel. The second argument is the action to take if the logical test evaluates TRUE. The third argument is the action to take if the logical test evaluates FALSE.

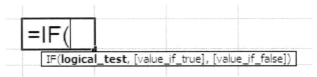

Figure 2.17 Logical IF syntax

Here is a Logical IF function used to display a message. A logical test is made to determine if cell B12 is greater than 1,000. If this is true then the message "TOO HIGH" is displayed in the cell where the Logical IF function is located. If function evaluates to False, the message "OK" is displayed.

	A	B	C	D	
	B16		*fx*	=IF(B12>1000,"TOO HIGH", "OK")	
4		January	February	March	
5	Expenses				
6	Salary	12.770.00	14,047.00	15,451.70	
7	Payroll Taxes	1,267.00	1.393.70	1.533.07	
8	Office Supplies	200.00	220.00	242.00	
9	Postage	50.00	55.00	60.50	
10	Insurance	100.00	110.00	121.00	
11	Telephone	1.023.00	1,125.30	1.237.83	
12	Rent	2.000.00	2.200.00	2.420.00	
13	Total	17.410.00	19.151.00	21.066.10	
14					
15					
16		TOO HIGH			
17					

Figure 2.18

USING PARENTHESES TO ORGANIZE COMPLEX FORMULAS

Sometimes it is necessary to use parentheses to organize complex formulas due to the precedence rules of operators. For example if we want to sum 5 plus 4 and divide that quantity by 2 the result will be 4.5. If we write our formula 5+4/2 the result will be 7. Due to operator precedence the division calculates first and the result is 5+2 = 7. To get the intended result we have to use parentheses. We must write our formula as (5+4)/2, resulting in 4.5. Expressions inside parentheses are evaluated first and then are subjected to other operators.

CELL AND RANGE REFERENCE

After you have created a formula you can use it anywhere in the worksheet by copying it from one cell to another. By default, Microsoft Excel will reinterpret the cell reference to fit the formula's new location. This is called "Relative" cell reference. There are four types of cell references: (1) Relative, (2) Absolute, (3) Row Absolute, and (4) Column Absolute.

RELATIVE CELL REFERENCE

B13	▾	fx =SUM(B6:B12)

	A	B	C
4		January	February
5	Expenses		
6	Salary	12.770.00	14.047.00
7	Payroll Taxes	1.267.00	1.393.70
8	Office Supplies	200.00	220.00
9	Postage	50.00	55.00
10	Insurance	100.00	110.00
11	Telephone	1.023.00	1.125.30
12	Rent	2.000.00	2.200.00
13	Total	17.410.00	
14			

C13	▾	fx =SUM(C6:C12)

	A	B	C
4		January	February
5	Expenses		
6	Salary	12.770.00	14.047.00
7	Payroll Taxes	1.267.00	1.393.70
8	Office Supplies	200.00	220.00
9	Postage	50.00	55.00
10	Insurance	100.00	110.00
11	Telephone	1.023.00	1.125.30
12	Rent	2.000.00	2.200.00
13	Total	17.410.00	19.151.00

Figure 2.19 Relative Cell Reference

The formula in cell B13 (=SUM(B6:B12)) sums the numbers in cells B6 to B12. If we copy that formula and paste it in cell C13 it becomes "=SUM(C6:C12)". Microsoft Excel has reinterpreted the formula to fit its new surrounding cells.

ABSOLUTE CELL REFERENCE

Sometimes we do not want Microsoft Excel to reinterpret the cells used in a formula after we copy it to a new location. To keep the same cell reference after copying a formula to a new location we have to make the cell reference fully "Absolute". Fully absolute means we want both the row reference and the column reference to stay the same after moving to a new location. A reference is made absolute by placing the dollar sign ($) in front of the cell reference. For example if we want the formula reference to remain "B6:B12" after moving to a new location we must write it as follows: $B$6:$B$12. In the following worksheet we calculate a variance in rows D5:D8. Variance is calculated by squaring the difference between a specific data point and the average of all data points. So data points (and the cell reference thereto) will change but the average remains the same (i.e. Absolute.) So in our example the cell references A5:A8 and B5:B8 will change as data points change but the average located in cell C9 will remain constant.

D5		▼	fx =((A5-$C$9)^2*B5)	
	A	B	C	D
1				
2			Asset X	
3	X_i	$P(X_i)$		Variance
4	Return	Probability	$X_iP(X_i)$	$[X_i-E(X)^2P(X_i)]$
5	8%	0.10	0.008	0.0000729
6	9%	0.20	0.018	0.0000578
7	11%	0.30	0.033	0.0000027
8	12%	0.40	0.048	0.0000676
9	Expected Rate of Return		10.70%	0.000201
10	= E(X)			

Figure 2.20 Example of Absolute Reference

ROW ABSOLUTE REFERENCE

If you only want the row reference to remain the same after moving to another location make the row absolute by placing a $ sign in front of the row reference. With this partial absolute reference the column reference will be reinterpreted when the formula is copied but the row reference will remain the same. For example to make row 1 absolute in the following cell reference A1 write as A$1.

41

COLUMN ABSOLUTE REFERENCE

To make a cell reference partially absolute with regards to the column only, place a $ sign in front of the column reference. Now when the formula is copied the row reference will be reinterpreted and the column reference will remain constant. To make the cell reference A1 partially absolute in regards to the column write as follows: $A1.

INSERT FUNCTION FEATURE

We have discussed a few of Microsoft Excel's built-in functions; the ones that I use the most. There are many, many more functions available. Microsoft Excel's built-in formulas can be accessed from the "FORMULAS" Tab on the RIBBON. There you will find formulas organized by type. If you don't see the function you want to use, click the cell where the function will be located and then click the "Insert Function" icon on the Formulas Tab. An "Insert Function" dialog box will appear and it lists all available functions. Pressing the shortcut key combination of SHIFT+F3 will also display the "Insert Function" dialog box.

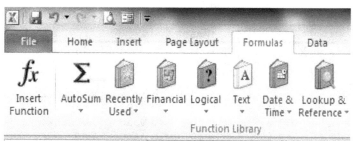

Figure 2.21

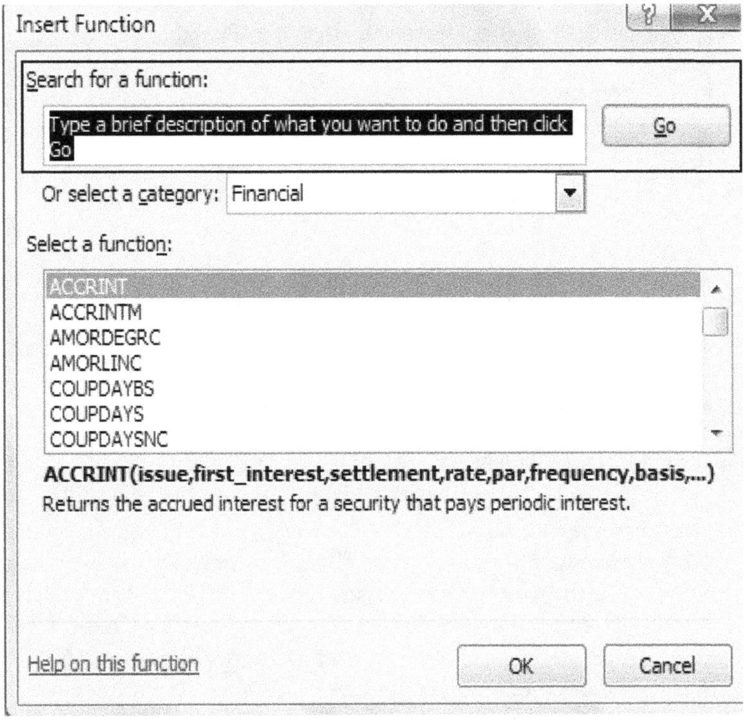

Figure 2.22

If you don't know what type of function you need to solve your problem, use Microsoft Excel's "Search for a function" feature. Enter a description of what you want to accomplish in this box and Microsoft Excel will suggest the appropriate function.

Let's revisit the Logical IF function. What if we did not know its syntax or order for entering required arguments? Select the Logical IF function from "Insert Function" dialog box and Microsoft Excel will help you through the process. Follow the on- screen directions.

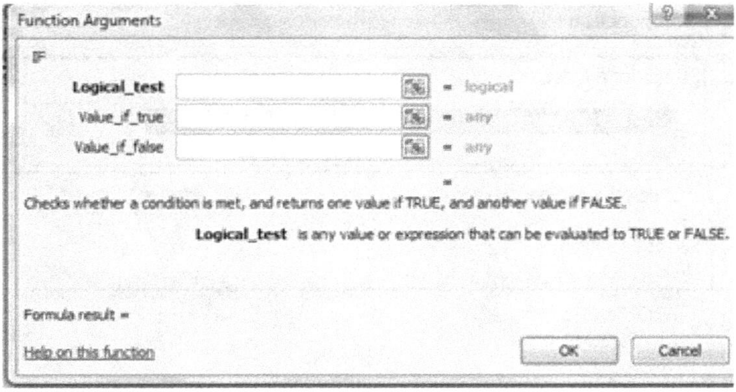

FIGURE 2.23

USING NAMES IN MICROSOFT EXCEL

A powerful feature of Microsoft Excel is the ability to give meaningful names to cells, rows, columns, ranges and other Microsoft Excel objects. This is especially useful when working with groups that consist of related data. On our 1st Microsoft Excel worksheet (the one we created in Chapter 1 – See Figure 1.12), January expenses occupy the range B6:B12. We can name this range "January" and use it whenever we need to reference that range. To define a name use the "Defined Names" group on the "Formulas" Tab on the RIBBON. Click the "Define Name" icon and the "New Name" dialog appears so that you can enter a name for the range.

Figure 2.24

Figure 2.25

Now that we have defined a name for range B6:B12, we can use it in a formula. If we want to know the total expenses for the month of January we can use "January" to represent the range in the following formula: **=SUM(January)**.

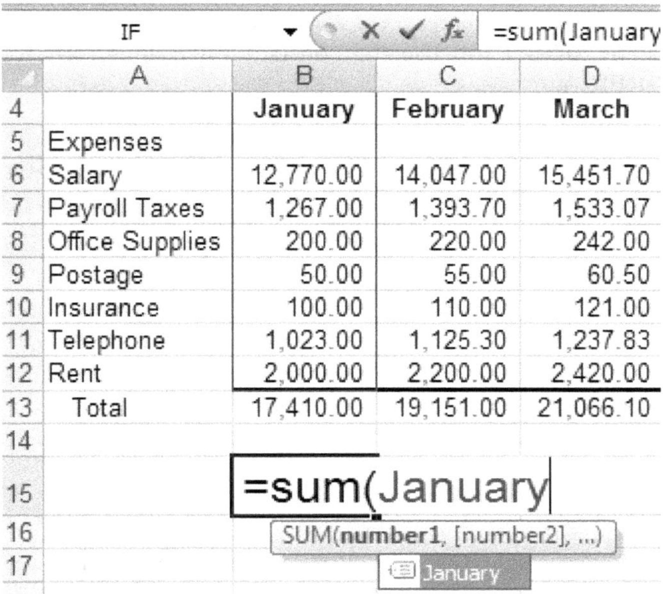

IF ▾ =sum(January

	A	B	C	D
4		January	February	March
5	Expenses			
6	Salary	12,770.00	14,047.00	15,451.70
7	Payroll Taxes	1,267.00	1,393.70	1,533.07
8	Office Supplies	200.00	220.00	242.00
9	Postage	50.00	55.00	60.50
10	Insurance	100.00	110.00	121.00
11	Telephone	1,023.00	1,125.30	1,237.83
12	Rent	2,000.00	2,200.00	2,420.00
13	Total	17,410.00	19,151.00	21,066.10
14				
15		=sum(January		
16		SUM(number1, [number2], ...)		
17		January		

Figure 2.26

Another way to define a name for a cell or range of cells is to select the cell or range and then type the name in the name box (Box that is to the left of the Formula Bar).

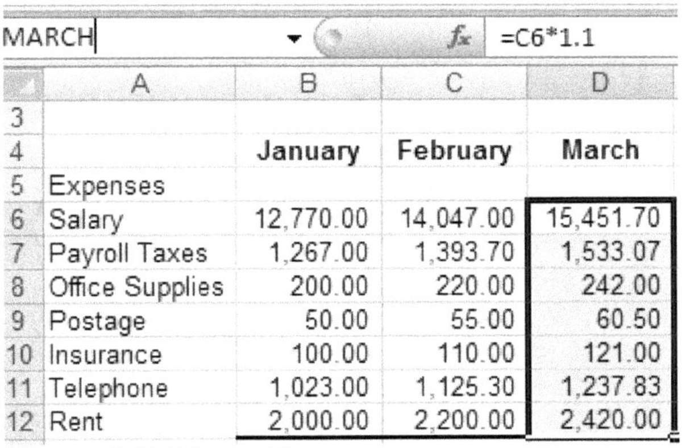

MARCH ▾ =C6*1.1

	A	B	C	D
3				
4		January	February	March
5	Expenses			
6	Salary	12,770.00	14,047.00	15,451.70
7	Payroll Taxes	1,267.00	1,393.70	1,533.07
8	Office Supplies	200.00	220.00	242.00
9	Postage	50.00	55.00	60.50
10	Insurance	100.00	110.00	121.00
11	Telephone	1,023.00	1,125.30	1,237.83
12	Rent	2,000.00	2,200.00	2,420.00

Figure 2.27 Name Box

Names can also be created for "Constants". Constants are names that refer to values that do not appear anywhere in your Worksheet. Constants are a quick way to use values in your formulas. When calculating payroll I use the constant FICA to represent the amount of payroll taxes to apply to a specific salary. So if I want to multiply a salary of $2,000 by .0765 I can use the constant FICA in a formula: =2000*FICA.

New Name		? ⋛
Name:	FICA	
Scope:	Workbook ▼	
Comment:		
Refers to:	.0765	
	OK	Cancel

Figure 2.28

To create a constant click the Define Name on the Defined Names Group on the Formulas Tab. In the New Name dialog box enter a name for your constant. And in the "Refers to" box enter a value for your constant. Now you can use the constant FICA whenever you want to multiply a specific salary amount by .0765 to calculate payroll taxes.

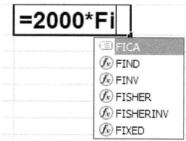

Figure 2.29

The function list in Figure 2.29 shows that the FICA constant is available for use in formulas. When you type a formula into a cell, a shortcut menu appears giving you a choice of available formulas and constants. Double-click the one you want to use.

You can also create names for formulas. In the New Name dialog box enter a name for your formula and in the

"Refers To" box enter your formula. Be careful using cell references in your formulas. Cell references are relative and will be reinterpreted when formula is pasted into a new cell.

USING DATE AND TIME FUNCTIONS

Dates and times are stored in Microsoft Excel using a serial number system. Day 1 is January 1, 1990. Of course since serial numbers are used to represent dates and time you can add and subtract dates and times. If cells B1 and B2 both contain dates you can calculate the number of days between them with the formula =B2-B1. You do not have to know serial numbers to work with dates or times in Microsoft Excel. All you have to do is enter data using a familiar date or time format and Microsoft Excel will make the conversion behind the scenes.

Use the shortcut key combination CTRL+; (semicolon) to enter the current date into a cell. Use the shortcut key combination CTRL+SHIFT+; to enter the current time in a cell. If you want both current date and current time in a single cell first type CTRL+;, then press space and type CTRL+SHIFT+;. Using these shortcut key combinations create static dates and times in your Worksheet. If you want updatable dates and times use the NOW Function (returns current date and time) and the TODAY Function (returns current date).

FORMULA ERRORS

Formula errors can occur when formula syntax is incorrect. When you enter a formula and receive an error message press the smart tag appearing next to the error message for information regarding that error and how to correct it.

Figure 2.30

47

Following is a table of errors that may appear in cells holding formulas.

Error message	Reason for Error
########	Column is not wide enough to display result. Not really an error just a problem
#DIV/0!	Dividing a number by zero also occurs when formula tries to divide by an empty cell
#NA	Using VLOOKUP or HLOOKUP functions and they do not return a match
#NAME?	Referring to a named range that does not exist, using worksheet function that does not exist or is spelled incorrectly, entering text without quotation marks, referring to another worksheet that does not exist.
#NULL!	Formula refers to intersection of two ranges that do not intersect
#NUM!	Passing the wrong argument to a formula
#REF	Referring to an invalid cell or cells that have been deleted.
#VALUE	Formula uses wrong data type, using text where a number is expected

On the Formulas Tab in the Formula Auditing Group are tools provided to help you locate formula Errors.

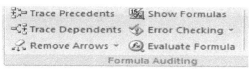

Figure 2.31

To determine that the desired cells are used in a formula click the Trace Precedents icon to identify the cells used in the Active Cell's formula. Microsoft Excel will draw a blue arrow from the precedent(s) to the Active Cell. Click the Remove Arrows icon to return the worksheet to normal.

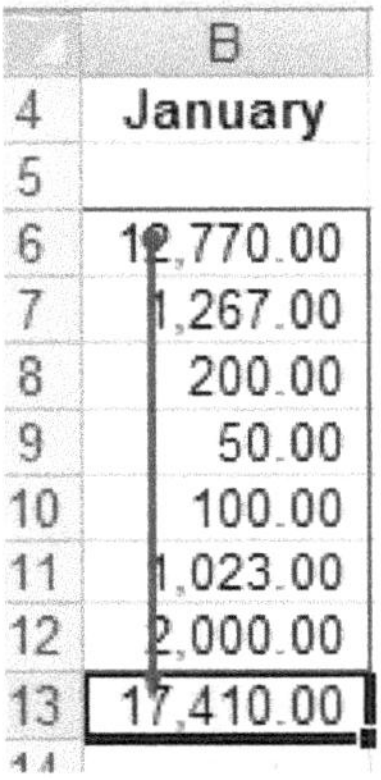

	B
4	**January**
5	
6	19,770.00
7	1,267.00
8	200.00
9	50.00
10	100.00
11	1,023.00
12	2,000.00
13	17,410.00

Figure 2.32

Dependents are cells that use another cell's values in their calculations. Click the Trace Dependents icon and Microsoft Excel will show arrows that indicate the cells that are dependent on the value in the Active Cell.

VLOOKUP FUNCTION

The VLOOKUP Function is very useful in working with complex lists of data arranged in a table. The VLOOKUP Function searches the first column of a range of cells and returns a value from any cell on the same row of the range.

	B13	▼	f_x	=VLOOKUP("JH1226",A6:C11,2,FALSE)	
	A	B		C	D
1					
2		PRODUCT LIST			
3					
4					
5	PRODUCT NO.	BOOK TITLE		PRICE	
6	JH0034	Individual income taxes		$ 125.00	
7	JH1106	Corporations, Partnerships, Estates		$ 130.00	
8	JH1226	Wiley GAAP Book		$ 55.00	
9	JH0324	SQL for Dummies		$ 49.00	
10	JH1109	U.S. Master Tax Guide		$ 100.00	
11	JH0327	Visual Basic Exam Guide		$ 110.00	
12					
13	LOOKUP	Wiley GAAP Book			
14					

Figure 2.33

Suppose you have a list of products with the following information in your worksheet: (1) Product Number, (2) Book Title, and (3) Price. If you know the Product Number, you can use it to find the related Book Title or Price. The "V" in VLOOKUP stands for vertical lookup. There is a related function, HLOOKUP, where the H stands for horizontal and works in a similar way. I want the Book Title so I wrote the formula as =VLOOKUP("JH1226",A6:C11,2,FALSE). The Product Number is text so I had to enclose it in quotation marks or formula would return a #NAME? error message. Using the Product Number JH1226, I was able to retrieve the Book Title: Wiley GAAP Book.

Syntax for the VLOOKUP function is as follows:
=VLOOKUP(lookup_value, table_array, col_index_num, [range_lookup])

ARGUMENT	EXPECTED VALUE
lookup_value	Required. The value to search in the first column of the table or range. Can be a value, cell reference, or text string. If supplied lookup_value is less than smallest value in the first column, a #N/A error results.
table_array	Required. The range of cells that contain the data. Either a range reference (for example A6:C11) or a

	range name is ok.
col_index_num	Required. The column number in the table_array argument containing the desired information.
range_lookup	Optional. (Remember that arguments enclosed in square brackets [ ] are optional). A logical value specifying if you want VLOOKUP to find an exact match or an approximate match. FALSE if exact match is required. TRUE if exact match or approximate match is OK. If argument is omitted it is assumed to be TRUE. If this argument value is FALSE and exact match is not found, function returns #N/A error. If there are two or more exact matches, function returns the first match found.

If col_index_num argument is less than 1, VLOOKUP returns the #VALUE! error. And if it is greater than the number of columns in the table_array then the #REF! error results.

A TRUE or omitted value in the range_lookup argument returns an exact or approximate match. However if an exact match is not found VLOOKUP returns the next largest value that is less than lookup_value. Also the values in the first column of table_array must be sorted in ascending order if the value in the range_lookup argument is TRUE or omitted.

ANOTHER VLOOKUP EXAMPLE

The Worksheet in Figure 2.34 holds data for students and their score on a recent exam. I want to assign a letter grade based on the score variable. The range D2:E6 shows the score needed to attain a specific grade (e.g. score of 90 and above warrants a grade of "A"). To make working with the VLOOKUP formula easier, the range D2:E6 was named "GRADES". The VLOOKUP formula was copied into C2:C17. Letter grades are assigned and posted in Column C by using the VLOOKUP formula. Look in column B for the score then look in the Grades table, column 2 to find an approximate match and then assign and post letter grade.

	A	B	C	D	E	F	G
1	STUDENT	SCORE	GRADE	SCORE	GRADE		
2	Student 1	98	A	40	F		
3	Student 1	60	D	60	D		
4	Student 2	65	D	70	C		
5	Student 3	70	C	80	B		
6	Student 4	100	A	90	A		
7	Student 5	50	F				
8	Student 6	40	F				
9	Student 7	75	C				
10	Student 8	85	B				
11	Student 9	95	A				
12	Student 10	70	C				
13	Student 11	78	C				
14	Student 12	60	D				
15	Student 13	69	D				
16	Student 14	55	F				
17	Student 15	90	A				
18							
19			=VLOOKUP(B2,GRADES,2)				
20							
21		NAME RANGE D2:E6 GRADES					
22		PUT VLOOKUP FORMULA IN COLUMN C					

Figure 2.34

ARRAY FORMULAS

An array is a group of cells or values that can be operated on at the same time. Actually it looks like a table as the group has rows and columns. An ARRAY formula lets you perform individual operations on each cell in the array. To enter an array formula in a cell you must press the key combination CTRL+SHIFT+ENTER. Indicating that this is an array formula, Microsoft Excel will enclose it with curly brackets ({ }). Do not type the brackets yourself.

	A	B	C	D	E
1	UNITS	PRICE	XTENSN		
2	2	10	20		
3	3	20	60		
4	4	15	60		
5	5	65	325		
6	6	3	18		
7	4	2	8		

Figure 2.35

Figure 2.35 shows a worksheet with information about the number of units sold and their respective prices. In accounting we call this calculating a price extension. We could put the extension formula (=A2*B2) in each of the cells from C2 to C7. Or we could make the calculation on all cells in the range C2:C7 at once using one formula (an array formula). First select the cell range C2:C7and in cell C2 type the formula: =A2:A7*B2:B7 and then press the CTRL+SHIFT+ENTER key combination. This formula will appear in all cells from C2 to C7 with the desired information. In the formula bar for cell C5 you see the curly brackets around the formula telling you that this is an array formula. If I want the total sales for the period I can use SUM function with an array formula. See Figure 2.36.

	C9			▼	f_x	{=SUM(A2:A7*B2:B7)
	A	B	C	D	E	
1	UNITS	PRICE	XTENSN			
2	2	10	20			
3	3	20	60			
4	4	15	60			
5	5	65	325			
6	6	3	18			
7	4	2	8			
8						
9			491			

Figure 2.36

USING ARRAY FORMULAS WITH THE SUM FUNCTION

You can do things with an array formula that is not possible with regular formulas. Suppose you have a Worksheet listing job categories and related payroll information. Looking at the Worksheet can you quickly determine how many managers (MGR) make more than $2,300.00? You could scan the Worksheet, look at salary for each manager and include in your count each manager who makes more than $2,300.00. Or you could use an array formula and get the answer. In cell B14 enter the formula: =SUM((A3:A12="MGR")*(B3:B12>2300)) and press the CTRL+SHIFT+ENTER keys for the correct answer of 3. Don't forget to enclose MGR in quotes as it is text.

	B14				fx	{=SUM((A3:A12="MGR")*(B3:B12>2300))}		
	A	B	C	D	E	F	G	
1								
2	EMPLOYEE	SALARY	FICA	MED	FED	STATE	NET PAY	
3	MGR	2,300.00	142.60	33.35	805.00	69.00	1,250.05	
4	SUP	1,239.00	76.82	17.97	433.65	37.17	673.40	
5	MGR	2,500.00	155.00	36.25	875.00	75.00	1,358.75	
6	MGR	2,200.00	136.40	31.90	770.00	66.00	1,195.70	
7	MGR	3,000.00	186.00	43.50	1,050.00	90.00	1,630.50	
8	MGR	3,200.00	198.40	46.40	1,120.00	96.00	1,739.20	
9	SUP	1,234.00	76.51	17.89	431.90	37.02	670.68	
10	SUP	1,000.00	62.00	14.50	350.00	30.00	543.50	
11	SUP	1,500.00	93.00	21.75	525.00	45.00	815.25	
12	SUP	1,400.00	86.80	20.30	490.00	42.00	760.90	
13								
14			3	Num of mgrs with salary > 2300				

Figure 2.37

The Array formula, SUM function combination, can also help me determine the total salaries of the managers included in the list. Enter the following formula into cell B15: =SUM((A3:A12 ="MGR")*(B3:B12)) and then press the CTRL+SHIFT+ENTER keys. Total salary is calculated to be $13,200.

	B15				fx	{=SUM((A3:A12="MGR")*(B3:B12))}	
	A	B	C	D	E	F	G
1							
2	EMPLOYEE	SALARY	FICA	MED	FED	STATE	NET PAY
3	MGR	2,300.00	142.60	33.35	805.00	69.00	1,250.05
4	SUP	1,239.00	76.82	17.97	433.65	37.17	673.40
5	MGR	2,500.00	155.00	36.25	875.00	75.00	1,358.75
6	MGR	2,200.00	136.40	31.90	770.00	66.00	1,195.70
7	MGR	3,000.00	186.00	43.50	1,050.00	90.00	1,630.50
8	MGR	3,200.00	198.40	46.40	1,120.00	96.00	1,739.20
9	SUP	1,234.00	76.51	17.89	431.90	37.02	670.68
10	SUP	1,000.00	62.00	14.50	350.00	30.00	543.50
11	SUP	1,500.00	93.00	21.75	525.00	45.00	815.25
12	SUP	1,400.00	86.80	20.30	490.00	42.00	760.90
13							
14			3	Num of mgrs with salary > 2300			
15			13200	Total salary of managers			
16							

Figure 2.38

COUNTIF FUNCTION

Look at Figure 2.38. There is another way to count the number of managers who make more than $2,300. I could use the COUNTIF function. It takes two arguments: (1) the range that holds the data to be counted and (2) the criteria used to determine if the cell should be included in the count. See Figure 2.39 for the syntax of the COUNTIF function. Also Figure 2.39 shows the application of the COUNTIF function to count the number of managers who make more than $2,300. If the criteria argument is not a number it must be enclosed in quotation marks.

Figure 2.39

SUMIF FUNCTION

Following is a copy of a Microsoft Excel spreadsheet that a client uses to keep track of his financial activities. I had to summarize and categorize expense items to prepare his tax return. My options were to visually pick out each category and individually sum to get a total or to use a nifty Microsoft Excel function called **_SUMIF._** To get the individual categories I copied the worksheet (so as to not destroy all of my client's hard work) and sorted column D to get a list of categories.

	A	B	C	D	E	F	G	H
1								
2	Date	Number	Name	Description	a	Debit	Credit	Balance
3	1/1/07		Ending 2006 Balance					9,041.80
4	1/1/07	1065	La Tierra Investments	2nd Mortgage	x	632.07		8,409.73
5	1/2/07	1066	THE National Bank	1st Mortgage	x	4,538.04		3,871.69
6	1/2/07	1067	Peoples Gas	Gas Service	x	65.38		3,806.31
7	1/2/07	1068	Peoples Gas	Office Gas Service	x	371.80		3,434.51
8	1/2/07	1069	Peoples Gas	Gas Service	x	49.23		3,385.28
9	1/2/07	1070	Peoples Gas	Gas Service	x	60.23		3,325.05
10	1/2/07	1071	Peoples Gas	Gas Service	x	28.01		3,297.04
11	1/2/07	1072	Allied Waste Services	Garbage Collection	x	69.42		3,227.62
12	1/4/07 Dep		Deposit	Law Office Rent	x		3,072.10	6,299.72
13	1/8/07 Dep		Deposit	Apt. Rents	x		3,025.00	9,324.72
14	1/15/07	1073	City of Chicago	Water Bill	x	831.49		8,493.23
15	1/15/07	1074	Com Ed	Electric	x	54.70		8,438.53
16	1/15/07	1075	Com Ed	Electric	x	131.40		8,307.13
17	1/17/06 Dep		Deposit	Vicky's Salon	x		2,150.00	10,457.13
18	1/22/07 Dep		Deposit	Gas Reimbursment-Law	x		371.80	10,828.93
19	1/30/07	1076	Peoples Gas	Gas Service		78.27		10,750.66
20	1/30/07	1077	Peoples Gas	Gas Service		32.75		10,717.91
21	1/30/07	1078	Peoples Gas	Gas Service		127.44		10,590.47
22	1/30/07	1079	Peoples Gas	Gas Service		69.95		10,520.52
23	1/30/07	1080	Peoples Gas	Gas Service		34.13		10,486.39
24	2/1/07	1081	Allied Waste Services	Garbage Collection		69.57		10,416.82
25	2/2/07	1082	Cook County Treasurer	Property Taxes		4,906.88		5,509.94
26	2/1/07	1083	La Tierra Investments	2nd Mortgage		632.07		4,877.87

What we want to do is search column D and get a total for each category. For example, for the category "Gas Service" we want a total. Also for the category of "Garbage Collection" we want a total. Actually for each individual category we want a total.

My client has some accounting skills and I am sure you noticed that he identified items as either debit items or credit items. He knew the difference between revenue and expenses.

In a separate section of the spreadsheet we are going to copy each category using the Microsoft Excel copy function. That way when we do a search we will be sure to search the exact category.

J	K
Mortgage	$ 35,767.25
1st Mortgage	$ 17,713.02
2nd Mortgage	$ 6,952.77
3rd Mortgage	$ 198.58
	$ 60,631.62
Gas Service	$ 3,477.57
Garbage Collection	$ 956.73
Water Bill	$ 1,978.62
Electric	$ 9,505.00
Property Taxes	$ 11,499.58
Bounced Check	$ 80.00
Partnership Taxes	$ 1,000.00
Windows	$ 2,477.00
Building Insurance	$ 2,972.00
Bug Spray	$ 275.00
Pest Control	$ 420.00
Ceiling Fan/Sink Repair	$ 200.00
Furnaces	$ 2,400.00
	$ 37,241.50

In column J we copy from column D the individual categories. Column K is where the magic of the **SUMIF** function will be applied.

Start the function with the equal sign (=), then the function name (**SUMIF**) followed by the open parentheses symbol. Microsoft Excel will ask you for the arguments of the function.

A	B	C	D
1 =sumif(			
SUMIF(range, criteria, [sum_range])			
2			

Type the SUMIF function in Column K.

The range argument asks which cells we want to search. Our category items are in column D, Cell D3 to Cell D209 so D3:D209 is the desired range. We precede both the Column name "D" and the Row number "3" with the dollar sign ($) because we want the range to be absolute and not relative. So enter the range as **$D$3:$D$209.** Place a comma after the first argument and then enter the next argument **"Criteria".** In our example criteria is the category item we want to sum. Criteria must be relative because we are going to use the SUMIF function to search through all of the categories (J1:J18). Thus, the criteria argument is found in Column J. We want the SUMIF function to work for each category. So enter J1 as criteria and follow it with a comma. Microsoft Excel then asks for the final argument "[sum_range]". "[sum_range]" is where the numbers are; the dollar amount for each category. We want this argument to be absolute so we can copy the function to all of the categories. "[sum_range]" is found in Column F. Enter **$F$3:$F$209** as the final argument, type closing parenthesis and hit Enter Key. Now we can copy the SUMIF function from K1 to K18 to apply to all categories. We have obtained a total for each category as shown in the picture above.

REFERENCE OPERATORS FOR RANGES

OPERATOR	WHAT IT DOES
: COLON	Specifies a range A1:A20
, COMMA	Specifies the union of two ranges
SPACE	Specifies the intersection of two ranges. (cells that are common to two ranges)

TEXT WORKSHEET FUNCTIONS

In addition to performing calculations on numbers you can also manipulate text. We will discuss a few of the text functions shipped with Microsoft Excel. The following table lists the most common text functions. (This table is modified from a table found in the Microsoft Help feature).

FUNCTION	DESCRIPTION
CONCATENATE	Joins multiple text items into one text item
FIND	Finds one text value within another (case sensitive)
LEFT	Returns leftmost characters from a text value
LEN	Returns the number of characters in a text string
LOWER	Converts text to lowercase
MID	Returns a specific number of characters from a text string

	starting at the position you specify
PROPER	Capitalizes the first letter in each word of a text value
RIGHT	Returns the rightmost characters from a text value
TEXT	Formats a number and convert it to text
TRIM	Removes spaces from text
UPPER	Converts text to uppercase
VALUE	Converts a text argument to a number

CONCATENATE FUNCTION

We can join together the contents of cell A2 "Employee" and the contents of B2 "Salary" to form "Employee Salary". In the function we must include arguments for spaces, (" ").

=CONCATENATE(A2," ",B2)   EMPLOYEE SALARY
CONCATENATE(text1, [text2], [text3], [text4], ...)

Figure 2.40 Syntax of Concatenate Function

FIND FUNCTION

Use the Find function to locate the position of a text string that is located in another string. For example if I want to find the character "P" that is located in the string "Employee" the "Find" Function will return a value of 3. The string "Employee" is located in cell A2. To find the location of "P" use the following formula: **=FIND("P",A2,1)**. The arguments in this function are:

find_text	Required. Text you want to find
within_text	Required. Look in this text string
start_num	Optional. Where in text string to start looking

FIND(**find_text**, within_text, [start_num])

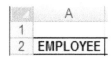

	A
1	
2	**EMPLOYEE**

Figure 2.41

LEFT FUNCTION

Use the Left function to locate the leftmost characters in a text string. If I want to return the left four characters of the string "Employee" I would use the following formula: =LEFT(A2,4). The arguments in this formula are:

text	Required. Where to look
num_chars	Optional. How many characters do you want? If omitted, only the first leftmost character is returned.

LEFT(**text**, [num_chars])

Figure 2.42

LEN FUNCTION

The LEN function tells you how many characters are in a text string. If I wanted to know how many characters are in the text string "Employee" I would use the following formula: =LEN(A2). This function takes one argument: where is the text string located.

LEN(**text**)

Figure 2.43

EXAMPLE USING FIND, LEFT, LEN, AND RIGHT TEXT FUNCTIONS

These text functions can be used in combination to solve some interesting problems. Suppose you have a Worksheet with first and last names in the same column. See Figure 2.44. Assume that you want to sort the column by last

59

names. To do so you have to get the last name and first name into individual columns. Using the Find, Left, Len, and Right text functions in combination makes this an easy task. As you will see, functions can be used within functions.

	A
1	Name
2	Washington, George
3	Jefferson, Thomas
4	Wallace, George
5	Grant, David
6	Bush, George

Figure 2.44

Set up the Worksheet to hold the number of characters to reach a space, and a column to hold last and first names. Use the "Find" to find the first space in the name string and place the number of characters leading up to space in column B.

NORMINV ▾ X ✓ fx =Find(" ",A2,1

	A	B	C	D
1	Name	letter Count	last name	first Name
2	Washington, George	12	Washington	George
3	Jefferson, Thomas	11	Jefferson	Thomas
4	Wallace, George	9	Wallace	George
5	Grant, David	7	Grant	David
6	Bush, George	6	Bush	George
7				
8	Formula for Column B			
9	=Find(" ",A2,1			
10	FIND(find_text, within_text, [start_num])			

Figure 2.45

Now we use the "Left" function to separate last name out and place it in column C.

	A	B	C	D
1	Name	letter Count	last name	first Name
2	Washington, George	12	Washington	George
3	Jefferson, Thomas	11	Jefferson	Thomas
4	Wallace, George	9	Wallace	George
5	Grant, David	7	Grant	David
6	Bush, George	6	Bush	George
7				
8	Formula for Column C			
9	=LEFT(A2,B2-2			
10	LEFT(text, [num_chars])			
11	Subtract -2 to handle comma			

Figure 2.46

Finally we use the "Right" function with the "Len" function embedded within to separate out the first name and place the results in column D.

NORMINV	▼ ✕ ✓ *fx*	=RIGHT(A2,LEN(A2)-B2+1)		
	A	B	C	D
1	Name	letter Count	last name	first Name
2	Washington, George	12	Washington	George
3	Jefferson, Thomas	11	Jefferson	Thomas
4	Wallace, George	9	Wallace	George
5	Grant, David	7	Grant	David
6	Bush, George	6	Bush	George
7				
8	Formula for Column D			
9	=RIGHT(A2,LEN(A2)-B2+1)			
10				
11	Add 1 to handle comma			

Figure 2.47

LOWER FUNCTION

Lower function converts a text string to all lower case. Formula takes only one argument which is: what text do we want to convert (a cell reference where text is located).

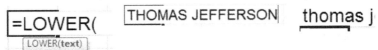

=LOWER(THOMAS JEFFERSON   thomas j
LOWER(text)

Figure 2.48

MID FUNCTION

The MID function returns a specific number of characters from a text string starting at the position the user

61

specifies. I want to return the text string "JEFF" from the "Thomas Jefferson" string shown in Figure 2.48. Assume that text string is located in cell I14. I would use the following formula: =MID(I14,8,4). Arguments for this formula are:

Text	Required. Where is the text you want to perform this operation
start_num	Required. Where in the text string do we want to start, which character number
num_chars	Required. How many characters do we want to return

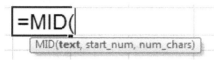

Figure 2.49

The rest of the text functions are easy to understand. You should, however, spend some time exploring these useful text functions. I am sure you will find a use for them.

CONSOLIDATING DATA FROM MULTIPLE SOURCES

If you organize your work among multiple Worksheets and Workbooks you need a way to combine and summarize data into one place to facilitate data analysis. If you work with the same Workbooks all the time you can save them in one place and Microsoft Excel will remember their location when you begin a new session. Also if you organize your work among multiple Worksheets you can summarize them into a master worksheet. For example you could have twelve Worksheets with each representing expenses for each month of the year. You can combine the twelve Worksheets into one to represent the entire year.

WORKSPACE FEATURE

To have Microsoft Excel remember the layout of Workbooks you use all the time in your data analysis activities use the Workspace feature found on the VIEW tab: WINDOW group.

Figure 2.50

CREATING WORKSHEET TEMPLATE

If you have created a Worksheet with all the features that you plan to use over and over, would it be nice to avoid recreating the wheel every time you start Microsoft Excel? If your Worksheet has the desired formatting and all of the needed formulas you can create a template for future use.

To create a template click the "FILE TAB" then click "Save As". Enter an appropriate name in the "File Name" box. Choose "Microsoft Excel Template" from the "Save as type" box and then click save. Later when you want to use the template, click Microsoft FILE TAB and choose "New" and then click "My Templates".

REFERENCING OTHER WORKSHEETS AND WORKBOOKS

Formulas can reference cells and ranges that are not in the same Worksheet as the formula. If your formula uses cells in another Worksheet, precede the cell reference with the Worksheet name and follow with the exclamation point. Cell B6 on our Budget Worksheet is dynamically linked to Cell B10 on the Salary Worksheet. See Figure 1.17 and 1.18. If the value of B10 on Salary Worksheet changes then Cell B6 on the Budget Worksheet is automatically updated. To reference Cell B10 on the Salary Worksheet from the Budget Worksheet type the following reference: =Salary!B10. There are two ways to link these worksheets in these cells. One is to type the aforementioned formula in Cell B6 in the Budget Worksheet. Another way is to type the equal sign in Cell B6 of the Budget Worksheet, then click the tab for the Salary Worksheet and click Cell B10 and press the enter key. You will automatically be returned to the Budget Worksheet and the cells will be linked.

Formulas can also link to cells in a different Workbook. To effect the link, precede the cell reference with the Workbook name in square brackets [ ] next add the Worksheet name then the exclamation point. For example to link to Workbook Expense type the following:

=[Expense.xlsx]Sheet1!A1

If the Workbook name in the reference contains spaces, you have to enclose it (and the Worksheet name) in single quotation marks. For example :

='[Expense for 2007.xlsx]Sheet1'!A1

If the Workbook you want to link to is closed then you must add the complete path to the Workbook reference. For example:

='C:\MSOffice\Microsoft Excel\[Expense for 2007.xlsx]Sheet1'!A1

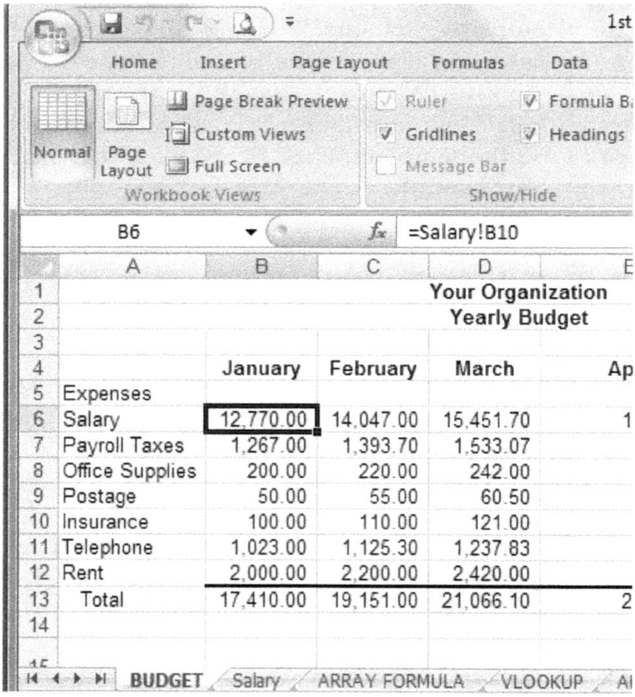

Figure 2.51

COMBINE DATA IN MULTIPLE WORKSHEET AN EASIER WAY

If you organize your work among multiple Worksheets you need an easy way to consolidate them into one summary sheet. We have already discussed linking individual cells. There is a way to consolidate multiple cells from multiple Worksheets all in one step. The

"CONSOLIDATE" feature found on the Data Tools group on the DATA tab will handle this task for you. This feature is useful especially if the Worksheets are organized so that data is in the same place on each Worksheet. I am thinking that the Worksheets were created using a template.

Figure 2.52

On the Worksheet to be used to hold the consolidated data, click the upper-left cell where you want the consolidated data to appear. Leave enough room to the right and below this cell to hold the consolidated data. Next click the Consolidate icon in the Data Tools group to display the Consolidate dialog box. You can now tell Microsoft Excel how you want to consolidate the data. Select the "Function" box and select from the drop-down list the function to use to consolidate the data. Function choices are: (1) SUM, (2) COUNT, (3) AVERAGE, (4) MAX, (5) MIN, (6) PRODUCT, (7) COUNT NUMBERS, (8) STDDEV, (9) STDEVP, (10) VAR, and (11) VARP. Next move to the first Worksheet that you want to include in the consolidation, select the desired cells and click the "ADD" button to store the reference. Do the same for the remaining Worksheets. If you decide not to include a stored reference in the consolidation select that reference and hit the "Delete" button to remove. If the Worksheets you want to consolidate are in different Workbook(s) you can check the "Create links to the source data" box and the consolidation will update automatically whenever the source data changes. To complete consolidation process click "OK" button. Microsoft Excel will summarize the data to your master Worksheet. You are limited to one data consolidation Worksheet per Workbook.

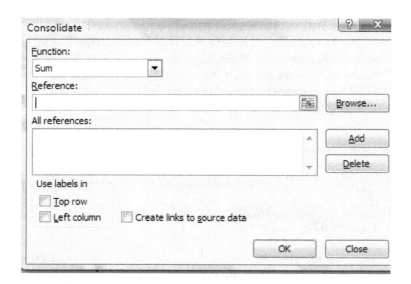

SUMMARY

What makes Microsoft Excel useful is its ability to perform calculations on data to get answers to important business questions. Any calculation that you can perform on a calculator can be done faster and easier in Microsoft Excel. Microsoft Excel has many types of built-in functions available to do calculations. Included are mathematical, financial, statistical, and user defined functions.

CHAPTER 3
FORMATTING WORKSHEETS

How you want your Worksheet to appear is a personal preference. What you strive for is data that is easy to read. Microsoft Excel has many features which help you make data in your Worksheet both easy to read and easy to understand. Font type, size, and color can be changed to draw attention to important cell contents. Borders can be placed around cells. You can change the look of your worksheet by turning on or off gridlines. Alignment of cell contents can be manipulated. Graphics can be added to the Worksheet. And numbers can be formatted to clearly show exactly what it represents.

One of the easiest ways to make data understandable is to use labels that describe the contents of cells. In Figure 3.1 column and row labels tell us that we have expenses (and the type of expense) for the months of January to April. We also see the total expenses for each month. It is pretty clear what this worksheet shows.

Your Organization
Yearly Budget

	January	February	March	April
Expenses				
Salary	12,770.00	14,047.00	15,451.70	16,996.87
Payroll Taxes	1,267.00	1,393.70	1,533.07	1,686.38
Office Supplies	200.00	220.00	242.00	266.20
Postage	50.00	55.00	60.50	66.55
Insurance	100.00	110.00	121.00	133.10
Telephone	1,023.00	1,125.30	1,237.83	1,361.61
Rent	2,000.00	2,200.00	2,420.00	2,662.00
Total	17,410.00	19,151.00	21,066.10	23,172.71

Figure 3.1

ADDING BORDERS TO CELLS

Another way to highlight cells content is to put borders around the cell. In Figure 3.1 cells holding expense information is surrounded by borders. You can put borders around the entire cell or you can have borders only around its top, bottom, left, or right side. The border formatting feature is found on the "Format Cells" dialog box. This dialog box can be accessed from the RIBBON, HOME Tab, from either of the following groups found there: (1) Font group, (2) Alignment group, or the (3) Number group. Clicking the down arrow on any of these groups displays the "Font Cells" dialog box. On this dialog box are tabs that let you change the format of cell contents. There is a tab to access Number formatting, a tab to change Alignment, a tab to change Font, a tab to change Border, a tab to change Fill, and a tab to change protection features of the Worksheet.

On the "Border" Tab there is a rectangle with the label "Text" enclosed therein. This rectangle represents an Active cell or range of selected cells. First decide on and then click the line weight (from the Line Style area) you want to use and then click the location in the rectangle where you want to apply the border. For example, if you want to place a border of the top of a cell click the top of the rectangle. If you want to surround the cell on all sides click the "Outline" icon. Also available are shortcut icons to place borders anywhere you want around a cell or selected range of cells.

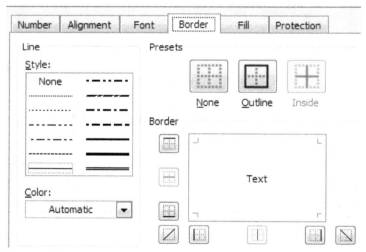

Figure 3.2

FORMATTING NUMBERS

Numbers in our Worksheet shown in Figure 3.1 are formatted in the accounting form. There are a number of ways to format numbers so that what they represent is clear. Click the Number tab on the Format Cells dialog box and let's explore the different number types.

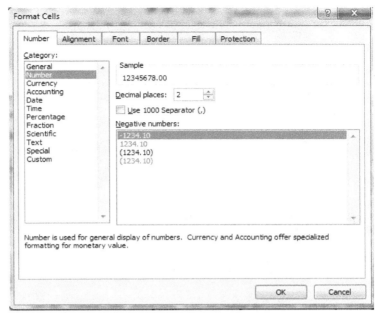

Figure 3.3

Number formats are organized around Categories. Look at Figure 3.3 to see the different ways you can format numbers. Next to the selected category is a sample of what that category looks like. Pick a category to get the desired result. If you already know what number format you want, you don't have to use the "Format Cells" dialog box . You can change the number format by clicking the text box found on the HOME tab, Numbers group. Figure 3.4 shows that numbers in the selected cells are formatted using the General Category. Click the down arrow to select other categories.

Following are examples of Number format categories.

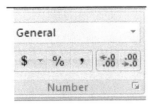

Figure 3.4

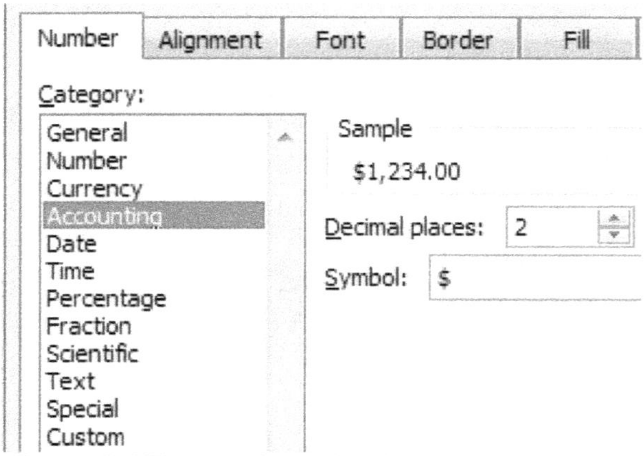

Figure 3.5 Formatting Numbers using Accounting Category.

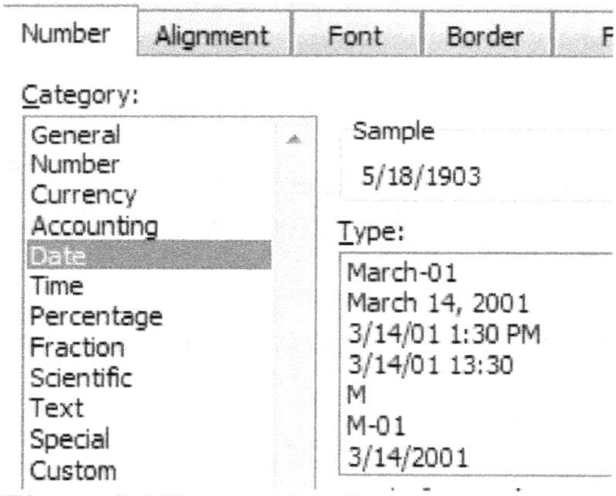

Figure 3.6 Formatting Dates

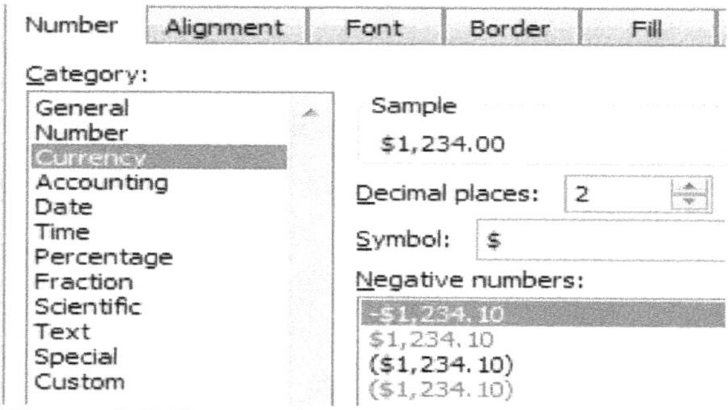

Figure 3.7 Formatting Numbers using Currency Category

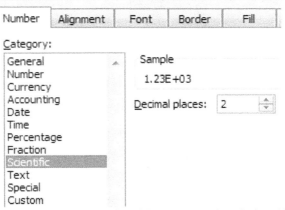

| Number | Alignment | Font | Border | Fill |

Category:

General
Number
Currency
Accounting
Date
Time
Percentage
Fraction
Scientific
Text
Special
Custom

Sample

1.23E+03

Decimal places: 2

Figure 3.8 Formatting Numbers using Scientific Category.

Scientific notation allows Microsoft Excel to display very large numbers and very small numbers in a cell. Scientific notation displays the first non-zero digit of a number then a fixed number of digits (usually the next 2 digits) and then shows what power of 10 that number needs to be multiplied by to generate the original number. Thus the number .0004 becomes 4.00×10^{-4}. Microsoft Excel displays the number as 4.00E-04. The power number is negative because the first non-zero digit is to the right of the decimal point. If the first non-zero number is to the left of the decimal point the power would be a plus. So the number 500 would be written as 5.00×10^{2} and displayed by Microsoft Excel as 5.00E+2. By the way, the formula bar will display the number as originally written while the cell where the number is located displays the number in scientific notation.

The "Text" category tells Microsoft Excel to treat the numbers in this cell or range of cells as text. No mathematical calculations are allowed on contents treated as text. And the "Custom" category allows you to create your own number format. You could add the text "Per Quarter" after another number format and number in a cell will be followed with the string "Per Quarter" (for example $5,000 Per Quarter).

The "Special" category formats numbers for four common items: (1) Zip Code, (2) Zip Code +4, (3) Phone Number, and (4) Social Security Number (for security purposes Social Security Numbers should rarely appear in

71

anyone's spreadsheet). The original number appears in the formula bar while the formatted number appears in the cell.

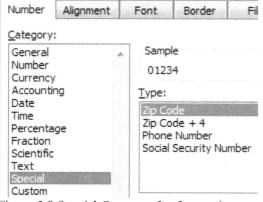

Figure 3.9 Special Category for formatting numbers

FORMATTING ALIGNMENT IN CELLS

Alignment of cell contents can be changed by clicking the Alignment tab on the Format Cells dialog box. Look at Figure 3.10 to see the different alignment options.

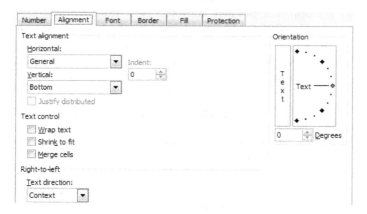

You don't have to drill down to the Format Cells dialog box to change the most common alignment features. The most common alignment features are on the Ribbon in the Alignment Group.

Figure 3.11

FORMATTING FONTS

Like other formatting options, there are two ways to change the format of Fonts. You can use the Font group found on the Ribbon or you can use the Format Cells dialog box. The most common formatting features for fonts are found on the ribbon.

Figure 3.12

From the Ribbon you can change font, font style, size, font color and the characteristics of: Bold, Under-line, or Italics. To change other features you have to invoke the Format Cells Dialog Box.

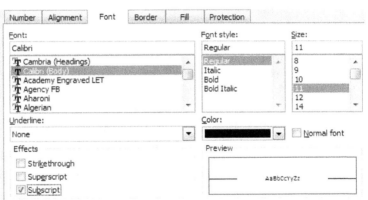

Figure 3.13

When displaying statistical data in cells it is useful to be able to show Subscripts and Superscripts. See the following Worksheet where both are employed. See Figure 3.14.

	A	B	C	D
1				
2			Asset A	
3	X_i	$P(X_i)$		Variance
4	Return	Probability	$X_iP(X_i)$	$[X_i\text{-}E(X)^2P(X_i)]$
5	11%	0.30	0.033	0.0010443
6	18%	0.45	0.081	5.445E-05
7	22%	0.25	0.055	0.00065025
8				
9	Expected Rate of Return		16.90%	0.001749
10	= E(X)			
11		Standard Deviation		
12		=Square Root of Var.		0.041821047
13				
14				
15		Coefficient Variation =.041821047/.1690		

Figure 3.14 Example of Superscripts and Subscripts

Applying superscripts and subscripts is a little tricky and requires multiple trips to the Font tab on the Format Cells dialog box. When you are ready to type a superscript or subscript visit the Font tab on the Format Cells dialog box and click the check box for the feature desired (Superscript or Subscript). These features are found in the "Effects" area of the dialog box. See Figure 3.13. Click OK to return to the Worksheet. Next step is to type in the desired superscript or subscript. Now you have to return to the Font tab on the Format Cells dialog box and click (to de-select) the feature you just employed. Finally you press OK to return to the Worksheet and continue typing cell content.

On the Font tab are features that let you pick a "Font Style". Available Font Styles are: (1) Regular, (2) Bold, (3) Italic, and (4) Bold Italic. Also present there, is a feature that allows you to change the Font size from a minimum of 8 to a maximum of 72. Finally, on this tab is the ability to change the color of the font for the contents of the cell or for a range of selected cells. Click the down arrow in the "Color" box to display available colors.

Color:

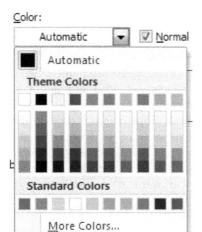

Figure 3.15

CHANGE TAB COLOR OF WORKSHEET

Since we are discussing changing the color of items on a Worksheet this is a good time to discuss changing the color of Worksheet tabs. Click the tab you want to change. Next right-click and select from the resulting shortcut menu the item "Tab Color". Available colors will be displayed. Click the desired color.

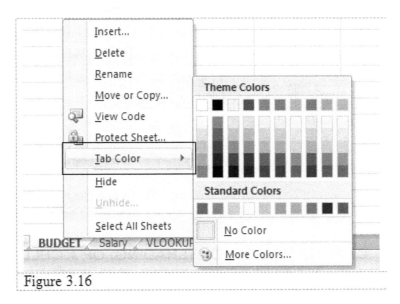

Figure 3.16

INSERT SYMBOLS AND SPECIAL CHARACTERS

This is really not a formatting feature, but it does change the appearance of a Worksheet so I am going to discuss it now. Sometimes there are symbols and special characters you want to use in your Worksheet but they do not appear on your keyboard. This feature is found on the INSERT tab in the TEXT group. Click the Symbol icon to display the "Symbol" dialog box. And then click the desired symbol or special character you want to insert into your Worksheet. Click the INSERT button.

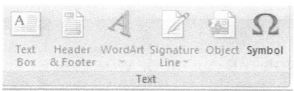

Figure 3.17

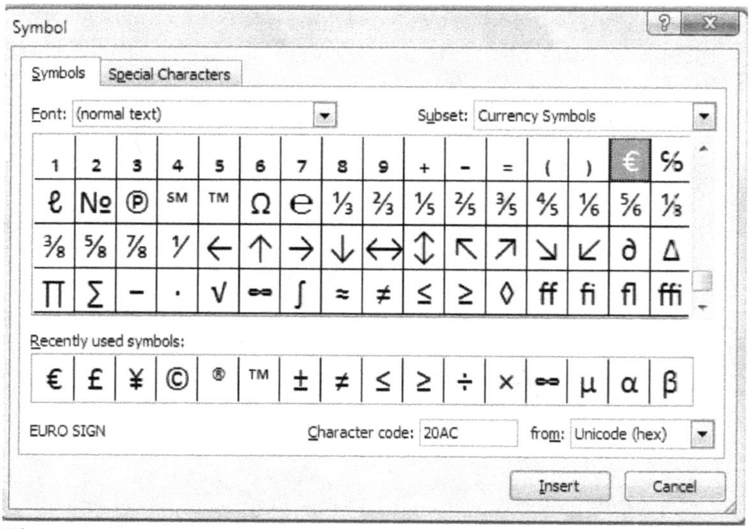

Figure 3.18

CHANGE FILL COLOR (SHADING) OF A CELL

Background coloring (shading) which is called Fill color by Microsoft Excel can be changed. Click the Fill icon on the HOME tab, Font group, and available colors will be displayed. Figure 3.19 shows how cells look with the yellow fill color selected.

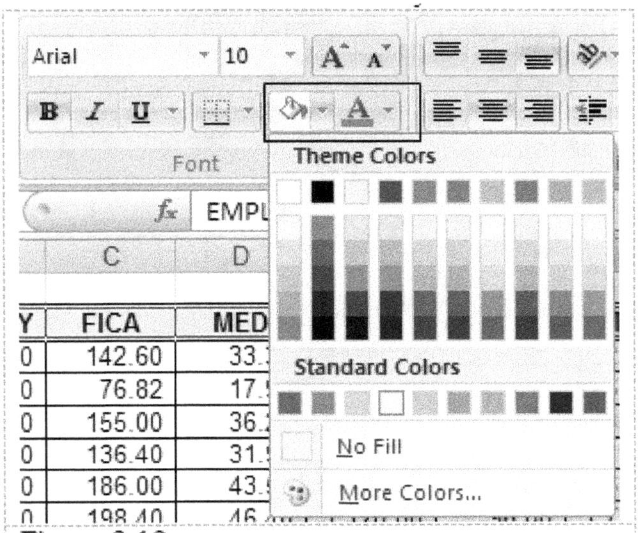

Figure 3.19

APPLY A CELL STYLE

Remember earlier I said that Worksheet appearance is based on personal preference. As you become more experienced using Microsoft Excel you will develop your personal way of formatting labels, titles, and other Worksheet items. You can format target cells one characteristic at a time or you can use predefined formats provided by Microsoft Excel's Style feature. Using the style feature changes all format characteristics at once. And if you don't like any of the predefined formats, you can create and save your own style. The newly created style will be available in any Worksheet in the current Workbook.

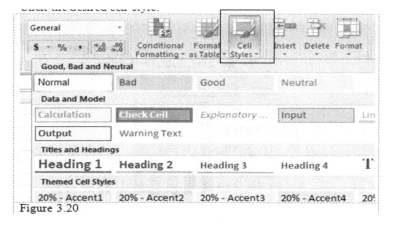

Figure 3.20

The "Style" feature is found on the HOME tab, in the Styles group. Click the Cell Styles icon and available styles are displayed. Click the desired cell style.

To create a new style, go to the bottom of the Style Dialog box and click "New Cell Style. Enter a descriptive name in the "Style Name Box" and then click Format. Existing styles will be presented in the new style dialog box. Clicking Format displays the Format Cells dialog box. Make desired changes and press OK. You will be returned to the New Style dialog box and format elements will have been updated to the new style. Click OK to apply the new style.

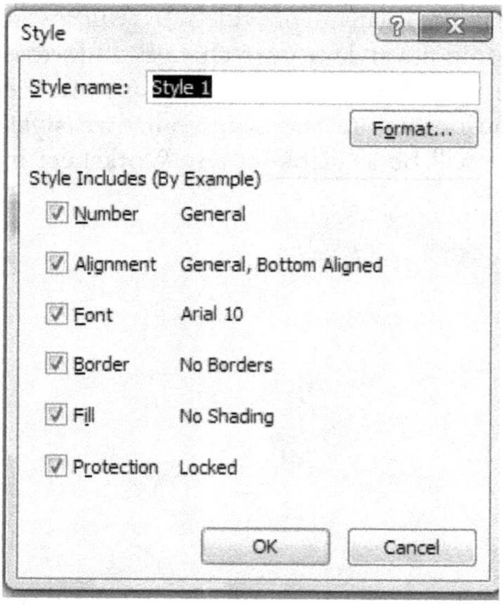

Figure 3.21

USE THE FORMAT PAINTER

The Style feature is a powerful tool for applying multiple format characteristics to a range of cells. Its use is overkill if all you want to do is copy the format changes made to one cell into another cell. The "Format Painter" is found on the HOME tab, Clipboard group. To use, click the cell containing the format you want to copy. Next click the Format Painter icon and then select the target cells. The format will be successfully copied from the source cell into the target cell.

Figure 3.22

ADD OR REMOVE GRIDLINES

Gridlines are what makes a Worksheet look like a Worksheet. Gridlines are the light colored lines that define rows and columns intersections (i.e. cells) on the Worksheet. By default, gridlines do not appear on the printed Worksheet. Sometimes you want a clearer presentation of data in the Worksheet and want to remove gridlines from the worksheet displayed on the screen. Gridlines apply to the entire Worksheet so you cannot remove them from portions of the Worksheet. They must be removed from the entire Worksheet. The "Add / Remove" gridlines feature is found on the VIEW tab, SHOW/HIDE group. To add gridlines add a check mark (click the icon) to the Gridline check box. To remove gridlines remove the check mark in the gridlines checkbox.

UNITS	PRICE	XTENSN
2	10	20
3	20	60
4	15	60
5	65	325
6	3	18
4	2	8

Figure 3.23   Gridlines removed from Worksheet

SUMMARY

Formatting Worksheets is a matter of personal preference. Following are just a few of the many formatting features that are available in Microsoft Excel. Borders can be added to cells. Numbers can be formatted to clearly show what they really mean. Alignment of cell content can be changed. Text fonts and size can be changed. Color can be added to fonts, backgrounds, and to Worksheet tabs. Special characters and symbols can be inserted in the Worksheet. And if you don't see any style that you like, you can create and save a custom style.

CHAPTER 4
USING FILTERS AND SORTING LISTS

With large Worksheets it is important to control the amount of data seen on the screen. You can decide what data is important for a particular analysis and have your Worksheet display only that data. You can also perform calculations on the subset of data appearing on the Worksheet. And you can limit types of data input into cells to reduce or eliminate errors.

SHOWING ONLY THE DATA YOU WANT ON THE SCREEN

Create a Filter to limit the data displayed on a Worksheet. A filter uses criteria suggested by you to select rows to be shown in a Worksheet. Rows not meeting the criteria are hidden from view. These rows still exist on the Worksheet. You just cannot see them while the filter feature is employed. When you turn-on the filter feature, Microsoft Excel treats the entire column where the Active Cell is located as a range. So if you know that you will be using the Filter feature always put a label on the columns that will be included in the filter. Rows meeting the criteria and displayed on the Worksheet is called a "Subset". You can copy, chart, edit, find, format, and print the resulting subset. However, when the filter is employed the find feature only works on the subset.

The Filter feature is found on the Ribbon, Data tab, Sort & Filter group. To turn-on a filter click into a cell in the column you want filtered. Next click the Filter icon. A "Down Arrow" will then be placed next to each column label as an indication that the columns are filter enabled but not yet applied. The filter icon changes color when clicked to indicate the Filter feature is 1employed. To turn-off Filter feature re-click the icon.

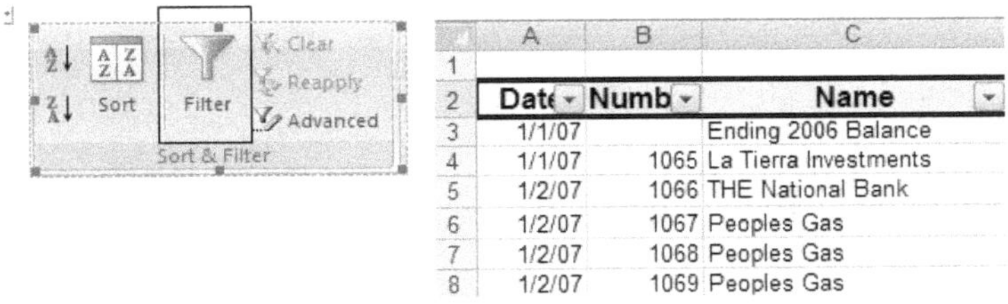

Figure 4.1

81

If you hover over a column heading that has been filter enabled, you will see a screen tip that displays "(Showing All)".

Figure 4.2

Click the down arrow of the column you want to subject to the filter criteria. This will deploy the Filter feature. All cells in the selected column will be displayed in a drop down box. Since the selected column content is text, Text Filters will be employed. Also notice that the items in the filter drop down box are in alphabetical order. If the contents were numbers they would be in ascending sort order. When you first deploy the Filter feature the "(Select All)" box is checked. First remove check mark from the "Select All" box. This removes check marks in all of the other boxes (there is one box for each item in the column and there can be up to 10,000 items in the list). Next put a check mark in the box next to the desired item and it is included in the subset. You can filter more than one column at a time. Additional column filters are additive. Subsequent filters are based on the preceding filter and further reduce the subset.

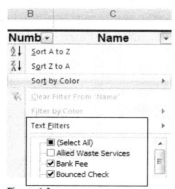

Figure 4.3

Name

Ending 2006 Balance
La Tierra Investments

Filter icon next to label indicates that filtering is deployed on the column.

After you have selected your subset click the Text Filters menu item to access comparison operators. These operators further define which items will appear in the filtered subset.

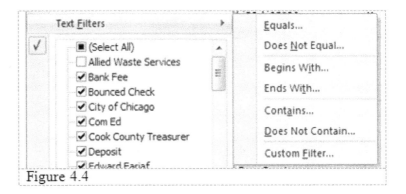

Figure 4.4

Below is a Worksheet that a client uses to track his finances. It is a large Worksheet. Suppose I only wanted to see information about payments to Peoples Gas for the month of January. I would have to deploy the Filter feature on two columns, (1) first on the name column and then (2) on the date column. The resulting subset would contain rows that met both criteria.

Date	Numb	Name
1/2/07	1067	Peoples Gas
1/2/07	1068	Peoples Gas
1/2/07	1069	Peoples Gas
1/2/07	1070	Peoples Gas
1/2/07	1071	Peoples Gas

Figure 4.5 Filter 2 columns

There are many more Filter features available; too many to discuss. You should spend some time exploring all of the Filter features.

CALCULATIONS ON FILTERED DATA

Now that you have the desired subset you can use eleven different functions to perform calculations on the data.

We use the SUBTOTAL function which takes as its first argument a choice of eleven different Worksheet functions.

Figure 4.6 Subtotal Syntax

"ref1, ref2,….." are 1 to 254 ranges or reference that you want to subtotal.

You can perform eleven different calculations on the filtered subset by using as the first argument the desired function. You can calculate the average, count, maximum, minimum, standard deviation, sum, and variance of the subset items. Following table shows the function number used for each function.

function_num (Includes hidden value)	function_num (Ignores hidden value)	Function
1	101	AVERAGE
2	102	COUNT
3	103	COUNTA
4	104	MAX
5	105	MIN
6	106	PRODUCT
7	107	STDEV
8	108	STDEVP
9	109	SUM
10	110	VAR
11	111	VARP

	F213			f_x	=SUBTOTAL(4,F6:F23)		

	A	B	C		D	E	F
1							
2	Date	Numb	Name		Description		Debit
6	1/2/07	1067	Peoples Gas		Gas Service	x	65.38
7	1/2/07	1068	Peoples Gas		Office Gas Service	x	371.80
8	1/2/07	1069	Peoples Gas		Gas Service	x	49.23
9	1/2/07	1070	Peoples Gas		Gas Service	x	60.23
10	1/2/07	1071	Peoples Gas		Gas Service	x	28.01
19	1/30/07	1076	Peoples Gas		Gas Service		78.27
20	1/30/07	1077	Peoples Gas		Gas Service		32.75
21	1/30/07	1078	Peoples Gas		Gas Service		127.44
22	1/30/07	1079	Peoples Gas		Gas Service		69.95
23	1/30/07	1080	Peoples Gas		Gas Service		34.13
211							
212							917.19
213						◊	371.80
214							

Figure 4.7 Performing calculations on filtered subset

I have a filtered subset consisting of payments made to Peoples Gas for the month of January 2007. I have several questions about the payments. First I want to know how much was paid to Peoples Gas during the month of January 2007. Using the SUBTOTAL function with 109 as the first argument (function_num for the SUM function) and the range of the subset (F6:F23), I calculated the total payments as $917.19. Changing the first argument to 4 (function_num for MAX) I calculated the largest payment to be $371.80. By changing the number of the first argument I can perform eleven different calculations on the data in the subset. See Figure 4.7.

DATA INPUT VALIDATION

You can control the type of content users can enter into a cell. Data input can be limited to whole numbers, numbers fitting within a range, dates within a range, or a choice by using a list. The Data Validation feature is very useful when sharing Workbooks with co-workers. With the Data Validation feature you can ensure that all users are inputting the same type of data into the cells. The Data Validation feature is found on the RIBBON, DATA tab, Data Tools group.

85

Figure 4.8 Data Validation

To deploy the Data Validation feature click the Data Validation icon to display the Data Validation dialog box. This is where the data validation magic takes place. The Settings tab is where you set Validation Criteria. Start by setting criteria in the "Allow" box and then refine the criteria using the "Data, Minimum, and Maximum" boxes.

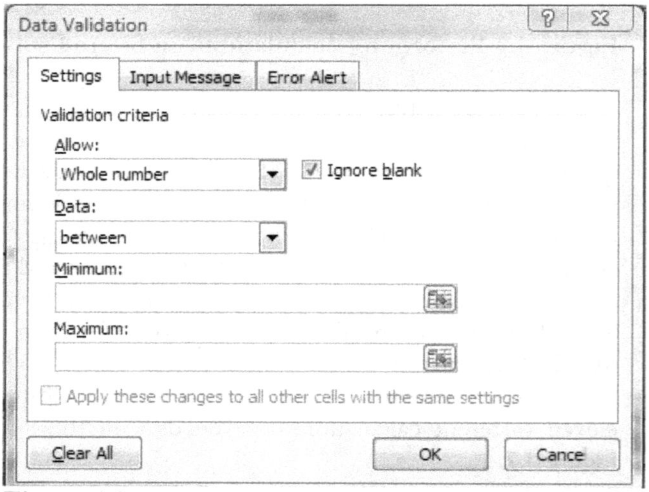

Figure 4.9

In the Allow box, you tell Microsoft Excel to only accept this type of data. Choices are: (1) Any value, (2) Whole number, (3) Decimal, (4) List, (5) Date, (6) Time, (7) Text length, and (8) Custom. We are going to use this feature and tell the user what is acceptable input in a specific cell or group of cells and give user a warning if our suggestions are ignored. First click into the cell or range of cells where you want to use the Data Validation feature. Next click the Data Validation icon and in the Allow box, click Whole number. In the Minimum box type 900 and in the Maximum box type 1600. Next click the "Input Message" tab of the Data Validation dialog box and enter your message.

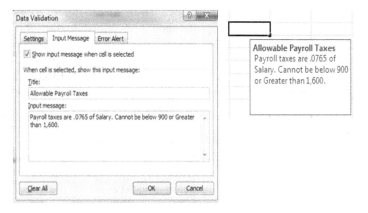

Figure 4.10

If user ignores our posted suggestions an error message is displayed and gives user options as to what can be done next. We create error messages on the "Error Alert" tab and can choose three warning symbols to display with the error message: (1) Stop, (2) Warning, or (3) Information.

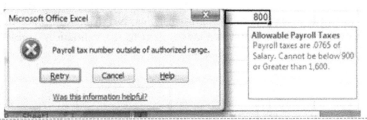

Figure 4.11

The user is allowed to take different action depending on the type of error message displayed. The following table shows the warning icon, type of error alert, and allowable action user can take after trying to enter invalid data into a data validation enabled cell.

Icon	Type	Allowable Action
	Stop	Does not allow user to enter invalid data in a cell. Gives user two options (1) Retry, or (2) Cancel.

	Warning	Warns user that entered data is invalid but allows the input anyway. User given three choices: (1) Click "Yes" to accept invalid entry, (2) Click "NO" to edit the entry, or (3) "Cancel" to delete invalid entry.
	Information	User is told that entry is invalid. User is given two choices: (1) Click "OK" to accept invalid entry or (2) Click "Cancel" to delete invalid entry.

DATA VALIDATION USING A DROP-DOWN LIST

Users can be restricted to picking data input from a list. To create input list select "List" from the "Allow" box. Next click the "Source" box and type list values separated by commas. Click "Input Message" tab and enter desired message. Complete the validation rule by clicking "Error Alert" tab and choosing desired type of error alert. In our example, user is provided choices: Yes, No, Maybe. To see the choices click on the down arrow next to the validation enabled cell.

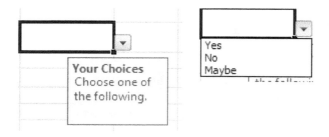

Figure 4.12

DATA VALIDATION BASED ON THE CONTENT OF ANOTHER CELL

You can limit data input based on a calculation. Select cell or range of cells where you want to deploy data validation feature. Click "Settings" tab and enter type of data you want in the "Allow" box. Next select type of restriction you want from the Data box (I used comparison of "less than or equal to" in my example. Next use the Minimum or the Maximum box to specify what is allowed. For example, if you don't budget for Rent Expense to exceed Salary expense (located in cell B6 on our worksheet) type in =B6 in the Maximum box. Remove check mark from "Ignore blank" box to prevent any type of values to be entered in the validated cell if you are using named ranges. Complete validation process by entering message and error alert information.

USE A FORMULA TO RESTRICT INPUT INTO A CELL

Data Validation of a cell can be based on the evaluation of a formula. From the Settings tab, select Custom from the Allow box. In the Formula box enter a formula that calculates a logical value (TRUE if valid or FALSE for invalid entries). For example:

Limiting factor	Formula
Data in cell range A5:A13 contains unique values	=COUNTIF($A$5:$A$13,A5)=1
A cell contains text only. Assume Cell A5	=ISTEXT(A5)
The cell for Payroll taxes (B7) can only be updated if there is a value for Salary (B6) and cannot exceed .0765 x B6.	=AND(B6>0, B7<.0765*B6)

Don't forget to enter validation message and error alert information.

SORTING

An important part of data analysis is sorting. You usually are not concerned with any particular order when entering data into your Worksheet. The order of things becomes important when you have to analyze the inputted data. You might want to arrange your customer list alphabetically to see how many of them have the same last name. You might want to list students in order of grades received on an exam from highest to lowest. Sorting improves the organization of data and allows for better data analysis.

89

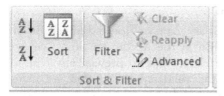

Figure 4.13

The SORT feature is found on the DATA tab of the RIBBON in the SORT & FILTER group.

Figure 4.14
Click the Sort icon to display the SORT Dialog box.

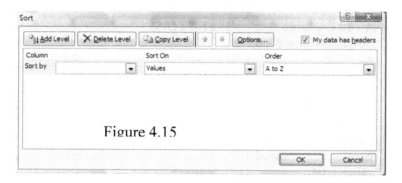

Figure 4.15

	A	B	C
1	FIRST NAME	LAST NAME	SCORE
2	George	Washington	100
3	John	Adams	95
4	Teddy	Roosevelt	90
5	Franklin	Roosevelt	100
6	Grover	Cleveland	60
7	Ike	Eisenhower	99
8	Richard	Nixon	80
9	John	Kennedy	98
10	Lyndon	Johnson	75
11	Thomas	Jefferson	99
12	William	Clinton	79
13	George	Bush	77

In our Worksheet we have a list of students and their scores. Suppose we want to arrange the list in alphabetical order by last name. Click anywhere in the range and then click the Sort icon to display the Sort dialog box. Click the "Column Sort By" box and choose from the resulting drop-down list the column you want to sort by. I chose Last Name. Next click on the "Sort On" box and choose from the resulting drop-down list. Your choices are (1) Values, (2) Cell Color, (3) Font Color, or (4) Cell Icon. I chose values. Next choose desired order. Click into "Order" box and pick from the resulting drop-down list: (1) A to Z, (2) Z to A, or (3) Custom list. If we were sorting numbers, sort order (1) and (2) would be replaced by (1) Smallest to Largest and (2) Largest to Smallest. Click "OK" to complete the sort.

Figure 4.16

Our Worksheet has two students with the same last name. We can apply levels to our sort so that we order our list by last name but student with the highest score will appear first in the list.

A	B	C
FIRST NAME	LAST NAME	SCORE
John	Adams	95
George	Bush	77
Grover	Cleveland	60
William	Clinton	79
Ike	Eisenhower	99
Thomas	Jefferson	99
Lyndon	Johnson	75
John	Kennedy	98
Richard	Nixon	80
Teddy	Roosevelt	90
Franklin	Roosevelt	100
George	Washington	100

Click the "Add Level" button to display sort levels. You can add multiple sort levels. Click the down arrow for the "Then By" box and pick "Score" from the resulting drop-down list. Now student Teddy Roosevelt with a score of 90 (we picked smallest to largest criteria) will appear before Franklin Roosevelt who had a score of 100.

Figure 4.17

USING THE OUTLINE FEATURE

After you sort data you can perform calculations on the reordered list. The SUBTOTAL function is used for calculations on the reordered list. The following functions are available for use: (1) Sum, (2) Count, (3) Average, (4) Max, (5) Min, (6) Product, (7) Standard Deviation for a sample (stdev), and for population (stdevp), and (8) Variance for sample (var) and population (varp). The OUTLINE feature is found on the DATA tab of the RIBBON.

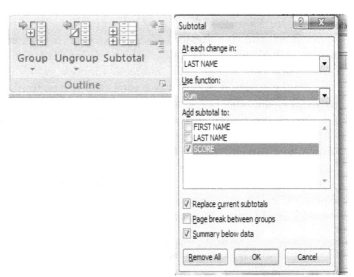

Figure 4.18

To perform calculations on reordered list, click the Subtotal icon and in the "Use function" box pick the type of calculation you want to perform. Set other criteria as desired and press "OK" button to apply. See Figure 4.18.

	A	B	C	D	E
1					
2	CUSTOMER	PROD NO.	PRODUCT	SALES	REGION
3	Richard Daley	JH1001	Individual income taxes	4,000.90	NORTH
4	Jane Burns	JH1002	Programming Excel Using VBA	7,895.00	EAST
5	Jackie Robinson	JH1003	A Brief History of Time	5,432.00	WEST
6	Michael Jordan	JH1004	Visual Basic Exam Guide	3,456.70	NORTH
7	Michael Reese	JH1005	SQL for Dummies	9,876.23	EAST
8	Michael Jackson	JH1006	U.S. Master Tax Guide	8,765.43	SOUTH
9	Sandra Jones	JH1007	Cost Management Controls	7,654.32	WEST
10	Lynnette Smith	JH1008	Intermediate Accounting	6,543.21	WEST
11	Ann Burkke	JH1009	CHH Federal Taxation	5,432.10	SOUTH
12	Dorothy Byrnes	JH1010	MCSD Access	4,321.09	NORTH
13	Constance Williams	JH1011	Tony Hawke Exercise Program	3,210.98	EAST
14	Jennifer Kane	JH1012	Sony Guide to Computers	2,109.88	WEST
15	Vanessa Smyth	JH1013	Satellite Design and Build	1,987.65	NORTH
16	David Grant	JH1014	Glucerna Food Cook Book	9,765.43	NORTH
17	Fred Jones	JH1015	Oxford Guide to Chemistry	8,976.70	EAST
18	Danny Ulman	JH1016	Rhode Scholar Prep Guide	7,645.40	SOUTH
19	Ricky George	JH1017	Sanford Biology	6,789.80	WEST
20	Johnny Walker	JH2009	Jefferson College Chemistry	5,678.90	SOUTH
21	Jack Daniel	JH2010	Algebra for Dummies	4,567.60	EAST
22	Harold Washington	JH2340	Excel 2003 Guide	5,674.80	SOUTH

Figure 4.19

In Figure 4.19 is a Worksheet showing sales to Customers and the Region where customer is located. To prepare marketing budget it would be helpful to know the total sales per region. The Subtotal function will help us answer the question of "What are total sales per region?" Click any cell in the table range and deploy the Sort feature and sort by region. Next click Subtotal icon and set criteria as follows: (1) in the "At each change in" box select Region from drop-down box (there is an item for each column label). We want to accumulate totals for each region. (2) in the "Use function" box select Sum. We want totals per region. (3) in the "Add Subtotal to" box, select Sales. We want the Sales column totaled. See Figure 4.21 for results.

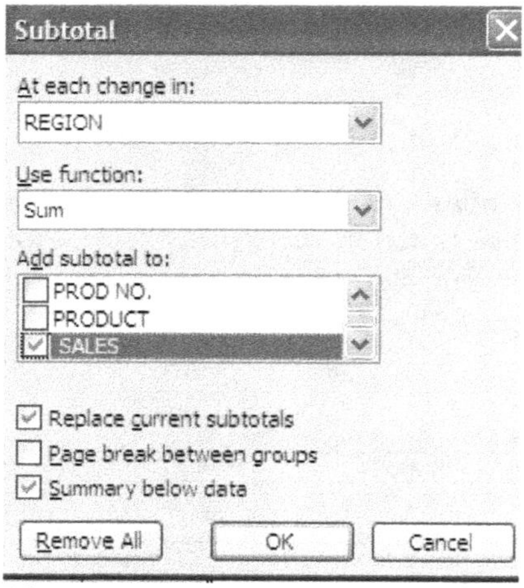

Figure 4.20

	CUSTOMER	PROD NO.	PRODUCT	SALES	REGION
1					
2	CUSTOMER	PROD NO.	PRODUCT	SALES	REGION
3	Jane Burns	JH1002	Programming Excel Using VBA	7,895.00	EAST
4	Michael Reese	JH1005	SQL for Dummies	9,876.23	EAST
5	Constance Williams	JH1011	Tony Hawke Exercise Program	3,210.98	EAST
6	Fred Jones	JH1015	Oxford Guide to Chemistry	8,976.70	EAST
7	Jack Daniel	JH2010	Algebra for Dummies	4,567.60	EAST
8				34,526.51	EAST Total
9	Richard Daley	JH1001	Individual income taxes	4,000.90	NORTH
10	Michael Jordan	JH1004	Visual Basic Exam Guide	3,456.70	NORTH
11	Dorothy Byrnes	JH1010	MCSD Access	4,321.09	NORTH
12	Vanessa Smyth	JH1013	Satellite Design and Build	1,987.65	NORTH
13	David Grant	JH1014	Glucerna Food Cook Book	9,765.43	NORTH
14				23,531.77	NORTH Total
15	Michael Jackson	JH1006	U.S. Master Tax Guide	8,765.43	SOUTH
16	Ann Burkke	JH1009	CHH Federal Taxation	5,432.10	SOUTH
17	Danny Ulman	JH1016	Rhode Scholar Prep Guide	7,645.40	SOUTH
18	Johnny Walker	JH2009	Jefferson College Chemistry	5,678.90	SOUTH
19	Harold Washington	JH2340	Excel 2003 Guide	5,674.80	SOUTH
20				33,196.63	SOUTH Total
21	Jackie Robinson	JH1003	A Brief History of Time	5,432.00	WEST
22	Sandra Jones	JH1007	Cost Management Controls	7,654.32	WEST
23	Lynnette Smith	JH1008	Intermediate Accounting	6,543.21	WEST
24	Jennifer Kane	JH1012	Sony Guide to Computers	2,109.88	WEST
25	Ricky George	JH1017	Sanford Biology	6,789.80	WEST
26				28,529.21	WEST Total
27				119,784.12	Grand Total

Figure 4.21

SUMMARY

Filters are used to limit the data displayed on the screen. Calculations can be performed on filtered data. You can control type of content that can be entered in a cell. Formulas can be used to restrict input into a cell. Data can be sorted (put in Alpha or Rank order). And calculations can be performed on sorted data.

CHAPTER 5
WHAT IF ANALYSIS

Data that has been entered into a Worksheet can be analyzed to answer all sorts of questions. The analysis, however, is limited to the data already entered in the Worksheet. Microsoft Excel does a good job of answering the question of "what were annual sales per region, per salesman". This is a "what happened question". What if we want to know what happens to sales volume if we increase advertising (a what if question). To answer this question we could save an alternative data set in our Worksheet and create formulas to calculate the impact of our changes. Microsoft Excel has "What-if" features that allow you to define one or more alternative data sets and lets you switch between original data and the new data that you create. You can use different data sets in one or more formulas to arrive at various outcomes (i.e. you change values in cells and see how the changes affect the results of formulas on the Worksheet). Microsoft Excel provides three different "What-if analysis" features: (1) Scenarios, (2) Data Tables, and (3) Goal Seek. Both the Scenarios and Data Table features use input values of formulas to determine alternative results. A data table works with one or two variables, but can accept many values for those variables. A Scenario can have as many variables as needed but values are limited to 32. Goal Seek works backwards. It starts with a result and determines the input values that produced the result. With Goal Seek if you know net pay, employee exemptions, and tax rates, you can "Gross it up" to determine the gross pay.

The "What-if" features are found on the DATA tab, Data Tools group of the RIBBON. Click the "What-if" icon and the three choices are displayed.

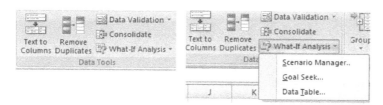

Figure 5.1

USING SCENARIOS TO ANALYZE DIFFERENT VARIABLES

In Figure 5.2 is a Worksheet that holds a "Variable Type" income statement. We want to see what happens to Operating Income when either of the following items is changed: (1) Variable expenses, (2) Fixed manufacturing overhead, or (3) Fixed marketing overhead. Make sure the Worksheet is not hard coded and that the appropriate cells contain formulas. After all, the Scenario manager is used to show changes in formula results as the cells holding the input for the formulas change.

	A	B	C
1	GEORGE ELECTRONICS		
2			
3	Sales	$ 60,000	
4	Less: Variable expenses	24,250	Formulas
5	Contribution Margin	35,750	=B3-B4
6			
7	Less: Fixed manufacturing overhead	20,000	
8	Less: Fixed marketing overhead	12,000	
9	Operating income	$ 3,750	=B5-(B7+B8)

Figure 5.2

Scenarios change cell content in the Worksheet. If you accidentally save the Worksheet after applying the scenario feature you will lose the original data. Therefore it is important to first create an "undo" scenario that will restore the Worksheet to its original state. To use the Scenario feature click the down arrow on "What-if" icon to display the Scenario Manager dialog box. Next click the "Add" button to display the "Add Scenario" dialog box. Enter a descriptive name in the "Scenario name" box. I usually enter "Original" here, so that I know this is the scenario I need to run to return my Worksheet to its original state. In the "Changing cells" box enter B4, B7, B8 separated by commas. These are the cells I will be changing during the scenario process so I want a way to restore them to their original values. Next press "OK" button and in the displayed "Scenario Values" dialog box will be the original values for our Worksheet. Accept these values as is and click "OK" button to update Scenario Manager. Now the "Original Values" scenario is listed in the Scenario Manager.

Figure 5.3

When we are done or whenever we want to restore original values, select the 'Original values choice in the "Scenarios box" and then hit the "Show" button. Worksheet will be returned to its original state.

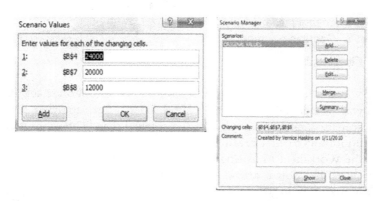

Figure 5.4

Follow the same process to see the effect of changing Variable expense to a new value. Click What-if icon and select the Scenario Manager icon from the drop-down list. On the Scenario Manager dialog box click the add button to display Add Scenario dialog box. Enter a descriptive name in "Scenario name" name box. I entered "Change Variable Expense". Next in the "Changing cells" box enter the cell you want to change. Since Variable expenses are located in cell B4 I entered B4 in this box. Click "OK". The Scenario Values dialog box appears. Enter the new value for cell B4 and click OK. I entered 24000. Now that Change Variable Expense is in the Scenario Manager we can select it and press the Show button to see the changes on our Worksheet. See Figure 5.6 to see that Variable expenses changed from $24,250 to $24,000. As a result of changing Variable expenses, Operating income changed from $3,750 to 4,000.

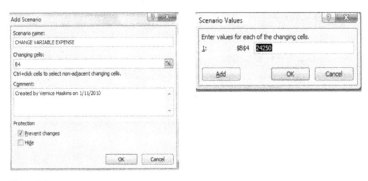

Figure 5.5

	A	B
1	**Geoge Electronics**	
2		
3	Sales	$60,000
4	Less Variable expenses	24,000
5	Contribution margin	36,000
6		
7	Less Fixed manufacturing overhead	20,000
8	Less Fixed marketing overhead	12,000
9	Operating income	$ 4,000

Figure 5.6

We follow the same process to see the effect of changes in "Fixed manufacturing overhead" and "Fixed marketing overhead". Now that desired scenarios are listed in the Scenario Manager, we can toggle between them and see the respective outcomes. And when we are done, select "Original Values" from the Scenario Manager to restore Worksheet to original state. When you save the Worksheet, Scenario Manager is saved also and will be available the next time you open the Worksheet.

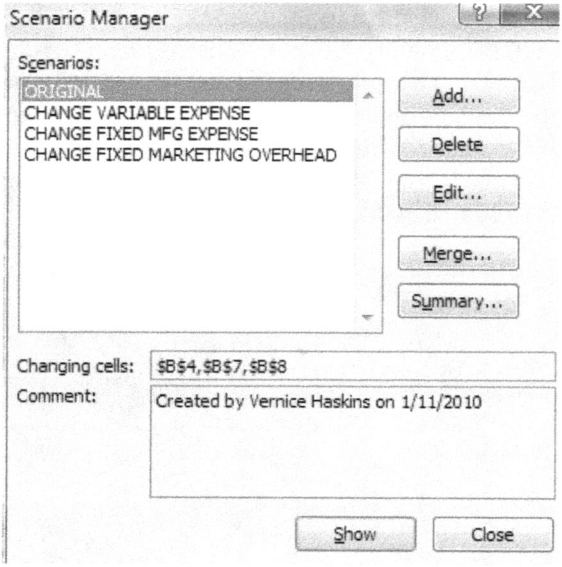

Figure 5.7

SCENARIO SUMMARY

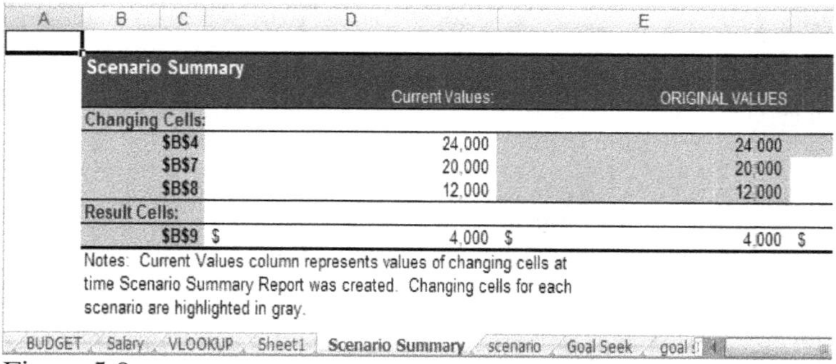

Figure 5.8

Scenario Summary allows you to see all of the created scenarios side-by-side in a new Worksheet that is created when you use Scenario Summary feature. See Figure 5.8. New Worksheet is automatically named "Scenario Summary" by Microsoft Excel. To use Scenario Summary click the "Summary" button on the Scenario Manager. The "Scenario Summary" dialog box is then displayed. Select the "Report Type" and enter an appropriate cell reference (cell holding the different results after applying the different scenarios). Hit "OK" and Microsoft Excel creates new Worksheet with summary information.

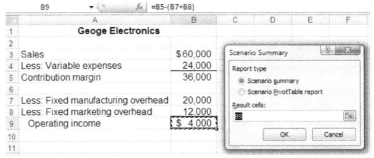

	A	B	C	D	E	F
1	**Geoge Electronics**					
2						
3	Sales	$60,000				
4	Less: Variable expenses	24,000				
5	Contribution margin	36,000				
6						
7	Less: Fixed manufacturing overhead	20,000				
8	Less: Fixed marketing overhead	12,000				
9	Operating income	$ 4,000				
10						
11						

Figure 5.9

USE GOAL SEEK TO DETERMINE HOW TO GET A DESIRED RESULT

Goal Seek is used to determine the necessary inputs to make a formula calculate to a specific outcome. Suppose you have an income statement in a Worksheet which shows "operating income" of $360,000 based on variable expense (always a percentage of sales) and fixed expense of $800,000. Your CFO comes to you late in the evening and says "Quickly I need to know what sales level will generate an operating income of $424,000. If you are an experienced accountant you can use cost-volume-profit analysis to answer this question. I will show you how in a later chapter. If you don't know cost-volume-profit analysis techniques you can still answer the CFO's question using the Goal Seek feature. Goal seek only allows you to input one value. If you want to work with more than one input value you have to use the Solver add-in (more on this later).

	A	B	C
1		Dollars	Pecent of Sales
2	Sales	$2,900,000	100%
3	Variable Expense	1,740,000	60%
4	Contribution Margin	$1,160,000	40%
5	Less: Fixed Expenses	800,000	
6	Operating income	$ 360,000	
7			
8	Breakeven point	$2,000,000	
9	Target income	$ 424,000	
10	Sales to reach Target	$3,060,000	
11			
12	Contribution Margin is sales minus variable expenses		

Figure 5.10

101

You have to set up your Worksheet first. Remember that Goal Seek works by changing the value in a formula to get a different result. Worksheet must have formulas for this to work. In cell B1, type "Dollars". In cell C1, type Percent of Sales. I am thinking ahead to when we discuss Cost-Volume-Profit Analysis. I am going to use this same Worksheet when we have that discussion. We really don't need cells B1 and C1 unless we want to label our columns so other users know what we are trying to show.

In the cells A2:A6 type in the following: A2 type Sales, A3 type Variable Expense, A4 type Contribution Margin, A5 type "Less: Fixed Expenses, A6 type operating income.

Now enter column B items. In cell B2 enter $2,900,000. This is what we want Goal Seek to resolve. In cell B3 enter the formula: "=B2*.60". We are saying that Variable Expense always equal 60% of sales. In cell B4 enter the formula: "=B2-B3" to calculate Contribution Margin. Contribution Margin is Sales minus Variable Expense. In cell B5 enter $800,000 which represents value for Fixed Expenses. And in cell B6 which represents Operating income, enter the formula: "=B4-B5". Operating income is Contribution Margin minus Fixed Expense. Save Worksheet with appropriate name.

Now we are ready to answer the CFO's question of what sales level with our present sales and cost relationships will generate operating income of $424,000. Access the Goal Seek feature from the Data tab, Data Tools group on the RIBBON. Select Goal Seek and the Goal Seek dialog box will be displayed. We enter B6 in the "Set cell" box. We want to change the value in cell B6 which holds the value for operating income. The new value in cell B6 should be set to $424,000 the desired operating income. Type this value in the "To Value" box. Click "OK". Goal Seek runs and attempts to come up with an answer. Results are shown in the "Goal Seek Status" dialog box and the cells on the Worksheet are updated to new values.

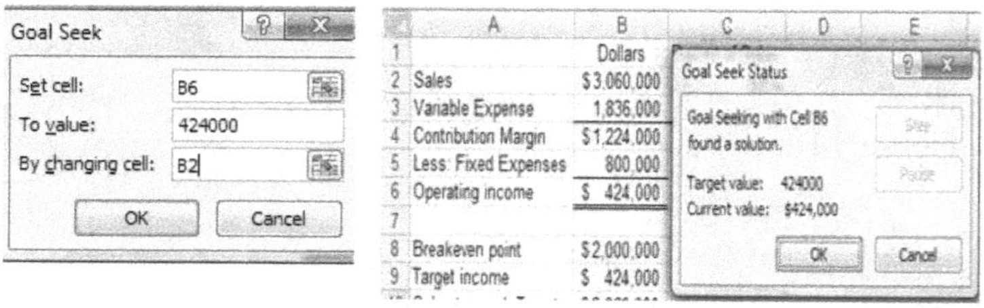

Figure 5.11

The answer to the CFO's question is that Sales must be $3,060,000 for operating income to be $424,000. Click OK to close Goal Seek feature. Also press CTRL+Z (undo feature) to return Worksheet to original state.

USING DATA TABLES

If you have a range of related cells that contain formulas, a Data Table can be used to show the effect of changing one or two (Maximum allowed) of the variables in the formulas. Multiple results of the changes to the variables can be viewed and compared side-by-side in your Worksheet. Only two types of Data Tables are possible in Microsoft Excel (One variable data table, or Two- variable data table).

One-variable data table is used when you want to see the outcome effect of changing just one variable. In our first example we will show the effect of changing the number of units sold has on operating income. Variable values are entered in one column or row and results are displayed in an adjacent column or row. Data Table can be column-oriented (variable values are listed down a column) or row-oriented (variable values are listed across a column).

Set up the Worksheet and then type the list of variables you want to substitute in the input cell either down a column (column oriented) or across one row (row oriented). For appearance sake, it is probably a good idea to leave a few empty columns or rows on either side of the values.

Set up the worksheet as displayed in Figure 5.12. For this to work we have to use formulas to represent the relationship between sales, variable expense, fixed expense, and operating income. We want to see how changing sales amounts affects operating income. So in cell C3 enter the current sales amount. And in cells C4:C6 enter different sales amounts to see how operating income is affected. The resulting effect on operating income will be shown in cells D3:D6.

	A	B	C	D	E
1	Verns Sales corporation		Sales	Operating income	
2					
3	Sales	$4.050.000	Formulas		
4	Less: Variable Expenses	2,430.000	=B3* 60		
5	Contribution Margin	1,620.000	=B3-B4		
6	Less: Direct fixed Expenses	200.000			
7	Operating income	$1,420.000	=B5-B6		
8					

Figure 5.12

103

Steps to create a One-Variable Data Table:

1.   For column-oriented table, type the formula to be
    evaluated in the cell one row above and one cell to the
    right of the column of values. If you want to see
    effects of various other values on other formulas, type
    additional formulas in cells to the right of the first
    formula. In our example we would type the formula in
    cell D2. Since we want to see how changing sales
    would impact operating income we enter the formula
    to   calculate   operating   income   here   (=B3-
    ((B3*0.60)+B6). Sales − Variable expenses (60% of
    sales) minus Fixed Expenses.

2.   For a row-oriented table, type the formula in the cell
    one column to the left of the first value and one cell
    below the row of values. If you want to see effects of
    various   other   values   on   other   formulas,   type
    additional formulas in cells to below the first formula.

3.   Select range of cells that contain the formulas and
    values you want to substitute. Select range C2:D6.

4.   Click "What-if Analysis" on the Data tab, Data Tools
    group, then click "Data Table".

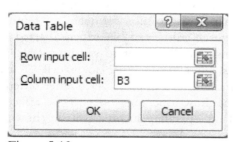

Figure 5.13

5.   For a column-oriented table, enter the cell reference
    for the input cell in the "Column input cell" box. For
    a row-oriented table, enter the cell reference for the
    input cell in the "Row input cell" box. The input cell
    for our example is cell B3. Enter this reference in

"Column input cell". Click "OK" to see results. And you can format result cells as desired.

	A	B	C	D	
1	Verns Sales Corporation		Sales	Operating Income	
2				1,420,000	
3	Sales	$4,050,000	4,050,000	1,420,000	
4	Less: Variable expenses	2,430,000	3,240,000	1,096,000	
5	Contribution Margin	$1,620,000	1,620,000	448,000	
6	Less: Direct fixed Expenses	200,000	1,350,000	340,000	
7	Operating Income	$1,420,000			
8					

Figure 5.14 Resulting Data Table shown in range D3:D6.

The Data Table performs its magic using Array Formulas. Look at the formula bar for cell D3. The curly brackets around the formula {=TABLE(,B3)} reveals that this is an array formula. As with all array formulas you cannot edit individual cells in the array formula range. It is an "All or Nothing" proposition.

D3		f_x {=TABLE(,B3)}			
	A	B	C	D	E
1	Verns Sales Corporation		Sales	Operating Income	
2				1,420,000	
3	Sales	$4,050,000	4,050,000	1,420,000	
4	Less: Variable expenses	2,430,000	3,240,000	1,096,000	
5	Contribution Margin	$1,620,000	1,620,000	448,000	
6	Less: Direct fixed Expenses	200,000	1,350,000	340,000	
7	Operating Income	$1,420,000			
8					

Figure 5.15

Steps to create a Two-Variable Data Table
    Two-Variable data table has a formula with two different input cells and two different lists of input values. The Worksheet in Figure 5.16 is set up to answer question of what happens if we not only vary sales but also vary Direct Fixed Expenses. Originally they were $200,000. What happens to operating income if we also reduce Direct fixed expenses to $150,000, and then to $125,000.

1. Put the formula we used in the One-Variable data table example to calculate operating income. "=B3=((B3*0.60)+B6 into cell C2. In the same column below the formula enter the list of varying sales values.

105

2. Enter the second list (the one for the varying Direct Fixed Expenses) on the right of the formula in the same row.

3. Select the range of cells that holds formula and both input lists, C2:F6 (this defines our table).

4. Click "What-If Analysis" icon on Data Tab, Data Tools Group.

5. Enter B6 in the "Row input cell" box. This is the input cell for the list located in the row to the right of the formula. In our example, this input cell holds Direct Fixed Expenses.

6. Enter B3 in the "Column input cell" box. This is the input cell for the list located in column just below the formula. This input cell holds varying values for Sales. Click "OK" to process and then format results as desired. Column E6 shows that operating income is $390,000 when sales are $1,350,000 and fixed expenses are $150,000.

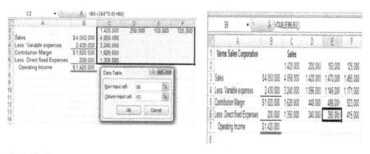

Figure 5.16

SUMMARY

Microsoft Excel has three "What-if Analysis" features: (1) Scenarios, (2) Data Tables, and (3) Goal Seek. Both Scenarios and Data Tables use input values of formulas to obtain alternate results. Goal Seek works backwards from known results to input values. In a later chapter we will discuss sensitivity analysis. In sensitivity analysis we change one or more inputs to get alternative results.

CHAPTER 6
CREATING PIVOT TABLES

The appearance of data in a Worksheet can be changed using Microsoft Excel's many formatting features. What you can't change is the organization of data on the page in the Worksheet. You cannot change for instance, row information to column information. Worksheet layout is static. All is not lost if you change your mind about the layout of a Worksheet. Microsoft Excel has a powerful feature that allows you to create dynamic lists that can be rearranged to meet any of your organizational requirements. The dynamic list is called a "Pivot Table". We use the Pivot table to change Worksheet layout so that we can answer different types of questions about one data set.

For the Pivot table feature to be useful, the Worksheet setup must conform to a few rules. There should be no blank rows or columns in the range of cells to be included in the Pivot table. Also all columns should be labeled. Keep in mind that the range is really a table. In the table, columns represent fields (attributes about a unique object), and rows represent a record (a collection of all of the fields for a unique object). You can create a Pivot table from a list found on your Worksheet or from an external list or database.

Figure 6.1 shows a Worksheet with recorded activity for salesmen. The table matrix consists of Salesman's name, Region where salesman is located, Month sale was made, and the amount of the sales. Even though you cannot see the entire Worksheet on the screen, I will tell you that the last occupied cell in the Worksheet is D34. Cell D34 holds the value for the Grand Total sales. Here is the question: Can I reorganize the data so that sales per salesman per month are summarized. Also can I get this summarized information for each "region"? Finally, is there a way to see all this and total sales per month and the grand total on one screen. The answer to all of the above is "YES" with the use of a Pivot Table.

	A	B	C	D
1	Salesman	Region	Month	Sales
2	George Washington	North	Jan	44,000
3	George Washington	North	Feb	30,000
4	George Washington	North	Mar	50,000
5	George Washington	North	May	60,000
6	John Adams	South	Jan	40,000
7	John Adams	South	Feb	25,000
8	John Adams	South	Mar	34,000
9	John Adams	South	May	22,000
10	Teddy Roosevelt	West	Jan	70,000
11	Teddy Roosevelt	West	Feb	69,000
12	Teddy Roosevelt	West	Mar	55,000
13	Teddy Roosevelt	West	May	45,000
14	Jimmy Carter	South	Jan	22,000
15	Jimmy Carter	South	Feb	23,000

◄ ◄ ► ►I   Goal Seek   goal seek cvp   Data Table   2

Figure 6.1

The Pivot Table feature is found on the Insert tab, Tables group. Following are the steps to create a Pivot Table:

1.   Click any cell in a range of cells. Don't forget that columns must have column headings.

2.   On the Insert tab, Tables Group, click the Pivot Table icon. And choose between PivotTable and Pivot Chart. This determines the type of report you want to create. For now choose PivotTable. After choosing PivotTable, the "Create PivotTable" dialog box will be displayed. Notice that the option "Select a table or range" is clicked. This tells you that the Pivot Table is using a list located on a Worksheet. If you want to create a Pivot Table from external sources click the option "Use an external data source" and follow the on-screen instructions. Review the information in the "Table/Range" box. This should be the range of data that you want in the PivotTable. Change if necessary.

3.   Choose where you want to place PivotTable. Your choices are "New Worksheet" (the default), or "Existing Worksheet" (if you select this option you must put a cell reference indicating where PivotTable

will start). Click "OK" and Microsoft Excel (if you selected New Sheet option) will insert a new Worksheet into your Workbook and therein will display the PivotTable layout.

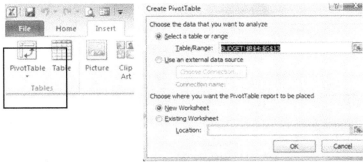

Figure 6.2

4. In addition to the PivotTable layout the "PivotTable Field List" is displayed. Remember earlier we said columns must have header labels. The PivotTable Field List has an item for each column heading. In our example there is an item for (1) Salesman, (2) Region, (3) Month, and (2) Sales. Now we have to decide which of the headings will be records (Row Labels) and which of the headings will be fields (column Labels). When we select heading, text will automatically be placed in leftmost cells and numeric data will be placed to the right of text cells. Note if you click anywhere in the Worksheet outside of the lay-out grid, the PivotTable Field List will disappear. To re-display it click into the lay-out grid.

Figure 6.3

5. Next you have to decide which of the fields you want displayed in the PivotTable. I decided that for this PivotTable, Salesman would be the record, thus I need a row for each salesman. There are two ways to get a field to our PivotTable. In earlier versions of Microsoft Excel you had to select and drag a field to the layout grid. If it was a Row Label there was an identified location to drag the field. And if it was to be a Column Label there was a different location on the layout to drag the field. The "PivotTable" layout grid did not change in version 2010, but the methods of getting fields to the layout grid did change. The new way of getting fields to the grid is to right-click the field and select from the drop menu where in the PivotTable you want to put the field. Your choices are (1) Add to Report Filter (works just like the Filter feature we discussed in Sorting and Filter chapter), (2) Add to Row Labels (for fields that we want to be records), (3) Add to Column Labels (for fields that we want to be record fields, and (4) Add to Values (cells that will hold our numeric values. Right-click Salesman and choose "Add to Row Labels". The field is made bold to indicate that it has been placed on the layout grid. At the bottom of the PivotTable Field List box is an area to drag fields to be placed in the lay-out grid (in deference to earlier versions I guess). So alternatively, I could have selected the Salesman field and dragged it to the Row Labels box at the bottom of the PivotTable Field List box.

6. Since I want Months to be record fields (here they are column headings in our PivotTable), I right-clicked and selected "Add to Column Labels.

7. Right-click Sales and choose "Add to Values" to populate the PivotTable with sales numbers.

8. Finally I want to filter the PivotTable by Regions. I want to be able to see a summary of all regions together, and a summary for individual regions. So right-click Region and select "Add to Report Filter. Now our PivotTable is complete and you can format it as desired.

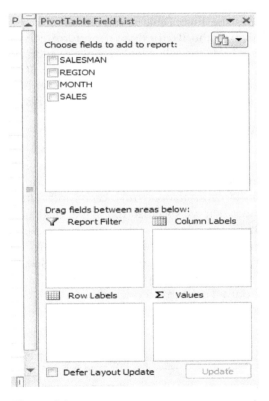

Figure 6.4

A3   fx   Sum of Sales

	A	B	C	D	E	F		G	H	I	J
1	Region	(All)						PivotTable Field List			✗
2											
3	Sum of Sales	Month						Choose fields to add to report:			
4	Salesman	Jan	Feb	Mar	May	Grand Total		☑ Salesman			
5	David Grant	90000	89000	76000	95000	350000		☑ Region			
6	George Washington	44000	30000	50000	60000	184000		☑ Month			
7	Jimmy Carter	22000	23000	40000	19000	104000		☑ Sales			
8	John Adams	40000	25000	34000	22000	121000					
9	Ricky Smits	19000	18000	19500	17000	73500					
10	Sahara Williams	50000	45000	69000	35000	199000		Drag fields between areas below:			
11	Teddy Roosevelt	70000	69000	55000	45000	239000		▼ Report Filter		Column Labels	
12	William Taft	20000	21000	22000	23000	86000		Region ▼		Month ▼	
13	Grand Total	355000	320000	365500	316000	1356500					
14								Row Labels	Σ Values		
15											
16								Salesman ▼	Sum of Sales ▼		
17											
18								☐ Defer Layout Update	Update		
19											

Figure 6.5

9. After the PivotTable is created an "Options" tab is added to the RIBBON. To perform actions on the PivotTable the following Groups are added to the tab: (1) Active Field, (2) Group, (3) Sort, (4) Data, (5) Actions, (6) Tools, and (7) Show/Hide. Most of the action features added have obvious effect, but you should explore each one to see how to perform different actions on the PivotTable

Our resulting PivotTable now shows information summarized for all regions. Using the "Report Filter" we can show information for each individual region. Remember that we specified the region field as the report filter. Let's see what the sales were per salesman in the North region. Click the down arrow next to the Region field. From the resulting drop-down list select " North". Now the PivotTable displays information for the North Region only. To return to original view, click down arrow and choose "All".

	A	B	C	D	E	F
1	Region	North				
2				Figure 6.6		
3	Sum of Sales	Month				
4	Salesman	Jan	Feb	Mar	May	Grand Total
5	George Washington	44000	30000	50000	60000	184000
6	Sahara Williams	50000	45000	69000	35000	199000
7	Grand Total	94000	75000	119000	95000	383000
8						

Most things you can do on a regular Worksheet is possible also on the PivotTable Worksheet. In Figure 6.6

you can see that I applied some conditional formatting to the Salesman cell. Based on some specified criteria, George Washington has a different background color. Another great feature is found on the Active Field Group of the Options tab. What if I wanted my PivotTable to average sales instead of summing cells? Click the "Field Settings" icon to display the "Value Field Settings" dialog box. The usual calculation options are found in the "Summarize value field by" box.

Figure 6.7

CREATE A PIVOTCHART REPORT

You have created a good looking and highly functional PivotTable. The CFO asks you to make a presentation regarding the information in the PivotTable. And as a parting shot tells you that some charts would be nice for the presentation. After all, they say a picture is worth a 1,000 words. No problem you say, because you know how easy it is to create a PivotChart from a PivotTable.

1. Click anywhere in the PivotTable. From the Charts group on the Insert tab select the type of chart you want to create.

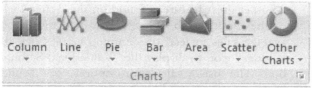

Figure 6.8

2. A "PivotChart" will be displayed. On this chart are selection boxes to set criteria for the chart. You can change (1) Report Filter, (2) Row Fields, and (3)Column Fields.

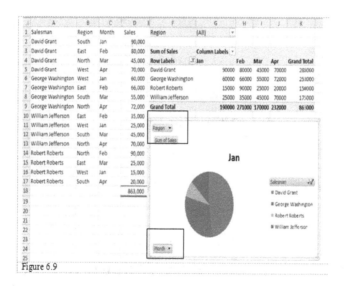

Figure 6.9

AUTOMATIC PIVOTTABLE UPDATE

PivotTables can be updated if the data list used to create them is changed. Assume that the CFO gives you information on a salesman who was left off of the original data list and says that he needs an updated PivotTable for a meeting in the next ten minutes. Not a problem to you the expert Microsoft Excel power user. The salesman Billy Bob from the North region is a new hire and only had sales for the month of May. Billy Bob's sales were $80,000.

1. First thing to do is update original data list with this new information. Then click sheet where

PivotTable is located. Click anywhere in the PivotTable.

2. Microsoft Excel will change the RIBBON to add a new tab named "Options". Click the Refresh icon found there and PivotTable will be updated to reflect the new information. Figure 6.10 shows the updated PivotTable.

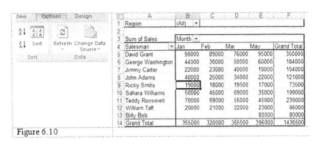

Figure 6.10

USING FORMULAS IN PIVOTTABLES

If calculations found under the summary functions feature that work on value fields do not satisfy your needs, you can create your own formulas in calculated fields and in calculated items. We can for example calculate commissions in a calculated item and have a different commission for each region. Results of commission calculations would automatically be included in the PivotTable subtotals and grand totals.

Formulas used in PivotTables must conform to the following rules:

1. Operators and expressions are allowed just as in regular Worksheets.

2. Use of constants is Ok, but you cannot use cell references or defined names.

3. Worksheet functions that require cell references or defined names as arguments cannot be used.

4. Array functions are not allowed.

115

5. Field and item names are used to identify elements of a report in your formulas.

6. The difference between Calculated field and a Calculated item follows:

    A. Calculated Fields are calculations based on the fields found in the PivotTable field list. Calculated fields are added to the PivotTable Field list after they are created. A Calculated Field must reside in the Values area of a PivotTable. Using a Calculated Field is just a way to show new information in a PivotTable. It is equivalent to creating a new column field in your source data.

    B. Calculated Items are calculations based on the items found on the drop-down list for each field that has been added to the PivotTable Report. In Figure 6.11, Month is the field and "Jan", "Feb", "Mar", and "May" would be items. Calculated items must reside in the Column Labels, Row Labels, or Report Filter sections of the PivotTable. **CAN NOT** use Calculated item in the Values area of the PivotTable. A Calculated Item is equivalent to adding a new row to the data source; i.e. rows that hold formulas that refer to other rows. Should turn-off Grand Total feature to avoid double counting. (To turn off Grand Total feature navigate to PivotTable Tools, Design, Layout, Grand Totals).

7. Formulas for calculated fields operate on the sum of the underlying data and not on the individual elements of that field. In our example if we create a formula on the Sales Field (=Sales *1.5). The formula multiplies the sum of the sales for each region by 1.5.

8. Formulas for calculated items do however, operate on the individual records. So the formula: ="JAN" * 200% would multiply each individual item in "JAN" and then summarize together in the Values area.

9. If the name of a field includes more than one field, the fields can be in any order. You must surround names that use more than one field or contain numbers or symbols with single quotation marks.

10. Formulas cannot refer to totals such as Grand Total in our example.

11. Field names can be included in a reference to an item. Item name must be enclosed in square brackets, for example Region[North].

12. Also you can refer to an item by its current sorted position.

Figure 6.11

STEPS TO CREATE FORMULAS IN PIVOTTABLES

1. Decide if you want a calculated field or a calculated item within a field.

2. Calculated field should be used when you want to use data from another field in the formula.

3. Calculated item should be used when you want formula to use data from one or more specific items within a field.
4. **To add a calculated field do the following:**
   (1) Click PivotTable and on the Options tab, click "Calculations Group, and then click "Fields, items, & Sets" icon
   (2)

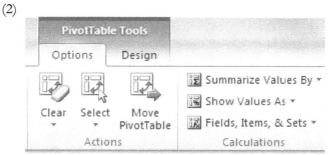

   (3) In the Name box, enter appropriate name for the field.
   (4)

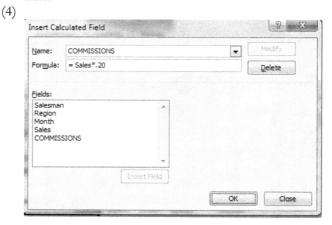

   (5) Enter the formula for the field into the Formula box.
   (6) To use data from another field in the formula, click the Fields box, and then click "Insert Field. In our example we will be calculating a 20% commission on each value in the Sales field. Therefore our formula will be "=Sales*20%".
   (7) Click Add.

DELETE PIVOTTABLE FORMULA

To delete a PivotTable Formula do the following:

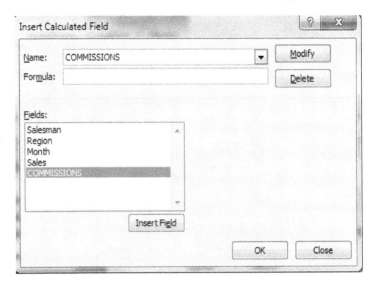

1. Determine if formula is a Calculated field or Calculated Item
2. On the Options tab, Calculations group, Click Fields, Items, & Sets.
3. Select the element you want to delete from the Name box.
4. Click Delete.

USING THE GROUPING FUNCTION

The Worksheet in Figure 6.13 lists students and their scores for a recent exam To evaluate how well the exam was constructed we need to know how many students were in each of the typical grade ranges (i.e., groups) We can use a PivotTable and the Grouping feature to construct a frequency distribution, which in statistics is defined as a summary table with numerically numbered groups. Frequency distributions make it easier to draw conclusions about large data sets. For example you can get an answer to the question: "how many students earned an "A" on the exam (score of 90-100).

119

Figure 6.13

To create a frequency distribution using PivotTable and the related Group feature do the following:

1. Click anywhere in the data range holding students and their scores.

2. From Insert tab click PivotTable icon and then click PivotTable to display "Create PivotTable" dialog box. This time choose to put PivotTable in existing Worksheet. Tell Microsoft Excel where to put PivotTable in existing Worksheet (enter a cell reference indicating where the upper left corner of PivotTable should be). I entered cell D3. Click OK.

3. On the "PivotTable Field List dialog box, put score in "Row Labels" box. Put a second instance of score in the "Values" box.

4. We want to apply grouping to the score in the "Row Labels" area of the PivotTable. So click anywhere in that area and then on the Options tab, "Group" group, click "Group Selection. On the displayed "Grouping" dialog box, Microsoft Excel makes a guess that you want to start your first group at the lowest score and have grouping end at largest score. Based on the characteristics of the number series, it makes a guess as to what you want the group interval to be. Click OK.

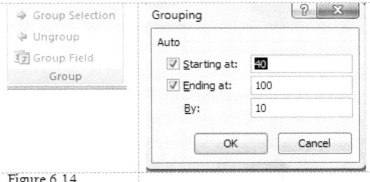

Figure 6.14

5. To get the count in each group, go to "Calculations Group", then click "Summarize Values By" icon and select "Count". Figure 6.13 shows resulting PivotTable. Six (6) students received a score of "90-100".

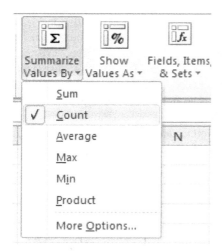

SUMMARY

One of the most powerful features of Microsoft Excel is the PivotTable. It changes your Worksheet from a static to a dynamic presentation of data. Data can be rearranged to answer most questions you can think of. A PivotChart can be constructed from PivotTable data. Also PivotTables can be updated if underlying data changes. Finally, you can perform calculations on the data in the PivotTable.

CHAPTER 7
CREATING CHARTS

Charts and graphs are useful when analyzing categorical data. Categorical data is where you count the number of items in a category and summarize by frequency or by percentage. A chart or graph is another way to communicate to users what the data means. Charts are especially useful in showing trends in large data sets. Charts can be created on the Worksheet where the data is located or on a separate special "Chart Sheet". The quickest way to create a chart is to press the F11 key and Microsoft Excel will create a chart on a separate Chart Sheet putting your data in visual form. My personal preference is not to use this shortcut because I like my charts next to the actual data that was used to create the chart.

Using Worksheet where we stored student and score data press F11 key and a chart sheet will be inserted in your Workbook.

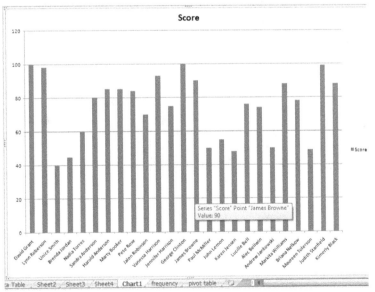

Figure 7.1

Figure 7.1 shows a new separate Worksheet named "Chart1". This is an example of a "Column Chart". There are many different types of charts that you can create. The problem I have with displaying a chart in a separate Worksheet is that underlying data is not shown. You have to switch back to the original Worksheet holding the data to get a good understanding of what the chart is illustrating.

Here is a better approach in my opinion. To create a chart on the Worksheet holding the data, select the range that you want to chart.

1. Go to the "Insert tab", "Charts Group" and select the type of chart you want to create.

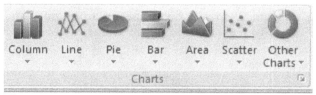

Figure 7.2

2. For comparison purposes choose the "Column type" chart. See the improvement of having chart displayed next to the underlying data?

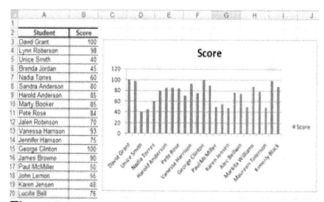

Figure 7.3

BAR CHART

It is election time and pollsters are accumulating data regarding who voters prefer. The following Worksheet holds data on voter preference. A "Bar" chart will be used to present voter preference visually. A Bar chart has a bar for each category. Length of the bar represents the amount, frequency, or percentage of data falling into that category. With a Bar chart you can compare percentages of the various categories.

1. Select the range you want to chart. On the "Insert" tab, "Charts" group, select the Bar Chart icon.

2.

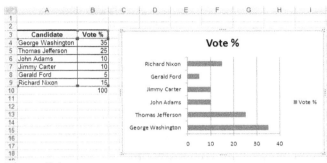

Figure 7.4

PIE CHART

Another way to visually present voter preference is to use a "Pie Chart". A Pie chart is based on a circle. Pie slices are used to represent categories. Size of each slice presents the percentage in each category. There are three different layouts for the Pie chart. Layout 1 shows percentages on the pie for each category. Chart layout is found on the "Design" tab, Charts Layouts group.

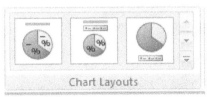

Figure 7.5

125

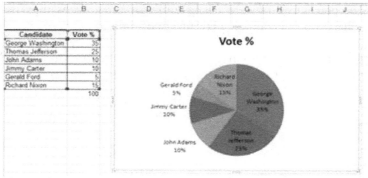

Candidate	Vote %
George Washington	35
Thomas Jefferson	25
John Adams	10
Jimmy Carter	10
Gerald Ford	5
Richard Nixon	15
	100

Figure 7.6

BREAKEVEN CHART

A very important piece of information for business managers is the breakeven point. Breakeven point is where total sales equal total expenses (i.e., zero profit, but also zero loss). The breakeven point can easily be determined by creating a breakeven chart. You need to know the selling price per unit, variable cost per unit, and fixed costs to calculate breakeven point. Set up Worksheet to show a range of units to be sold, and related Total Revenue, Total Variable Cost, Total Fixed Costs, and Total Cost. Select the range for this information (B6:F14). Select line chart from the Charts group on the "Insert" tab. If we look at the breakeven chart based on the sales price, variable cost, and fixed costs which we entered on our Worksheet, we see that breakeven point is 25 units. That is the point where the total revenue line intercepts the total cost line.

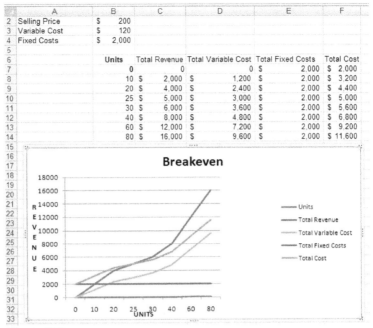

	A	B	C	D	E	F
2	Selling Price	$ 200				
3	Variable Cost	$ 120				
4	Fixed Costs	$ 2,000				
5						
6		Units	Total Revenue	Total Variable Cost	Total Fixed Costs	Total Cost
7		0	0	$ 0	$ 2,000	$ 2,000
8		10	$ 2,000	$ 1,200	$ 2,000	$ 3,200
9		20	$ 4,000	$ 2,400	$ 2,000	$ 4,400
10		25	$ 5,000	$ 3,000	$ 2,000	$ 5,000
11		30	$ 6,000	$ 3,600	$ 2,000	$ 5,600
12		40	$ 8,000	$ 4,800	$ 2,000	$ 6,800
13		60	$ 12,000	$ 7,200	$ 2,000	$ 9,200
14		80	$ 16,000	$ 9,600	$ 2,000	$ 11,600

Figure 7.7

FORMATTING THE CHART

Our breakeven chart did not look like Figure 7.7 when we first created it. We had to apply some formatting to get it to look like that. The first thing we added were labels. The Label feature is found on the "Layout" tab, Labels group.

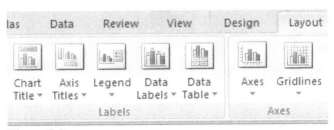

Figure 7.8

To add a title to your chart, click the down arrow on the "Chart Title" icon. There you have choices as to where to locate the title. The "Centered Overlay Title" option was chosen. And we entered a title of "Breakeven".

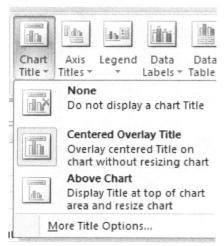

Figure 7.8

Next we entered labels for the horizontal axis and for the vertical axis. We put the label "Revenue" on the vertical axis to identify that series of numbers. We put the label "Units" on the horizontal axis to identify that series of numbers. Click the down arrow by the "Axis Title" icon to access this feature.

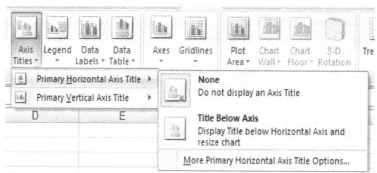

Figure 7.9

Microsoft Excel automatically added a legend on the right-side of the chart. Clicking the "Legend" icon down arrow gives you a choice of where to put the legend.

Figure 7.10

CHANGE CHART COLOR

On the "Format" tab, "Shape Styles" group, are features that let you change "Shape Fill" (background color of chart), "Shape Outline" (color of the border of the chart), and "Shape Effects" (special effects, like shadow, etc.).

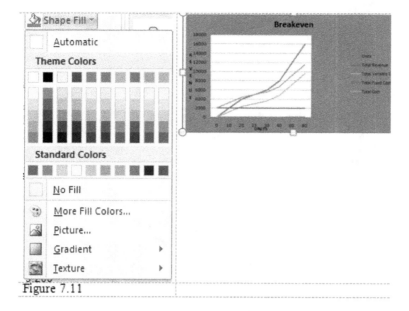

Figure 7.11

ADD UP DOWN ARROWS TO CHART

Drop Lines can be added to the chart to improve visual presentation. Click the Lines icon on the Layout tab, Analysis group to add drop lines to the chart. Drop Lines show where the vertical and horizontal points intercept.

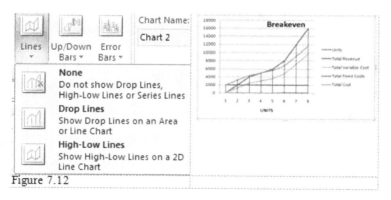

Figure 7.12

ADD GRIDLINES TO CHART

Gridlines can be added to the chart. Gridline feature is found on the "Layout" tab, "Axes Group. You can choose to add Horizontal or Vertical Gridlines or both.

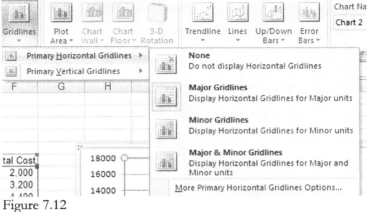

Figure 7.12

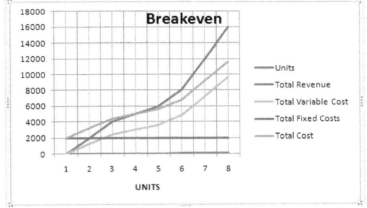

Figure 7.13 Example of Vertical Gridlines

SET GAP ON BAR CHART USED AS A HISTOGRAM

Another way to display frequency or percentage of numerical data is to create a Histogram. A Histogram is just a bar chart without a gap between adjacent bars. Variable of interest is plotted along the horizontal (X) axis. And frequency or percentage of values for each group interval is plotted along the vertical (Y) axis. See figure 7.16.

131

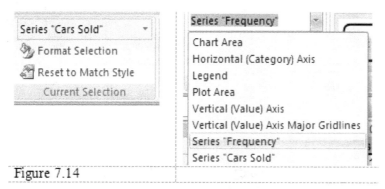

Figure 7.14

STEPS TO REMOVE GAP BETWEEN BARS

1. On the "Format" tab, "Current Selection" group, click the down arrow to display selection options. Choose one of the two series (Frequency or Cars Sold). Next click "Format Selection" icon and the "Format Data Series" dialog box will be displayed.

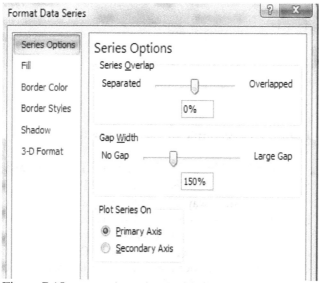

Figure 7.15

2. Select the "Series Options" category and then set the "Gap Width" to zero % and click "Close" button.
3. Do the same with the Frequency series but select "Secondary Axis" in the "Plot Series On" frame.

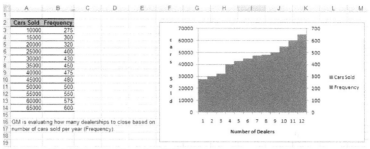

Figure 7.16 Example of a Histogram

SCATTER DIAGRAMS

Sometimes managers need to know the relationship between two numerical variables. A "Scatter Diagram" will show the relationship if there is one. One variable is plotted along the horizontal axis and the other along the vertical axis. On your Worksheet put the independent variable in the left column and the dependent variable in the right column to prepare for the scatter graph. Scatter graph will tell us if the relationship between the dependent variable and independent variable is linear.

1. Select data range holding Machine Hour data and Manufacturing Cost data. On the "Insert ", "Charts" group, click the down arrow of the Scatter Chart icon. Select the type of scatter chart you want. Format as desired.

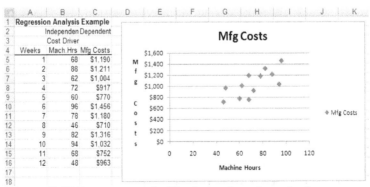

Figure 7.17 Scatter graph. Horizontal and vertical axes formatted with labels.

CHANGE CHART TYPE

After you have created a chart and find yourself unhappy with it, you can change to another type of chart. To change chart type go to the "Design" tab, "Type Group, and click the "Change Chart Type" icon. The "Change Chart Type" dialog box will be displayed so that you can select a different type of chart.

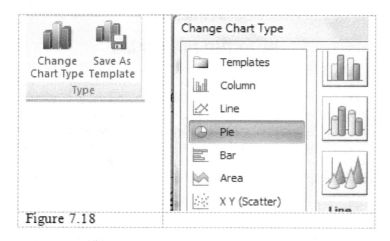

Figure 7.18

SUMMARY

They say a picture is worth a thousand words. Microsoft Excel's chart feature lets you display numerical data in a visual way. Many types of charts are available and they can be changed to meet your needs.

CHAPTER 8
PRINTING

Your Worksheet may not be perfect, but it contains the data you need and is in the right form to facilitate analysis. You are ready to prepare reports to share with your colleagues or to present to your boss. One way to get your reports in the hands of others is to print your Worksheets to paper. All or part of a Worksheet can be printed. Also, you can change the way a Worksheet looks when printed.

There are four ways to access the "Print" feature that allows you to put your Worksheets to paper. The quickest way is to press the shortcut key combination of CTRL+P. This shortcut key combination will display the "Print" dialog box so you can select printing options. The CTRL+F2 key combination also displays "Print " feature. Click the "Print" icon to process the printing operation.

Figure 8.1

The second way is through the "File Tab". Click the File Tab and then select "Print" and you will be taken to the same print area as shown in Figure 8.1.

PRINT PREVIEW

The third way to start the printing process is through the "Print Preview" feature. If you remember one of the first modifications I made when first starting Microsoft Excel was to put the "Print Preview" feature on the Quick Access Bar. I wanted this feature handy because I use it a lot. Click "Print

Preview" and print feature as shown in Figure 8.1 will appear on your screen.

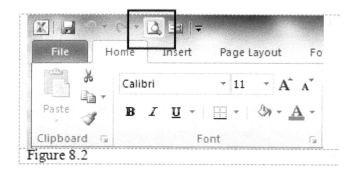

Figure 8.2

The fourth way to access the "Print" feature is through the RIBBON, "Page Layout" tab, "Page Setup" group. Click the group's down arrow to display the "Page Setup" box. Select either "Print" button or "Print Preview" button to display print feature.

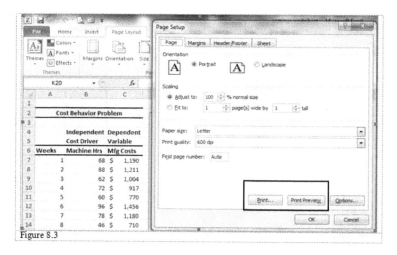

Figure 8.3

SETTING MARGINS

Margins determine where the Worksheets contents will be located on the printed page; how far from the top, bottom, left, and right edge of the page. On "Page Layout" tab, select "Page Setup Group" and click "Margins. There you can use predefined margins, or you can create Custom margins. To create custom margins, enter margin size in the Top, Bottom, Left, and Right boxes. Header and Footer settings must be set smaller than your Top and Bottom margin settings and equal to or larger than the minimum printer margins.

Figure 8.4

To see results of new margin settings, Click 'Show Margins" icon at the bottom of the Print screen. Worksheet will be surrounded by black margin handles. You can manually set margins by dragging these handles to different locations.

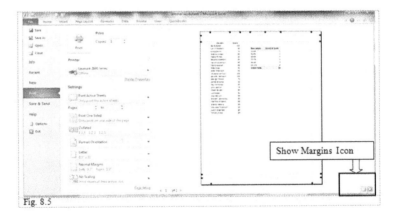

Fig. 8.5

PAGE SETUP FEATURE

Access this feature from the "Page Layout" tab, "Page Setup" group. Click the down arrow for this group to display the "Page Setup" dialog box.

On the "Page Setup" dialog box are tabs containing features for modifying the printed page, changing margin settings, adding a header and footer, and changing print characteristics on the Worksheet. See Figure 8.3.

CHANGE PAPER ORIENTATION

On the "Page" tab you can change the orientation of the paper from "Portrait" to "Landscape" or from "Landscape" to "Portrait" by selecting the appropriate button.

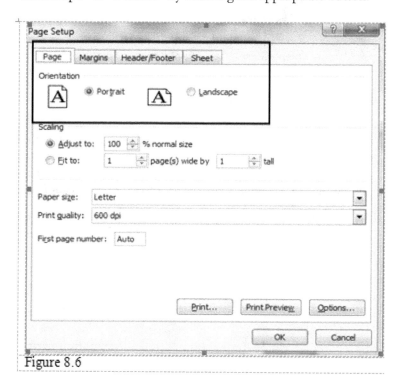

Figure 8.6

Orientation can also be changed by clicking the "Orientation" icon on the "Page Layout" tab, "Page Setup" group.

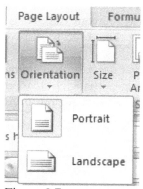

Figure 8.7

CHANGE PAPER SIZE

There are two ways to change paper size of the printed output: (1) Click the "Size" icon on the "Page Layout" tab, "Page Setup" group and select desired paper size, and (2) Click the down arrow on the "Paper Size" box on the "Page Setup" dialog box (See right side of Figure 8.8).

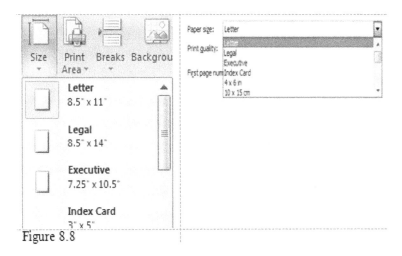

Figure 8.8

SET PRINT AREA

Most Worksheets are bigger than what can fit on the printed page. You can control what part of the Worksheet is printed by using the "Set Print Area" feature. The "Set Print Area" feature is found on the "Page Layout" tab, "Page Setup" group.

Figure 8.9

To set a print area, select the area that you want to print. Then click the down arrow of the "Print Area" icon to display two choices: Set Print Area, Clear Print Area. Select "Set Print Area" option to establish a print area. Select "Clear

Print Area" option to delete a previously set print area. On the Worksheet, a dotted line will enclose the "Set Print Area" that was established. When the Worksheet is printed to paper only the data enclosed in the dotted lines (the Set Print Area) will be printed to paper. "Print Area" can also be established from the "Sheet" tab of the "Page Setup" dialog box. Be careful of how you access the "Page Setup" dialog box. If and only if you access this dialog box through the "Print" feature, the "Print Area Box" and the "Print Titles Box" do not work. Always access the "Page Setup" dialog box from the "Page Layout tab".

	A	B	C	D	E	F	G
				Your Organization Yearly Budget			
		January	February	March	April	May	June
	Expenses						
	Salary	12,770.00	14,047.00	15,451.70	16,996.87	18,696.56	20,566.21
	Payroll Taxes	1,267.00	1,393.70	1,533.07	1,686.38	1,855.01	2,040.52
	Office Supplies	200.00	220.00	242.00	266.20	292.82	322.10
	Postage	50.00	55.00	60.50	66.55	73.21	80.53
	Insurance	100.00	110.00	121.00	133.10	146.41	161.05
	Telephone	1,023.00	1,125.30	1,237.83	1,361.61	1,497.77	1,647.55
	Rent	2,000.00	2,200.00	2,420.00	2,662.00	2,928.20	3,221.02
	Total	17,410.00	19,151.00	21,066.10	23,172.71	25,489.98	28,038.98

Figure 8.10

SET PAGE BREAKS

A page break is where Microsoft Excel stops printing data on one page and starts printing subsequent data on a new page. You can control when this happens by using the "Set Page Break" feature. This feature is found on the "Page Layout" tab in the "Page Setup" Group. Click the down arrow of the "Breaks" icon to display page break choices. If you choose "Insert Page Break" option, location of page breaks will appear on Worksheet as a dotted line, starting at row just above the active cell.

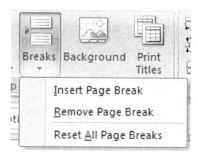

Figure 8.11

Setting page breaks allows you to print a Worksheet with the exact number of pages you want. While you can set page breaks in the Worksheet from the "Normal" view, it is better to set page breaks from the "Page Break Preview. To access this feature go to the "View Tab ", "Workbook Views Group".

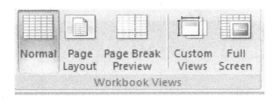

Figure 8.12

Click the "Page Break Preview icon. In this view the Worksheet shows the page number that will be printed. The numbers that appear here, however, will not make it to the printed page. Page breaks can be dragged to the desired location.

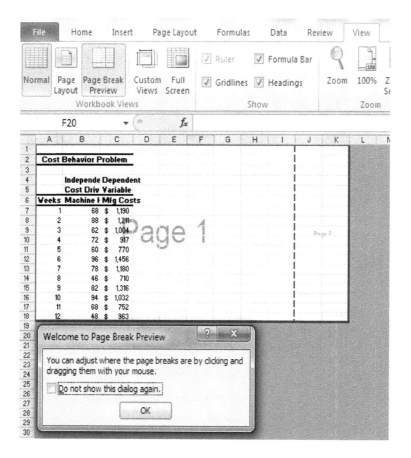

Figure 8.13

ADD BACKGROUND GRAPHIC TO WORKSHEET

While I find this feature distracting; for amusement purposes you can add a background to your Worksheet. Pick a picture that will not keep you from getting your work done. To add a background picture, click the "Background" icon on the "Page Layout tab", "Page Setup Group".

The "Sheet Background" dialog box will be displayed. There you can choose the picture to serve as background for your Worksheet.

PRINT TITLES

The "Print Titles" feature provides a way to specify which Rows to repeat at the top of each printed page and or which Columns to repeat at the left of each printed page.

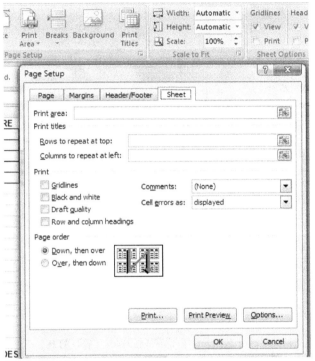

Figure 8.14

To use this feature, click the "Print Titles" icon on the "Page Layout tab", "Page Setup Group" and the "Sheet tab" of the "Page Setup" dialog box will be displayed. To set repeating rows at the top of the Worksheet, enter a range reference in the "Rows to repeat at top" box. To set repeating columns on the left of the Worksheet, put a range reference in the "Columns to repeat at left" box.

USING THE SCALE TO FIT FEATURES

Worksheet Scaling can also be changed here. Scaling is the amount (Size) of the Worksheet that will appear on the printed change. With this feature you can reduce the scale of the Worksheet so that it appears in its entirety on one printed page. The smaller you adjust the Worksheet as a percent of its normal size the more of it you can fit on one printed page. Using the "Fit to" option you can make a large Worksheet fit on one page or more as desired. Paper Size and Print quality can also be modified here. Click the down arrow of "Width" icon to shrink width of printed output to fit maximum number of pages. Click the down arrow of the "Height" icon to shrink the height of printed output to fit a maximum number of pages. Click the spinner up or down to stretch or shrink the printed output a percentage of its actual size. Note that to use this feature the Width feature and the Height feature must be set to "Automatic".

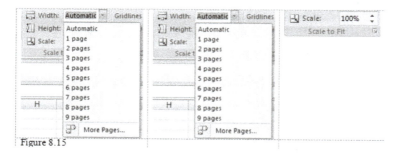

Figure 8.15

USING THE SHEET OPTIONS GROUP

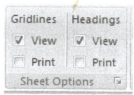

Figure 8.16

Sheet Option Group is found on the "Page Layout" tab. Here you can set options for viewing Gridlines (shown on Worksheet but not printed on outputted page), and for printing the Gridlines on the outputted page. Header options can also be set here. To create a header or footer click the down arrow of the Sheet Options group to display the "Page Setup" dialog box.

ADDING HEADER/FOOTER TO PRINTED WORKSHEET

On the "Header/Footer tab you can add headers and footers to the printed Worksheet.

Figure 8.17

Click the "Custom Header" button to add a header to the printed Worksheet. Enter header text in either the "Left section", "Center section", or "Right section". This positions the header in the left, center, or right side of the printed page. After entering text in one of the sections, text can be formatted by clicking the Format icon. This will cause the standard "Format Cells" dialog box to be displayed so that the text can be set to your desired taste.

Header

To format text: select the text, then choose the Format Text button.
To insert a page number, date, time, file path, filename, or tab name: position the
  insertion point in the edit box, then choose the appropriate button.
To insert picture: press the Insert Picture button. To format your picture, place the
  cursor in the edit box and press the Format Picture button.

Left section: Center section: Right section:

&[Page]&[Date]&[Path]&[File]   **Budget Worksheet**

OK   Cancel

Figure 8.18

There are options, (shown left to right, and in order), on Figure 8.18 to: (1) Insert page number, (2) Insert number of pages, (3) Insert a date, (4) Insert time, (5) Insert file path, (6) Insert file name, (7) Insert sheet name, (8) Insert picture, and (9) Format picture.

Format Text

Figure 8.19 Options to modify Header

The same process is available to add a "Footer" to the printed Worksheet. The options that are available for the header are also available for use with the footer feature.

11/19/2010E:\Excel Book\1st excel worksheet **Budget Worksheet**

	January	February	March	April	May	June
		Your Organization Yearly Budget				
Expenses						
Salary	12,770.00	14,047.00	15,451.70	16,996.87	18,696.56	20,566.21
Payroll Taxes	1,267.00	1,393.70	1,533.07	1,686.38	1,855.01	2,040.52
Office Supplies	200.00	220.00	242.00	266.20	292.82	322.10
Postage	50.00	55.00	60.50	66.55	73.21	80.53
Insurance	100.00	110.00	121.00	133.10	146.41	161.05
Telephone	1,023.00	1,125.30	1,237.83	1,361.61	1,497.77	1,647.55
Rent	2,000.00	2,200.00	2,420.00	2,662.00	2,928.20	3,221.02
Total	17,410.00	19,151.00	21,066.10	23,172.71	25,489.98	28,033.98

Figure 8.20 Example of Header created in Figure 8.18

SUMMARY

A Worksheet that has all of the data needed and formatted in the right way can be output to paper. The user controls how the Worksheet looks on paper. There are a number of ways to control output appearance. Margins can be manipulated, headers and or footers can be inserted, gridlines can be printed to paper. And the size of the Worksheet actually put to paper can be controlled.

CHAPTER 9
USING MACROS TO AUTOMATE REPETITIVE TASKS

There are some things that you do repeatedly when you work on Worksheets. Most of these repetitive tasks are easy and can be done quickly. Some repetitive tasks, however, take a lot of work to accomplish. The Microsoft Excel Macro feature can make your life easier when performing repetitive tasks. The Macro feature records the related steps required to perform a task. Later when you need to perform the same task again, run the Macro and the task is completed automatically. Macros use the Visual Basic for Applications (VBA) programming language to record and store a series of actions needed to perform a task. VBA has been the major scripting language used in Microsoft Office Products since Office 95.

RECORDING A MACRO

The Macro feature is found on the "View" tab, Macros group. When you click the down arrow for this feature you are presented with three choices. You can View a previously recorded Macro, you can Record a new Macro, and you can change Macro record mode from "record absolute cell reference (the Default)" to use Relative cell references. The "View Macros" choice also allows for editing and deleting Macros. With absolute reference, when you select a cell, the Macro will remember the exact cell (not the cell relative to current active cell) used to perform some action. Sometimes you want the Macro to operate on a different range of cells, therefore you would choose the "Use Relative References" menu item.

Figure 9.1

As I said earlier, a Macro uses the VBA programming language to record and store the series of steps needed to accomplish a task. Macros are recorded and stored in Modules. I want you to see the background action that takes place in VBA as a Macro is recorded. We are going to record a Macro and look at how the actions are converted to VBA programming instruction. Follow these steps.

1. Open up a blank Workbook. Make sure it is not maximized.

2. Press ALT+F11 to open the Visual Basic Editor (VBE). This is where we write VBA programming instructions. Make sure VBE is not maximized.

3. Resize and arrange both windows next to each other so that both are visible. Your screen should look like Figure 9.2.

Figure 9.2

4. To start the Macro recorder click into the Microsoft Excel Worksheet and from the "View" tab, click the down arrow and select "Record Macro". The "Record Macro" dialog box will be displayed. In the "Macro name" box you can enter a descriptive name for the Macro or you can accept the name Microsoft Excel provides. You can assign a Shortcut Key to run the Macro by entering a letter in the "CTRL+" box. If you enter a lower case letter here, press CTRL+(whatever key you entered) to run the Macro. If you enter a upper case letter you must press CTRL+SHIFT+(the letter entered) to run the Macro. Be very careful when assigning the shortcut key as this combination overrides shortcut keys previously

149

designated by Microsoft Excel. For example if you assign CTRL+P to run the Macro, CTRL+P will no longer work to start the Print feature. Next you have to decide where you want to store the Macro. Store Macro in the active Workbook ("This Workbook") is the default. You could choose to store Macro in a new Workbook, or in the "Personal Macro Workbook". If you choose to store Macro in the "Personal Macro Workbook", it will be available for use in any Workbook when you open Microsoft Excel. Click "OK" to continue.

Figure 9.3

5. Now Microsoft Excel inserts a new module (named Module1) into the VBE and starts recording the steps performed to accomplish a task.

6. Click into the VBE window, scroll the Project Explorer window (it is the top window in the left pane of the VBE) until you see Module1. Double-click Module1 to move it into the editing window.

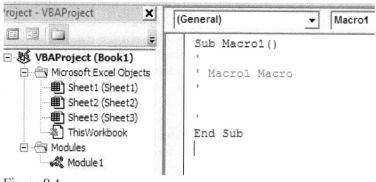

Figure 9.4

7. Notice the sub-procedure wrapper [Sub Macro1 ( ), End Sub] that was inserted in the VBE editor window. VBA programming instructions will be entered here (between the sub-procedure wrapper) as the Macro Recorder records steps to complete a task. A sub-procedure is where we record VBA instructions. More on this concept when we explore in detail VBA programming in a later chapter. The name of this sub-procedure, Macro1 was provided when we entered a descriptive name in the "Macro name" box on the "Record Macro" dialog box.

8. Close the Project Explorer window to maximize the editor window.

9. Click back into Microsoft Excel window and start performing some action. For this example I will select a range of cells and format them. Cell A1 was formatted to change its font to "Times New Roman", "Bold", and number format was changed to "Currency". Click the Macro icon on the view tab and stop the Macro recorder.

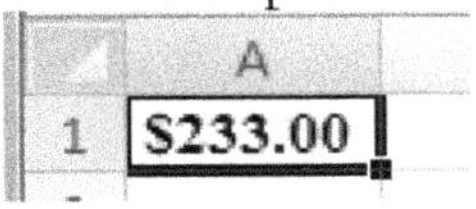

Figure 9.5

Figure 9.6 shows what VBA recorded when the Macro was recorded. There were a lot of VBA instructions written just to make three formatting changes to cell A1. Recording a Macro can sometimes be very inefficient. The more lines of VBA programming instructions (called Code by programmers) in a Macro, the slower it will run. We can edit the Macro to make it run faster. Here is a more efficient Macro that I wrote to do the same formatting, but is more efficient.

Sub Macro1( )
Range ("A1").Select
With Selection.Font
        .Name = "Times New Roman"
        .FontStyle = "Bold"
        .Size = 11
End With
Selection.NumberFormat = "$#,##0.00_) ; ($#,##0.00) "
End Sub

151

To test the revised Macro, click anywhere in the wrapper and press the F5 key. It works!

```
Sub Macro1()
'
' Macro1 Macro
'

    Range("A1").Select
    With Selection.Font
        .Name = "Times New Roman"
        .FontStyle = "Bold"
        .Size = 11
        .Strikethrough = False
        .Superscript = False
        .Subscript = False
        .OutlineFont = False
        .Shadow = False
        .Underline = xlUnderlineStyleNone
        .ThemeColor = xlThemeColorLight1
        .TintAndShade = 0
        .ThemeFont = xlThemeFontNone
    End With
    Selection.NumberFormat = "$#,##0.00_);($#,##0.00)"
End Sub
```

Figure 9.6

Why is the Macro recorder inefficient? Take a look at the "Format Cells" dialog box. On the "Font" tab are numerous "Font" characteristics that can be changed. You can change Font, Effects (Strikethrough, Superscript, and subscript), Font Style, Size, and Color. Now look at the instructions in Figure 9.6. In programming parlance "Font" is an object with properties (characteristics that define the object and make it unique from other objects). The Macro writes a line of instruction to describe the state of each of the properties of the Font object. If we changed one of the properties the line of instruction showing its changed state is mandatory. If we did not change the state of a property the line of instruction is optional, but the Macro records it anyway. Therefore, usually it is safe to eliminate those lines where property was not changed. For example all of the properties that were set equal to "False" can be eliminated (because they were not changed).

HOW TO REVISE A MACRO

On the View tab, click the Macros icon and select View Macros. The Macro dialog box will be displayed. In the Macro name box select the Macro that you want to manipulate. Maybe we want to see how it works before we edit it. Click the "Step into" box and you run each instruction (in order) of the Macro by repeatedly pressing the F8 key. Selecting the "Step into" command button displays the VBE code window so you can see each line of instruction. Press F8 and an instruction runs. Press F8 key again and the next instruction runs. As you step through the Macro check out how each step affects the Worksheet. To do this put the Worksheet and VBE side by side in the window.

If you are satisfied that you know how the Macro works then you are ready to edit the Macro. Click ALT+F4 to return to the Macro dialog box and choose "Edit".

Figure 9.7

Click the "Edit" button and the VBE editor is displayed. Make your changes and press ALT+4 key and you will be returned to the Worksheet.

If you want to delete a Macro, click the "Delete" button on the Macro dialog box.

153

RUN THE MACRO

To run the Macro click the Macro icon on the View tab, and from the resulting dialog box select the Macro you want and then click "Run". Or you can use the shortcut key ALT+F8 to display Macro Dialog box and choose run command from there.

MICROSOFT EXCEL 2010 SECURITY PREVENTS RUNNING MACROS

One of the new features in Microsoft Excel, since version 2007, is the security feature that prevents running Macros of unknown sources which may contain viruses. If your Worksheet will not let you work with Macros you have to turn on the "enable Macros" feature. To enable Macros click the "Options" button on the File tab. Next select the "Trust Center" button and click "Trust Center Settings". Click the "Macro Settings" button and select "Enable all Macros". Click "OK" button.

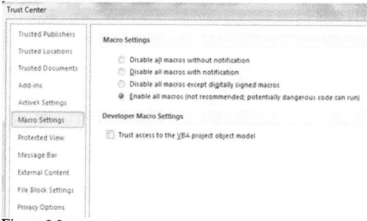

Figure 9.9

PRACTICAL EXAMPLE OF A MACRO

Macros are useful whenever you have complex repetitive tasks to complete. For example if you have a budget on a Worksheet and you want to create a chart to include in your presentation package to the Board of Directors, a Macro would make creating the chart an easy task. Turn on the Macro recorder, create the Macro. Now whenever you need a chart for the Budget data, just run the Macro.

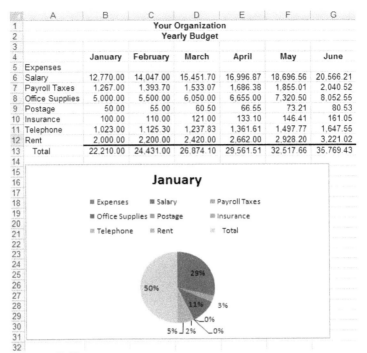

	A	B	C	D	E	F	G
1				Your Organization			
2				Yearly Budget			
3							
4		January	February	March	April	May	June
5	Expenses						
6	Salary	12,770.00	14,047.00	15,451.70	16,996.87	18,696.56	20,566.21
7	Payroll Taxes	1,267.00	1,393.70	1,533.07	1,686.38	1,855.01	2,040.52
8	Office Supplies	5,000.00	5,500.00	6,050.00	6,655.00	7,320.50	8,052.55
9	Postage	50.00	55.00	60.50	66.55	73.21	80.53
10	Insurance	100.00	110.00	121.00	133.10	146.41	161.05
11	Telephone	1,023.00	1,125.30	1,237.83	1,361.61	1,497.77	1,647.55
12	Rent	2,000.00	2,200.00	2,420.00	2,662.00	2,928.20	3,221.02
13	Total	22,210.00	24,431.00	26,874.10	29,561.51	32,517.66	35,769.43

Figure 9.12

```
Sub BUDGETCHART_JAN()
'
' BUDGETCHART_JAN Macro
'

'
    Range("A4:B13").Select
    ActiveSheet.Shapes.AddChart.Select
    ActiveChart.SetSourceData Source:=Range("'MACROS'!$A$4:$B$
    ActiveChart.ChartType = xlPie
    ActiveChart.ApplyLayout (2)
End Sub
```

Figure 9.13

The VBA instructions to create the chart are surprisingly simple.

155

SUMMARY

Repetitive steps can be recorded for use at a later time. The Macro feature uses Visual Basic for Applications to write instructions for the steps it takes to perform some action. Macros can be edited and when no longer useful, they can be deleted. A quick and easy way to learn how to program using VBA is to record a macro and check the VBE to see how action steps are written in code.

CHAPTER 10
PREPARING AND ANALYZING FINANCIAL STATEMENTS

Microsoft Excel has become the essential tool of accountants. The electronic Worksheet created in Microsoft Excel has replaced the pen and pencil worksheets that have been around for hundreds of years. One of the final steps in the accounting cycle is the preparation of a trial balance so that financial statements can be prepared. In the old days this was quite a chore, taking many hours to complete. A trial balance and financial statements can be quickly prepared using a Microsoft Excel Worksheet.

	A	B	C	D	E	F	G
1							
2							
3		Trial Balance		Income Statement		Balance Sheet	
4	Cash	261,435	187,760			73,675	
5	Accounts Rec	7,500				7,500	
6	Furn & Equipment	20,935				20,935	
7	Accum Depr		4187				4187
8	Accts Payable						
9	Notes Payable		50935				50935
10	Owners Equity		6000				6000
11							
12	Sales		212,000		212,000		
13	Salary	138,252		138,252			
14	Payroll taxes	10,572		10,572			
15	Rent	12,000		12,000			
16	Advertising	900		900			
17	Utilities	1,500		1,500			
18	Insurance	600		600			
19	Interest Exp	1,620		1,620			
20	Telephone	1,380		1,380			
21	Deprec Expense	4187		4,187			
22		460,882	460,882	171,012	212,000	102,110	61,122
23				40,988			40,988
24				212,000	212,000	102,110	102,110

Figure 10.1

Figure 10.1 shows a Microsoft Excel Worksheet used to facilitate the preparation of an Income Statement and a Balance Sheet for a company. The trial balance is entered in the first two columns (Column 1 holds Debit values, and Column 2 holds Credit values). Each statement requires the use of two columns (one for Debit amounts, and one for Credit amounts). If you remember from your accounting classroom days, Debits must always equal Credits at the end of an accounting period. Our Worksheet makes it easy to see that Debits do in fact equal Credits and thus we can proceed to prepare the period ending financial statements. Notice that the Worksheet only shows the Income Statement and the Balance Sheet. The Statement of Cash Flows is not shown because it requires further analysis of period activities to complete.

Completed financial statements tell users a story about a company's financial position at a certain point in time and for a period of time. The Balance Sheet tells how well off or not a company is at a particular point in time (i.e. at the end of the year, quarter, or month). The Income Statement reveals financial performance of the company over a period of time. For example, did we make money or lose money over the past year, quarter, or month.

FINANCIAL RATIOS

Microsoft Excel can be used to analyze financial statements and explain in detail the financial condition of a company. We can perform intra-company analysis (comparing different periods for one company), or we can perform inter-company analysis (comparing our company to other companies in the same industry). The analysis is performed by calculating financial ratios. This task was made for Microsoft Excel. Formulas are used to calculate the ratios. And we know what a good tool Microsoft Excel is in working with formulas.

We are going to discuss various financial ratios and learn how to use Microsoft Excel to calculate their formulas. Since we use the same formulas a lot to calculate financial ratios (over and over again, at the end of each accounting period) at the end of this chapter I am going to teach you how to convert these formulas to functions. Functions make formulas easy to use.

Financial ratios are divided into four categories. Each category tells us something different about the financial health or performance of a company. The categories are: (1) Liquidity, (2) Profitability, (3) Efficiency, and (4) Leverage.

LIQUIDITY RATIOS

Liquidity Ratios describe the relationship between the current assets of a company and its current liabilities. They are used to evaluate the "Liquidity" of the company. Liquidity is the ability of the company to pay its short-term bills when they become due. There are two liquidity ratios: Current ratio, and Quick Acid Test ratio.

The Current Ratio is Current Assets divided by Current Liabilities. As a rule of thumb, accountants consider that a current ratio less than 2 indicates liquidity problems. Enter this formula in the Worksheet to calculate Current Ratio: =CA/CL.

$$\text{Current Ratio} = \frac{\text{Current Assets}}{\text{Current Liabilities}}$$

Your Company	
Current Assets	$50,000.00
Current Liabilities	$45,000.00
Current Ratio	1.11

Figure 10.2

A better ratio for calculating liquidity is the "Quick Ratio". The Quick ratio uses Quick Assets in the equation. Quick Assets are cash, Securities, and Receivables. These assets are quickly and easily converted into cash. Therefore, inventory, which may take longer to convert to cash is omitted from Quick Assets. The formula to compute Quick Ratio that as used in the Worksheet is "=(Cash+Securities+Receivables) / Currentliabilities".

$$\text{Quick Ratio} = \frac{\text{(Cash+Securities+Receivables)}}{\text{Current Liabilities}}$$

Figure 10.3

PROFITABILITY RATIOS

Ok you are looking at a company's income statement and it reported $575,000 of net income. Is this good or bad? It depends on the amount of investment that was used to generate this level of net income. There are two profitability ratios to help you evaluate the net income level; Return on Assets and Return on Investment.

The Return on Assets Ratio (ROA) measures the net income generated by Total Assets. It is calculated with the formula: ROA = Net income / Total Assets. Interpret ROA as the number of dollars earned per dollar of assets invested.

The Return on Equity Ratio (ROE) measures the net income generated by Stockholders Equity. ROE takes into account leverage and is calculated with the formula: ROE = Net income /Stockholders Equity. Interpret ROE as the amount earned per dollar of equity investment.

EFFICIENCY RATIOS

Efficiency ratios tell us how well we are using assets to generate sales. Examples are Accounts Receivable turnover, Average collection period, Inventory turnover, and Number of days' sales in inventory. All of these ratios are based on various average assets. Average assets are calculated by adding ending balance to beginning balance and dividing the sum by 2.

LEVERAGE RATIOS

Leverage tells us the extent to which borrowed funds are used to buy assets. Buying assets without using up owners' investment is considered a good thing. There are three leverage ratios: (1) Debt ratio, (2) Debt-to-Equity ratio, and (3) Times interest earned.

CREATING USER-DEFINED FUNCTIONS

You are probably using these formulas a lot. Would it be easier to use functions to calculate the financial ratios than formulas? Well you say, I looked into the Microsoft Excel Formula feature and I did not see functions to calculate financial ratios. You are right, but you can create your own functions using the Visual Basic for Applications programming language. I know I am jumping the gun here, VBA has not been discussed yet. However, creating your own Microsoft Excel functions (called "User Defined Functions") does not take a lot of programming skill or knowledge.

I am going to teach you how to create functions to calculate some of the following financial ratios:

Financial Ratio	How Calculated	Description
(1) Return on Sales	Net income / Sales	Amount earned per dollar of sales
(2) Asset turnover	Sales / Total	Sales generated

		Assets	by Total Assets
(3)	Accounts Receivable turnover	Sales / Average Accts Receivable	Number of sales/collection cycles during the year
(4)	Average Collection period	Average AR/ Avg. daily sales	How long does it take to collect credit sales
(5)	Inventory turnover	Cost of goods sold /Avg. inventory	Number of purchase / sales cycles during the year
(6)	Number of days' sales in inventory	Avg. inventory / Avg. daily cost of goods sold	Using present inventory stock how many days of sales to stock-out
(7)	Debt ratio	Total Liabilities/Total Assets	Percent of borrowed funds used to buy assets
(8)	Debt Equity Ratio	Total Liabilities / Stockholders Equity	Amount of Debt as a percentage of Equity

There are more financial ratios but you get the idea. Let's create some functions to replace the formulas in the above table.

Press the SHIFT+F3 key combination to display the "Insert Function" dialog box.

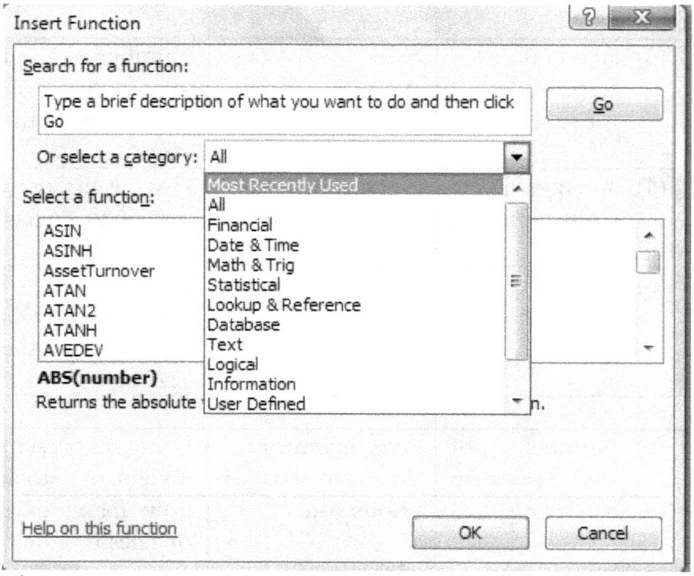

Figure 10.4

Listed in the "Or select a category list" are the functions available in Microsoft Excel organized by category. Notice the "User Defined" category at the bottom of the list. That is where we will house the functions that we will create from the formulas listed in the above table.

User defined functions are created using VBA and are housed in modules. We have to get into the Visual Basic Editor to write VBA instructions (i.e., do some programming, write some code). This is our second trip to the VBE. If you remember, when we viewed recorded Macros it was through modules in the VBE. Now we are going to create our own functions and do it in modules located in the VBE.

To reach the VBE press the key combination ALT+F11. Your screen should look like Figure 10.5. Next you have to insert a module into the blank Visual Basic Editor window. From the Visual Basic Menu (There is no Ribbon to make menu choices) select "Insert", then "Module.

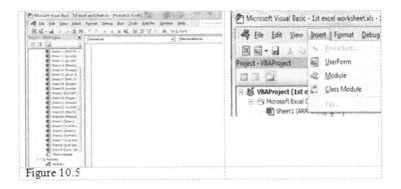

Figure 10.5

Now we are ready to write some code to create our own user defined function.

1. First, type in the keyword "Function" and then type in a name for the function. Name should be descriptive of what the function calculates. Follow name with open parentheses. Between the parentheses enter the arguments for the function and tell Microsoft Excel their data type (string, number). Arguments are inputs (variables) needed to calculate a formula. The following code tells Microsoft Excel to expect a big number as an argument input: FUNCTION CURRRATIO (CurrAsset As Double). Multiple arguments must be separated by commas. This example has one argument.

2. After you enter function arguments and closing parentheses, press ENTER and Microsoft Excel completes the Function Wrapper by entering "END FUNCTION". We write the programming instructions within the wrapper.

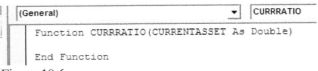

```
(General)                                    CURRRATIO

     Function CURRRATIO(CURRENTASSET As Double)

     End Function
```

Figure 10.6

3. The Function will return one and only one value. Returned value is the result obtained by calculating a formula. So you must use the Function name as the

163

variable to be calculated. See the following function that I wrote to calculate the current ratio.

```
(General)                                    ▾  CurrRatio

Function CURRRATIO(CurrAsset As Double, CurrLiab As Double)
CURRRATIO = CurrAsset / CurrLiab
End Function
```

Figure 10.7

4. Let's test the function on the Worksheet. Press ALT+F4 to return to the Worksheet. At the Worksheet press SHIFT+F3 to insert a function. In the "Or select a category" box select "User Defined" and the "Select a function" box will be populated with and will display all of the functions that you created.

5. Click the "CurrRatio" function and the "Function Arguments" dialog box appears. Enter the required arguments and immediately see calculation results. Arguments can be values or cell references. I used cell references in this example. So if I change the value in one of the cells referenced in the function, result will automatically update. Look at the formula bar in Figure 10.9. Alternatively, I could have calculated the current ratio by writing the following in a cell: "=CurrRatio(B2,B3). Remember that multiple arguments must be separated by commas.

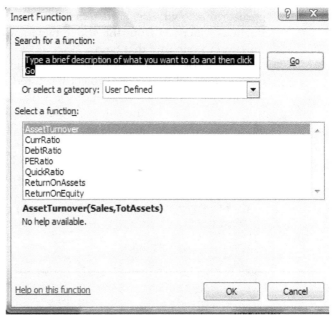

Figure 10.8

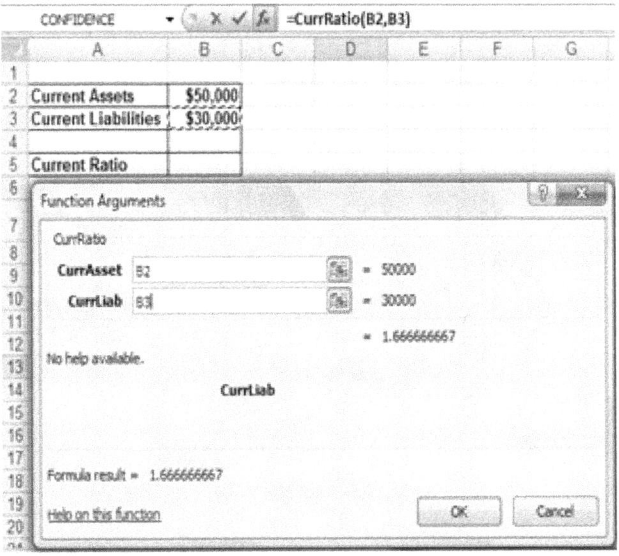

Figure 10.9

User defined functions are used in the Worksheet just like Microsoft Excel's built-in functions. To make sure you understand how to

165

create your own user functions, pick one of the financial functions from the above table and create a function to calculate that ratio.

All of the functions that I created in modules can be accessed from the "Project Explorer" window. It is located on the left margin of the VBE. There you will find listed all of the sheets in the Workbook and all of the modules that were inserted. Click on a module to access the code that was written to create the user defined functions. To delete a module, right-click it and select the "Remove Module" menu item.

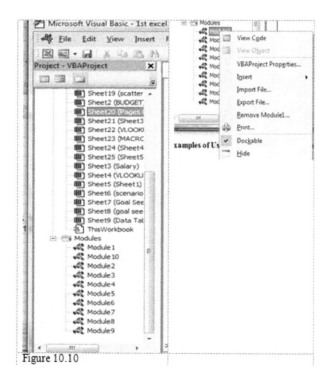

Figure 10.10

EXAMPLES OF USER DEFINED FINANCIAL RATIOS

I clicked on each module containing a user defined function and copied the code. Here are the functions I created.

ASSET TURNOVER RATIO

```
Function AssetTurnover(Sales As Double, TotAssets As Double)
AssetTurnover = Sales / TotAssets
End Function
```

Figure 10.11

It is important to note that spaces are not allowed in Function names or in arguments. If a name requires two words, combine them and capitalize first letter of second word.

QUICK ACID TEST RATIO

```
Function QuickRatio(Cash As Double, Securities As Double, Receivable:
QuickRatio = (Cash + Securities + Receivables) / Liabilities
End Function
```
Figure 10.12

RETURN ON ASSETS RATIO

```
Function ReturnOnAssets(NetIncome As Double, TotAssets As Double)
ReturnOnAssets = NetIncome / TotAssets
End Function
```
Figure 10.13

RETURN ON EQUITY RATIO

```
Function ReturnOnEquity(NetIncome As Long, Stkholdrs As Long)
ReturnOnEquity = NetIncome / Stkholdrs
End Function
```
Figure 10.14

PRICE EARNINGS RATIO

```
Function PERatio(Price As Double, EPS As Double)
PERatio = Price / EPS
End Function
```
Figure 10.15

DEBT RATIO

```
Function DebtRatio(Totliab As Double, TotAssets As Double)
DebtRatio = Totliab / TotAssets
End Function
```
Figure 10.16

RETURN ON SALES

```
Function ReturnOnSales(NetIncome As Double, Sales As Double)
ReturnOnSales = NetIncome / Sales
End Function
```
Figure 10.17

ACCOUNT RECEIVABLE TURNOVER

```
Function AccountsReceivableTurnover(Sales As Double, _
AcctsRecBeg As Double, AcctsRecEnd As Double)
AccountsReceivableTurnover = Sales / ((AcctsRecBeg + AcctsRecEnd) / 2)
End Function
```
Figure 10.18

AVERAGE COLLECTION PERIOD

```
Function AvgCollPeriod(AcctsRecBeg As Double, _
AcctsRecEnd As Double, Sales As Double)
AvgCollPeriod = ((AcctsRecBeg + AcctsRecEnd) / 2) / (Sales / 365)
End Function
```
Figure 10.19

INVENTORY TURNOVER

```
Function InventoryTurnover(CostGoodsSold As Double, _
InventoryBeg As Double, InventoryEnd As Double)
InventoryTurnover = CostGoodsSold / ((InventoryBeg + InventoryEnd) _
/ 2)
End Function
```
Figure 10.20

NUMBER OF DAYS SALES IN INVENTORY

```
Function NumDaysSalesInventory(InventoryBeg As Double, _
InventoryEnd As Double, CGS As Double)
NumDaysSalesInventory = ((InventoryBeg + InventoryEnd) / 2) _
/ ((CGS) / 365)
End Function
```
Figure 10.21

DEBT EQUITY RATIO

```
Function DebtEquity(TotLiab As Double, Stkholders As Double)
DebtEquity = TotLiab / Stkholders
End Function
```

Figure 10.22

USING MICROSOFT EXCEL'S DEPRECIATION FUNCTIONS

To calculate depreciation you have to know (1) cost of the asset, (2) salvage value, (3) useful life, and (4) pattern of use. Two major categories of calculating depreciation are (1) passage of time method and (2) units used method.

There are two passage of time depreciation methods: (1) Straight-line depreciation and (2) Accelerated methods (Declining-balance method and the Sum-of-the-years digits method). Units used method also has two depreciation methods (1) Service-hours depreciation and (2) productive output depreciation.

Straight-line depreciation assumes that asset will be productive on an equal basis over its useful life. Accelerated methods assume that asset will be productive in the early periods of its useful life and decline in productiveness in later years.

CALCULATE STRAIGHT LINE DEPRECIATION

To calculate Straight-line you have to know (1) cost of asset, (2) salvage value, and (3) useful life. The formula to calculate Straight-line depreciation is: "(Cost – Salvage) / Useful life". Microsoft Excel's "SLN Function" is used to calculate Straight-line depreciation. All of Microsoft Excel's depreciation functions are found in the "Financial" category of functions.

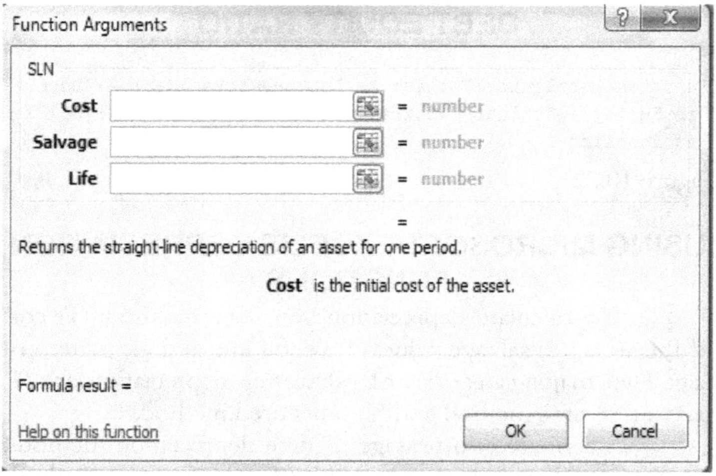

Figure 10.23

CALCULATE DECLINING-BALANCE DEPRECIATION

Declining balance depreciation methods calculate depreciation costs as a constant percentage of the declining book value of an asset. Usually the rate used is twice the straight-line rate, thus the popular name for this method is "Double-Declining Balance depreciation or DDB". Another method required by the Internal Revenue Code on certain assets is 150% declining balance. To determine the straight-line depreciation rate, divide 100 by the asset's useful life. For example the straight line rate for an asset with a useful life of 5 years is 20% (100 / 5). DDB rate would then be 40%. And to calculate DDB depreciation you would multiply 40% by the book value of the asset. Salvage value is not used in DDB calculation, but you of course cannot depreciate any asset below its salvage value. Also you should switch to the straight-line method when the remaining depreciation calculated by the straight-line method exceeds depreciation calculated by declining-balance method.

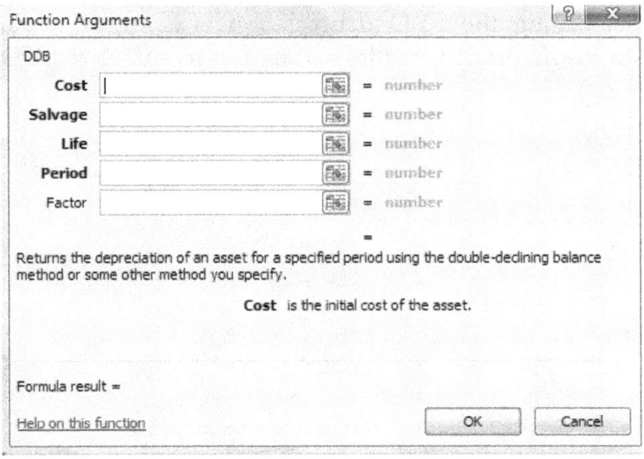

Figure 10.24

To calculate declining-balance depreciation, use the DDB Function. This function requires five arguments: (1) cost, (2) salvage, (3) useful life, (4) period, and (5) factor. Cost, salvage, and life are self-explanatory. Period is used to tell Microsoft Excel which year of depreciation is being calculated. Use this function to calculate depreciation for any year, from year one to end of useful life. Factor argument specifies what percentage of straight-line rate is to be used. Default is 2 (leave blank) for Double-declining balance.

SUM-OF-THE-YEARS-DIGITS DEPRECIATION (SYD)

Another method of declining-balance depreciation method is the Sum-of-the-years-digits method. We teach this method in school, but frankly I have never seen it in the real world. This method uses a fraction (becoming smaller each year) multiplied by (cost − salvage) to calculate a declining depreciation expense. Numerator of fraction is number of years of useful life and the denominator is the sum of all digits from one to the end of the original useful life. For example denominator for an asset with useful life of 5 years would be 15 (1+2+3+4+5). And the fraction to calculate depreciation in the first year would be "5/15". Multiply this fraction by declining book value of asset to calculate depreciation. In our example, year two "fraction" would be "4/15". How long would it take to calculate the denominator if useful life was long, say 20 years? Not very long if you use the following formula: "[n(n+1)] /2. The "n" stands for useful life.

171

Calculating the SYD depreciation is a lot of work. Luckily Microsoft Excel provides a function to calculate SYD depreciation.

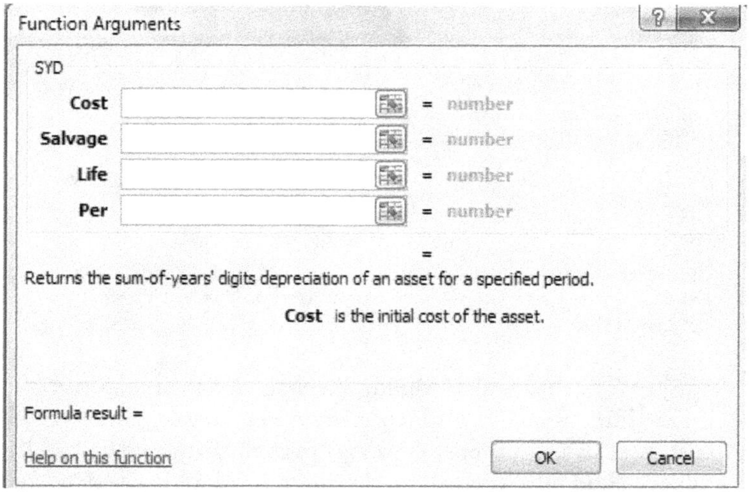

Figure 10.25

The arguments for cost, salvage, and life are self-explanatory. The argument "Per" tells Microsoft Excel the year you want to calculate depreciation for.

SUMMARY

Microsoft Excel is a good tool for preparing and analyzing financial statements. A worksheet is the starting point for preparing a trial balance and subsequent financial statements (Income Statement and Balance Sheet). Analyzing financial statements consists of calculating financial ratios. Formulas are used to calculate these ratios and we know how good Microsoft Excel is at calculating formulas. Formulas that are frequently used can be converted into functions and used just like Microsoft Excel's built-in functions. Converting formulas into functions requires a little Visual Basic for Applications programming skill. Microsoft Excel has built-in depreciation functions to handle most depreciation problems.

CHAPTER 11
TIME VALUE OF MONEY

When making decisions about money received (cash inflows) and money paid (cash outflows) in future periods, interest and changing prices must be considered. For example would you rather receive $100 today or $100 one year from today? The correct answer should be "Show me the money now"! Why will become clear in a moment. Let's consider a mortgage on your house and the fact that mortgage interest is tax deductible. When the mortgage payments are made, there needs to be a way to separate interest payments from principal payments so that we know how much interest expense we can deduct on our taxes. To make the separation is a time value of money problem.

The "Time Value of Money" (TVM) concept is used to answer questions regarding future value verses present value. There are four ways to handle TMV problems: (Mathematical Formulas, TVM tables, Business Calculators, and Microsoft Excel Spreadsheets). What is the value today of money that is to be received or paid in the future? This is a "Present Value" question. Money received or paid in the future must be "discounted" or adjusted to its value today. The opposite question is, "what will money accumulate to in the future if invested today". This is a "Future Value" question. For comparison purposes the two questions must be stated at their respective present values.

CALCULATING INTEREST

Underlying the process of calculating present value and future value is the concept of *interest*. Interest is the money you must pay to use someone else's money. On the other side of the coin, interest is amount earned by letting someone else use (borrow) your money. There are two types of interest: (1) Simple interest, and (2) Compound interest.

SIMPLE INTEREST

If you borrow $1,000 today and have to pay it back one year from today, how much do you have to pay back if you are required to also pay interest at 10%? This is a "Simple Interest" problem. Let's define some terms. The amount borrowed is called the "Principal Amount" ($1,000 in our example). The percentage of the principal that you have to pay

173

to borrow the money (10%) is the "Rate". And the length of time allowed before you have to pay back the money and interest is called "Time". These are the factors we need to calculate simple interest. The formula for calculating simple interest is: $i = p \times r \times t$. For example (i = 1000 x .10 x 1 =$100).

where:
i   Amount of simple interest
p   Principal amount
r   Interest rate (per period)
t   Time (number of periods)

COMPOUND INTEREST

Most present value and future value transactions are based on compound rather than simple interest. With compound interest, the interest earned (or paid) in a period is added to the principal for the next period and interest is computed on that sum. Already you can see that compound interest for multiple periods will be greater than simple interest. Usually compound interest is stated for a period of a year. This is called the compound period. Sometimes interest is stated (compounded) for different periods. Interest can be compounded monthly, quarterly, or semi-annually. For compounding periods other than a year you must adjust interest rate and time by the frequency of compounding. To make the adjustment to rate, divide the rate by the number of compounding periods per year. For example if rate is 8% and interest is compounded quarterly (4 periods per year), divide 8% by 4 to get an adjusted rate of 2% per quarter. To adjust time, multiply time by number of compounding periods per year. Multiplying factor must be the same as was used to calculate adjusted rate. For example if interest is compounded quarterly, multiply time by 4. Time is now adjusted to 4 periods per year.

CALCULATING FUTURE VALUE AND PRESENT VALUE

The answer to the earlier question of "what is your preference, receive $100 today or receive $100 a year from today" is show me the money today. The $100 received today is more valuable. The money received today can be invested for a year and can earn interest. So one year from today you would have $100 + interest. The concept of the Time-Value-of-Money is the comparison of money paid or expected to be received at different time periods.

The comparison of future value to present value is made from two perspectives, (1) Present time-frame and (2) Future time-frame. If you choose to evaluate alternatives from today (present time-frame), all cash flows must be discounted from the future to the present. The value of Cash flows today will be smaller than Cash flows in the future. That is how I know my present values (PV) calculations are right (PV is always smaller than Future Value (FV)). When the future time frame is chosen, all Cash flows must be accumulated to the future period. Value of Cash flows in the future period will always be greater then the value of present Cash flows. Again that's how I know my calculations are right (FV always is greater than PV).

There are four (4) types of present and future value problems. Two types deal with a single payment or single receipt (either present or future values) and two types deal with annuities (either present or future values). An annuity is an equal amount of payments received or paid over a specified number of equal time periods. We can use a formula to calculate each type. Actually there are two types of annuities. If payment is made or received at the end of a period that is called an "Ordinary Annuity". If payment is made or received at the beginning of a period that is call an "Annuity Due". In calculations Annuity Due always has one more period than an Ordinary Annuity. The following is an annuity: required payments of $7,000 per year for 4 years. The following is not an annuity: required payments of $1,000 in year 1, payment of $5,000 in year 2, payment of $500 in year 3, and payment of $500 in year 4.

USING TVM FORMULAS

1. Calculate Future Value of a Single Payment: $FV = P(1 + i)^n$ where:

   FV   Future Value
   P   Principal amount to be accumulated
   i   Interest rate per period
   n   Number of periods

A FV example: Calculate future value of $2,000 to be accumulated at 12% annual interest for 10 years. $FV = PV \times (1+i)^n$

$FV = \$2,000(1+0.12)^{10}$
$FV = \$6,211.70$

2. Calculate Present Value of a Single Payment: $PV = FV(1/(1+i)^n)$

Where:
PV   Present value
FV   Accumulated amount to be discounted
I   Interest rate per period
N   Number of periods

A PV example: Calculate present value of $6,212 discounted at a rate of 12% per year for 10 years. $PV = FV / (1+i)^n$

$PV = \$6,211.70(1 / (1 +.12)^{10})$
$PV = \$2,000$

3. Calculate Future Value of an Annuity : $FV_n = A((1+i)^n -1)/ i)$ where:

FV$_n$ Future value of an annuity
A   Annuity payment to be accumulated
i   Interest rate per period
n   Number of periods

A FV of Annuity example: Calculate future value of annuity of $2,500 for 10 years at a rate of 12% annual interest.

$FV_n = \$2,500((1 + .12)^{10} - 1) / .12)$
$FV_n = \$43,871.84$

4. Calculate Present Value of an Annuity: $PV_n = A(1- (1/(1+i)^n)) /i$ where:

PV$_n$ Present value of an annuity
A   Annuity payment to be discounted
I   Interest rate per period
N   Number of periods

A PV of Annuity example: Calculate present value of an annuity of $7,000 for three years discounted at 10% annual interest.

$$PV_n = \$7,000(1 -(1/(1+.10)^3))/.10$$
$$PV_n = \$17,407.95$$

USING TABLES OR A BUSINESS CALCULATOR TO CALCULATE PRESENT VALUE AND FUTURE VALUE

Using tables are beyond the scope of this book. Besides I can never find a book with the tables when I need it. And I can never find my calculator when I need it.

Microsoft Excel can be used to calculate present value and future value problems with Built-in functions. I always have my notebook computer loaded with Microsoft Excel with me.

To calculate the Future value of a Single Payment using the same factors as used in the above example: press SHIFT+F3 to insert a function:

Figure 11.1

Microsoft Excel Function Argument	What you enter
Rate	Interest rate in decimal form, i.e. 10% entered as .10
Nper	Number of periods
Pmt	Amount of each annuity payment

177

	(leave blank for single amounts, i.e. for initial lump sum)
Pv	The Single initial amount
Type	If cash flows occur at end of period (default) this is an ordinary annuity. Leave blank or enter zero. If cash flows occur at beginning of the period, this is an Annuity Due. Enter 1 to indicate Annuity Due.

If you know the function you need just enter the equal sign, followed by function name, followed by opening parentheses as follows:

Figure 11.2

EXAMPLE USING MICROSOFT EXCEL TO CALCULATE FV OF A SINGLE AMOUNT

FV example. Calculate future value of $2,000 to be accumulated at 12% annual interest for 10 years.

$FV = \$2,000(1+0.12)^{10}$
$FV = \$6,212$

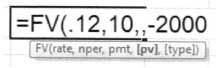

Figure 11.3 Microsoft Excel FV Function

Figure 11.3 shows the syntax for the Future Value Function. Same Function is used to calculate both Future value of a Single Amount and Future Value of an Annuity. The arguments of the function are just different.

For Future Value of Single Amount, omit "pmt" argument and enter an amount in the "pv" argument. Notice in Figure 11.3 that I used a comma as a placeholder to tell the Function that "pmt" argument is zero. Or I could have easily entered zero (0) here. Also always precede both pmt argument and pv argument (when used) with a minus sign. This will yield a positive number as the function result.

EXAMPLE USING MICROSOFT EXCEL TO CALCULATE PV OF A SINGLE AMOUNT

A PV example: Calculate present value of $6,212 discounted at a rate of 12% per year for 10 years.

$PV = \$6,212(1 / (1 + .12)^{10})$
$PV = \$2,000$ (rounded)

=PV(.12,10,0,-6212|
PV(rate, nper, pmt, [fv], [type])

Figure 11.4 Microsoft Excel PV Function

As was the case for the FV Function, the PV function is used to calculate both Present value of a Single Amount and Present Value of an Annuity. Different arguments are used. In Figure 11.4, notice that zero is entered for pmt argument and an amount is entered for the fv argument.

EXAMPLE USING MICROSOFT EXCELTO CALCULATE FV OF AN ANNUITY

A FV of Annuity example: Calculate future value of annuity of $2,500 for 10 years at a rate of 12% annual interest.
$FV_n = \$2,500((1 + .12)^{10} - 1) / .12)$
$FV_n = \$43,872$ (rounded)

=FV(.12,10,-2500|
FV(rate, nper, pmt, [pv], [type])

Figure 11.5 FV of Annuity Function

To calculate the FV of an annuity enter an amount in the pmt argument but leave the pv argument blank.

EXAMPLE USING MICROSOFFT EXCEL TO CALCULATE PV OF AN ANNUITY

A PV of Annuity example: Calculate present value of an annuity of $7,000 for three years discounted at 10% annual interest.

$PV_n = \$7,000(1 - (1/(1+.10)^3))/.10$
$PV_n = \$17,408$ (rounded)

=PV(.10,3,-7000,0,0|

PV(rate, nper, pmt, [fv], [type])

Figure 11.6 PV of Annuity Function

To calculate PV of an Annuity, enter an amount in the pmt argument but leave the fv argument blank.

USING TVM TECHNIQUES TO SOLVE BUSINESS PROBLEMS

Example 1 – Future Value of a Single Payment

Your CFO wants to know how much the company will earn if it invests its excess cash of $250,000 in a 4 year CD that pays 8% compounded quarterly. This is a future value of a single payment problem. Since compounding is quarterly we must adjust both interest rate and period arguments.

	A	B
1	Principal	$ 250,000
2	Interest Rate	8%
3	Period	4 yrs
4	Compounded	Quarterly
5		
6	Future Value	$ 343,196.43
7	Less Investment	$ 250,000.00
8	Interest Earned	$ 93,196.43

| 9 | =FV(.08/4,16,,-250000| |
| 10 | FV(rate, nper, pmt, [pv], [type]) |

Figure 11.7

Example 2 – Present Value of a Single Payment

John James holds a note receivable from a customer. The note is for $30,000, which includes principal and interest. The note is scheduled to be paid in three years. Customer wants to pay off note now. What is pay-off amount if John James and customer agree that discount should take place at 12%.

PV   PV of a single payment
A   30,000
I   12%
N   3 yrs

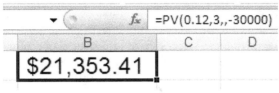

Figure 11.8

Pay-off amount is $21,253.41.

Example 3 – Future Value of an Annuity

CFO asks you to compute how much an investment of $5,000 per year will grow to if invested at an interest rate of 10% for 5 years.

FV   FV of an annuity
A   Annuity   payment
       $5,000
I   10%
N   5 yrs

$5,000 per year invested at a rate of 10% for five years accumulates to $30,525.50.

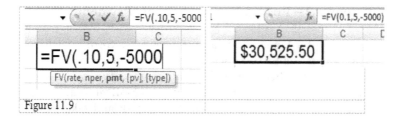

Figure 11.9

Example 4 – Present Value of an Annuity

    I am looking to rent an office for the coming tax season. I investigate two alternatives. Alternative (1) "Building A" offers the office for an annual payment of $24,000, payable at the end of the year, (2) "Building B" offers to rent the office for $2,000 per month, payable at the end of each month. Which alternative should I choose? "Building A" is a present value of single amount problem. "Building B" is a present value of annuity problem. To compare alternatives we must discount both to the present period. Use an interest rate of 12%. Choose "Building A" as it is the cheaper option.

	Payment Cycle	Amount	PV
Building A	Annual	24000	$21,428.57
Building B	Monthly	2000	$22,510.15
int. compounded		0.12	
monthly			
Building A	=PV(.12,1,-24000)		
Building B	PV(rate, nper, pmt, [fv], [type])		

	Payment Cycle	Amount	PV
Building A	Annual	24000	$21,428.57
Building B	Monthly	2000	$22,510.15
int. compounded		0.12	
monthly			
Building A	$21,428.57		
Building B	$22,510.15		

Figure 11.10

Find unknown Interest, Number of Periods, and Payment Amount

    While using the four (4) formulas to calculate Future value and Present value amounts we always knew three of the formula factors and we solved for the fourth. The same thing is true when using Microsoft Excel's TVM functions. Sometimes in business transactions we may not know one of the following factors: (1) Interest rate, (2) Time, or (3) payment amount. Those of you with knowledge of Algebra know that if you have a formula that has four factors and you know three of them, then you can solve for the fourth. That's a lot of work. Microsoft Excel makes it easy for you as there are built-in functions that can be used to find missing (1) interest, (2) time period, and (3) payment amount.

USE THE NPER FUNCTION TO FIND UNKNOWN PERIODS

William Jefferson wants to buy a new car that costs $80,000. He has bad credit so he must pay cash. William has $60,000 now. How long will it take him to get together the $80,000 needed to buy the car if he can invest the $60,000 today at 8% compounded quarterly?

Rate	.02 (8% / 4)
Pmt	0
PV	-60,000 show as negative to represent cash outflow
FV	80,000

CHIINV	▼ X ✓ ƒ =NPER(.02,0,-60000,80000)		
	A	B	C	D
1	Rate	.02 (8% /4)		
2	Pmt	0		
3	PV	$ (60,000)		
4	FV	$ 80,000		
5	NPER	14.52746992		
6				
7	=NPER(.02,0,-60000,80000)			

Figure 11.11

William will have to wait 14.5 quarters or 3.62 years.

DETERMINE UNKOWN INTEREST RATE

Use Microsoft Excel's RATE Function to determine unknown interest rate. Suppose you can buy a bond for $200 today and it will pay you $1,000 at the end of 30 years. What is the interest rate? We know three of the four factors needed to solve this problem. First, let's use the PV formula and solve for interest rate. Then we will see how much easier it is to use the Microsoft Excel "Rate Function". If you look in the formula bar, you see that I also created a user defined function to calculate unknown interest for investments of a single amount.

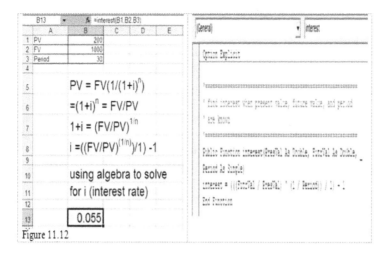

Figure 11.12

A quirk of the Microsoft Excel Rate Function is that you must enter the fv argument as a negative number.

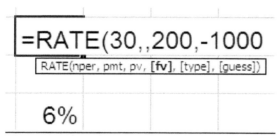

Figure 11.13

DETERMINE PAYMENT AMOUNT

Use Microsoft Excel's PMT Function to determine unknown payment. David Grant purchased a house for $400,000. He made a 10% down payment and financed the rest with a 4% mortgage, compounded monthly. He will pay off the mortgage in monthly payments for 15 years. First payment is due in one month. What are the monthly payments?

Rate   .04 / 12 compounded monthly
Nper   (15 x 12) = 180 months
Pv $400,000 –(400,000-(.10 x 400,000)) = $360,000
Fv   0

Monthly payments are $2,662.88.

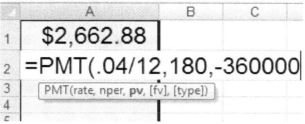

Figure 11.14

PRICING BONDS

Whether you are using bonds to borrow operating funds or are purchasing bonds as an investment you need to know how to calculate the market price of bonds. Market price depends on the credit-worthiness of the bond's seller and the current market interest rate for similar types of bonds available in the market place.

There are two interest rates associated with bonds. There is the market rate for similar bonds and there is the rate included in the bond contract. The rate in the bond contract is the amount of interest that the bond issuer promises to pay the investor for using their funds for the term of the bond issue. Underwriters who package, market, and sale a bond issue will try to make the contract interest (sometimes called stated interest) as close to the market interest as possible.

If the underwriters are on target and the contract interest equals market interest, the bonds will sale at par value (face value of the bond). So a $1,000 bond will sale at $1,000. If the contract rate of interest is less than the market interest for similar bonds, investors will not be willing to pay par value. Investors will only buy these bonds if they are offered a discount from par value. If the contract interest is greater than the market interest on similar bonds, investors will flock to the bond issue and will be willing to pay more than the par value (a bond premium) to acquire the bonds. The question for both the issuer and the buyer of the bonds is "what price should the bonds sell for?"

To price a bond you must calculate the present value of the maturity value of the bond (amount to be paid when the bonds become due) and the present value of remaining interest payments. The discount calculations must use the market rate of interest for similar bonds at that date. We have two components to calculate: (1) present value of maturity

185

value is a present value of a single payment problem, and (2) present value of interest payments is a present value of annuity problem. To get the price, add the two components together.

For example assume that JeffCo wants to sell 10 year 10% bonds of $100,000 on January 15, 2010. Also assume that on this date, market interest for similar bonds is 8% compounded semiannually. At what price will the bonds sale?

1.   Calculate present value of bond maturity value

PV   Present value of bond maturity value
FV $100,000
I   .08/2 = .04, semiannual compounding
N   10yrs x 2 = 20 periods
     Present value of bonds maturity value is $45,638.69.

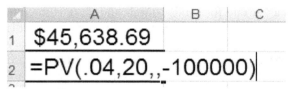

	A	B	C
1	$45,638.69		
2	=PV(.04,20,,-100000)		

Figure 11.15

2.   Calculate present value of 20 remaining interest payments.

PV   PV of interest payments
FV   0
Pmt   ($100,000 x .10) / 2 = $5,000
I   .04
N   20
      Present value of remaining interest payments is $67,951.63.

	A	B
1	$67,951.63	
2	=PV(.04,20,-5000)	
3	PV(rate, nper, **pmt**, [fv], [type])	

Figure 11.16

JeffCo's bond issue will sell for $113,590.32 ($45,638.69+$67,951.63), resulting in a considerable premium of $13,590.32.

Present Value of bond maturity	$ 45,638.69
Present Value of interest payments	67,951.63
Price of the bonds	$113,590.32

When calculating the price of a bond issue, Microsoft Excel does a good job. And it's a pretty quick process, even though you have to perform two present value calculations. Both the present value of the maturity value of the bonds and the present value of the remaining interest payments have to be calculated and then added together to get the price of the bonds.

What if I told you that you could calculate the price of bonds much quicker and in one step using a "User Defined" function? Would that make your life easier if you had to frequently calculate bond prices? Following is a function I wrote to calculate bond prices. To create this function requires a little more skill and knowledge of the Visual Basic Programming language.

BONDPRICE FUNCTION

Steps taken to create BondPrice Function (remember that VBA does not like spaces in names):

1. I know that I can calculate bond price by using the formula for the present value of a single amount and the present value of an annuity and combine the results.
2. What factors do I need to calculate the formulas? The factors needed to calculate Bond Price will become the arguments for my function.

Factors Needed	VBA Argument Name	Amount for our Example
Maturity Value of Bonds	MaturityValue	100000
Market Interest	MktInterestRate	.08

Rate		
Term of Bonds	TermOfBonds	10
Compounding Period	CompoundPeriod	2
Interest payments	Pmts	5000

3. From the Worksheet press ALT+F11 to display the Visual Basic Editor. Functions are written in modules. From the Visual Basic menu choose "Insert" and then "Module". Now you are ready to write some code.

4. Type the word "FUNCTION" and then type a "beginning parentheses". Now we have to tell Visual Basic the input arguments that the function requires to solve the problem. We also have to tell Visual Basic the maximum size of the input argument. Visual Basic uses this information to set space aside in memory to hold the argument variable.

5. Enter the first argument: "MaturityValue as Double". This tells Visual Basic the argument name "MaturityValue" and its size "As Double". A double is a big number. Enter the rest of the arguments and their size.

6. So that I can remember the next week what my program was supposed to do, I document the program with comments. Start a line of code with the single quotation mark and Visual Basic assumes that what follows is a comment and is not to be processed. Comments remind me of what the instructions following the comment are supposed to accomplish. Comments are shown in green type.

7. Variables are used in the formulas. You need to tell Visual Basic what variables you will be using in the formulas and their size. Use the "Dim" statement to declare your variables and use the "As" operator to report their size.

8. Now you are ready to enter your first formula. Remember if interest is compounded on any period other than a year you have to adjust both the interest rate and the number of periods. Divide interest rate by number of compound periods in a year and multiply the number of periods by the same number of compound periods. Thus if interest is compounded quarterly, divide the interest rate by 4 and multiply the periods by 4. The first two formulas ("intrate" and "Perod") adjust interest rate and periods by the compounding factor.

9. Enter the formula to calculate the present value of a single amount. This is the present value of the maturity value of the bonds. $PV = A(1/(1+i)^n)$. Write it in a way that Microsoft Excel and Visual Basic understands. See Figure 11.17 for an example of how the formula should be written. Formula results are assigned to the variable "PVMaturity".

10. Next enter the formula for the present value of an annuity. This calculates the present value of the remaining interest payments. $PV_n = A(1-(1/(1+i)^n))/i$. Again, write it in a way that Microsoft Excel and Visual Basic understands. Formula results are assigned to the variable "PayAmt".

11. Add the present value of bond maturity to the present value of the remaining interest payments: TotBondPrice = PVMaturity + PayAmt

12. Use the name of the Function to return the BondPrice variable to the Worksheet. I got fancy and created a customized number format to be displayed in the Worksheet. The "Format ( )" function is used by Visual Basic to format numbers.

13. Final step is to test the function against known results to see if it works.

189

```
Function BondPrice(MaturityValue As Double, MktInterestRate _
As Single, TermOfBonds As Single, CompoundPeriod As Integer, _
Pmts As Double)
' Declare variables for formulas
Dim intrate As Single, perod As Single, PVMaturity As Double, _
PayAmt As Double, TotBondPrice As Double

' calculate Present value of Maturity value of bonds
intrate = MktInterestRate / CompoundPeriod
perod = TermOfBonds * CompoundPeriod
PVMaturity = MaturityValue * (1 / (1 + intrate) ^ perod)
  ' Calculate Present value of remaining interest payments
PayAmt = Pmts * (1 - (1 / (1 + intrate) ^ perod)) / intrate
'Add pv bond maturity to pv of interest payments
TotBondPrice = PVMaturity + PayAmt
BondPrice = Format(TotBondPrice, "###,###,##0.00")

End Function
```

Figure 11.17

After creating the BondPrice Function I realized that I could have made it easier to use by including features to automatically calculate amount of periodic interest payments. That's an assignment for you to complete.

USING THE BONDPRICE FUNCTION

Let's test the BondPrice function using data previously discussed.

For example assume that JeffCo wants to sell 10 year 10% bonds of $100,000 on January 15, 2010. Also assume that on this date, market interest for similar bonds is 8% compounded semiannually. At what price will the bonds sale?

Press the SHIFT+F3 key to display the "Insert Function" dialog box. Select "BondPrice from the "User Defined" section. Enter values for the required arguments in the "Function Arguments" dialog box and the price of the Bonds is calculated to be $113,590.33. Ok I am a penny off due to rounding.

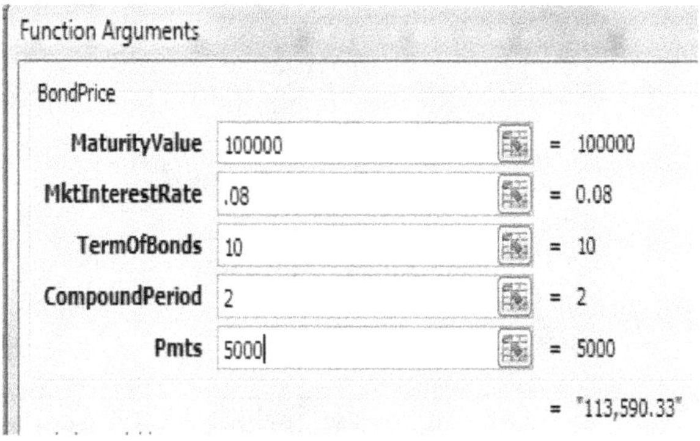

Figure 11.18

USING TIME VALUE OF MONEY TO SOLVE LEASE PROBLEMS

A lease is a contract between the owner (lessor) of an asset and the user (lessee) of an asset which allows the lessee to use the asset for a set period of time. There are two types of leases. 'Operating lease" is treated by both lessor and lessee as an ordinary rental agreement. Lessor records as rental income the payments received. The lessee records rental expense for the amounts paid. The other type of lease is a "Capital Lease". Under accounting rules, for a capital lease, on the day the lease contract is signed, the lessor has a sale of asset transaction. Lessor makes an entry to record a sale and to reduce inventory. And the lessee has a purchase of asset with a loan agreement transaction. Lessee records both the asset and liability on its books. In a moment I will show you the criteria used to classify a lease as operating or as a capital lease.

Time-value-of-money techniques are used by both lessor and lessee to evaluate lease transactions. Present value concepts are used by the lessor to determine lease payments. And both the lessor and lessee use present value concepts to determine if lease is a capital lease or operating lease. Each party makes the evaluation independently as the same lease may be a capital lease to one party and an operating lease to the other party.

LESSOR CALCULATES LEASE PAYMENTS

I admit that I have not researched how a lessor actually determines lease payments. Here is a suggested approach for academic purposes. Following are the factors the lessor must know to determine a payment amount.

191

(1)	Fair Market Value of the asset (FMV)
(2)	Estimate of the required (Guaranteed) Residual value This is amount lessee guarantees and if FMV of asset at end of lease is less than guaranteed residual, then lessee pays the lessor the difference.
(3)	Interest rate to be included in lease payments. This is usually the return the lessor expects to earn on the transaction.
(4)	Term of the lease, how long should lessee be allowed to use asset.

One way to determine residual value is to calculate depreciation (using method lessor typically uses) over the useful life of the asset. Calculate book of asset at end of lease. You want lessee to guarantee an amount at least equal to book value. For example an asset with a FMV of $100,000 and a useful life of seven years would have straight line depreciation of $14,286 a year. If lease term was five years, book value of asset would be $28,570 ($100,000 – (14,286 x 5). You want lessee to guarantee this amount.

To calculate lease payment we first calculate the present value of the FMV of the asset and then calculate the present value of the guaranteed residual. Accounting rules require that we add these two values together. The sum will be used in the Microsoft Excel PMT FUNCTION to calculate lease payments. Following are the factors needed to make the calculation of lease payment:

FMV of Asset	$100,000
Guaranteed Residual Value	$28,570
Lease Term	5 years
Required Interest Rate	12% Compounded monthly

The required factors were put on the Worksheet shown in Figure 11.19 to calculate lease payments. Lease payment required by lessor is $1,574.27 per month.

	A	B
1	FMV OF ASSET	$ 100,000.00
2	GUARANTEED RESIDUAL	$ 28,570.00
3	LEASE TERM	5 Years
4	INTEREST	12% compounded monthly
5		
6	Present Value of Asset	$55,044.96
7	=PV(.12/12,60,,-100000	
8	PV(rate, nper, pmt, [fv], [type])	

	A	B
1	FMV OF ASSET	$ 100,000.00
2	GUARANTEED RESIDUAL	$ 28,570.00
3	LEASE TERM	5 Years
4	INTEREST	12% compounded monthly
5		
6	Present Value of Asset	$55,044.96
7		
8	Present Value of Guarantee	$15,726.35
9	Total Present Value	$70,771.31
10	Use this amount in PMT	
11	function.	
12		
13	Calculate lease payment	$1,574.27
14	=PMT(.12/12,60,-70771.31	
15	PMT(rate, nper, pv, [fv], [type])	

Figure 11.19

Now the question is: What kind of lease is this, Operating or Capital lease? The criteria used to classify leases are in the following table. A lease is a capital lease to the lessee if it meets any one of the following criteria:

1.	Title transfers from lessor to lessee at end of lease.
2.	There is a Bargain Purchase Option.
3.	Term of lease is equal to or greater than useful life of the asset
4.	Present value of minimum lease payments are equal to or greater than 90% of the FMV of the Asset

The lease is a capital lease to the lessor if any one of the above criteria are met and both of the following conditions are true: (1) It is reasonably predictable that minimum lease payments will be collected, and (2) There are no important uncertainties regarding the amount of unreimbursable costs yet to be incurred by the lessor. Minimum lease payments generally are lease payment per period x number of periods.

Criteria 1 to 3 are pretty easy to figure out. Criteria number 4 requires the use of Present Value concepts. In our example, total minimum lease payments are $94,457 ($1574 x 60). Accounting rules (FASB #13) requires the lessee to use as a discount factor the interest rate implicit in the lease if known by the lessee. The implicit rate is the rate used by the lessor to calculate the lease payments. In our example it was 12% compounded monthly. Use PV of an annuity to calculate present value of lease payments. Accounting rules requires that the minimum lease payments for the lessee include the guarantee of residual value. Therefore must also calculate present value of guarantee using PV of a single amount. Add together and compare to FMV of asset. As present value of minimum lease payments in our example ($86,497.71) is less than 90% of the FMV of our asset ($100,000 x .90 = $90,000) criteria number 4 is not met.

Minimum lease Payments	$	94,457.00
Interest Rate		12%
Present Value of Min.Pymts		$70,771.37
Use PV of annuity $1,574		
PV of Guarantee, $28,570		$15,726.35
		$86,497.71

Figure 11.20

USE MICROSOFT EXCEL PMT FUNCTION TO CREATE AMORTIZATION SCHEDULE

An amortization table gives pertinent information about a loan. For each period that the loan is outstanding, amortization tells you (1) beginning loan balance, (2) scheduled payment, (3) principal portion of payment, (4) interest portion of the payment, (5) ending loan balance for the period, and (6) cumulative interest.

To create the following amortization table the following Microsoft Excel features must be used:

1.	Use Microsoft Excel PMT function
2.	Format numbers, surround cells with borders
3.	Use absolute cell reference so formulas can be copied
4.	Use Merge and Center function, also use Alignment feature
5.	Use Fill function to change background color of a range of cells
6.	Make formulas dynamic and interactive by using cell references in formulas
7.	Use sum function to total columns
8.	Create an input area for data, lock all other cells (Protection Feature)

1. Set up Input Area on Worksheet and format. Use "Merge and Center" feature and then left Alignment. Change Fill color of cells holding input values. Put a

thin border around input area. Now input area should look like graphic in Figure 11.21. Perform same steps for a Summary area. I got the idea for the layout of the amortization table from a template that accompanied Microsoft Excel 2007.

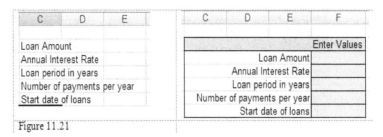

Figure 11.21

2. We are going to use Microsoft Excel's PMT Function in two places. Remember that if we know the loan amount, interest rate, and periods; we can calculate the payments required to liquidate the loan. We put the PMT Function in the cell holding the "Scheduled Payment" value in the "Loan Summary" section of the amortization Worksheet. We also put the PMT Function in the Scheduled Payment cell, row 1 of amortization table (D12 in our example). Notice two things here: (1) The function is not hard-coded; instead cell references are used to make the amortization table dynamic and interactive (we can change the amortization table just by changing one or more of the input values, (2) we want the results of the PMT Function to stay constant over a range of cells so we use "absolute" cell references. Remember to put dollar sign before both the column reference and row reference to make the cell reference "absolute".

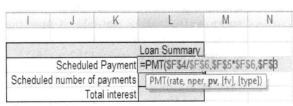

Figure 11.22

195

3. So that we can evaluate the amortization table as we create it, add some data into the input area. Ok let's build the first two rows of the table. Again so that table is dynamic we are going to use cell references in row 1 and 2 of the table. In the "Beginning Balance column", enter the formula: =F3. Cell F3 is where the input value for the "Loan Amount" is located. We already have the PMT Function in the column for the "Scheduled Payment" so skip to the "Interest "Column (E12) and enter the formula for simple interest (i =PRT). Use cell absolute cell reference where appropriate. The interest formula, therefore is: "=C12*($F$4/$F$6)*$A$12". C12 is the cell reference for the principal in the interest formula. F4 is the cell reference for the interest rate amount. F6 is the number of payments in a year. F4 is divided by F6 to adjust interest for the compounding period. A12 is the time component in the interest formula.

"Principal" column shows how much of the scheduled payment was a reduction of the loan balance. Calculate this column by subtracting interest from the Scheduled payment value. The formula is "=D12 – E12". The "Ending Balance" column is the Beginning loan balance minus principal reduction for the period ("=C12 – F12"). For first row of the amortization table, "Cumulative Interest" equals row 1 interest ($833.33 in our example). So I entered the formula "=E12" in this cell.

Row two (2) is a little tricky. Beginning Balance for row 2 is the Ending Balance of Row one (1). This relationship will occur in all following rows (Beginning Balance of row is Ending Balance of previous row). Put "=H12" in cell C13. Scheduled Payment does not change from row to row. In our example put $1,321.51 in row D13. Copy the interest formula from E12 to E13. Copy the "Principal" formula from F12 to F13. And copy "Ending Balance" formula from H12 to H13. To calculate "Cumulative Interest", add current row interest to prior row Cumulative Interest. Put this formula here: "=J12+E13". After row two is complete, select it and copy down as many periods as you desire.

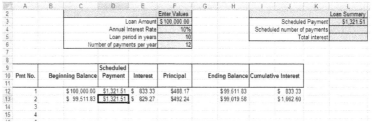

Figure 11.23

Figure 11.24 shows a completed amortization table for 12 periods.

	Enter Values			Loan Summary	
Loan Amount	$100,000.00		Scheduled Payment	$1,321.51	
Annual Interest Rate	10%		Scheduled number of payments		
Loan period in years	10		Total interest	$ 63,811.91	
Number of payments per year	12				

Pmt No.	Beginning Balance	Scheduled Payment	Interest	Principal	Ending Balance	Cumulative Interest
1	$100,000.00	$1,321.51	$ 833.33	$488.17	$99,511.83	$ 833.33
2	$ 99,511.83	$1,321.51	$ 829.27	$492.24	$99,019.58	$ 1,662.60
3	$ 99,019.58	$1,321.51	$ 825.16	$496.34	$98,523.24	$ 2,487.76
4	$ 98,523.24	$1,321.51	$ 821.03	$500.48	$98,022.76	$ 3,308.79
5	$ 98,022.76	$1,321.51	$ 816.86	$504.65	$97,518.11	$ 4,125.65
6	$ 97,518.11	$1,321.51	$ 812.65	$508.86	$97,009.25	$ 4,938.30
7	$ 97,009.25	$1,321.51	$ 808.41	$513.10	$96,496.15	$ 5,746.71
8	$ 96,496.15	$1,321.51	$ 804.13	$517.37	$95,978.78	$ 6,550.84
9	$ 95,978.78	$1,321.51	$ 799.82	$521.68	$95,457.10	$ 7,350.66
10	$ 95,457.10	$1,321.51	$ 795.48	$526.03	$94,931.07	$ 8,146.14
11	$ 94,931.07	$1,321.51	$ 791.09	$530.42	$94,400.65	$ 8,937.23
12	$ 94,400.65	$1,321.51	$ 786.67	$534.84	$93,865.82	$ 9,723.90

Figure 11.24

SUMMARY

Time Value of Money (TVM) concepts are used to make decisions about money received and to make decisions about money paid in business transactions. You need to know how much to pay or receive, and when should the payment or receipt of cash flows occur. TMV must be considered to answer questions about future value of cash flows as compared to present value of those cash flows. Interest (more specifically compound interest) is the deciding factor in our decision model.

There are four types of TVM problems: (1) future value of a single amount, (2) future value of a series of payments, (3) present value of a single amount, and (4) present value of a series of payments. Microsoft Excel has built-in functions to solve each of these problems.

197

CHAPTER 12
USING MICROSOFT EXCEL TO SOLVE COST BEHAVIOR PROBLEMS

When making decisions, business managers have to deal with three types of costs: (1) fixed costs, (2) mixed costs, and (3) variable costs. How these costs behave when activity levels change affect planning, control, and decision making. Planning, control, and decision making are the major daily functions performed by managers.

FIXED COSTS

Fixed costs in total do not change as activity level changes. For example the amount of rent would be the same for when 1,000 units are produced or if 20,000 units are produced. However the fixed cost per unit produced would change based on the change in activity. If fixed costs are $1,000 and 1,000 units are produced, then fixed cost per unit would be $1 ($1,000 / 1000). And if instead 20,000 units were produced, fixed cost per unit would be $0.05 per unit. Fixed cost would be $1,000 regardless of the number of units produced. We have to define a time period where the costs will remain constant. Even fixed costs change in the long run. Rent increases after a lease expires and becomes fixed at a higher level for the duration of the lease. We define the period for when the costs will remain fixed as the "relevant range". So when evaluating a cost as fixed we have to keep in mind the relevant range.

VARIABLE COSTS

Total variable costs vary in direct proportion to changes in activity level. Variable costs per unit do not change as activity level changes. Assume that a gallon of milk is used to make four pounds of ice cream, and that a gallon of milk costs $1.75. If a hundred gallons of milk are used during a time period, total variable costs would be $175 (100 x $1.75). If only fifty gallons were used, then total variable costs would be $87.50 (50 x $1.75). The variable cost per gallon of milk would be $1.75 in either case.

MIXED COSTS

Mixed costs have both a fixed and a variable component. I have a client who owns a restaurant in downtown Chicago, Illinois. His rent expense is a mixed expense. He pays a fixed amount each month. Additionally the lease requires that he pay a percentage of his sales each month as an extra amount of rent. The percentage of sales is a variable cost.

EVALUATING COST BEHAVIOR OF FIXED, VARIABLE, AND MIXED COSTS

Cost behavior is the term used to describe how costs change as activity level changes. For evaluation purposes it helps to be able to represent the different behaviors in equation form. We make an assumption that the behavior of costs is linear at different levels of activity.

For a given relevant range, Total Fixed costs can be represented by the linear equation: "F = Total Fixed costs", where "F" is fixed costs. For Total Variable costs the linear equation is: "$Y_p = VX$." "Y_p" stands for total variable costs during the period. "V" stands for Variable cost per unit. And "X" stands for number of units produced during the period. To represent mixed costs in a linear equation we use this formula: "Y =Fixed Cost +Total variable Cost, i.e. "Y=F +VX, where "Y" is total cost.

DETERMINE FIXED AND VARIABLE PORTIONS OF MIXED COST

Why is it important to separate the fixed portion from the variable portion of a mixed cost? Many of the expenses that appear in our income statement are mixed costs. If we are to evaluate how a change in activity level will affect a mixed expense we need to know what portion is fixed and what portion is variable. We want to be able to take some action toward an expense if the activity level changes. This taking action is part of the planning and control responsibility of managers. Remember that over the relevant range, fixed costs are constant regardless of activity level. So we will not be taking any action regarding fixed costs in the relevant range. We can only apply planning and control activity over variable costs.

There are several methods we can use to separate mixed costs into its fixed and variable portions. All of the methods revolve around evaluating the mixed cost linear formula "Y = F+VX". Mixed cost is the sum of total Fixed cost and total Variable cost. The most popular methods are (1) "High-Low method", (2) Scatter plot method, and (3) the

Method of Least Squares. Wondering what all this accounting discussion has to do with Microsoft Excel? Well, we are going to use Microsoft Excel with each of these methods to separate mixed costs into fixed costs and variable costs components.

First we have to understand how the variables of the mixed cost formula interact with each other. "Y", the total cost value depends on the changing value of "X". Decision making means evaluating different alternatives and choosing one. Fixed costs are not relevant to the decision as it will be the same in each alternative. Since "Y" (total cost) depends on the changing value of "X" we define it as the "dependent variable" in the equation. And since "X" (level of activity) does not depend on any other variable for its value we define it as the "independent variable". This is the variable that measures activity and explains changes in total cost. For analysis purposes it is important for the manager to find an independent variable that is closely related to the dependent variable. Microsoft Excel needs this delineation of variables to do its job. Variable "V" (variable cost per unit) determines the rate of change in total mixed costs as activity level changes. Mathematically, the rate of change is defined as a slope. The "V" is the slope parameter of the linear equation. "F" is defined as the "intercept parameter". Graphically it is where the mixed cost line intercepts the cost (vertical) axis. Or you can interpret it as the amount of "Y" where "X" is zero. For example "F" would be the amount of manufacturing overhead at no activity.

I know most accountants are math challenged but let's for a moment explore the relationship between independent and dependent variables. It is important information to know before we continue with our analysis of cost behavior.

VARIABLES AND THE RELATIONS AMONG THEM

Variables are things that can change or be different. Constants do not change. If you have a group of variables you can calculate how each variable is different from the group average (Mean) and this difference is called a variance. We discuss variance in more detail in a later chapter. Variance is calculated by the following formula: (Sum of squares divided by the number of items [n] in the group). You calculate "Sum of squares" as follows: Σ(variable $-$mean)^2. We are trying to answer the question: How are the variables in the group related to each other? **This analysis is called Descriptive statistics.**

Some variables can be used to predict (or cause) other variables. These predictor variables are called **independent variables.** The thing you are trying to predict (or the variable that is caused by another variable) is called the **dependent variable.** Sometimes the independent variable and dependent variable are both caused by another variable. This variable is said to **mediate** (link) the relationship between the independent and dependent variable. Mediating variables answer the why question (why are the independent and dependent variables related?). Or it asks how does the independent variable affect the dependent variable?

A causal model is a description (visual – picture) of the relationship among variables. Models can also be depicted with formulas. If the purpose of the model is to only predict a relationship, then we do not care about mediating variables. For example, how the change in activity level affect total costs. If purpose of the model is to explain the relationship, then we care about mediating variables. **Moderating** variables are variables that affect the magnitude (size) of the link between variables. Moderating variables act like a multiplying effect.

Models can be converted into formulas. **"Y"** is used to symbolize the dependent variable and **"X"** is used to symbolize the independent variable. If there are more than one variable, express them with subscripts: X_1, X_2, ...X_n. By convention we put the dependent variable on the left of the equation and the independent variable on the right side of the equation: $Y = X_1 + X_2$. Formulas are necessary to test models with quantitative evidence.

After defining variables you have to figure out how to measure them. How do you determine **how much effect the** independent variable has on the dependent variable.

The design of a model is just the plan for gathering evidence on how the variables are related. We obtained mixed cost information from our accounting system.

There are three criteria for assessing causation. Independent variable X caused dependent variable Y if: (1) X precedes Y (cause comes before effect), (2) X covaries with Y (X and Y change together, they are correlated), and (3) other possible causes of Y are ruled out (this is the hardest criteria to meet, can you be sure that all other causes have been eliminated?)

201

We are not only interested in if X causes Y. We want to know how strongly X causes Y (measuring the size of the effect).

Accounting records only show total costs "Y" and activity level "X". Using algebra and geometry we can use these two variables to calculate the "F" and "V" variables in the mixed cost equation and predict what total costs will be at different levels of activity.

Assume that accounting records for JeffCO report manufacturing overhead cost and units produced for the past 10 months. The CFO needs to accumulate information in order to prepare the annual budget for the coming year. He has checked with the VP of sales to get information on estimated sales for the coming year. Based on estimated sales the VP of manufacturing has informed the CFO of the possible levels of production. The CFO knows that there is a relationship between production level and manufacturing overhead and will use this information to predict manufacturing costs for the coming year. To be precise, the CFO needs to separate the fixed cost component from the variable cost component of the manufacturing overhead cost.

JeffCO' accounting records report the following information:

	A	B	C
1			
2	**Month**	**Mfg Overhead**	**Units Produced**
3	January	$ 3,000	153
4	February	4,000	200
5	March	2,800	168
6	April	1,950	200
7	May	5,000	500
8	June	4,350	300
9	July	6,100	387
10	August	1,875	400
11	September	3,200	480
12	October	5,275	430
13			
14			
15			
16			
17			5.763688761
18			2120

Figure 12.1

HIGH-LOW METHOD

Geometry tells us that two points are needed to determine a straight-line (a linear line). We can calculate the equation of a line if we know two points on that line. Looking at Figure 12.1 we see that we know two points on the line that describes manufacturing overhead. We know "Y" and we know "X". With this information we can calculate "F" (intercept) and "V" (slope) and form the equation for the mixed cost line as "Y = F + VX". The "High-Low" method selects the high level of activity and the low level of activity and related costs at each level as the two points.

Defining (X_1, Y_1) as the low point and (X_2, Y_2) as the high point and putting each into an equation for a straight line results in following formulas:

$$Y_1 = F + VX_1 \text{ and } Y_2 = F + VX_2$$

Using algebra we can solve either of the two equations for V and F as follows:

V = Change in cost / change in activity
  $= (Y_2 - Y_1) / (X_2 - X_1)$
F = Total mixed cost –Variable cost
  $= Y_2 - V X_2$

We used the high point equation but we could also use the low point equation.

Use the Microsoft Excel MAX Function to determine the highest level of activity and the MIN Function to determine the lowest level of activity. Highest point was calculated to be ($5,000, 500) and the lowest level was calculated to be ($3,000, 153). Substitute these values into our equation.

V = ($5000 -$2000) / (500-153)
  = $5.76
F = $Y_2 - VX_2$
  = $5,000-($5.76 x 500) = $2,120

	A	B	C
1			
2	**Month**	**Mfg Overhead**	**Units Produced**
3	January	$ 3,000	153
4	February	4,000	200
5	March	2,800	168
6	April	1,950	200
7	May	5,000	500
8	June	4,350	300
9	July	6,100	387
10	August	1,875	400
11	September	3,200	480
12	October	5,275	430
13			
14			
15			
16			
17			5.763688761
18			2120

Figure 12.2

Substitute the calculated values into the linear equation for mixed costs and we now have the cost formula for manufacturing overhead: Y= $2,120 + $5.76X. Now at any level of production activity, the CFO can predict manufacturing overhead cost. For example, if the VP of production tells the CFO that expected production will be 600 units, CFO will be able to estimate manufacturing cost using the cost formula. Using the cost formula, manufacturing costs at production level of 600 units will be $5,576 (=$2,120+($5.76 x 600)).

The High-Low method is really easy. You should however be careful when you use it. This method can return a biased result if the high point and / or low point is not representative of the rest of the data points. The Scatterplot Method supposedly fixes this problem.

SCATTERPLOT METHOD

Following are the steps needed to separate mixed costs into fixed and variable portions using the scatter plot method:

Step 1 is to plot the data points to graphically show the relationship between Manufacturing overhead and units produced. We want to see if the relationship really is linear. Our schedule is not really set up the way Microsoft Excel likes it. Microsoft Excel wants the independent variable to be in the left column of the chart selection area. The independent variable in our example, units produced, is presently in the right column (C3:C12). Don't worry we will fix this problem after we create the chart.

1. Select the range B2:C12. Click the insert tab and select Scatter from the chart group. The chart that is created assumes that Manufacturing overhead is the independent variable and puts it on the x axis (horizontal axis). This is clearly wrong. Manufacturing cost is actually the dependent variable and should be on the y axis (vertical axis).

2. You have two choices here: (1) you can rearrange your schedule so that units produced is in the left column of the schedule. This is where Microsoft Excel assumes the independent variable to be located. Or (2) you change the axis orientation using the features provided in Microsoft Excel. I chose option (2).

3. On the Design tab (it shows up when you click anywhere inside the chart), Data Group, click the Select data icon.

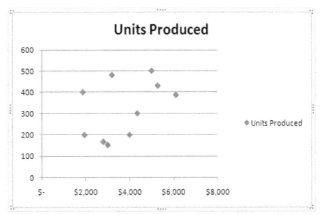

Figure 12.3

4. The "Select Data Source" is then displayed. Click the "Switch Row/Column button to change the axis orientation.

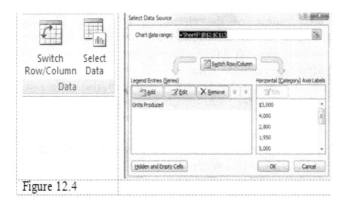

Figure 12.4

5. Now the "Select Data Source" dialog box looks like Figure 12.5. In the "Legend Entries(Series)" window, click each series and then click remove button.

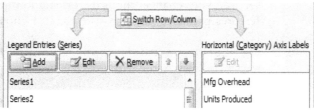

Figure 12.5

6. This action will display the "Edit Series" dialog box. Give the series a name. I am going to use Mfg Overhead Costs. Enter the correct range in "Series X values" box. Enter the range for Units Produced (C3:C12). Remember the x-axis (horizontal axis) is for the independent variable. In the "Series Y values" box enter the range for Mfg Costs (B3:B12). Remember that the y-axis (vertical axis) is for the dependent variable. Microsoft Excel changes the axis of the chart to display the data as we desire.

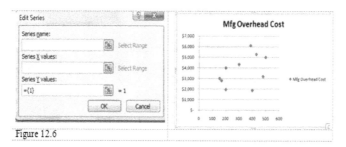

Figure 12.6

7.	You can fix the format of the chart if you desire. For now I clicked on the legend label (Mfg Overhead Cost) located on the right side of the chart and deleted it to have more room in the chart area.

8.	Does the ScatterPlot look linear? It looks somewhat linear as manufacturing overhead costs go up as units produce go up. But it appears that the relationship between manufacturing overhead and activity is weak.

9.	Before Microsoft Excel, the manager would choose two points on the graph that appear in his/her opinion to represent all of the data. The manager would use past experience to make this decision. Data points, (i.e. costs) that seem out of place (outliers – data points that don't fit with what we know about the typical data set) can be eliminated from the data set. Next the cost function would be estimated using the same formulas and techniques used in the High-low method.

10.	Now that we have Microsoft Excel, we will let it plot and draw the "Trend line" on the ScatterPlot chart. From the "Layout" tab, Analysis group, click the down arrow for the Trend line icon to see the trend line options. I picked the "Linear Trendline". If you hover over each choice, Microsoft Excel will tell you when to use each type.

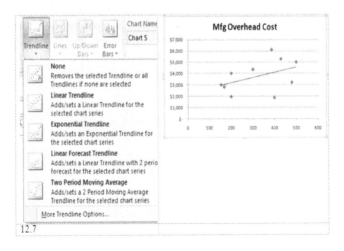

12.7

11. Looks like Microsoft Excel picked the same two points we used in the High-low method: ($3,000, 153) and ($5,000, 500). So the cost line would be: Y= $2,120 + $5.76X. Caution! Don't expect this to happen too often.
12. Allowing the cost analyst to view the data graphically is an advantage over the High-low method. And with Microsoft Excel drawing the Trendline, this method is not as subjective as it was in the past.

METHOD OF LEAST SQUARES

The Trendline that Microsoft Excel plotted and placed on our ScatterPlot is supposed to be the line that "best fits" the data points. The "best-fit" line is supposed to be the line where the data points are closest to the line. We can measure the closeness as the vertical distance of the data point to the line. Vertical distance is the distance between the actual cost and the predicted cost based on the calculated cost formula. This difference is called the deviation. Sometimes the deviation will be positive and sometimes it will be negative. To calculate the deviation of all the data points, we need to calculate deviation for each point and sum the deviations. Mathematically this does not work because we would be adding positive and negative numbers. To overcome this problem we simply square each deviation and the result is a positive number. Now we can sum the deviations. You must compare lines from different cost formulas and calculate the sum of deviations for each line. The line with the least sum of deviations is the best-fitting line. It is the line that best displays the relationship of the underlying data points. Following is how our Worksheet looks after applying the "Method of Least Squares" techniques.

	A	B	C	D	E	F
1						
2	Month	Mfg Overhead	Units Produced	Predicted Cost	Deviation	Dev. Sqrd
3	January	$ 3,000	153	$ 3,002	$ (2)	$ 4.00
4	February	4,000	200	$ 3,273	$ 727	$ 528,910.38
5	March	2,800	168	$ 3,088	$ (288)	$ 83,116.72
6	April	1,950	200	$ 3,273	$ (1,323)	$ 1,749,635.16
7	May	5,000	500	$ 5,002	$ (2)	$ 4.00
8	June	4,350	300	$ 3,849	$ 501	$ 250,894.17
9	July	6,100	387	$ 4,351	$ 1,749	$ 3,060,583.87
10	August	1,875	400	$ 4,425	$ (2,550)	$ 6,504,925.30
11	September	3,200	480	$ 4,887	$ (1,687)	$ 2,844,520.41
12	October	5,275	430	$ 4,598	$ 677	$ 457,806.28
13						$ 15,480,400.29
14						
15						
16						
17			5.763688761			
18			2120			
19			Use cost formula and units produced as X			
20			to calculate predicted cost.			
21			Deviation is actual cost - Predicted cost			

Figure 12.8

REGRESSION ANALYSIS

A regression model minimizes the sum of squares of deviations. Regression calculations are tedious. Again you are in luck. Microsoft Excel has an "Add-in" that performs a host of statistical calculations. We just have to tell Microsoft Excel to make the Add-in available. Here's how:

1. Click the **FILE TAB** and select "Options". From the "Microsoft Excel Options" dialog box select Add-ins category. From the Add-ins list box select "Analysis ToolPak". Click "GO" Button. Add-Ins dialog box will be displayed. Check Analysis ToolPak and OK. Microsoft Excel will load and make available a bunch of statistical tools. After loading Add-Ins, Microsoft Excel adds a new group to the Data tab on the Ribbon. The Data Analysis group is where we find the new statistical features. Click the Data Analysis icon to display Data Analysis dialog box and choose Regression from the Analysis Tools list box.

209

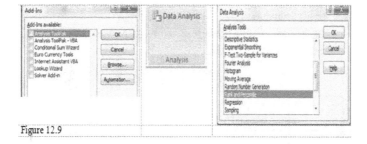

Figure 12.9

2. The regression model is an advanced version of the method of least squares. In addition to calculating the parameters (called coefficients in the Microsoft Excel regression program) "F" and "V", regression tells you how reliable the cost formula is. And since the regression cost formula is the best-fitting line it should do a better job of predicting costs than the High-low method and the ScatterPlot method.

3. To use the regression feature, click the Data Analysis icon on the Data tab of the ribbon. From the Data Analysis dialog box select Regression. The Regression dialog box will be displayed. Enter the range that holds the dependent "Y" variable (Mfg overhead) in the "Input Y Range" box. In our example it is B2:B11. Enter the range for the independent variable (Units produced) in the "Input X Range" box. In our example it is C2:C11. Next decide how good you want results to be. I always want to be 95% sure that my results are correct, so I check the Confidence Level box and accept the default of 95%. Now decide where you want to locate regression results: (1) on same Worksheet, click Output Range option and enter a cell reference for the desired location, or (2) on a New Worksheet, or (3) in a New Workbook. Don't worry about the other statistical options now. Click Ok and results will be displayed in the location specified.

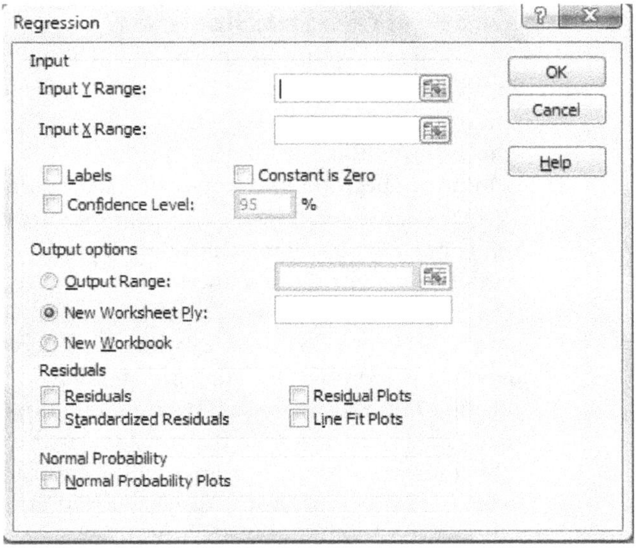

Figure 12.10

I entered the required data in the Regression dialog box and asked that results be placed in Cell E2 on the Worksheet. My preference is to have results on same Worksheet as input data. Look at the bottom 2 rows of the Regression Summary Output (See Figure 12.11). The Intercept Coefficient (2245.82) is "F" in our cost formula. The "X Variable 1" Coefficient (4.69) is "V" in our cost formula. Regression thus computed a cost formula of: "Y = 2,245.82 + 4.69(X). Compare this to the cost formula that was calculated using the High-Low method and the ScatterPlot method (Y = $2120 + $5.76X).

The regression method computed the best-fitting line, but how good is it? How well does it predict manufacturing overhead cost based on units produced? We can use three statistical results provided by the regression model to evaluate the reliability of the cost formula: (1) hypothesis test of cost parameters, (2) goodness of fit, and (3) confidence interval. I will explain how to calculate these statistics in a later chapter.

211

HYPOTHESIS TEST

The hypothesis test of cost parameters (how and why is discussed in chapter 19) tells us if the parameters ("F" and "V") are statistically significant. The information for the hypothesis test is found in column I, bottom two rows of our results (Figure 12.11). A p-value of .091776 for the Intercept and a p-value of .203858 were calculated by the regression model. We want the p-value to be as low as possible. The hypothesis test tells us the extent to which a parameter explains the relationship between the dependent variable and the independent variable in forming the cost formula. This number should be less than .10. In our example the p-value for the intercept (.09) indicates that it is statistically significant, and it explains the aforementioned relationship. The p-value for "V" is too high (.203858), and thus is not a good indicator. This means that the model does not have confidence that the "V" parameter is correct. I suspected as much because the ScatterPlot graph didn't look very linear.

GOODNESS OF FIT

The Goodness of Fit statistic tells the percentage of total variability in a cost formula that is explained by an independent variable. In our example, what percentage of changes in manufacturing overhead cost is caused by the change in units produced? The percentage of variability is called the "Coefficient of Determination". It is a measure of the goodness of fit. The higher the percentage, the better is the explanation of variability. As it is a percentage, the coefficient of determination is always between 0 and 1.0. Look at Figure 12.11 and find "R Square" in the Regression Statistics section (Cell E6). R Square is the coefficient of determination. The value found there in cell F6 (.19309033) tells us that 19% of the change in manufacturing overhead cost is caused by the number of units produced. R-Square is calculated by dividing SS for the Regression by Total SS. These values are found in the "ANOVA" section of the regression worksheet (3544366.09 / 18356000). So 81% of the variability is unexplained. It is telling us that some other independent variable (or variables) is driving the change in manufacturing overhead cost. And we should find some other activity driver (independent variable) to create a cost formula to predict future manufacturing overhead cost.

	A	B	C	D	E	F	G	H	I	J
1	Month	Mfg Overhead	Units Produced							
2	January	$ 3,000	153		SUMMARY OUTPUT					
3	February	4,000	200							
4	March	2,800	168		Regression Statistics					
5	April	1,950	200		Multiple R	0.439420447				
6	May	5,000	500		R Square	0.19309033				
7	June	4,350	300		Adjusted R Square	0.092226621				
8	July	6,100	387		Standard Error	1360.681535				
9	August	1,875	400		Observations	10				
10	September	3,200	480							
11	October	5,275	430		ANOVA					
12						df	SS	MS	F	Significance F
13					Regression	1	3544366.09	3544366	1.914369	0.203857922
14					Residual	8	14811633.91	1851454		
15					Total	9	18356000			
16										
17						Coefficients	Standard Error	t Stat	P-value	Lower 95%
18					Intercept	2245.82115	1172.559484	1.915315	0.091776	-458.1058662
19					X Variable 1	4.68980376	3.389548678	1.383607	0.203858	-3.126509501

Figure 12.11

CONFIDENCE INTERVAL

Most of the time, the predicted value will be different from actual cost. First, because we only used one independent variable in building the cost formula. Maybe other important factors that affect the dependent variable were ignored. Secondly, the cost formula was built from a sample of known data points. Maybe the sample is somehow not representative of the population. Using statistics we can measure the variance caused by these two reasons and create an interval that we know with a certain amount of confidence the predicted value of "Y" will be within.

To build the confidence interval we need to know the standard error and the "t-statistic" for a certain degree of freedom. The interval is built by multiplying the standard error by the t-statistic and adding the product to the "Y" variable and subtracting the product from the "Y" variable. This creates an upper and lower range for the "Y" variable. The t-statistic is calculated as an area under a normal distribution curve (usually the tail), but don't worry about the math. You can find a table of "t" values in most statistics books. Look up the "t" statistic using the degree of freedom and the confidence level you desire. The degree of freedom is the number of

213

observations of data points (see Figure 12.11, cell F9) minus the number of parameters (two in our example: intercept and X variable 1; see bottom 2 rows of regression model output). So in our example the degrees of freedom would be 8 (10-2). If you look in a t-statistic table for 8 degrees of freedom and a confidence level of 95%, the t-statistic is 2.306. Or you can use the Microsoft Excel TINV Function to determine the t-statistic. The TINV Function takes two arguments (1) probability, (use 1-confidence level as probability) and (2) degrees of freedom. The standard error in our example is 1360.68 (regression model output, cell F8). Standard error is calculated by taking the square root of (Residual SS / n-2). Residual is the difference between the observed "Y" and the predicted "Y" (predicted "Y" is value calculated using the calculated cost formula "Y = F +V(x)". Standard error tells us if there is a significant relationship between the two variables and lets us make inferences about future values of Y. Now we are ready to create our confidence interval.

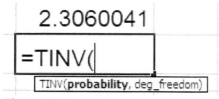

Figure 12.12

$$Y \pm tS$$

where:

Y = predicted cost, t = t-statistic, and S = standard error.

Using the cost line created by the regression model: Y = 2245.82+ 4.49(x), the cost of manufacturing overhead at 500 units produced is $4,490.82. If you remember the actual cost at this level of activity was $5,000. At 95% confidence we think the calculated "Y" will fall within the range Y±2.306 x ($1360.68) or $1,353.09≤Y≤$7,628.55. Wow! This is a wide range. The cost equation computed by the regression model is not looking good. It tells us to use some other independent variable to build a cost formula for manufacturing overhead costs in the future.

MULTIPLE REGRESSION ANALYSIS

If you find that one independent variable does not sufficiently explain the change in "Y" then use one or two more independent variables. When using Microsoft Excel to perform multiple regression analysis, enter the "Y" values as was done in the single regression. To enter the independent variables select the entire range that holds them and enter in the regression box labeled "X" input. Everything else works the same.

SUMMARY

Managers need to understand the behavior of costs in order to make decisions. Costs are classified as fixed, variable, or mixed. Accounting records have mixed cost information. To make decisions about the future we must separate the mixed cost into its fixed and variable portions. There are three methods available to separate mixed costs into fixed and variable components: (1) High-Low Method, (2) ScatterPlot Method, and (3) Method of Least Squares. The method of least squares is the best method to use to separate mixed costs into its fixed and variable components.

CHAPTER 13
COST-VOLUME-PROFIT ANALYSIS

Costs, units sold, and price of products are interrelated and when analyzed together consolidate the financial information of a company. Analyzing the relationship between these three items allows managers to perform their primary duty (planning, decision making and control.) Cost-volume-profit analysis allows managers to see what happens to profit if one, or all of the items (cost, units sold, and price) are changed. It allows managers to use feedback about operations to make changes before it's too late. Unfortunately the most common answer is to reduce costs; usually a code word for reducing staffing. Cost–Volume-Profit (CVP) analysis requires the use of formulas. And by now we know that when there are formulas to be solved, Microsoft Excel is the tool of choice.

We start our CVP with the calculation of Breakeven. Breakeven in units can be calculated or just as easily breakeven sales can be directly calculated. I used the term directly calculated because breakeven sales can be indirectly calculated by multiplying breakeven units by sales price.

So what is breakeven? It is the point where total revenue equals total cost. At breakeven there is no profit or loss. There are two alternative formulas for calculating breakeven. We could use the "Operating Income Approach" formula or the "Contribution Margin" formula to calculate breakeven.

OPERATING INCOME FORMULA

The formula to calculate breakeven sales follows:

Sales = Sales – (variable costs +fixed costs)

If you try to solve this formula in Microsoft Excel you will get a circular reference error. First set sales on the left side of the equation to 0 and with a little algebra magic we can change the formula to "fixed costs / (sales –variable costs)". Microsoft Excel can work with this formula. This formula will give you breakeven point in units.

A	B	C	D	E	F
Selling Price	$ 200				
Variable Cost	$ 120				
Fixed Costs	$ 2,000				
	Units	Total Revenue	Total Variable Cost	Total Fixed Costs	Total Cost
	0	0	0	$ 2,000	$ 2,000
	10	$ 2,000	$ 1,200	$ 2,000	$ 3,200
	20	$ 4,000	$ 2,400	$ 2,000	$ 4,400
	25	$ 5,000	$ 3,000	$ 2,000	$ 5,000
	30	$ 6,000	$ 3,600	$ 2,000	$ 5,600
	40	$ 8,000	$ 4,800	$ 2,000	$ 6,800
	60	$ 12,000	$ 7,200	$ 2,000	$ 9,200
	80	$ 16,000	$ 9,600	$ 2,000	$ 11,600

Figure 13.1

Figure 13.1 has a Worksheet with the data we will be using to calculate breakeven units and breakeven sales.

Using the operating income formula: fixed costs / (sales − variable costs) yields a breakeven point of 25 units.

A	B	C
1	=2000/(200-120)	

To calculate breakeven dollars multiply 25 units x sales price ($200) and the result is $5,000. I prepared a mini-income statement to see if the sale of 25 units would result in zero profit.

Income Statement	
Breakeven sales	$ 5,000
Variable costs (25 x $120)	3,000
Contibution Margin	2,000
Fixed Costs	2,000
Operating income	$ 0.00

Figure 13.2

CONTRIBUTION MARGIN FORMULA

Look at Figure 13.2. Notice that contribution margin equals fixed costs at breakeven point.

Contribution margin is defined as Sales minus variable costs.

Contribution margin formula:

BE =fixed costs /contribution margin.

SETTING PROFIT TARGETS

As a manager you would not be happy earning zero profits. Usually your bonus is based on earning a profit. We can use the breakeven formula to calculate the number of units we need to sell to achieve a target profit. The formula is:

Units = (Fixed Cost + Target income) / Contribution Margin

For example, how many units are needed to be sold to achieve a profit of $100,000? Plug this into formula: = ($2,000 + $100,000) / 80 =1,275 units.

Income Statement		
Target sales (1,275 x $200)	$	255,000
Variable costs (1275 x $120)		153,000
Contibution Margin		102,000
Fixed Costs		2,000
Operating income	$	100,000

Figure 13.3

As you can deduce, every dollar of contribution margin above breakeven equals a dollar profit per unit.

SETTING PROFIT TARGETS AS A PERCENT OF SALES

Sometimes we want to set profit targets as a percentage of sales. For example, how many units do we have to sale to earn a profit equal to 20% of sales. Use the following formula (CM stands for contribution margin) :

$$\frac{\textbf{Fixed Costs}}{\textbf{(CM - (\% x sales price))}}$$

Figure 13.4

Using the numbers in our spreadsheet and plugging in the required numbers: =2,000 / ($80 – (20% x $200)) the result is 50 units. To test, plug into a mini income statement.

Income Statement		
Target sales (50 x $200)	$	10,000
Variable costs (50 x $120)		6,000
Contibution Margin		4,000
Fixed Costs		2,000
Operating income	$	2,000
Operating income as percent of sales 2000/10000 = 20%		

Figure 13.5

CALCULATING BREAKEVEN POINT IN DOLLARS

So far we have calculated breakeven point in units. We can directly calculate breakeven sales. To do so we have to define variable costs as a percentage of sales. Variable cost percentage using the information in our spreadsheet would be: $120 / 200 = .60. Next we have to calculate a contribution margin ratio. Contribution margin ratio = 1 – variable cost percent. In our example the contribution margin is .40 (1-.60). If we already know the contribution margin we can calculate the contribution ratio by dividing it by sales price. Contribution margin is 40% ($80 / $200).

Breakeven in sales dollars is "Fixed costs / CM Ratio". Or in our example $2,000 / .4 = $5,000.

CALCULATING PROFIT TARGETS IN DOLLARS

Use the same concept to directly calculate target dollars as was used to calculate units required to generate target profit. How many sales dollars are needed to generate a $100,000 profit? Use the formula: = (Fixed costs + target profit) / contribution ratio.

= ($2,000 + $100,000) / .40 = $255,000. See Figure 13.3.

Since the contribution ratio behaves like a profit ratio and every dollar above breakeven is profit, we can use cost-volume-profit analysis to answer planning questions. For example what would happen to profits if we increase sales by a

219

specific amount. To answer this question, multiply change in sales by contribution margin ratio. What is the increase in profit if we increase sales by $10,000? The answer is profits will increase $4,000 ($10,000 x .4).

GRAPHIC REPRESENTATION OF CVP

A Cost-Volume-Profit graph can be created from sales, variable cost, and fixed cost information. Using sales of units from 0 to 80 units the graph in Figure 13.6 was created. Breakeven is where the total cost line intercepts the total revenue line. By visual inspection you can determine profit or loss generated by any unit of sales. Just draw a line from units (horizontal axis) to the total revenue line. If at that point the total revenue line is above the total cost line there is a profit. The distance between the two lines represents profit.

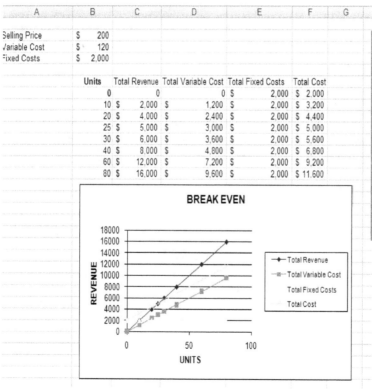

A	B	C	D	E	F	G
Selling Price	$ 200					
Variable Cost	$ 120					
Fixed Costs	$ 2,000					

Units	Total Revenue	Total Variable Cost	Total Fixed Costs	Total Cost
0	0	0	$ 2,000	$ 2,000
10	$ 2,000	$ 1,200	$ 2,000	$ 3,200
20	$ 4,000	$ 2,400	$ 2,000	$ 4,400
25	$ 5,000	$ 3,000	$ 2,000	$ 5,000
30	$ 6,000	$ 3,600	$ 2,000	$ 5,600
40	$ 8,000	$ 4,800	$ 2,000	$ 6,800
60	$ 12,000	$ 7,200	$ 2,000	$ 9,200
80	$ 16,000	$ 9,600	$ 2,000	$ 11,600

Figure 13.6

A USER DEFINED BREAKEVEN FUNCTION

If you have to compute breakeven point on a regular basis it is a good idea to create a user defined function. Do you remember how? Follow these steps:

1. From the Worksheet click ALT+F11 to display the VBE. From the Visual Basic menu select insert module.
2. Type "FUNCTION FunctionName ("
3. Enter argument(s) name and size followed by ending parentheses. Visual Basic will add closing end wrapper (End Function).
4. Enter required formulas. Give final function the same name as Function Name. To return to Worksheet press ALT+F4. Test to see if user defined function works.

Let's demonstrate the building of a function to calculate Breakeven. Following factors are needed to calculate Breakeven. See Figure 13.7. These factors will become the required arguments in the function.

	A	B
1		
2	Sales Price per unit	$ 200
3	Variable Cost per unit	$ 120
4	Fixed Cost	$ 2,000
5	Target Profit	$ 100,000

Figure 13.7

Let's create the function for breakeven units. Give the function name as "BreakEvenUnits". Remember that Visual Basic does not like spaces between combined words. In between the parentheses tell Visual Basic the names and sizes of required arguments. Because I wanted the results to be nicely formatted I had to do two additional things: (1) tell Visual basic that I would be using another variable (BE) in my function and it needed the size of a double number (see the Dim statement), (2) use the additional variable to hold results of breakeven calculation. Then I used the "Format" function to make results look as desired. Finally, I assigned the "BE" results to the BreakEvenUnits Function Name.

221

```
Function BreakEvenUnits(Sales As Double, varCost As Double, _
fixedCost As Double, targetprofit As Double)
Dim BE As Double
BE = (fixedCost + targetprofit) / (Sales - varCost)
BreakEvenUnits = Format(BE, "###,##0")
End Function
```
Figure 13.8

OK, let's test to see if it works. Press SHIFT+F3 to display the Insert Function dialog box. From the User Defined section select BreakEvenUnits. On the displayed Function Arguments dialog box enter values for all arguments (if there is no target profit in this problem, enter a "0" in its box). Answer is displayed in dialog box. Hit OK and results are pasted to the Worksheet.

Create a function to calculate breakeven point sales.

```
Function BreakEvenSales(Sales As Double, varCost As Double, _
fixedCost As Double, targetprofit As Double)
Dim cmratio As Single, BE As Double
cmratio = (Sales - varCost) / Sales
BE = (fixedCost + targetprofit) / cmratio
BreakEvenSales = Format(BE, "$###,###,##0")
End Function
```
Figure 13.9

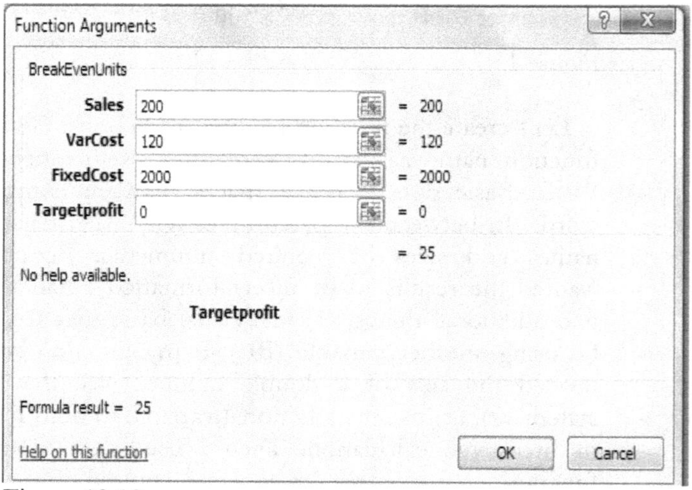

Figure 13.10

SENSITIVITY ANALYSIS

The user defined functions makes it easy to perform sensitivity analysis. If you set up your Worksheet correctly and use cell references, you can dynamically answer questions as to what happens to breakeven if we change any of the argument values.

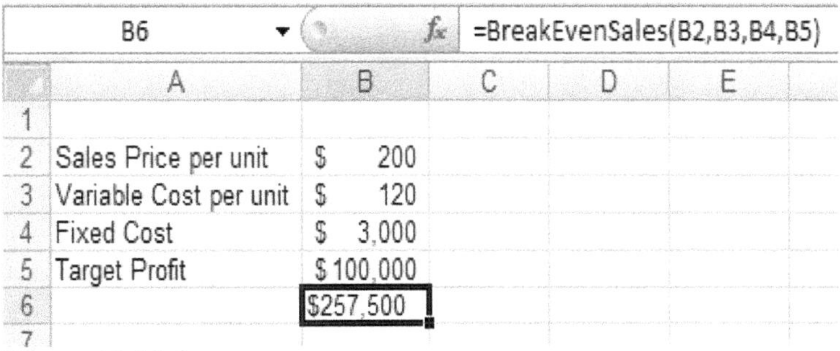

	B6	▼	f_x	=BreakEvenSales(B2,B3,B4,B5)	
	A	B	C	D	E
1					
2	Sales Price per unit	$ 200			
3	Variable Cost per unit	$ 120			
4	Fixed Cost	$ 3,000			
5	Target Profit	$ 100,000			
6		$257,500			
7					

Figure 13.11

In Figure 13.11 cell references were used as arguments. Enter new values in the appropriate cells and new results will immediately be revealed. Fixed costs were increased from $2,000 to $3,000 and immediately a new breakeven sales point was calculated.

SUMMARY

Managers use cost-volume-profit analysis for planning and control purposes. The process begins with the calculation of the breakeven point. Breakeven is where there are zero profits and zero costs. Breakeven sales can be calculated or breakeven units can be calculated.

CHAPTER 14
CAPITAL INVESTMENTS

Organizations sometimes have to invest in long-term assets to sustain future operations. When confronted with different investment alternatives managers must choose the one that provides the best net cash flows. There are two types of cash flows to consider (1) outflows i.e. the initial investment, and (2) cash inflows, return on the investment. We will discuss four methods used to evaluate long-term projects. Two methods are easy to calculate but have shortcomings.

Also there are two categories of long-term investments. The first is called "Independent" projects. Acceptance of one project does not prevent you from also accepting another project. The second types are "mutually exclusive" projects. If you choose one project you are precluded from accepting another project.

Of the four methods for evaluating long-term projects, two take into account the time-value of money and two do not. Let's first discuss the two methods that do not consider time-value-of –money. The first of the two non-discounting methods is called the "Payback Period" method. The payback period method is used to tell the analyst how fast the initial investment will be recovered. It is calculated by dividing initial investment by period cash flows. For example if we make an investment of $200,000 and it provides positive net cash flows of $40,000 a year, we will get our money back in 5 years ($200,000 / 40,000). This is a popular method and is very easy to use. However it has two major shortcomings: (1) it does not take into account the time-value-of money and (2) it ignores the economic performance of the investment after the payback period has been reached.

The second non-discounting method is called the "Accounting Rate of Return" method. Unlike the payback method it does take in account economic performance. The formula to calculate Accounting Rate of Return is: Average income / Original investment. Average income is the average of the total positive cash flows. It ignores the time-value-of money.

The "Net Present Value" method and the "Internal Rate of Return" method both take into account the time value of money when evaluating long-term projects. When the projects are independent they yield the same answer but when the projects are mutually exclusive, Net Present Value yields the best answer.

NET PRESENT VALUE METHOD (NPV)

With the Net Present Value method you determine the present value of future cash flows and then subtract out the original investment. The company's cost of capital rate should be used in the present value function. The company's cost of capital is the rate it pays to borrow money and to use stockholders' equity. How cost of capital is calculated is found in most beginning finance textbooks. If the net present value calculation results in a positive number, the project returned an amount that exceeded the cost of capital rate. That project will be accepted as it yields a return better than what the company could get by investing in something else. If you are evaluating alternative projects, choose the one with the highest net present value. If net present value (NPV) is zero, managers would be indifferent as to whether to accept the project. NPV of zero means that returns from the project exactly matched the cost of capital. If NPV is negative reject that project. The formula for NPV is $= [\sum CF_t / (1+i)^t]-I$ where:

CF_t	Cash Flow to be received in period t and t=1...n
n	Useful life of the project
I	Original investment
i	Required rate of return, should be cost of capital
t	The time period

This formula should look familiar as it is the formula for calculating the present value of a single amount. It is applied against the cash flow of each period and then summed. The present value of an annuity is not used because cash flows are usually not equal.

Let's use the formula to evaluate a project which requires an original investment of $900,000. Project has positive cash flow in years 1 – 4 of $300,000 each year. In year 5, positive cash flow is $500,000. Use 12% as the required rate. NPV is positive so accept this project. Notice that I used relative cell reference so that I could calculate present value for each period, just by copying the formula through the range C3:C8.

225

NPV	▾	X ✓ f	
	A	B	C
1			
2	Year	Cash Flow	Present Value
3	0	$(900,000)	$ (900,000)
4	1	$ 300,000	267,857
5	2	$ 300,000	239,158
6	3	$ 300,000	213,534
7	4	$ 300,000	190,655
8	5	$ 500,000	283,713
9	Net Present Value		$ 294,918
10			
11	Formula in Column C		
12	=B3/(1+.12)^A3		

=NPV(0.12,300000,300000,300000,300000,500000)-900000

$294,918.23

Figure 14.1

It took time to set up the NPV Worksheet. I could have gotten an answer in much quicker time by using Microsoft Excel's NPV Function. It is found in the financial category in the "Input Function" dialog box. The first function argument is rate. Enter as a decimal. Then there are 2 boxes shown for entering cash flow values. Don't worry if you have more than 2 periods. After entering a value for Value2, press tab key and an additional box "Value3" appears so you can enter cash flow for the third period. You can repeat this process until Value254 is reached. So you can enter a maximum of 254 cash flow periods. Using this function is a little tricky. It will return the wrong answer if you include the negative original investment as value1. This makes sense to me now after taking a second look at the NPV formula. First you calculate the present of each cash flow period, then you sum those present values, and then and only then, do you subtract out the original investment. So when using the Microsoft Excel NPV function, leave out original investment and subtract it at the end. Figure 14.1, the right side pane shows how I handled original investment.

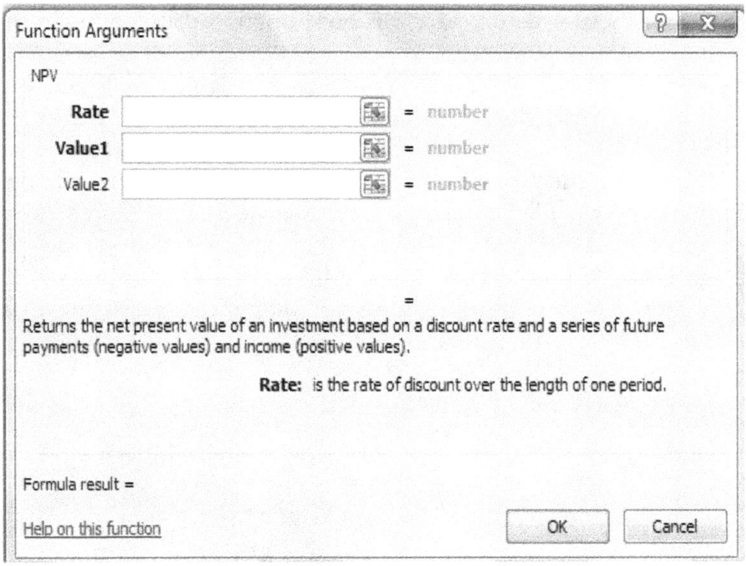

Figure 14.2

INTERNAL RATE OF RETURN

The second discounting method, "Internal Rate of Return" (IRR) is more popular than NPV. Most people incorrectly assume that IRR represents the true rate of return of a project. But it only calculates the interest rate that sets NPV to zero.

The formula to calculate IRR is:

$$I = \sum CF_t / (1+i)^t$$

Left side of equation is set to " I", original investment. Right side of equation is the sum of the present value of cash flows for each period. We know the value for every variable in formula except for the interest rate. Solving equation by hand requires substituting many different values for interest into the equation until both sides are equal. This is called the trial and error method. If you have a business calculator use it. Most of them come with the IRR function built-in. I am going to use Microsoft Excel's IRR Function.

After computing IRR, compare it to the company's cost of capital. Accept the project if the IRR is greater than the cost of capital. If IRR equals cost of capital, manager is indifferent to acceptance or rejection. And finally, if IRR is less than cost of capital reject the project. Using our Worksheet in Figure 14.1 let's calculate the Internal Rate of Return using the Microsoft Excel IRR Function. It is found in

227

the financial category of the Input Function dialog box. Some rules for using the IRR function. The Values box holds an array of cash flow values. You can enter a cell range in this box, but cash flow amounts must be entered in the order received or paid. Value range must include at least one negative value (usually the first value in the range) and one positive value. Whether you enter a value in the "Guess" box (must be a decimal version of the expected rate) or not is optional. If you leave it blank, Microsoft Excel assumes that your guess is 10%. If IRR cannot find the interest rate that sets NPV to zero, it returns a "Value Error".

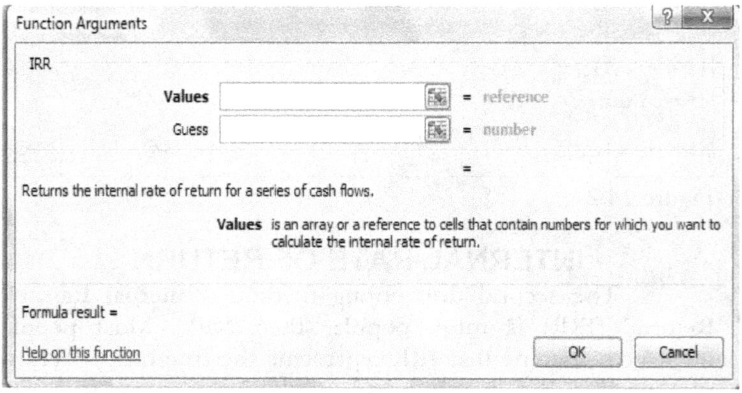

Figure 14.3

The result of the IRR formula is an interest rate of 24%. This project should be accepted because it is greater than the cost of capital. Accept this project is the same answer that the NPV method yielded.

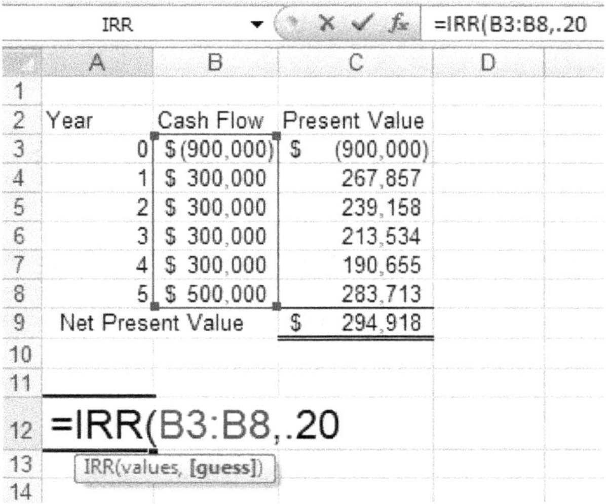

	IRR	▼	× ✓ fx	=IRR(B3:B8,.20	
	A	B	C	D	
1					
2	Year	Cash Flow	Present Value		
3	0	$ (900,000)	$ (900,000)		
4	1	$ 300,000	267,857		
5	2	$ 300,000	239,158		
6	3	$ 300,000	213,534		
7	4	$ 300,000	190,655		
8	5	$ 500,000	283,713		
9	Net Present Value		$ 294,918		
10					
11					
12	=IRR(B3:B8,.20				
13	IRR(values, [guess])				
14					

Figure 14.4

SUMMARY

Managers have four methods to evaluate long-term projects: (1) payback method, (2) Accounting Rate of Return, (3) Net Present Value, and (4) Internal Rate of Return. Methods (3) and (4) give the best answer as they consider the time-value-of-money.

CHAPTER 15
INTRODUCTION TO BUSINESS STATISTICS

The Microsoft Excel Analysis ToolPak add-ins is used to solve statistics problems. We showed you how to load it in Chapter12 when we discussed regression analysis.

Statistics is a part of mathematics. Statistics deals with the process of collecting, categorizing, summarizing, analyzing, and presenting data to users. Users draw conclusions from the data and employ those conclusions to make decisions.

A first step in understanding statistics is to have definitions for the items that we will be working with in our statistical processes. The things we want to study are called **data.** Data has characteristics that distinguish one piece of data from another. Those distinguishing characteristics are called **variables.** So that we are on the same page while discussing variables, all variables should have a widely accepted meaning.

Because we are interested in cost-benefit analysis, we know that often it is impossible to study all data in a particular universe that we want to draw conclusions about. The technical term for the universe we want to study is **population.** A population contains all members of a group from which we want to study and draw conclusions. We sometimes have to study a portion of the population (called a **sample**), draw conclusions from the sample, and then project those conclusions to the population. A **parameter** is a numeric measure that describes a characteristic of a population. A **statistic** does the same for a characteristic of a sample.

TYPES OF VARIABLES

Depending on the type of answer we seek we divide variables into four (4) categories. If we seek a **yes** or **no** answer we have to use a **categorical variable.** If we seek a how much or number answer we have to use a **numerical value.** A **discrete variable** is used when we seek a numerical response resulting from a counting process. And we use a **continuous variable** when we seek a numerical response resulting from a measuring process. Continuous variables can be any value in an interval. A discrete variable can only be a specific value.

USING TABLES AND CHARTS TO PRESENT DATA

Categorical Data Tables and Charts

To get vast amounts of categorical data into useable form, we can construct a **Summary Table**. A summary table shows the frequency, amount, or percentage of items in a group of categories so that differences are highlighted.

	A	B	C
1			
2	Who are you voting for in the election?		
3	Party	Percentage	
4	Democrat	55	
5	Republican	40	
6	Independent	4	
7	Undecided	1	
8		100	
9			

Figure 15.1

We could also use a Bar Chart to display the same information. Each category is displayed and its length represents the amount.

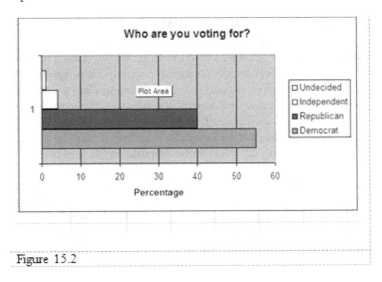

Figure 15.2

See Chapter 7 for detailed instructions on how to create charts.

A pie chart can also be used to display the same data. A circle is divided into slices that represent a category. Size of slice indicates percentage in each category.

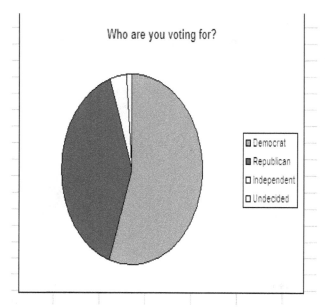

Figure 15.3

NUMERICAL DATA TABLES AND CHARTS

A *Frequency Distribution* is a summary table that is used to draw conclusions from a large set of data. Data are arranged into numerically ordered (sorted) class groupings. Everything revolves around correctly creating class groupings. Decisions you must make are: (1) What is the appropriate number of class groupings (from 5 to 15 class groupings, the more data you have the higher the number of class groupings not to exceed 15), (2) what is the suitable width (interval) of a class grouping, and (3) what are the lower and upper boundaries of each class grouping. Each class grouping must have equal width. To calculate width, divide range (highest value to lowest value of data) by the number of class grouping desired. Boundaries should be chosen for readability and interpretation (round up to whole number if necessary).

$$\text{Width of interval} = \frac{\text{range}}{\text{number of desired class groupings}}$$

Suppose that a class of 50 students was given an exam. As their teacher I am interested in how the classed performed. Grades ranged from 50 to 100. See the following frequency distribution to determine how well the class performed. I used letter grade ranges to determine class grouping: (A = 90% or better, B = 80% - 89%, C = 70% to 79%, D = 60% to 69%, and F = 50% - 59%). Assume that the lowest grade possible was 50. To get more useful information, have Microsoft Excel calculate the percentage totals for each class grouping. Our frequency distribution tells us that the class did well with 60% of the students earning a grade of "B" or better.

Class Groupings		Frequency
A	90 - 100	10
B	80 - 89	20
C	70 - 79	10
D	60 - 69	5
F	50 - 59	5

Class Groupings		Frequency	Percentage
A	90 - 100	10	20%
B	80 - 89	20	40%
C	70 - 79	10	20%
D	60 - 69	5	10%
F	50 - 59	5	10%

Figure 15.4

There are a number of ways to handle frequency calculations in Microsoft Excel. If you remember we discussed frequency calculations in Chapter 6 when we discussed PivotTables. We also discussed frequency distributions when we described the uses of the VLookUp function in Chapter 2.

DESCRIPTIVE STATISTICS

Descriptive statistics are used to summarize large amounts of data and present it in a way to make the data easier to use. Some descriptive methods to summarize numerical variables are (1) central tendency, (2) variation, and (3) shape. Central tendency describes how a group of variables cluster around a central value. There are three ways to describe central tendency: (1) mean, (2) median, and (3) Mode. Central tendency is a measure of location. Variation tells us the pattern and how far variables of a group are from the central value. There are three ways to describe or measure variation (dispersion): (1) range, (2) variance, and (3) standard deviation. And shape, visually shows the pattern of the distribution of values from lowest to highest value.

233

MEASURES OF CENTRAL TENDENCY

You already know what this measure means. Central tendency is the average value of a group of values. The "**Mean**" is known to most of us as the "Average". Let XBar represent the sample mean; and the formula to calculate the mean is XBar = Sum of the values / n-1. Where "n" is the total count of the group of values. There is no need to use the mean formula as Microsoft Excel's AVERAGE Function will calculate the mean for you. As you would suspect, all the values in the group of values, will have an equal role in calculating the mean. So outliers (values greatly different from other values in the group) may make the mean less useful in measuring the values in the group. When outliers are present, median is a better measure of location than mean. To calculate mean (μ) for a population, sum the values and divide by N (where N is the number of items in a population).

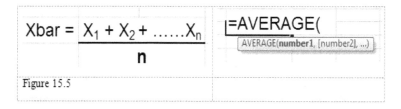

Figure 15.5

THE MEDIAN

If you have a group of values, ranked from lowest value to highest value, the Median is the point half way from lowest to highest value. It is the value in the middle of the group. If the number of values in the group is odd, median is the middle observation. If the number of values in the group is even, median is the mean of the two middle values. For example if we have 12 values the mean of the middle two (the 6th and 7th values) would be the median. Extreme values will not affect the calculation of the median, so it is still a useful measure when outliers exist. Median = (n)/2. Median is sometimes called the 50 percentile or the second quartile. A quartile is another descriptive measure of location. Most of the time it will be easier to calculate median if you use Microsoft Excel's Median Function.

8		
8		
8		
9		
9	Median is 10.5	
10	(10+11)/2	10.5
11		
11		
11		
12		
12		
12		

Figure 15.6

Following is Microsoft Excel's Function to calculate the median.

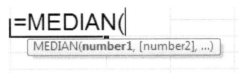

Figure 15.7

THE MODE

Mode, the final measure of location is the value that appears the most times in the group of values (i.e. value with greatest frequency). Mode is not affected by outliers. Mode is different from sample to sample and thus should only be used for descriptive purposes. Use Microsoft Excel's MODE Function to calculate.

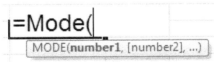

Figure 15.8

QUARTILES

Quartiles divide the group of values into four equal parts. First Quartile divides the first 25% of the smallest values from the other 75% larger values. Second Quartile is the median, 50% of the values are smaller than the median and 50% of the values are larger than the median. And the third Quartile separates the smallest 75% of the values from the largest 25%. Quartile is used to indicate the location of a value in the ranked group. Figure 15.9 shows formulas for Quartile 1, Quartile 3, and the Microsoft Excel Quartile Function.

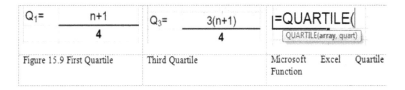

$Q_1 = \dfrac{n+1}{4}$	$Q_3 = \dfrac{3(n+1)}{4}$	=QUARTILE(QUARTILE(array, quart)
Figure 15.9 First Quartile	Third Quartile	Microsoft Excel Quartile Function

MEASURES OF DISPERSION

RANGE

Range is the difference between the largest value and smallest value in a data set. Look at figure 15.6. The range of that data set is 12 − 8 = 4. Range really is not a good measure of dispersion because only extremes (largest and smallest) are considered. Therefore no information is provided about the variability of the in between values.

VARIANCE

Variance measures how values cluster around the mean. Variance is the mean of the sum of the squared deviations. A deviation is the difference between a value of an item in a data set and the mean of the data set. It shows the pattern of how far variables vary from the average value in the group. Since a variable can be either greater than or less than the average we have to square the difference and then sum the squared differences. This is called the sum of the squares (**SS**). The sum of the squares is divided by (**n-1**) to calculate a sample variance (**S²**). To calculate population variance substitute μ for XBar and divide by N (total number of items in population) rather than by "n − 1". Microsoft Excel has a function to calculate variance and works a lot faster than the formula.

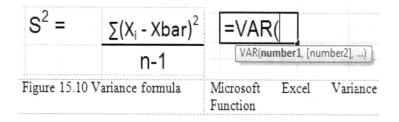

$S^2 = \dfrac{\sum(X_i - Xbar)^2}{n-1}$	=VAR(VAR(**number1**, [number2], ...)
Figure 15.10 Variance formula	Microsoft Excel Variance Function

STANDARD DEVIATION

Like the variance, the Standard Deviation measures how values cluster around the mean. It has an advantage over the variance as a measure. The variance is a squared quantity, while the standard deviation is always in the same units as the original values in the group. Sample Standard Deviation **(S)** is the square root of the sample variance. And σ (sigma) is the standard deviation of a population. Of course Microsoft Excel also has a function to calculate standard deviation.

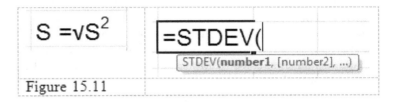

Figure 15.11

COEFFICIENT OF VARIATION

The Coefficient of Variation is a relative measure of variation and is always expressed as a percentage rather than in terms of the units of the values in the group. Coefficient of Variation **(CV)** measures the scatter of the value relative to the mean. CV is useful when comparing two or more groups of values when those groups are measured in different units. Coefficient of variation is standard deviation divided by the mean and then multiplied by 100%.

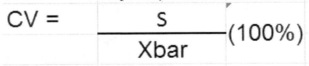

Figure 15.12

Z SCORES

Z scores are used to identify outliers. The Z score is the difference between the value and the mean which is then divided by the standard deviation. The larger this number the farther the value is from the mean. A Z score should be calculated for each value. A Z score greater than **+3.0 or less than -3** is considered an outlier.

237

$Z =$	$X_i - Xbar$
	S

Figure 15.13

SHAPE

Shape is another statistic that describes a set of numerical data. Is shows the pattern distribution of all data values from the smallest value to the largest value. It graphically displays the relationship of the mean to the median. The shape can be symmetrical if the low values and high values balance each other out around the median. The shape can be skewed (to the left or to the right). A skewed shape has an imbalance of low or high values. Shape and its relationship to median:

(1) Mean < Median; negative or left-skewed shape

(2) Mean = Median; symmetric or zero skewness

(3) Mean > Median; positive or right-skewed shape

MICROSOFT EXCEL DESCRIPTIVE STATISTICS

Microsoft Excel's Descriptive Statistics feature is found on the Data tab, Analysis Group. The Analysis group becomes available only after the Analysis ToolPak has been installed. You must access Microsoft Excel options from Microsoft Office **FILE TAB**. Select Add-Ins category and then click box for Analysis ToolPak. Click GO button and Microsoft Excel's statistical package (Analysis ToolPak) will be added to the Microsoft Excel program. From the Data Tab, Analysis Group, click the Data Analysis icon. Enter requested values in input boxes and Microsoft Excel will display a host of Descriptive Statistics.

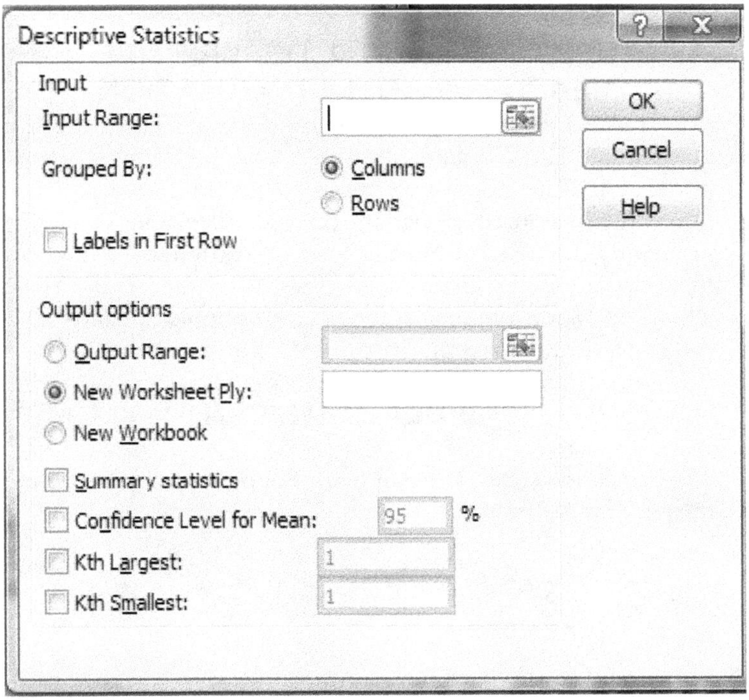

Figure 15.14

Using Microsoft Excel's Descriptive Statistic package yields results much quicker than calculating individual statistics.

	A	B	C	D
	Month	Mfg Overhead	Units Produced	
January		$ 3,000	153	
February		4,000	200	
March		2,800	168	
April		1,950	200	
May		5,000	500	
June		4,350	300	
July		6,100	387	
August		1,875	400	
September		3,200	480	
October		5,275	430	

Column1		Column2	
Mean	3755	Mean	321.8
Standard Error	451.6143881	Standard Error	42.31490413
Median	3600	Median	343.5
Mode	#N/A	Mode	200
Standard Deviation	1428.130091	Standard Deviation	133.811476
Sample Variance	2039555.556	Sample Variance	17905.51111
Kurtosis	-1.061790704	Kurtosis	-1.861970425
Skewness	0.217646505	Skewness	-0.025029033
Range	4225	Range	347
Minimum	1875	Minimum	153
Maximum	6100	Maximum	500
Sum	37550	Sum	3218
Count	10	Count	10
Confidence Level(95.0%)	1021.622721	Confidence Level(95.0%)	95.72296326

Figure 15.15

239

USING NUMERICAL DESCRIPTIVE
MEASURES WITH A POPULATION

We have discussed numerical descriptive measures for a sample. Those same measures can be applied to a population. The population mean, population variance, and population standard deviation can be calculated using the previously discussed formulas. The only difference is that for the population the denominator is "N" rather than "n-1", where "N" is the number of items in the population and "n" is the number of items in the sample.

POPULATION MEAN

The Greek lowercase letter mu, symbol **μ,** is used to represent the population mean.

$$\mu = \frac{\sum X_i}{N}$$

Figure 15.16

The Microsoft Excel **AVERAGE** Function works just as well.
Population Variance
The Greek lowercase letter sigma squared, symbol σ^2, is used to represent the population variance.

$$\sigma^2 = \frac{\sum(X_i - \mu)^2}{N}$$

Figure 15.17

The Microsoft Excel VARP Function works just as well.

X_i	$(X_i - \mu)^2$	
M	N	O
4.5	4.2436	
7.3	0.5476	
4	6.5536	
7	0.1936	
10	11.8336	
	23.372	
6.6	4.6744	

$$=VARP(M2:M6)$$

Consider the population (4.5, 7.3, 4, 7, 10). The population mean is 6.6. Using the Population variance formula in Figure 15.17, variance was calculated to be 4.6744. The Microsoft Excel VARP Function was used and yielded the same result.

Figure 15.18

POPULATION STANDARD DEVIATION

The Greek symbol σ, lowercase letter sigma is used to represent the population standard deviation. Just like the calculation of the sample standard deviation, the population standard deviation is the square root of the population variance. The population standard deviation is the square root of 4.6744 which equals 2.162.

$$\sigma = \sqrt{\frac{\Sigma(X_i - \mu)^2}{N}}$$

Figure 15.19

The Microsoft Excel Function **STDEVP** works just as well as the formula.

M	N	O	P
X_i	$(X_i - \mu)^2$		
4.5	4.2436		
7.3	0.5476		
4	6.5536		
7	0.1936		
10	11.8336		
	23.372		
6.6	2.162036077		

$$=STDEVP(M2:M6)$$

Figure 15.20

THE COVARIANCE

In chapter 12 we discussed cost behavior and talked about the relationship of a data set which contained a dependent variable and independent variable. The Covariance statistic can be used to measure the strength of the linear relationship between these numerical variables (Y and X). A major shortcoming of the Covariance statistic is that it can have any value, so it is not possible to determine the relative strength of the relationship. We will fix this problem by using the "Coefficient of Correlation" statistic.

Sample covariance is calculated by following formula:

$$cov(X,Y) = \frac{\Sigma(X_i - Xbar)(Y_i - Ybar)}{n - 1}$$

Figure 15.21

Following is the Spreadsheet example of calculating sample covariance.

	A	B	C	D
1	Month	Mfg Overhead	Units Produced	(X-Xbar)(Y-Ybar)
2	January	$ 3,000	153	127,444
3	February	4,000	200	(29,841)
4	March	2,800	168	146,879
5	April	1,950	200	219,849
6	May	5,000	500	221,859
7	June	4,350	300	(12,971)
8	July	6,100	387	152,894
9	August	1,875	400	(147,016)
10	September	3,200	480	(87,801)
11	October	5,275	430	164,464
12			SUM	755,760
13	**Mean**	$ 3,755	322	
14				
15		Calculations		
16	Xbar	=Average (B2:B11)		$ 3,755
17	Ybar	=Average (C2:C11)		322
18	n-1	=Count(B2:B11) - 1		9
19	Sum	=Sum(D2:D11)		755,760
20	Covariance	=D12 /D18		83973.33333

Figure 15.22

As you would guess, Microsoft Excel has a built-in function that also calculates covariance.

Figure 15.23

COEFFICIENT OF CORRELATION

To measure the relative strength of the linear relationship between two numerical variables you have to calculate the "Coefficient of Correlation". The result will range from -1 for perfect negative correlation to +1 perfect positive correlation. Perfect is defined as all data points on a scatter graph were able to be connected with a straight line. Use "r" to represent sample coefficient of correlation in the following formula:

243

$$r = \frac{cov(X,Y)}{S_X S_Y}$$

Where S_x is the standard deviation of variable X

S_y is the standard deviation of variable Y

Figure 15.24

According to the sample coefficient of correlation, Mfg Overhead and Units Produced are positively correlated but the relationship is not very strong ($r = .439420447$).

	A	B	C	D	E	F
1	Month	Mfg Overhead	Units Produced	$(X\text{-Xbar})^2$	$(Y\text{-Ybar})^2$	(X-Xbar)(Y-Ybar)
2	January	$ 3,000	153	28493.44	570.025	127,444
3	February	4,000	200	14835.24	60.025	(29,841)
4	March	2,800	168	23654.44	912.025	146,879
5	April	1,950	200	14835.24	3,258.025	219,849
6	May	5,000	500	31755.24	1,550.025	221,859
7	June	4,350	300	475.24	354.025	(12,971)
8	July	6,100	387	4251.04	5,499.025	152,894
9	August	1,875	400	6115.24	3,534.400	(147,016)
10	September	3,200	480	25027.24	308.025	(87,801)
11	October	5,275	430	11707.24	2,310.400	164,464
12			SUM	161149.6	18356000	755,760
13	Mean	$ 3,755	322			
14						
15			Calculations			
16	Xbar	=Average (B2:B11)		3,755		
17	Ybar	=Average (C2:C11)		322		
18	n-1	=Count(B2:B11) - 1		9		
19	Covariance	=F12 /D18		83973.33333		
20	S_X	=SQRT(D12/D18)		133.811476		
21	S_y	=SQRT(E12/D18)		1428.130091		
22	r	Correl(B2:B11,C2:C11)		0.439420447		
		or =D19/(D20 *D21)				
				0.439420447		

Figure 15.25

Microsoft Excel's **CORREL** Function will give you the same answer.

$$=CORREL(C3:C12,D3:D12)$$

Figure 15.26

SUMMARY

Business statistics are used to solve many different types of problems. Statistics make sense of large amounts of information. There are two types of statistics: (1) descriptive statistics and (2) inferential statistics. Variables are used to describe different types of data. There are several methods that can be used to summarize large amounts of data: (1) central tendency, (2) variation, and (3) shape. Statistics can be used to determine the relationship between variables.

CHAPTER 16
DISCRETE PROBABILITY DISTRIBUTIONS

In this chapter we discuss techniques to answer a question accountants regularly are asked regarding events. For example: "What is the probability of finding a defined outcome in a sample of a specific size". As an auditor you might be interested in how many times an internal control feature is violated. For example, sales invoices require the signature of a supervisor indicating that the sales invoice has been reviewed and approved. If we have a sample of a specific size, how many sales invoices will lack a supervisor's signature? To answer these types of questions we will build a statistical model and draw conclusions from the model.

PROBABILITY DISTRIBUTION FOR A DISCRETE RANDOM VARIABLE

In chapter 15 we defined a numerical variable as one that yielded numerical responses to a survey. There are two types of numerical variables: (1) discrete and (2) Continuous. A discrete variable yields outcomes out of a counting process. While a continuous numerical value yields an outcome from a measuring process. A probability distribution for a discrete random variable is a list of all possible outcomes for that random variable along with the probability of occurrence of each outcome.

Suppose you are the new CFO of HuntCo printing company and the VP of manufacturing asks you to evaluate two different printing presses. She needs to decide which press to purchase. She has already evaluated usage and performance. The chief accountant has told her that based on past performance the two presses generated different amounts of revenue. The chief accountant has prepared a list of the returns for each printing press and based on past experience has assigned a probability of each yield occurring. This is a probability distribution and the chief accountant gives it to you for review and to determine which of the two presses would be the best purchase if financial consideration is the final criteria for the decision. Figure 16.1 has the probability distribution for the first printing press. Your task is to evaluate the yield of each press and decide which has the best expected yield. To perform this task you need to calculate three statistics: (1) expected value of the discrete random variable,

(2) variance of the discrete random variable, and (3) standard deviation of the discrete random variable.

1	B	C	D	E
2	PRINTING PRESS 1			
3	X_i	$P(X_i)$		Variance
4	Return	Probability	$X_iP(X_i)$	$[X_i-E(X)]^2P(X_i)$
5	8%	0.10	0.008	0.0001225
6	9%	0.20	0.018	0.000125
7	11%	0.30	0.033	7.5E-06
8	14%	0.40	0.056	0.00025
9	Expected Rate of Return		11.50%	0.000505

Figure 16.1

For this example the return X_i for each press is the discrete random variable. The mutually exclusive list is a return of 8%, 9%, 11%, or 14%. In column C is the probability of each discrete random variable.

CALCULATE EXPECTED VALUE OF A DISCRETE RANDOM VARIABLE

The expected value of a probability distribution is just the population mean μ of the distribution. Why use the population mean. Well, remember that probability distribution is a mutually exclusive list of all the variables in the population, thus we have to use the population mean. The formula is:

$$\mu = E(x) = \Sigma X_i P(X_i)$$

Figure 16.2

Where X_i is the ith outcome of the discrete random variable X and

$P(X_i)$ is the probability of occurrence of the ith outcome of X

The expected rate of return for printing press 1 is 11.50%. See column D9, Figure 16.1.

247

CALCULATE VARIANCE OF A DISCRETE RANDOM VARIABLE

To calculate the variance of a discrete random variable you (1) subtract the expected value E(X) from each individual outcome (X_i) and square this number, and then (2) multiply each of the squared number by their related probability $(P(X))$. The sum of (1) and (2) is the variance.

$$\sigma^2 = \Sigma[X_i - E(X)]^2 P(X_i)$$

Figure 16.3

The variance of the returns for printing press 1 is .000505. See column E9, Figure 16.1.

CALCULATE STANDARD DEVIATION OF A DISCRETE RANDOM VARIABLE

The standard deviation of a discrete random variable is the square root of the variance of a discrete random variable. For printing press 1, the standard deviation is .02247 (SQRT (E9)).

$$\sigma = \sqrt{\Sigma[X_i - E(X)]^2 P(X_i)}$$

Figure 16.4

In summary for printing press 1, the mean return is 11.5%, variance is .000505, and the standard deviation is .02247. Perform the same calculations for printing press 2 and compare.

BINOMIAL DISTRIBUTION

What if you did not know the probabilities of the discrete random variables that were used in the previous example? What if you wanted to calculate the exact probability of each occurrence of the discrete random variable? The **Binomial Probability distribution mathematical model** is going to be used to calculate probability of occurrence for each discrete random variable.

First we have to discuss some rules:
1. The sample consists of a fixed number of observations, n.
2. Each observation is classified into one of two mutually

exclusive categories called success or failure.

3. Both success "P" and failure "1-P" are constant from observation to observation.

4. The outcomes of any observation are independent of the outcome of any other observation.

Returning to the previous example, we have four possible returns. Based on prior experience there has always been a 10% chance that returns would be 11%. What we want to know is the exact probability of the return being 11%.

The formula is tedious because it requires the solving of factorials. The formula for calculating the number of successes (X), given the values of n and p is:

$$P(X) = \frac{n!}{X!(n-X)!} P^{X(1-P)n-x}$$

Figure 16.5

Where:
P(x) is the probability of X successes given "n" and "p"

n is the number of observations,

p is the probability of success

1-p is the probability of failure

X is the number of successes in the sample (X = 0, 1, 2, 3,…,n)

Like I said, the computation of this formula is tedious, let's just make a spreadsheet and instead use the Excel **BINOMDIST Function.**

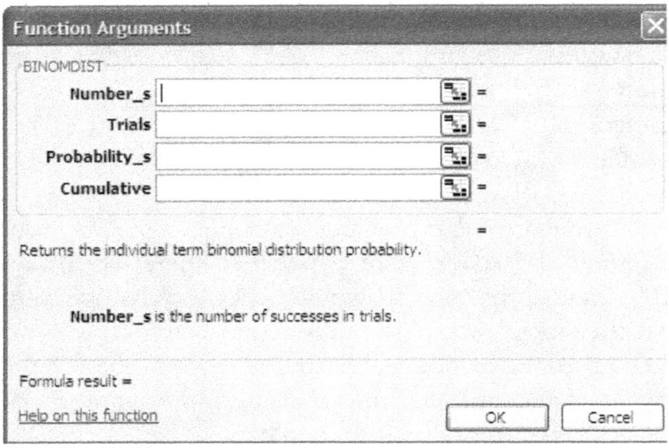

Figure 16.6

The Binomdist Function is found in the statistical category in the "Insert Function" dialog box. The four arguments need a little explanation:

1. Number_s. How many times does variable appear in the sample
2. Trials. Number of independent trials (i.e. sample size)
3. Probability_s. Probability of success on each trial
4. Cumulative. A logical value. TRUE for cumulative distribution function, FALSE for the probability mass function (looking for discrete answer not cumulative answer)

	A	B	C
1	Return 11%		
2			
3	Data		
4	Sample Size	4	
5	Probability of Success	0.1	
6			
7	Statistics		
8	Mean	0.4	=B4*B5
9	Variance	0.36	=B8*(1-B5)
10	Standard deviation	0.6	=SQRT(B9)
11			
12	Binomial Probabilities Table		
13	x	P(x)	
14	0	0.6561	=BINOMDIST(A14,$B$4,$B$5, FALSE)
15	1	0.2916	=BINOMDIST(A15,$B$4,$B$5, FALSE)
16	2	0.0486	=BINOMDIST(A16,$B$4,$B$5, FALSE)
17	3	0.0036	=BINOMDIST(A17,$B$4,$B$5, FALSE)
18	4	0.0001	=BINOMDIST(A18,$B$4,$B$5, FALSE)

Figure 16.7

We have a sample of 4 discrete random variables which represent revenue yields for a printing press. What is the probability that in our sample of 4 variables, a return of 11% will occur? Answer (.2916 or 29.16%) is found in the Binomial Probabilities Table. What is the probability that a return of 11% does not appear in the sample of 4 variables (Zero (0))? That probability is .6561 or 65%.

THE MEAN OF THE BINOMIAL DISTRIBUTION

The mean is equal to the sample size, n, multiplied by the probability of success.

$$\mu = E(X) = np$$

Variance of the Binomial Distribution

Variance $(X) = np(1-p)$

$$\sigma^2 = np(1-p)$$

Figure 16.8

STANDARD DEVIATION OF BINOMIAL DISTRIBUTION

Standard deviation of the Binomial Distribution is the square root of the variance of Binomial Distribution.

$$\sigma = \sqrt{np(1-p)}$$

Figure 16.9

POISSON DISTRIBUTION

The "Poisson Distribution" examines the number of times an event occurs during a specified interval. An interval can be anything; a unit of time, length, volume. For example how many times did the internal control feature over sales invoice preparation fail during the month of November.

Characteristics of using "Poisson Distribution":
1. You are interested in counting the number of times a particular event occurs in the interval.
2. Average rate of success is known.
3. Probability that a single success will occur during the interval is proportional to the size of the interval.

251

4. Probability that an event occurs in one interval is independent of event occurring in any other interval.

POISSON PROBABILITY DISTRIBUTION FORMULA:

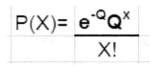

$$P(X)= \frac{e^{-Q}Q^X}{X!}$$

Figure 16.10

Where:
P(X) is the probability of X events in an interval.

Q is the expected number of events

e is a mathematical constant approximated by 2.71828

X is the number of events

Here we go again with a tedious formula to calculate. Let's get Excel to do the work for us. Set up your Worksheet as follows and use the **Excel "POISSON( )"** FUNCTION. As an auditor we are testing the internal control over the sales invoice process. We expect to find 3 instances out of a sample of twenty invoices where the internal control feature failed.

	A	B	C	D	E
1	Failure of internal control feature				
2					
3		Data			
4	Average/ Expected number of Successes				3
5	(Defined here as control failure)				
6					
7	Poisson Probabilities Table				
8	X	P(X)			
9	0	0.049787	=POISSON(A9,$E$4, FALSE)		
10	1	0.149361	=POISSON(A10,$E$4, FALSE)		
11	2	0.224042	=POISSON(A11,$E$4, FALSE)		
12	3	0.224042	=POISSON(A12,$E$4, FALSE)		
13	4	0.168031	=POISSON(A13,$E$4, FALSE)		
14	5	0.100819	=POISSON(A14,$E$4, FALSE)		
15	6	0.050409	=POISSON(A15,$E$4, FALSE)		
16	7	0.021604	=POISSON(A16,$E$4, FALSE)		
17	8	0.008102	=POISSON(A17,$E$4, FALSE)		
18	9	0.002701	=POISSON(A18,$E$4, FALSE)		
19	10	0.00081	=POISSON(A19,$E$4, FALSE)		
20	11	0.000221	=POISSON(A20,$E$4, FALSE)		
21	12	5.52E-05	=POISSON(A21,$E$4, FALSE)		
22	13	1.27E-05	=POISSON(A22,$E$4, FALSE)		
23	14	2.73E-06	=POISSON(A23,$E$4, FALSE)		
24	15	5.46E-07	=POISSON(A24,$E$4, FALSE)		
25	16	1.02E-07	=POISSON(A25,$E$4, FALSE)		
26	17	1.81E-08	=POISSON(A26,$E$4, FALSE)		
27	18	3.01E-09	=POISSON(A27,$E$4, FALSE)		
28	19	4.76E-10	=POISSON(A28,$E$4, FALSE)		
29	20	7.14E-11	=POISSON(A29,$E$4, FALSE)		

Figure 16.11

Using the Poisson Probabilities Excel function requires some explanation.

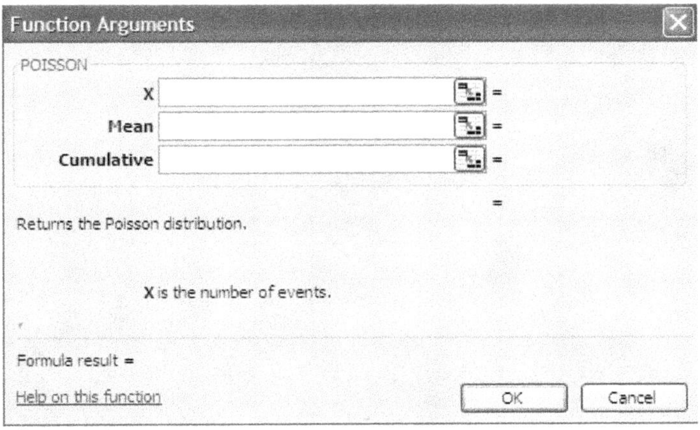

Figure 16.11

Function Arguments for Poisson Function:

1. "x". The discrete random variable that you want to calculate a probability for.
2. Mean. The number of times that variable will appear in the sample
3. Cumulative. TRUE if looking for cumulative number of times, FALSE if looking for the probability of one variable occurring.

The probability of finding 3 internal control failures is .224042 or 22.4042%.

SUMMARY

Discrete probability distributions are often used by auditors to answer the question "how many internal control failures will I find in a particular sample?" If you have a sample of events and the probability that each event will occur, then you can estimate the event that is expected to occur. Using statistics you can evaluate how good the estimate is in predicting the expected event. The binomial distribution is used when we do not know the probabilities that the events discussed above will occur. It helps us determine the probability of a particular event occurring. We use the poisson distribution to answer the question of how many times a particular event will occur during a specific time frame. We can use the poisson distribution to answer the question: "how many times did the internal control feature fail during the month of August?"

CHAPTER 17
NORMAL DISTRIBUTION

In Chapter 16 we talked about discrete random variables which dealt with results of a counting process. In this chapter we discuss continuous numerical variables which result from a measuring process. We will be using a mathematical model to define the distribution of values for a continuous random variable.

The 'Normal Distribution" is a type of continuous probability density function. It is symmetric and bell shaped. Most values in this continuous distribution cluster around the mean, which in this case is equal to the median of the distribution. The mean, median, and mode are all equal in a normal distribution. With the normal distribution you can calculate the probability that various values occur within certain ranges or intervals. You cannot however, calculate the probability of a discrete value from this continuous distribution as the probability of a particular value is zero. This is one of the things that differentiates a counting process from a measuring process.

The formula to calculate the Normal Distribution is:

$$f(x) = \frac{1}{\sqrt{2\pi\sigma}} e^{-(1/2)[(X-\mu)/\sigma]^{\wedge}2}$$

Figure 17.1

Where:
f(x) normal probability density function
e is the mathematical constant approximated by 2.17828
π Greek lower case letter pi which is used as a mathematical constant approximated by 3.14159
σ is the standard deviation
X is any value of the continuous variable, in between positive infinity and negative infinity

Do you want to try to solve this formula, even with Microsoft Excel? Not me! Let's try something else. First let's use the transformation formula to simplify the normal distribution function. The Transformation Formula is used to convert any normal random variable X to a standardized normal random variable Z. The standardized random variable Z will always have mean $\mu = 0$, and a standard deviation $\sigma = 1$. Look at Figure 17.2 to see how the transformation formula simplifies the normal distribution function.

$$Z = \frac{X - \mu}{\sigma} \qquad f(Z) = \frac{1}{\sqrt{2\pi}} e^{-(1/2)z^2}$$

Figure 17.2	Simplified normal distribution function

The Z value is used to find the area under the normal distribution curve. The area under the curve found by the Z value gives you the probability of the continuous variable. That's too much math for me so I just use Microsoft Excel to find normal probabilities.

Ok, now that we know the normal distribution formula and the transformation formula, let's use Microsoft Excel to calculate a normal probability. Suppose that student scores on a recent exam had a μ (population mean) of 70 and an σ (population standard deviation) of 6. What is the probability that X> 78 (that there will be a score of 78 in the distribution of grades)?

Looking at the mean of 70 and standard deviation of 6, I guess the probability is high.
Set up your Worksheet like Figure 17.3.

	A	B	C	D	E
1	Normal Probabilities				
2					
3	Input Data				
4	Mean	70			
5	Standard Deviation	6			
6					
7	Probabilitity for X>78				
8	X Value	78			
9	Z Value	1.333333	=STANDARDIZE(B8,B4,B5)		
10	P(X=78)	0.908789	=NORMDIST(B8,B4,B5,TRUE)		
11					

Figure 17.3

=Standardize(STANDARDIZE(x, mean, standard_dev) Figure 17.4	We use the Standardize Function to calculate Z.

We use the NORMDIST Function to calculate the Normal probability. The probability that 78 will be in the distribution is 90.88%.

Figure 17.5

SUMMARY

The normal distribution concept by itself does not seem all that important. Believe me it is important because it is the foundation of sampling and hypothesis testing which we will discuss in the next two chapters.

CHAPTER 18
USING MICROSOFT EXCEL TO SOLVE SAMPLING PROBLEMS

Sometimes you need to examine a population to evaluate its characteristics (called parameters by mathematicians). If the population is large it is not cost effective to examine every item in the population. What we really want to do is examine a small number of items drawn from the population, evaluate those items, and use the results to draw inferences about the population. How do we know that the inferences we make are correct and can we measure that? The small number of selected items is called a Sample and we can use statistics, more precisely sampling distributions, to answer the aforementioned question.

To be able to draw inferences about a population from sample results, the sample must be representative of the population. Therefore the first thing you have to do is correctly define the population, the entire population. Characteristics of the sample must be the same as found in the population for it to be a representative sample. For example assume that you are an auditor who needs to test the correctness of the recorded account receivables of a company for the entire year. What is the population? The population is the recorded customer accounts for the entire year. The recorded accounts receivable for the month of November would not be an appropriate population to determine whether the yearly accounts receivable are correctly recorded. So the sample should be drawn for customer accounts for the entire year, and not just from the month of November.

Even after we pull the sample, examine the items for the attributes that we are interested in, the inferences we draw may not be representative of the population. There are two risks that sample is not representative of the population: (1) Non-sampling risk and (2) Sampling Risk. Non-sampling risk occurs when the examiner of the sample fails to recognize the attributes that sample if supposed to identify. Therefore the wrong conclusions are made about the sample results. Statistics will not rescue you. Better training and adherence to quality control procedures are the only answer to this type of risk. Sampling risk occurs when the wrong conclusion is reached because the sample is not representative of the population. To control sampling risk you can increase sample size. The larger the sample, the smaller the sampling risk and vice versa.

There are two types of sampling. For those accountants reading this, either of the two types is perfectly acceptable when performing audits. The two types are: (1) Statistical sampling and (2) Non-statistical sampling. Statistical sampling applies mathematical rules to measure sampling risk and to evaluate sampling results. Non-statistical sampling relies on judgment of the sample taker and examiner and does not quantify sampling risk. Regardless of the type chosen you must perform the following steps for the sample to be successful:

1. Plan the sample; what are your objectives, what are you looking for?
2. Select the sample.
3. Perform tests on the sample items; inspect them to find what you are looking for?
4. Evaluate the results; draw inferences about the population.

How a sample is selected is divided into two types: (1) probabilistic or (2) non-probabilistic. With the probabilistic selection method, you randomly select a sample where the probability of a population item being in the sample is known. The non-probabilistic uses judgment to select sample items. Usually, the probabilistic sample results in less work as this sample selection method results in a smaller, more efficient, and less costly sample.

There are four ways to select a probabilistic sample: (1) simple random sample, (2) systematic selection, (3) probability proportional to size selection, and (4) stratified sample selection.

Now let's discuss the math behind statistical sampling. We will be calculating a sample mean (called a statistic by mathematicians) to estimate the population mean. We will also be calculating the sample proportion (another statistic) to estimate the population proportion (a parameter) of the existence of a particular attribute. For auditors the proportion might be "what is the proportion of sales invoices where the internal control measures were not applied". Remember that our goal is to draw inferences about the population, and not about the sample.

Because we assume that the population is normally distributed, one sample of a predetermined size will be enough to answer our business question. That is if the sample is randomly selected. Statistics allow us to use this one sample to

259

draw inferences about the population. This is possible because of the relationship of the single sample to every possible sample of a predetermined size that could be taken from the population. The results of every possible sample of a predetermined size, is called a sampling distribution. The sample mean of one randomly selected sample is an unbiased predictor of the population mean (μ); because the mean of the sampling distribution of all samples of a population of a given size (n) is equal to (μ). This measure (mean) of central tendency is what makes this work.

STANDARD ERROR FOR THE MEAN (SE)

Sample means are less variable than individual values in the population because each sample mean is averaged with all other possible samples means. The Standard Error of the mean is the value of the standard deviation of all possible sample means. The standard error of the mean tells you how the sample mean varies from sample to sample. Standard error of the mean σ_{XBar} is calculated by dividing the standard deviation of the population (σ) by the square root of the sample size n. The following equation defines σ_{XBar} when sampling with replacement, or for large or infinite populations, sampling without replacement.

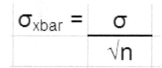

$$\sigma_{xbar} = \frac{\sigma}{\sqrt{n}}$$

Figure 18.1

What the sample taker needs to know is that as the sample size increases the standard error of the mean will decrease by an amount equal to the square root of the sample size. It is ok to use this formula when the sample is taken without replacement if the sample contains less than 5% of the population.

Sampling with replacement means that selected items are returned to the population and their chance of being selected again are equal to the chance all other items in the population have of being selected. Sampling without replacement means that items are selected only once and are not returned to the population. Thus there is no chance of that item being selected again.

Using the formula in Figure 18.1, if the population mean of account receivable values is $50 ($\sigma$) and the sample size (n) is 30, so then the standard error of the mean is 9. Thus the sample mean (9) is much less variable than the individual account receivable values.

SAMPLING FROM NORMALLY DISTRIBUTED POPULATIONS

If the population is normally distributed then the sample will be normally distributed. Thus you can use the Z values to find the area below any value X (i.e. finding the area under a normally distributed curve). All you need to know is the population mean and population standard deviation and you can use the Microsoft Excel function "**NORMDIST**" to calculate the Z value. Assume you have a population of accounts receivable with a mean of 70 and a standard deviation of 50. If you pull a sample of 30 items what do you think the average value of each receivable will be? Statistically you would assume that the sample mean would be very close to the population mean of 70. Suppose we want to know the percentage of all receivables in a sample of 30 items that would have a recorded value of less than the population mean? Specifically let's estimate the number of accounts with a recorded value of less than 65. Using the "Normdist" function we estimate that 46.02% of the receivables would have a value less than 65.

Figure 18.2

CENTRAL LIMIT THEOREM

The "Central Limit Theorem" basically says that when you have a sample size of 30 or more, the sampling distribution of the mean is normally distributed. That answers the question of what the minimum sample size should be to apply mathematics to measure sampling risk. Of course if you know for sure that the population is normally distributed, then you can use a smaller sample size.

SAMPLING DISTRIBUTION OF THE PROPORTION

Assume you are auditing sales invoices and take a sample of 30 items from the sales invoice population. You want to know the proportion of sales invoices where internal control measures were not applied. So for each invoice selected, control measures were either applied or not applied. It is either yes or no, control deviation or no control deviation. When you have a sample with two possible states (yes/no) you can use the Binomial Distribution model to calculate the sample proportion if you are sampling with replacement from a finite population.

The sample proportion is calculated and used to estimate the population proportion. Here is how it works. Assign the value 1 to the yes factor. Assign the value 0 to the no factor. Yes if there is a control deviation and No if there is no control deviation. Sum all the 1 and 0 values and divide by n to get sample proportion.

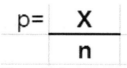

Figure 18.3

Where:
p = sample proportion
x = number of items having the characteristic of interest
n = sample size

Since this is a proportion, the value of "p" will be between 0 and 1. For example if 10 items of a sample of 30 sales invoices have no control measures in place, the value of "p" will be .3333. From this we infer that 33.33% of the sales invoices in the sales invoice population have no control measures applied.

SELECTING A SIMPLE RANDOM SAMPLE

In a simple random sample every item in the population has an equal chance of being selected. To use this method of sample selection, every item in the population must be numbered. Random numbered items can be selected by using a "Random Number Table" or you can let Microsoft Excel generate a list of random numbers.

USING THE MICROSOFT EXCEL RAND FUNCTION

Use the RAND function to generate random numbers for picking a simple random sample. Enter the Rand function in a cell and copy the function through the number of random values you need. Random numbers generated will have a value of 0 to 1. Thus you will have to format the generated numbers to reduce the number of decimal places.

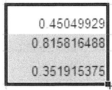

Figure 18.4

Figure 18.5

The result of the Rand function is volatile. This means that the random numbers will change every time the Worksheet is recalculated. Also if you save the Workbook and reopen it, new random numbers will be generated. So soon after you generate the random numbers print that Worksheet so you have a record of the generated random numbers. I will show a fix for this problem shortly.

If you know the range of numbers in the population (highest number and lowest number) it is better to use the "RANDBETWEEN" FUNCTION. This function takes two arguments: (1) Bottom, for the smallest number and (2) Top, for the largest number. Again results are volatile and will change each time Worksheet is recalculated.

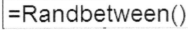

Figure 18.6

For example if you know that population items are numbered from 3454 to 6598; enter as the first argument, the number 3454 and as the second argument 6598.

Here is the fix for the volatility of the random functions. You have to write a new user defined function. I call my function STAYRANDOM. User defined functions are not volatile unless (in your Visual Basic code) you specifically tell them to be volatile.

```
Public Function STAYRANDOM(NUM)
STAYRANDOM = Int(Rnd() * NUM)
End Function
```

Figure 18.7

We have discussed creating user defined functions and how to use them on a worksheet in earlier chapters. This is a very easy function to create. It takes only one line of code. But first you have to tell Microsoft Excel what the function arguments are. This function takes one argument "NUM". NUM is the upper boundary (highest numbered item in the population). If I want a range of random numbers from 1 to 100, I enter 100 as the value of NUM. Because I want whole numbers, I used the INT Function with the argument VB RND( ) Function. RND is the Visual Basic built-in function that generates random numbers. STAYRANDOM works the same as Microsoft Excel's Rand and Randbetween functions. Enter it into a cell and one random number will be generated. Drag the fill handle across the number of cells equal to number of random values you want generated. Or just copy formula to the range of cells equal to the number of random values wanted. Random numbers generated with the STAYRANDOM function will not change when Worksheet is recalculated.

CREATING THE CONFIDENCE INTERVAL ESTIMATION

We have pulled our sample, performed tests on sample items and drawn conclusions about the sample results. And we have also drawn inferences about the population based on sample results. Now we ask the questions: (1) how good is the sample and (2) was the sample big enough. Was the sample representative of the population? We have used inferential statistics to estimate unknown population parameters using sample statistics. There are two types of estimates: (1) "Point Estimate", and (2) "Interval Estimates. We have already discussed the point estimates of mean and standard deviation. A point estimate is a single sample statistic.

An interval is a range built around a point estimate, with a lower boundary below the point estimate and an upper boundary above the point estimate. A "Confidence Interval Estimation" is a range around the point estimate built such that there is a known probability that the population parameter of interest will lie somewhere within that range.

CONFIDENCE INTERVAL FOR THE MEAN (σ known)

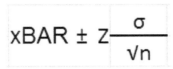

$$XBAR \pm Z\frac{\sigma}{\sqrt{n}}$$

Figure 18.8

XBar is the point estimate for the mean of a sample. Confidence interval is found by multiplying a Z value (remember population is normally distributed) by the quantity of the population standard deviation divided by the square root of the sample size. We know the Z value for any confidence level. For example for 95% confidence , Z value is 1.96 and for 99% confidence, Z value is 2.58. There is a table of Z values that can be found in any statistics book. The lower boundary would be found by subtracting the result of the above formula from the point estimate. Upper boundary is found by adding result of formula to the point estimate.

CONFIDENCE INTERVAL FOR THE MEAN (σ unknown)

If the mean of a population (μ) is unknown then it is unlikely that the standard deviation (σ) will be known. So we have to build a confidence interval estimate of μ using the sample statistics XBar and S (sample standard deviation).

STUDENT'S *t* distribution

For unknown σ use the student's *t* distribution instead of Z values.

265

$$t = \frac{(\text{Xbar} - \mu)}{(S/\sqrt{n})}$$

Figure 18.9

To build the confidence interval you first have to calculate the "DEGREES OF FREEDON" The Degree of freedom is sample size n minus 1. Substitute student's t distribution value for Z value to build the confidence interval estimation.

$$\text{xBAR} \pm t_{n-1} \frac{S}{\sqrt{n}}$$

Figure 18.10

Seems like a lot of work to me. Why don't we let Microsoft Excel help us calculate the confidence interval? The result of our Worksheet calculation shows the mean value of sales invoices in the sales invoice population lies within the range of $43.87 and $96.14. We are 95% sure of this. Since we want an upper boundary and a lower boundary we have to calculate an "Interval Half Width". The Interval Half Width is subtracted from and added to point estimate for the sample mean to build the confidence interval.

	A	B	C
1	Estimate of mean for sales invoices		
2			
3			
4	Sample Deviation	50	
5	Sample Mean	70	
6	Sample Size	30	
7	Confidence level	95%	
8			
9	Intermediate Calculations		
10	Standard Error of the Mean	12.78019	=B4/SQRT(B6)
11	Degrees of Freedom	29	=B6-1
12	t value	2.04523	=TINV(1-B7,B11)
13	Interval Half Width	26.13843	=B12*B10
14			
15	Confidence Interval		
16	Interval lower boundary	43.86157	=B5-B13
17	Interval upper boundary	96.13843	=B5+B13
18			
19	Explanation of TINV Function to calculate t value		
20	Use 1- probability to indicate what is not in the interval		
21	=TINV(		
22	TINV(**probability**, deg_freedom)		

Figure 18.11

CONFIDENCE INTERVAL FOR THE PROPORTION

The formula to calculate the confidence estimate for the proportion is:

$$p \pm Z \sqrt{p(1-p)/n}$$

Figure 18.12

Where "p" is sample proportion, Z is critical value (1.96 for 95% confidence, or 2.58 for 99% confidence), and n is sample size.

267

	A	B	C
1	Confidence of proportion of sales invoice errors		
2			
3		Data	
4	Sample size	100	
5	Number of errors in sample	5	
6	Confidence level	95%	
7			
8		Intermediate Calculations	
9	Sample Proportion	0.05	=B5/B4
10	Z Value	-1.95996	=Normsinv$_{probability}$((1-B6)/2)
11	Standard Error of the Proportion	0.021794	=SQRT(B9 *(1-B9)/B4)
12	Inteval Half Width	0.042716	=ABS(B10*B11)
13			
14		Confidence Level	
15	Lower Boundary	0.007284	=B9-B12
16	Upper Boundary	0.092716	=B9+B12
17			
18	=NORMSINV(		
19	NORMSINV(**probability**)		
20			

Figure 18.13

Be careful with the NORMSINV function. There are two in the statistical category. You have to pick the one that says ("probability"). You will know which one to choose based on the number of arguments required for the function. If more than one argument (probability) is required, you chose the wrong NORMSINV function.

Based on evaluating our sample we can say with 95% confidence that error rate in the sales invoice population is between 0.7% and 9.27%. It should be noted that the larger the confidence level, the larger the confidence interval.

CALCULATE SAMPLE SIZE FOR THE MEAN

Previously sample size was given in all of our calculations. In the real world you have to be able to calculate an appropriate sample size. Don't forget the cost-benefit factors surrounding taking and evaluating a sample.

Calculation of sample size requires two considerations: (1) the tolerable sampling error and (2) desired confidence level.

The sampling error is defined as:

$$e = Z(\sigma/\sqrt{n})$$

Figure 18.14

Plug e into the sample size function:

$$n = \frac{Z^2\sigma^2}{e^2}$$

Figure 18.15

Assume that ±$8 is the tolerable sampling error. We want a sample with 95% confidence level. And past data indicates that the population standard deviation has consistently been $30. Thus e =$8, σ = $30, and the Z value is 1.96 for 95% confidence. The required sample size is 55 items (54.0225); always round up.

$$n = \frac{Z^2\sigma^2}{e^2} = \frac{(1.96)^2(30)^2}{(8)^2}$$

Figure 18.16

Let's setup a Worksheet so Microsoft Excel can be used to determine sample size.

	A	B	C
1	Sample Size Calculation for Mean		
2			
3	Data		
4	Population Standard Deviation	30	
5	Sampling Error	8	
6	Confidence Level	95%	
7			Formulas
8	Intermediate Calculations		
9	Z Value	-1.95996	=NORMSINV((1-B6)/2)
10	Calculated Size	54.02051	=((B9*B4)/5)^2
11	Needed Sample Size	55	=ROUNDUP(B10,0)
12			

Figure 18.17

CALCULATE SAMPLE SIZE FOR PROPORTION

First calculate a value for e. Plug "e" into sample size formula for a proportion. Pie (π) is the unknown population proportion. Usually you have past experience as to the value of π but if you don't have past experience use $\pi = .5$ and sample will not be under estimated. You know that we are going to let Microsoft Excel determine the sample size.

$$e = Z(\sqrt{(\pi(1-\pi)/n)}) \qquad n = \frac{Z^2\pi(1-\pi)}{e^2}$$

Figure 18.18

⁄	A	B	C	D	E	F
1			Proportion of Errors in population			
2						
3	Input Data					
4	Estimate of True Porportion			0.08		
5	Sampling Error			0.12	Formulas	
6	Confidence level			95%		
7	Z value			-1.95996	=NORMSINV((1-D6)/2)	
8	Calculated Sample Size			19.63412	=(D7^2*D4*(1-D4))/D5^2	
9	Rounded sample size			20	=ROUNDUP(D8,0)	

Figure 18.19

SUMMARY

Sampling is a cost effective way to draw conclusions about a population. A sample is a subset of a population which will be examined. Characteristics found in the sample will be used to draw inferences about a population. Since you are not examining every item in the population with a sample there are risks that you will come to the wrong conclusion about the population. Risk can be reduced by drawing a larger sample, but don't lose sight of the cost benefit considerations. As sample size increases so does the cost of taking the sample.

There are two types of samples: (1) statistical samples where mathematics is used to determine sample size and to measure and control risk, and (2) non-statistical samples where judgment is used to calculate sample size and to evaluate sample results. There four ways to select a statistical sample (1) simple random sample, (2) systematic selection, (3) probability proportional to size selection and (4) stratified sample selection.

Sampling works because we assume that the population from which it is drawn is normally distributed. Results of the sample can be a point estimate or a confidence interval.

CHAPTER 19
HYPOTHESIS TESTING

Hypothesis testing is another inferential method which uses a sample to draw inferences about a population. Hypothesis testing is used to validate claims made about a population parameter. When the sample statistics validate the claim; this is called the null hypothesis. The mutually exclusive alternative is that the sample results do not validate the claim. The process involves evaluating difference between sample statistic and the results you expect to get if hypothesis is true.

HYPOTHESIS TESTING PROCESS

Start out with a theory or claim about a population parameter. For example, you believe that recorded sales invoices have a mean value of $70. Null hypothesis is the status quo and is represented by the symbol H_0. Thus our assertion about the mean value of sales invoices would be written as $H_0{:}\mu = 70$. If null hypothesis is false an alternative hypotheses must be true. This alternative hypothesis is represented by the symbol H_1. So the alternative hypothesis is written as $H_1{:}\mu \neq 70$. The alternative hypothesis is the conclusion reached by rejecting the null hypothesis. This occurs when there is sufficient evidence from the sample that the null hypothesis is false. Note that since hypothesis analysis is based on a sample you can never really prove that the null hypothesis is true. Therefore failure to reject the null hypothesis does not mean that it is true. All you can say is that there is insufficient evidence to cause a rejection.

This is how the process works. Take a sample and evaluate the results. Ask the question: "is the sample statistic close to the population parameter". For example, is the sample mean close to the stated population mean? If sample mean of sales invoices is $69 and population mean is $70; that is close. Therefore do not reject null hypothesis. The question is: what do you mean by close. We need a way to measure the difference precisely so that we have a probability of getting a particular sample result if the null hypothesis is true. Remember that all of our statistical analysis is based on the belief that the sample is normally distributed. Thus we can use the standardized normal distribution or the t distribution to determine if the null hypothesis is true. We will be calculating a *"Test Statistic"* based on the sample results.

Looking at a normal distribution curve, the test statistic is divided into two regions: (1) region of rejection (critical region) and (2) region of nonrejection. The region of rejection is usually found on each tail of the curve far from the population mean μ. This region consists of values of the test statistic that are unlikely to occur if the null hypothesis is true, and where they are more likely to occur if null hypothesis is false. Thus, if test statistic falls in this region reject the null hypothesis.

A critical value divides the two regions from each other. The critical value is related to the risks involved in using only sample evidence to draw inferences about a population parameter. Since you are using a sample there is the possibility you will reach the wrong conclusion regarding the population parameter. There are two types of errors: (1) Type 1 or alpha error (α) and (2) Type 2 or beta (β) error.

1. Type 1 error. Reject null hypothesis H_0 when it is in fact true and should not be rejected. The probability of this happening is an (α) error.

2. Type 2 error. Null hypothesis is not rejected (it is accepted) when it is in fact false. The probability of this occurring is a beta (β) error.

LEVEL OF SIGNIFICANCE (α)

The probability of committing a Type 1 error is called the "level of significance" of the statistical test. You control the Type 1 error by deciding the risk level α that you are willing to take in rejecting the null hypothesis when it is in fact true. Considering the cost of making a Type 1error, you pick alpha levels of 0.01, 0.05, or 0.10. The level you pick defines the size of the rejection region because α is the probability of rejection under the null hypothesis. If you know the rejection region then you also know the nonrejection region.

CONFIDENCE COEFFICIENT

The confidence coefficient is the complement of the probability of a Type 1 error $(1-\alpha)$. Multiply by 100% to get the confidence level we discussed when building the confidence interval estimate. $1-\alpha$ is the probability that you will not reject the null hypothesis when it is true and should not be rejected. The confidence coefficient is the probability that the value of the parameter specified in the null hypothesis is plausible when it is true. For example it is the probability that the population mean of sales invoices is $70 when it really is

$70. Type 1 risk can be reduced by selecting a smaller value for alpha.

TYPE 2 β RISK

Unlike the alpha risk you do not control the β risk. The beta error depends on the difference between the hypothesized value of the population parameter and the actual value of the population parameter. The probability of committing a beta error is big if the difference between the hypothesized value and actual value is small.

THE POWER OF A TEST

The complement of the probability of a Type 2 error is $(1-\beta)$. It denotes the probability that you will reject the null hypothesis when it is false and should be rejected, i.e. you made the right decision. You can reduce the probability of making a beta error by increasing the sample size so that you can better detect even small differences between hypothesized values and population parameters. Don't forget that this will also increase the cost of taking the sample and may affect your decision on how big a sample you can afford.

There is a trade-off relationship between α and β. When the negative consequences of making a Type 1 error are significant you should set α to 0.01 instead of 0.05 giving you a 99.9% confidence rather than a 95% confidence level. The trade-off is that when you decrease α, you increase β. So decreasing the α risk will increase the β risk. Conversely if you wish to reduce β then select a larger value for α. Thus if you want to avoid a Type 2 error pick an α of 0.05 rather than 0.01. The trade-off between the two types of risk must be considered in your decision making process. There are costs associated with each type of error. You have to decide which cost is necessary to avoid.

Figure 19.1 shows the four possible results of testing a hypothesis:

Four possible outcomes of a statistical test		
	Decision	
State of Hypothesis	Accept H_0	Reject H_0
H_0 True	Right - no error	Wrong - Type 1 error
H_0 False	Wrong - Type 2 error	Right - no error

Figure 19.1

Z TEST OF HYPOTHESIS FOR THE MEAN (σ KNOWN)

When standard deviation σ is known you use the Z test if the population is normally distributed. If population is not normally distributed but sample size is 30 or more items it is still ok to use the Z test (See the Central limit theorem which was discussed in chapter 18). The Z statistic is calculated by the following formula:

$$Z = \frac{Xbar - \mu}{\sigma / \sqrt{n}}$$

Figure 19.2

The number is how far observed sample mean XBar is from the hypothesized mean μ. Denominator is the standard error of the mean. So Z is the difference between XBar and μ in standard error units.

CRITICAL VALUE APPROACH TO HYPOTHESIS TESTING

Remember that picking an α level defines the rejection region. If we pick a level of significance of 0.05, each tail of the normal distribution curve will have a value of .025 (.05 / 2). So, the rejection region under the lower critical value is .025 and the rejection region below the upper critical value is 0.975 (100 - .025). These critical values equate to a 95% confidence level or ± 1.96. This leads to the decision rule:

Reject H_0 if $Z > +1.96$
or if $Z < -1.96$

otherwise do not reject H_0

Assume that a sample of sales invoices is taken and XBar was found to be $69. If based on past experience the population mean μ tended to be $70 with a standard deviation σ of 8. Assume also a sample size of 30 items. Null hypothesis is that μ is $70. Should the null hypothesis be accepted or rejected; remember we want to be 95% confident in the

275

correctness of our decision. Plugging these numbers in the Z test formula yields an answer of -0.6846532. Since this number is between -1.96 and +1.96 do not reject H_0. To consider the Type 2 error, all you can say is that there is insufficient evidence that the population mean is different than ($70).

p-VALUE APPROACH TO HYPOTHESIS TESTING

The p-value is the probability that the test statistic will equal sample result or will be more extreme than the sample result, if hypothesis H_0 is true. The p-value is called the "observed level of significance" and represents the smallest level at which H_0 can be rejected. Decision rules for using the p-value are:

1. Do not reject H_0 if p-value is greater than or equal to α.
2. Reject H_0 if p-value is less than α.

See figure 19.3 for a worksheet that calculates p-value. In this example, Hypothesis that mean of population is $65 is accepted based on sample results.

	A	B
1	Z-Test for calc of p-value	
2		
3	Null hypothesis H_0	$65
4	Level of significance α	0.05
5	Population Std.Deviation σ	$70
6	Sample size n	30
7	Sample Mean s	$69
8	Standard Error of Mean (σ/SQRT(n))	$12.78
9	Z Test Statistic (s-H_0)/std error of mean	($0.08)
10	Two tail test	
11	Lower boundary =Normsinv(α/2)	-1.959963985
12	Upper boundary =Normsinv(1-α/2)	1.959963985
13	p-value =2*(1-Normsinv(ABS(Z-Test Stat)))	$4.83
14	Accept or Reject H_0. Accept if p-value >α	Accept H_0

Figure 19.3

ONE-TAIL TESTS

Use a one-tail test when the alternative hypothesis focuses on a particular direction; when the entire rejection region is in only one tail. Also if the alternative hypothesis has the less than sign then critical value of Z must be less than zero. See example spreadsheet in Figure 19.4. Want to test if population mean is less than $65. There was enough evidence to state that population mean is not less than $65.

16	One-tail test	
17		
18	Null hypothesis H₀	($65)
19	Level of significance α	0.05
20	Population Std.Deviation σ	$70
21	Sample size n	30
22	Sample Mean s	$69
23	Standard Error of Mean (σ/SQRT(n))	$12.78
24	Z Test Statistic (s-H₀)/std error of mean	($0.08)
25	Two tail test	
26	Lower boundary =Normsinv(α)	-1.644853627
27		
28	p-value =Normsinv(Z Test Stat)	($1.42)
29	Accept or Reject H₀ Accept if p-value >α	Reject H₀

Figure 19.4

t TEST OF HYPOTHESIS FOR THE MEAN (σ UNKNOWN)

Use t-test if you do not know the population standard deviation σ. You have to use the sample standard deviation S in your calculations. Must assume population is normally distributed or sample size must be at least 30 so it does not matter. Following formula calculates the test statistic for determining the difference between the sample mean (XBar) and population mean (μ) when the sample standard deviation (S) is used.

$$t = \frac{Xbar - \mu}{S / \sqrt{n}}$$

with n-1 degrees of freedom

Figure 19.5

Let's return to the example where we are auditing sales invoices. Over the past three years the mean amount per sales invoice is $70. How do we prove that the mean per sales invoice is increasing or decreasing?

277

CRITICAL VALUE APPROACH

H_0: μ = $70

H_1: $\mu \neq$ $70 The alternative hypothesis is the statement that we are trying to prove.

We have selected a sample of 30 items and decide to use an α of 0.05. Since σ is unknown we have to use the t-distribution and t-test statistic. Evaluation of sample results in sample mean of $69. The degrees of freedom (n-1) are 29. We use the formula to calculate the t-statistic and then go to the Upper-Tail Areas table with 29 degrees of freedom and calculate the critical value. If p-value is within the range of critical values do not reject alternative hypothesis. This is a lot of work, so I turn to Microsoft Excel for assistance.

$$t = \frac{69-70}{69/\sqrt{30}}$$

$$-0.0793801$$

Figure 19.6

Set up Worksheet like Figure 19.7

32	Hypothesis re: mean amount per invoice	
33		
34	Null hypothesis H_0 μ =	70
35	Level of significance α	0.05
36	Sample size n	30
37	Sample Mean Xbar	69
38	Sample standard deviation S	8
39	Standard Error of Mean (S/SQRT(n))	1.46
40	Degrees of Freedom Df	29
41	t Test Statistic (Xbar-μ) /(std. Error of mean	-0.684653197
42	Lower critical value = -TINV(α,Df)	-2.045229611
43	Upper critical value = TINV(α,Df)	2.045229611
44	p-value =TDIST(ABS(t-stat),Df,2)	0.498998545
45	Accept or Reject H_0, ± critical value interval	Accept H_0

Figure 19.7

Critical values are calculated using the TINV Function. P-value is calculated using the TDIST function. Following are the two functions and required arguments.

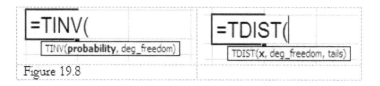

=TINV(

TINV(**probability**, deg_freedom)

=TDIST(

TDIST(**x**, deg_freedom, tails)

Figure 19.8

Z TEST OF HYPOTHESIS FOR THE PROPORTION

Used to test a hypothesis regarding a population proportion π. Start by taking sample and calculating the sample proportion, $p = X/n$, where X is the attribute you are interested in. Can use Z test for proportion if both X and n-X are at least five. This indicates that sample is normally distributed.

$$Z = \frac{p - \pi}{\sqrt{\pi(1-\pi)/n}}$$

Figure 19.9

Figure 19.10 shows the Microsoft Excel way to test hypothesis for the proportion.

0	Sales invoice Hypothesis	
1	Input Data	
2	Null hypothesis p =	0.5
3	Level of significance α	0.05
4	Attributes found in sample	370
5	Sample Size	900
6	Calculations	
7	Sampling Proportion= Attributes/sample size	0.411111
8	Standard Error = SQRT(α*(1-α)/sample size)	0.007265
9	Z Test Statistic= (SampleProportion -α)/StdError	49.70674
0	Two Tail Test	
1	Lower critical value =NORMSINV(α/2)	-1.95996
2	Upper critical value = NORMSINV(1-α/2)	1.959964
3	p-value =2*(1-NORMSDIST(ABS(Z-TESTSTAT)))	2
4	Reject or accept null hypothesis	Reject
5	p- value is outside of critical value range	

Figure 19.10

279

COMPARING MEANS OF TWO INDEPENDENT POPULATIONS

We now expand our knowledge of how samples behave to compare the statistics of samples drawn from two or more independent populations. Statistics from two random samples will be compared.

First some assumptions are in order; (1) the samples are randomly and independently drawn from normally distributed populations, (2) if the populations are not normally distributed, the sample size is at least 30 items so that the central limit theorem specifies that the samples are considered normally distributed regardless of the population distribution, and (3) the test statistic used to calculate the difference between the population means is the difference between the sample means $(XBar_1 - Xbar_2)$.

Now some definitions: (1) n_1 is the size of sample 1 and n_2 is the size of sample 2, (2) μ_1 and μ_2 represent the means of population 1 and population 2, respectively, (3) and σ_1 and σ_2 represent the standard deviations of population 1 and population 2 respectively. We can use the Z Test for the difference between two means. The formula is:

$$Z = \frac{(XBar_1 - XBar_2) - (\mu_1 - \mu_2)}{\sqrt{\sigma^2_1/n_1 + \sigma^2_2/n_2}}$$

Figure 19.11

POOLED-VARIANCE t- TO CALCULATE DIFFERENCE BETWEEN TWO MEANS

Rarely do you know the actual population variances (σ^2). You, however do know the sample means and variances. If the samples are randomly drawn from normally distributed populations, they can be used to determine the difference between means of populations. You also have to assume that the population variances are equal $(\sigma^2_1 = \sigma^2_2)$. If populations are not normally distributed then n_1 and n_2 must each be ≥ 30. In this situation you can use the pooled-variance t-test to test for the difference in two means.

The null hypothesis is that there is no difference in the means of two independent populations. The alternative hypothesis is that the means are not the same.

H_0: $\mu_1 = \mu_2$ or $\mu_1 - \mu_2 = 0$ Null hypothesis

H_1: $\mu_1 \neq \mu_2$ or $\mu_1 - \mu_2 \neq 0$ Alternative hypothesis

First you calculate the pooled variance of the two samples: S^2_p and substitute it into the pooled-variance t-test for the difference between two means formula.

$$S^2_p = \frac{(n_1-1)S^2_1 + (n_2-1)S^2_2}{(n1-1) + (n2-1)} \qquad t = \frac{(XBar_1 - XBar_2) - (\mu_1 - \mu_2)}{\sqrt{S^2_p(1/n_1 + 1/n_2)}}$$

Figure 19.12

Using these formulas, calculate t and get critical values for table found in statistics books. Or let Microsoft Excel do it for you.

	A	B	C	D
1	t-Test, two sample Assuming Equal Variances H_0			
2		Sample 1	Sample 2	
3	Mean	50.3	72	
4	Variance	350.6778	157.3333	
5	n	10	10	
6	Pooled variance	254.0056		
7	Hypothesized Mean Difference	0		
8	degrees of freedom	18		Formulas used
9	t stat	-3.04455		used t-stat formula
10	P(T<=t) one-tail	0.003487		=TDIST(ABS(B9),18,1)
11	t Critical one-tail	-2.10092		= -TINV(.05,18)
12	P(T<=t) two-tail	0.006975		=TDIST(ABS(B9),18,2)
13	t Critical two-tail	2.100922		=TINV(.05,18)
14	used α of .05 and p-value = .006975			
15	which is less than .05 so reject			
16	null hypothesis, accept alternative			
17	hypothesis that means are different.			
18	Also reject becsause t-statistic of -3.04455			
19	is less than critical value of -2.10092			

Figure 19.13

Following is additional useful information regarding drawing inferences from samples and applying to a population.

RELIABILITY AND VALIDITY

After coming up with research question, how do you accomplish research goals? Questions to be answered are (1) what is the overall design of the research project, (2) how will

281

variables be measured, and (3) what procedures will be employed to analyze collected evidence. Reliability and validity can be used to organize your thoughts in this area.

Reliability means consistency of either measurement or design. Will multiple measurements result in the same answer? Can experiment be replicated? Will different researchers come to same conclusion? The main measure of reliability is reliability coefficients. Reliability coefficients range from 0.0 (completely inconsistent) to 1.0 (entirely consistent). This should look familiar as this is just another way of defining correlation coefficients.

STATISTICAL INFERENCE

Statistical inference is when you make assertions about a population because of what you saw in a sample.

What makes a sample statistic significant (it is not due to random chance)? By convention we say that a statistic is significant if the result is likely due to chance less than 5% of the time (p<.05). Some researchers also use p<.01 and p<.10 to indicate significance. Significance is important in hypothesis testing (where we are concerned with the degree that data contradicts the null hypothesis). We use the label "p" in place of probability.

Statistical significance does not mean the same as substantive significance (magnitude of impact of the statistic on drawing inferences to the population).

There are two ways of inferring conclusions about a population based on sample statistics: (1) Confidence intervals (confidence and probable margins of error) and (2) hypothesis testing and statistical significance (p-values). So we have two questions: (1) what is the probability that I am wrong (significance testing approach) or (2) how confident am I that I'm right? (confidence interval approach). The two questions are interrelated. If you are 95% confident that you are right, that means the probability that you are wrong will be 5% (p = .05).

There is a difference between a two-tail test (two directions) and a one-tail test (one-direction). A two-tail approach tests the difference between two groups of variables but does not specify which one is bigger. A one-tail approach tests whether the mean of one group of variables is bigger than the mean of another group of variables. The two-tail approach (sometimes called nondirectional) is considered better. It is a more conservative, harder test to pass, because the mean difference has to be twice as big for a two-direction test to be statistically significant.

Standard Error (SE) is the estimate of how much sampling error you are likely to get in a sample of a particular size. Sampling error measures the difference between the sample value and its related population value. The t-statistic is calculated by dividing the mean difference (difference in means of the two groups) by the standard error (i.e. the sample statistic divided by its probable error). Therefore if a difference is statistically significant it will be bigger than the estimate of error (SE), usually at least 2 times bigger. Standard error of the mean is calculated as follows: STDev / SQRT of sample size. Since the SQRT of the sample size is the denominator in the equation, the bigger the sample size the smaller will be the sample error. The bigger the sample the likelihood of it being more representative of the population is increased.

Confidence interval is calculated by adding 2 SEs to the mean difference for the upper bound and subtracting 2 SEs for the lower bound.

There is a difference between a t-test and an ANOVA test. A t-test can only handle comparison of two groups of independent variables at a time. An ANOVA (analysis of variance) can handle three or more groups at a time. ANOVA tells you only that some difference in mean scores is significantly different. It does not tell you which means scores of which groups are significantly bigger than others.

SUMMARY

Hypothesis testing is another inferential method which uses a sample to make inferences about a population. A hypothesis is an assertion that you are trying to prove. It is the status quo. If the assertion (hypothesis) is false, then an alternative assertion must be true. Since the hypothesis is based on a sample there are two types of risks that exist. The alpha risk (Type 1 error) is when you incorrectly reject a hypothesis that is true. A beta risk (Type 2 error) is when you incorrectly accept a hypothesis that is false. The alpha risk can be controlled by the researcher, and the beta risk cannot. The risks are interrelated; changing one affects the other.

There are two methods for performing hypothesis testing: (1) critical value approach and (2) p-value approach.

And depending on your goal a test can either be a two-tail (considered the best approach) or a one-tail test.

CHAPTER 20
MISCELLANEOUS FINANCE PROBLEMS

HOW TO VALUE BONDS USING MICROSOFT EXCEL

In an earlier chapter we discussed how to price the issuance of bonds. We even created a user defined function to make calculating the price of a bond easier.

CURRENT YIELD AND YIELD TO MATURITY

Suppose you want to add a particular bond to your investment portfolio and this is what you know about the bond: (1) Annual interest payment (based on coupon rate of interest), (2) principal payment, (3) price of bond, (4) and number of years to maturity. Your question is "what is the yield if I purchase the bond and hold it until maturity". As I was cruising finance text books looking for things that I could turn into user defined functions I came across a cool formula to calculate approximate bond yields. See "Block, Hirt, Danielson, Foundations of Financial Management, 13th Edition, McGraw-Hill Irwin, 2009", pg 294). Figure 20.1 displays the formula. And Figure 20.2 is my user-defined function based on the formula.

	B5	▾	f_x	=(B1+((B2-B3)/B4))/((0.6*B3)+(0.4*B2))							
	A	B	C	D	E	F	G	H	I	J	K
1	ANNUAL INTEREST PAYMENT	110									
2	PRINCIPAL PAYMENT	1000									
3	PRICE OF BOND	932.21									
4	NUMBER OF YEARS TO MATURITY	15									
5	APPROXIMATE YIELD	0.1194									
6											
7	APPROX Yield[1] =	(Annual Int. Pymt +((Prin.Pmt - Price of Bond)/Yrs to Maturity))									
8		((0.6(Price of Bond) +(0.4(Prin.Pmt))									
9											
10											
11	[1] Formula was developed by Gabriel A. Hawawini and Ashok Vora										
12	"Yield Approximations: A Historical Perspective",										
13	Journal of Finance 37 (March 1982) pp. 145-56										
14											

Figure 20.1

Based on the information in column B, see Figure 20.1, the actual yield is 12%. Yield calculated by function is 11.94%, a pretty good approximation.

285

```
Public Function APPROXYIELD(ANNUAL_INTERST_PYMT As Single, PRINpAY As Double, _
BONDpRICE As Double, YRS_TO_MATURE As Single)

APPROXYIELD = (ANNUAL_INTERST_PYMT + ((PRINpAY - BONDpRICE)) / (YRS_TO_MATURE)) / _
((0.6 * BONDpRICE) + (0.4 * PRINpAY))

End Function
```
Figure 20.2

This function works if there are no compounding periods. To
adjust for compounding do the following:

1. Divide annual interest by number of compound
   periods (Semi-annual, quarterly, or monthly).

2. Multiply number of years by compound periods.

3. Divide approximate yield by number of compound
   periods.

If you are not inclined to write functions, you can use
Microsoft Excel's PRICE Function to calculate the price of a
bond and the YIELD Function to calculate a bond's yield to
maturity.

MICROSOFT EXCEL'S PRICE FUNCTION

Figure 20.3 has an example of the Microsoft Excel Price
Function.

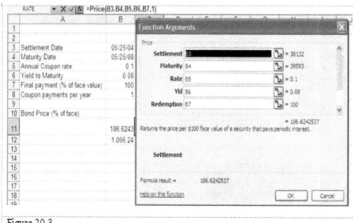

Figure 20.3

In cell B12 is the result of the user defined function
BONDPRICE which I showed you how to create in an earlier
chapter. The results are identical, but user defined function, in

my opinion is easier to use. If you use PRICE Function from Worksheet starting with equal sign, you must use Microsoft Excel's date functions to enter settlement date and then the maturity date.

Figure 20.4 Enter settlement date

MICROSOFT EXCEL'S YIELD FUNCTION

The yield to maturity is the rate that correctly prices a bond. It is the discount rate that caused the present value of the bond's payments to be equal to the bond's price. Microsoft Excel's Yield Function will calculate this amount. Again if you use this function on a Worksheet it is better to enter settlement date and maturity date by using a cell reference. Or you have to use the Microsoft Excel Date function where settlement data and maturity date are required.

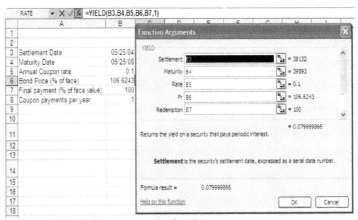

Figure 20.5 Yield to maturity is 8%.

Compare the results of the Microsoft Excel Yield function to the user defined "Approxyield" Function.

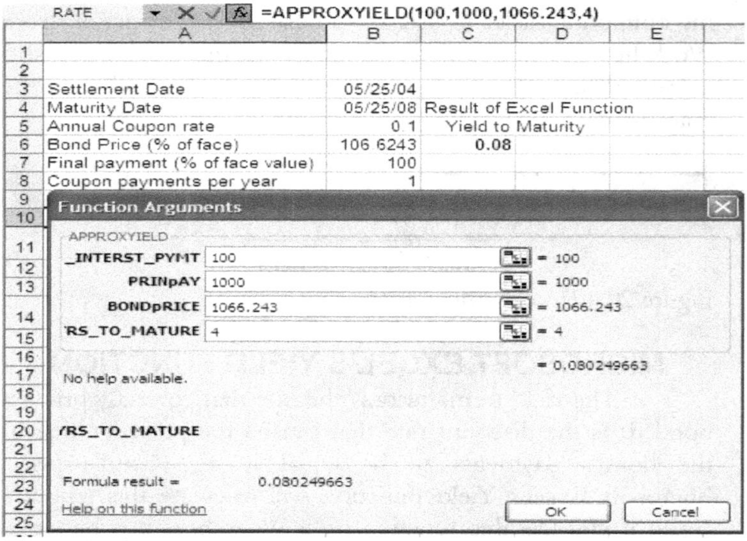

RATE	▾ × ✓ ∱	=APPROXYIELD(100,1000,1066.243,4)			
	A	B	C	D	E
1					
2					
3	Settlement Date	05/25/04			
4	Maturity Date	05/25/08	Result of Excel Function		
5	Annual Coupon rate	0.1	Yield to Maturity		
6	Bond Price (% of face)	106.6243	0.08		
7	Final payment (% of face value)	100			
8	Coupon payments per year	1			

Function Arguments [×]

APPROXYIELD

_INTERST_PYMT	100	🔢	= 100
PRINpAY	1000	🔢	= 1000
BONDpRICE	1066.243	🔢	= 1066.243
RS_TO_MATURE	4	🔢	= 4

= 0.080249663

No help available.

RS_TO_MATURE

Formula result =   0.080249663

Help on this function   [OK]   [Cancel]

Figure 20.6

SUMMARY

Microsoft Excel can used to value bonds, to determine current yield and yield to maturity, to determine the price of bonds, and to solve other miscellaneous problems.

CHAPTER 21
INTRODUCTION TO PROGRAMMING
MICROSOFT EXCEL USING VISUAL BASIC
FOR APPLICATIONS

WHAT IS VBA?

Visual Basic for Applications is a programming language used to extend the functionality of Microsoft Excel, Word, Access, and Outlook (products contained in Microsoft's Office Suites). Earlier versions of Microsoft Excel used a Macro language to automate Worksheet activity. VBA is not a Macro language. However, both Macros and VBA can automate an application. But VBA, unlike a Macro, can ask for and receive input from the user.

VBA is based on Microsoft's popular Visual Basic programming language. The only difference between VBA and Visual Basic is that a VBA program must reside inside a host (any of the aforementioned products in the Office Suite) and VBA cannot create a stand-alone application.

This book explores the use of VBA with Microsoft Excel. For data analysis and manipulation, Microsoft Excel is the most popular product on the market. After reading chapters in this part of the book, you will be able to use Microsoft Excel's powerful features to perform advanced and complex data analysis, manipulation, and reporting tasks. My goal here is not to make you a professional programmer. However, I hope to teach you enough to be a power user of Microsoft Excel.

Much of what we discuss will not be new to experienced Microsoft Excel users. In fact, some of the VBA instructions we will use to manipulate Microsoft Excel can also be performed manually. VBA allows Microsoft Excel to ask for input when needed to further processing activities.

We covered MACROS in an earlier chapter. Recording macros is a good way to learn how Microsoft Excel performs certain activities that you want to duplicate in your VBA code.

OBJECTS, PROPERTIES, AND METHODS

Microsoft Excel is a collection of objects. Objects are things that can be defined, manipulated, controlled, i.e. programmed. You can think of objects as nouns.

Microsoft Excel objects have characteristics, similar to the relationship of adjectives to nouns. These adjective values describe an object, making one object different from other objects. These Microsoft Excel adjectives are called **properties.**

We can manipulate an object and command it to do something. Objects are individuals and each has activities it is specifically capable of performing. We can command a pen to write, an airplane to take off, or a camera to snap a picture. The activities an object can perform (similar to the relationship of verbs to nouns) are called **methods.**

If we put objects, properties, and methods together in a sentence we have a VBA instruction that tells the computer to perform some action. To write a VBA program we have to add objects, get and set object properties, and call object methods. You are already familiar with the four (4) most common objects in Microsoft Excel that we will be manipulating. They are: Application, Workbook, Worksheet, and Range objects. The following illustration (Figure 21.1) shows the 4 objects: Application Object is the Microsoft Excel Program. Workbook object is the Microsoft Excel file that contains your Worksheet. Worksheet is where we enter data. Range is a subset of the Worksheet forming a group of cells that are related.

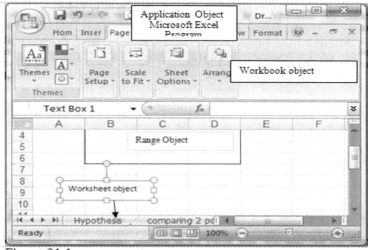

Figure 21.1

GETTING AND SETTING OBJECT PROPERTIES

The workbook object is commonly known as a Microsoft Excel file. We thus can use properties to describe a particular workbook. Following are 4 of the properties of a workbook. There are a lot more properties of a Workbook. I stopped counting after I reached twenty.

Property	Description
HasPassword	Boolean. True if workbook has a password, False if workbook has no password
EnableAutoRecover	Boolean. Saves changed files on a timed interval, True (Default) enables this feature
Path	String. Where the workbook is saved
ReadOnly	Boolean. True if workbook has been opened as read-only

291

SETTING OBJECT PROPERTIES

To assign characteristics that identify an object as different from other objects, we say in VBA lingo that we have to set an object's property. Actually what we are doing is changing the value of an object's built-in property as VBA provides various properties with each object that exists in the language. Note that some properties are Read-Only and thus cannot be changed. The syntax for setting an object's properties follows:

ObjectName.property = property value

The syntax consists of five (5) parts. For example, let's turn on the feature that allows Auto_Recover of the WorkBook. We start with the object name, followed by the dot operator, followed by the property name, followed by the equal operator, and finally followed by the new property value. The following VBA instruction sets the AutoRecover feature to true.

ActiveWorkBook.EnableAutoRecover = True

> Note our use of the <u>ActiveWorkBook</u> property which returns the workbook that is currently the Active Workbook. We can use this property to make changes to the currently Active workbook.

Analysis of Syntax:

Object name	ActiveWorkBook
Dot operator	.
Property name	EnableAutoRecover
Equals operator	=
Property value	True

GETTING OBJECT PROPERTIES

To use an object in a program, we need to know its characteristics. Retrieving Object characteristics in VBA lingo is called "Getting Object Properties". Before you can get a property of an Object, you first need to define a variable to hold the value of the property. The syntax is the same as setting an object property, but in the reverse order. So to get the name of a workbook requires the following VBA instruction.

WorkbookName = Workbooks("Budgets99.XLS").Name

Variable	WorkbookName
Equals operator	=
Object name	Workbooks("Budgets99.XLS")
Dot operator	.
Property name	Name

USING OBJECT METHODS

Since we are using the Workbook object to explain properties, let's continue to use the Workbook object as we explain the use of object methods. Following are a few workbook methods:

Method	Description
Close	Closes the workbook
PrintPreview	Shows a preview of the workbook as it would look when printed
Protect	Protects a workbook with a password
Save	Saves the changes to the specified workbook

If we want to get an Object to perform some action we have to call one of its methods. We call a method by first writing the <u>object name,</u> followed by the <u>dot operator</u> (it looks like a period), and then the <u>method name</u>. We will be using the term **Syntax** a lot in this book. Syntax is simply the structure of a programming language. Syntax for Object Methods is found in the VBA help feature. The syntax for calling a method follows:

ObjectName .method

For example, to close a Workbook we call its "close method" as follows:

Workbooks ("Budgets99").close

Additionally, most methods in Microsoft Excel have a set of **Arguments. Arguments** are additional items of information that specify how the method is to be carried out. Actually, Arguments (just like object properties) have built-in values that are either changed or ignored. During a method call, you can specify all, some, or none of the method's Arguments. If you call a method without passing its Arguments, Arguments will assume default values. Passing Arguments in VBA lingo, means changing the value of an argument in a method call.

PASSING ARGUMENTS BY NAME OR BY POSITION

Arguments can be specified in code either by position or by name. To pass Arguments by position, follow the exact order presented in the syntax, separating each argument with a comma. For example the full syntax to call the close method of a workbook object is:

Workbooks(1).Close(savechanges,filename, routeworkbook)

To close a Workbook , save changes made to the Workbook , save the workbook with the filename "Budgets.xls", and additionally not route the workbook to another Microsoft Excel user, requires the following VBA instruction:
Workbooks (1).Close True, "Budgets.xls", False

To pass Arguments by name, use the Argument name followed by a colon and an equal sign (: =), followed by the Argument's value. Passing Arguments by name makes code more readable. You can specify named Arguments in any order (syntax order does not have to be followed). For example, to close a workbook under the same circumstances as above, write the following VBA code:

Workbook.close   savechanges: =True, routeworkbook:=False, _ Filename:="Budgets.xls"

- Note that the entire syntax could not fit on one line, so we used the VBA line continuation character: a space followed by the underscore character (_) at the end of the line to indicate that the code is continued on the next line.

If passing Arguments by position and you want to omit one of the Arguments (you do not want to change its value), <u>you must include a blank space holder</u> for the omitted Argument. For example, to close a workbook and pass the first and third Arguments only, use the following VBA code:

Workbook.close True, , False

If your object's method has lots of Arguments, it makes sense to pass Arguments by name.

How did I know the properties and methods associated with a particular object? Believe me when I say it is unlikely anyone has this information in memory. Visual Basic has a feature that lists each object and its properties, methods, and events. It is called the "Object Browser". We will visit the Object Browser and discuss its usefulness soon.

REFERRING TO OBJECTS IN CODE

There are two types of objects in Microsoft Excel: **Singular Objects** and **Objects that are members of collections**. You refer to singular objects directly in code and you refer to an object in a collection by specifying its index number or its index name. A **collection** is a group of objects with the same characteristics.

A singular object has only one instance in a given context, while an object in a collection has multiple instances in a given context. How can you tell the difference? Since Microsoft Excel has over 100 objects, you certainly cannot be expected to remember which are singular and which objects are members of a collection. Thankfully you don't have to, because VBA help displays a hierarchical chart of all Microsoft Excel objects and shows which are singular and which are members of a collection (See Figure 21.2). For example, VBA help shows the hierarchy for WorkBook objects as one step below multiple objects which indicates that they are members of a collection

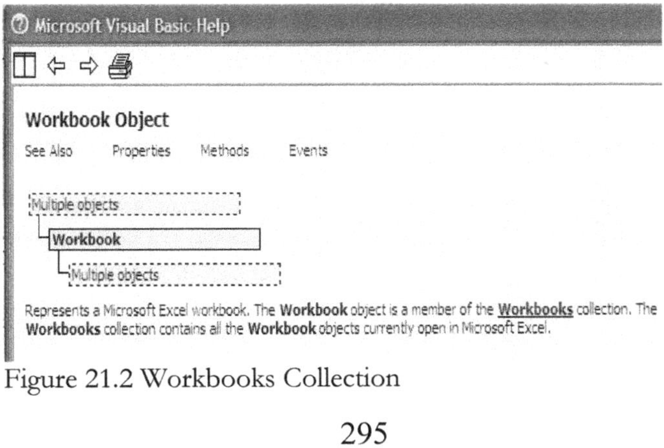

Figure 21.2 Workbooks Collection

295

Look at VBA help for the Application Object. It is a singular object. To manipulate the application object in code we refer to the application object directly. Let's change the caption property of the application object. First we have to create a procedure in a module. How we create procedures will be discussed later.

|(General)

```
Option Explicit



Public Sub examples()
Application.Caption = "My new Application"

End Sub
```

Figure 21.3 Use sub procedure to change caption

Application.Caption= "My New Application"

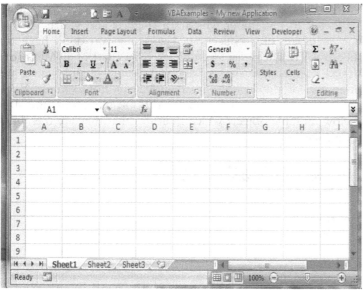

Figure 21.4

Notice how the title bar has changed to reflect the new application "caption", and the workbook name in this example is "VBAExamples". The caption property is a string so it must be enclosed in quotation marks.

Now let's manipulate an object that is a member of a collection. Index numbers for collections start at 1, unlike arrays whose index can start at 0, 1, or any other specified number (Arrays are discussed in Chapter 25). You can refer to an object in a collection by index number or by index name. For example let's change the name of the second worksheet to "QTR2Revenue". Referring to the second worksheet by its index number, we change its name by writing the following VBA code:

Worksheets(2).name = "QTR2REVENUE"

Note that Worksheets is a collection object and thus must be referred to in the plural.

Next, let's manipulate the 2nd worksheet by using its index name. We will make the Worksheet disappear from the screen by setting its visible property to false.

Worksheets("qtr2revenue").visible= false

Notice that **when indexing a collection by name, you must enclose the name in double quotation marks**. You may have also noticed that I changed the case of the name of the above object. It's ok. Unlike the **C programming language,** Visual Basic for Applications is not case sensitive. As long as the name is spelled correctly, Visual Basic for Applications does not care about the case; {UPPER CASE, lower case, it is all the same}.

THE RANGE OBJECT

The range object is a hybrid object. By definition it is a singular object, but sometimes the Range Object behaves like an object in a collection. For example, to refer to a cell or cells on a Worksheet, you must use an index of the range object address or you must use its defined name just like you would reference an object that is a member of a collection.

There are two (2) reference styles for referring to a cell or a range of cells. Most Microsoft Excel users are familiar with the **A1 notation** method, where column and row headings are used to refer to a cell. For example cell A1 is the cell that occupies the intersection of "column A" and "row 1". The second method uses the **Cells** property to refer to a single cell by using row and column index numbers. I will give examples of each, and you can obtain specific examples by invoking the VBA help feature.

Let's change the contents of a particular cell. We have to use the value property of the range object and the address of the range (the column and row of the cell) to change is contents. Using **A1 notation** change the value of Cell A1 to 57(See Figure 21.5). The range address, just like index names used with collections, must be enclosed in double quotes. We must enclose the VBA instruction to change cell A1 in a sub procedure. We discuss sub procedures in Chapter 23.

Sub EnterNewValue ( )
Worksheets ("Sheet1").Range("A1").value = 57
End Sub

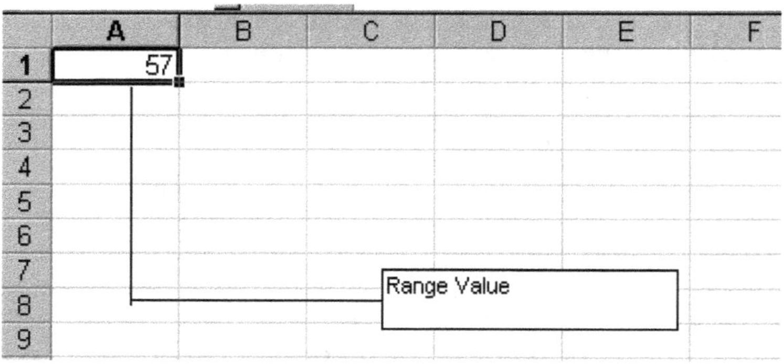

Figure 21.5

The contents of cell "A1" on the worksheet, now contains the value 57.

Writing the same procedure but referring to cells using the cells property, looks as follows:

Sub EnterNewValue ( )
Worksheets ("sheet1").Cells (1, 1).value = 57
End Sub

THE SYNTAX FOR THE CELLS PROPERTY

Cells (Row, Column)

The Cells Property is more convenient because you can use a variable for the Row or for the Column index. (I know we have not discussed variables yet, so again you have to take my word that this works until you see the example in a later chapter.)

USING NAMED RANGES

All Microsoft Excel users know that ranges are easier to identify by name than by A1 notation. To define a selected range (i.e. give it a name), click the name box at the left end of the formula bar, type in a name, and press the enter key. You can also give a range a name using VBA code (by changing the value of the range object's name property). If you have defined a name for a range using the above method or defined a name by using VBA code, you can index the range object using the defined name of a cell or the defined name for a group of cells, as follows:

Range ("A1").name = "TotalRevenue"
Range ("TotalRevenue").value = 5000

The first line defines cell "A1" as "TotalRevenue" and the second line assigns the value 5,000 to cell "A1".

For an address index that contains multiple cells, you would use the following code to set the value in each cell specified:

Range ("B1:G30").value = 5

Now every cell in the range "B1:G30" has a value of 5.

THE MICROSOFT EXCEL OBJECT HIERARCHY

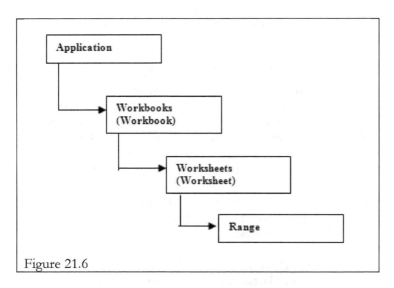

Figure 21.6

Microsoft Excel's object hierarchy affects the way you code objects. Depending on context, if you want to manipulate an object's properties and methods, you must sometimes refer to all the objects down the ladder to that object. You step down the path to a specific object by using the dot (.) operator. Notice that the two middle steps are collections and that the top and bottom steps are singular objects.

The object immediately up one step of the ladder is called the antecedent and can be omitted if Microsoft Excel considers it to be the default object. For example, to change the value of the first cell in the first worksheet of the first workbook using the full hierarchical path, write the following:

Application.workbooks(1).Worksheets (1).Range("A1").value=15

If executing this code inside Microsoft Excel it is assumed that the **application object** is the default. So the previous reference can be shortened to:

Workbooks (1).Worksheets (1).Range("A1").value =15

Continuing down the hierarchical ladder, if only one workbook is open and it is the one whose property you want to manipulate, omit the antecedent Workbooks (1) and write the following:

Worksheets (1).Range("A1").value =15

If there is only one worksheet in the open workbook, you can omit the antecedent Worksheets (1) and write the following:

Range ("A1").value = 15

You can continue down the ladder depending on the context in which object references are made.

SUMMARY
Microsoft Excel is a collection of objects whose properties and methods can be manipulated using Visual Basic for Applications.

Properties describe specific characteristics of objects and methods are the actions an object can perform. We use the syntax **"Objectname.property = value"** to set property values. And to get the property of an object we use the syntax: **"Variable = Objectname.property"**.

We cause objects to perform acts by calling their methods. The syntax for calling an object's method is **"Objectname.method"**. Most methods have Arguments which specify how the method is to be carried out. The Syntax for calling a method and invoking its Arguments follows:

Objectname.method arg1, arg2, arg3,…..argn.

Singular objects are referred to directly in code, while collection objects are referred to by index. The Range object is a hybrid object. It is defined as a singular object but sometimes behaves like a collection object.

The four (4) most common objects in Microsoft Excel in hierarchical order are: Application, Workbooks, Worksheets, and Range. Context determines how objects are referred to in code. Sometimes you have to include all the rungs in the hierarchical ladder to reference an object.

CHAPTER 22
THE VISUAL BASIC EDITOR

In this chapter we will discuss what you need to know to get started programming Microsoft Excel. Specifically we cover the Visual Basic Editor, Control and Event Procedures, Numbers, Variables, Strings, and Program planning and tools.

THE VISUAL BASIC EDITOR

Visual Basic for Applications comes with a powerful smart-editor and many debugging tools. The Visual Basic Editor (**VBE**) appears in its own window, separate from the host application. The VBE is where we write VBA code. To invoke the **VBE**: type **Alt+F11.** Your screen should now look like Figure 22.1.

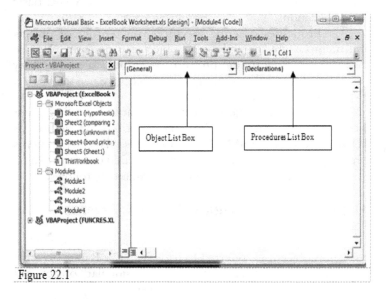

Figure 22.1

Let's write our first VBA program. All code is contained in modules so we first need to insert a module. Select **I**nsert, **M**odule from the VBE menu and your screen should look like Figure 22.2.

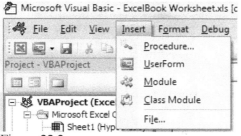
Figure 22.2

VISUAL BASIC CODE WINDOW

Inserting a module opens the code window. We will use the code window to write, display, and edit VBA code. You can open as many Code windows as you have modules. You can view the code in different forms or modules and copy and paste code between them.

The two boxes at the top of the Code window are very important. The **Object box** displays the name of the selected object that you are going to write code for. Clicking the arrow to the right of the list box displays all objects associated with the Module.

PROCEDURES AND EVENTS

The **Procedures /Events box** lists all the events recognized by Visual Basic for a form or control displayed in the object box. When you select an event, the event procedure associated with that event name is displayed in the code window. **What is an event?** It is an action that occurs in response to something the user does. For example, clicking the mouse is an event. **What is a procedure?** A procedure is a self-contained segment of VBA code (more on events and procedures later).

If (General) is displayed in the Object box, the Procedure box lists any declarations (variable definitions) and all of the general procedures that have been created for the object. When editing module code, the Procedures box lists all of the general procedures in the module. The procedure you select in the Procedures box is displayed in the Code window. The BondPrice Function is displayed in the code window in Figure 22.3. A function is a type of VBA routine and is also stored in the Procedures box.

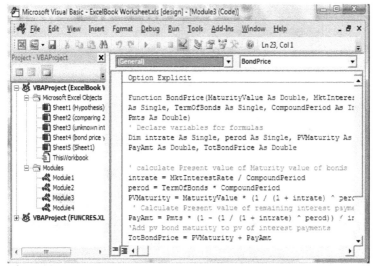

Figure 22.3

Notice the "**Option Explicit**" statement appearing at the beginning of the Code window in Figure 22.3. This is an optional statement that ensures that a variable is declared before it is used in code. Remember that when we were creating functions we had to tell VBA that we needed placeholders to store results of our calculations. Variables are those placeholders and we inform VBA (declare variables) of their type and size by using the DIM statement. Option Explicit also prevents misspelling of variables after they have been declared, when the variables are used again in code. You can type "Option Explicit" at the beginning of your module or set it along with other environment features by selecting **Tools, Options** from the Visual Basic menu.

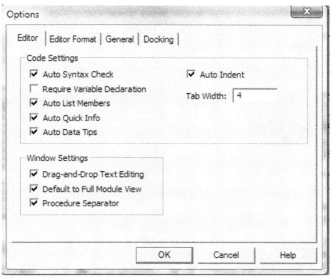

Figure 22.4

To the left of the code window is the "Project Window. The Project Window lists the "VBAProject" components. Components can be opened by clicking the icon next to the component name. All the Microsoft Excel Objects in the VBAProject are listed. All of the Worksheets in the Workbook are listed and the VBA code attached to a Worksheet can be read by clicking on the Worksheet icon next to the Worksheet name. Notice that both the Worksheet number and Worksheet name are listed in the Project Window. This will be important when we need to reference a Worksheet in our VBA code. The final Microsoft Excel Objected listed is "ThisWorkbook". Use this object to write code that affects entire Workbook. If you want the Workbook to do something when it is first opened, put start-up code in this object. Immediately below the Microsoft Excel Objects are the modules contained in the Workbook. Modules hold the VBA code that we have written. The item "VBAProject (FUNCRES.XLAM) tells us that there is an "ADD-IN attached to this Workbook.

If the "Project Window" is not visible on your system, press the CTRL+R key combination to make it visible. If you need more space and want to close the Project Window, click the close button on the top right side of the window. Or right-click anywhere in the Project Window to display a short-cut

305

menu and select "Hide". If you need to delete a Module, the "Remove Module" item should be selected from the short-cut menu. First you have to select the Module that you want to delete.

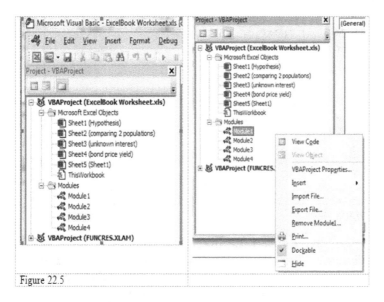

Figure 22.5

VBE MENU BAR AND TOOLBAR

Commands you need to work with the various features of VBA are found on the menu bar and toolbar. The appearance is different from the RIBBON found on the Microsoft Excel Worksheet. But it works the same. Just like in the Worksheet, shortcut keys are available to help you quickly access different features.

VBE IMMEDIATE WINDOW

The "Immediate Window" is used to run VBA instructions immediately when you are testing VBA code or debugging code. To display immediate window press the CTRL+G key combination. To hide the "immediate window", right-click anywhere in the immediate window and choose "Hide" from the resulting shortcut menu.

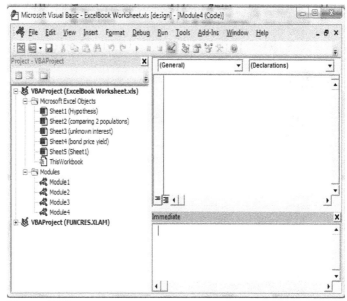

Figure 22.6

GETTING CODE INTO THE MODULE

There are three ways to get code into your Modules: (1) Record a Macro, (2) Cut and paste from other Modules, and (3) the old-fashion way of typing code directly into a Module.

We discussed Macros in Chapter 9. When you record a Macro, Microsoft Excel opens a new module to hold the code generated by recording the Macro. Figure 22.7 shows that Module5 was added to the VBE to hold the code for Macro1.

307

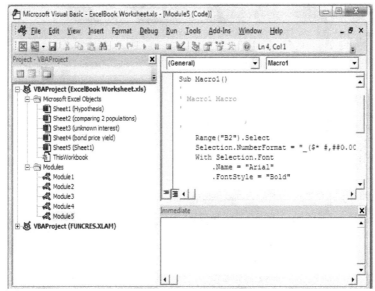

Figure 22.7

OK let's write some code. In most programming classes this is the first program that you are taught to write; the Hello routine. Look back at Figure 22.2. After we insert a Module we next have to insert a procedure to hold our VBA routine. We write code in VBA routines. Give your procedure a name and then tell Microsoft Excel which type of procedure you want to write: (1) Sub procedure, (2) Function, or (3) Property procedure. Accept the default Scope of "Public" if you want the procedure available to all Modules in the project. Select "Private" if you only want the procedure available in the Module where it is written.

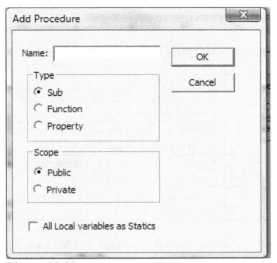

Figure 22.8

Oh I forgot to tell you that spaces are not allowed in procedure names. Press OK and VBA provides a "VBA Routine Wrapper" where you will write your code.

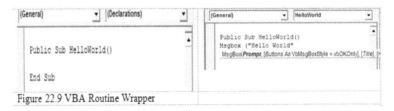

Figure 22.9 VBA Routine Wrapper

The "Msgbox" function will be used to display a message on the Worksheet. When a built-in function is written inside the wrapper its arguments are displayed to help you enter arguments correctly. The wrapper begins with the procedure name and scope. If procedure requires arguments, they are included within a set of parentheses following the procedure name. The wrapper ends with the "End Sub" statement.

The syntax for a procedure follows:

Sub ProcedureName ( )
    Statement(s)

309

End Sub

Syntax	Description
Sub	A Visual Basic Key word that starts a procedure.
ProcedureName	The name that identifies the procedure or macro.
( )	Where we list arguments used by the procedure. More on this later.
Statement(s)	Expressions that tell Visual Basic to perform some action.
End Sub	A Visual Basic key word that ends a procedure.

Now that we have written our first VBA program, how do we get it to run? There are four (4) ways to run a program. The fastest way is to hit **F5**. First make sure that the cursor is somewhere inside of the code block then press **F5** and your screen should look like Figure 22.10.

Figure 22.10

Our code created a **Message Box** with a message and a command button with the caption "OK". We will discuss Message Box functions in a later Chapter. Notice that you cannot perform any activities on the worksheet until after you press the "OK" button. The message box is said to be modal, and it must be attended to before any other action can take place. Message Boxes are used to give information to a user after he or she has done something.

The second way to run a program is to press the **"run button"** on the tool bar.

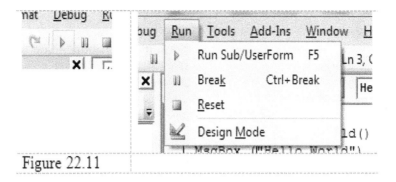

Figure 22.11

The third way is to select <u>R</u>un, **Run Sub/UserForm** from the VBE menu: See Figure 22.11.

And the fourth way is to return to Microsoft Excel **(ALT+Q or ALT+F4)** and select the Macro feature from the View Tab and run the procedure.

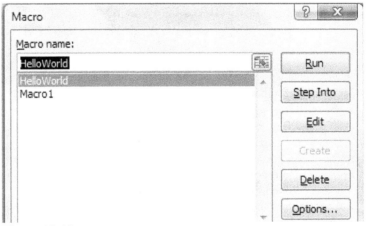

Figure 22.12

THE OBJECT BROWSER WINDOW

Another important window in the Visual Basic Editor is the **Object Browser** window. It displays the **classes**, properties, methods, events, and constants available from the **object libraries** that exist in your project. Found there are objects that you create and also objects from other applications. Help using the Object Browser is available from VBA on-line help. Sometimes when writing code to manipulate an Object, I forget some of the properties and methods for that object. The Object Browser comes to my rescue.

What is a class? "A class is the formal definition of an object. It acts as a template from which an instance of an object is created at run time. The class defines the properties of the object and the methods used to control the object's behavior." We will discuss Classes in more detail when we reach Chapter 30.

You invoke the Object Browser by selecting **View, Object Browser** from the VBE menu, or by pressing **F2**, or by pressing the **Object Browser button** on the tool bar.

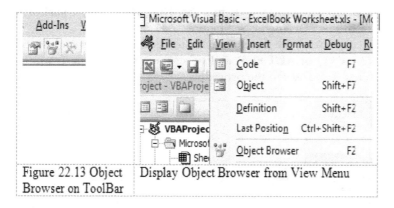

Figure 22.13 Object Browser on ToolBar	Display Object Browser from View Menu

In Figure 22.14 the Range Object is selected in the "Classes" list box. In the "Members of "Range" list box are all of the properties (looks like a hand holding a dollar bill) and methods (Functions, looks like a green brick) of the Range object are listed. The "Copy" function is selected and at the bottom of the Object Brower is a list of the arguments for that function. The argument "Destination" tells you where to deposit the copied contents.

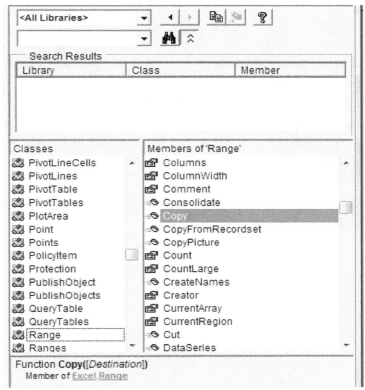

Figure 22.14

In the empty box below the box containing <All Libraries>, enter the string identifying the object you want to use in your search. Objects are displayed in the left window of the Object Browser. The "Members" window on the right side of the Object Browser displays in alphabetical order, all of the Properties, Methods, and Events of the object selected in the left window. If Properties, Methods, or Events already have code written for them, they appear bold. The bottom window of the Object Browser defines the object and gives code examples of selected Properties, Methods, and Events. If you select any item in the Object Browser and then hit the F1 key, VBA on-line help will give you detailed information on the selected item.

As you can see, the **Object Browser** can be very useful in writing VBA code.

313

DEVELOPER TAB

To continue with our discussion of VBA we have to discuss the "Developer Tab" on the Microsoft Excel Worksheet Ribbon. The tools found there are necessary to develop VBA applications. Don't see this tab on your ribbon? You have to add it. Access **FILE TAB** and select "Excel Options". Select "Customize Ribbon" and click the box under Main Tabs for "Developer", and then click OK Button. Microsoft Excel will add the Developer tab to the ribbon and tools for working with VBA will be made available.

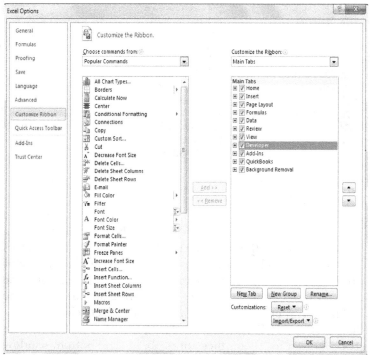

Figure 22.15

Spend some time investigating the tools on this tab. Most of the commands that we have used the shortcut keys to access are on this tab.

Figure 22.16

CONTROLS

Controls are objects that can be placed on Worksheets, Charts, and custom dialog boxes (userforms). Controls have properties, methods, and events for which VBA code can be written. To place controls on a Worksheet select the "Insert" icon from the "Controls" group, on the Developer Tab in the Ribbon. There are two types of controls: (1) Form Controls and (2) ActiveX Controls.

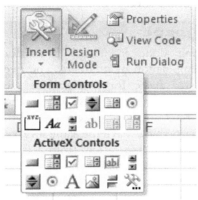

Figure 22.17

WORKING WITH CONTROLS ON A WORKSHEET

To place a control on a Worksheet, select design mode (press the button at the top left side of the Control ToolBar), then select the desired control and then click on the worksheet. For example let's put a command button on the Worksheet, assign a macro to it and change its caption.

315

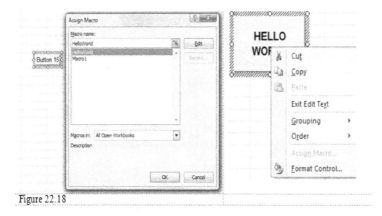

Figure 22.18

Since Worksheets can become big and cause you to scroll to different parts, I do not put controls on forms. There is a better way and I will show you how later.

NUMBERS

Most data processing done in Visual Basic for Applications involves the manipulation of numbers. The five arithmetic operations in Visual Basic for Applications are addition, subtraction, multiplication, division, and exponentiation. Arithmetic operators are listed below in precedence order. Where two operators have the same level of precedence, you must evaluate the expression from left to right. Use parentheses to clarify the meaning of an expression.

Arithmetic Operator

	Mathematical Notation	Visual Basic Notation
( ) Parentheses	Inside, start left to right	
^ Carat- Exponentiation		a ^ b
* Asterisk Multiplication / Division	a x b a ÷ b	a * b a / b
+ Addition and - Subtraction	a +b a − b	a + b a - b

Remember to move from the left to the right when evaluating expressions.
For practice, evaluate the following numeric expressions:

1.	4 * 12		2.	5 + (3 * 15)
3.	5 * 3 +2	4,	7 * (2^ 3+1)	

SCIENTIFIC NOTATION

Scientific Notation is used by VBA to write large numbers. Scientific Notation uses powers of 10 to stand for zeros. Numbers are written in the form b • 10^r , where b is a number from 1 up to 10, and r is a whole number. For Example 1,500,000,000 can be written as **1.5 •10^9**.

In Visual Basic **b • 10^r** is written as **bEr.** (The letter E is used as an abbreviation for exponent.) So **1.5 •10^9** would be written as 1.5E+09.

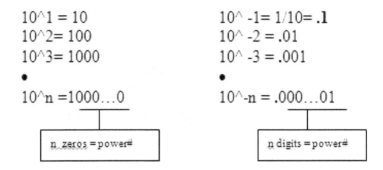

$$10^1 = 10 \qquad\qquad 10^{-1} = 1/10 = .1$$
$$10^2 = 100 \qquad\qquad 10^{-2} = .01$$
$$10^3 = 1000 \qquad\qquad 10^{-3} = .001$$
$$\bullet \qquad\qquad\qquad\qquad \bullet$$
$$10^n = 1000\ldots0 \qquad 10^{-n} = .000\ldots01$$

n zeros = power#   n digits = power#

VARIABLES

We need a way to refer to the results of arithmetic operations performed on expressions. For this we use **variables.** A variable is a name assigned to an item of data. The value of the variable may change during the execution of a program. A variable name must begin with a letter and can be up to 255 characters long. The variable name can only consist of letters, digits, and underscores. Variable names are not case sensitive. By convention we write variable names in lowercase letters except for the first letters of additional combined words such as **payRate** and **numberOfHoursWorked.** Variable names should be descriptive of the quantity to which they refer.

The combination of constants, variables, and arithmetic operations that are evaluated to yield a number is called a **numeric expression**. We use the assignment operator (=) to assign numeric expressions to variables. For example: X= 20+(2*2), assigns the value 24 to the variable X.

STRINGS

Another type of data processed by Visual Basic for Applications is a string. A string constant is a sequence of characters treated as a single item. Like numeric expressions strings can be assigned names with the assignment (=) operator. And the rules for naming string variables are the same as for numeric variables. Two or more strings can be combined to form a new single string by a process called **concatenation.** Use the ampersand **(&)** to combine the strings. You need to leave a space between the quote mark of the second string and the first letter of the second string. For example "Thomas" & " Jefferson" becomes "Thomas Jefferson".

When assigning values to a string, you must enclose the string constant in quotes. String variables, however, are never surrounded by quotation marks. For example:

> **Dim employeeFirstName As String**
> **EmployeeFirstName = "David"**

VISUAL BASIC FOR APPLICATIONS DATA TYPES

There are twelve (12) data types of values that variables can hold. Each type requires that a different amount of computer memory be set aside to hold the variable.

Data Type	Storage Size	Prefix	Possible Values
Boolean	2 bytes	Bln	True or False
Byte	1 byte	B	Unsigned integer between 0 and 255
Currency	8 bytes	Curr	Fixed point calculations Minus 922,337,203,685,477. to its positive same number
Date	8 bytes	Dat	Dates between 1/1/100 and 12/31/9999
Double	8 bytes	Dbl	Decimal #s with at most 14 digits to the right of a decimal point.
Integer	2 bytes	Int	Whole #s −32,768 to 32,767
Long Integer	4 bytes	Lng	-2,147,483,648 to 2,147,483,647
Object	4 bytes	Obj	Any Microsoft Excel object
Single	4 bytes	Sng	Decimal #s at most 6 digits to the right of a decimal point.
Strings	1 byte /char	Str	2 Billion characters
Variant	16 bytes + 1 byte for each string char.	Var	Any data type except user defined data types
User defined	Depends on definition		

HOW VBA DECLARES A VARIABLE

Variables are declared or dimensioned to tell VBA to set aside memory to hold the variable while a procedure executes. The amount of memory set aside is indicated in the above table. The following syntax is used to declare variables:

- **Syntax**:
  [Private | Public | Dim] variablename As Type

When you see items written this way, with the items separated by the piping (|) symbol, it means choose one of the items.

Analysis of the syntax:

- The **Private, Public, and Dim** statements are used to declare a variable of varying scope.

- The **Private** keyword declares a module level variable accessible only by procedures in the module where declared.

- The **Public** keyword creates a program-wide variable that can be used in any module and any procedure in the program.

- The **Dim** keyword, depending where it is used, creates a variable that can be used by the procedure in which it is declared and by other procedures.

- *variablename* is the name by which the variable is known.

- **Type** is the data type of the variable. If omitted VBA sets **Type** as variant.

Should always try to declare a variable locally if possible.

Sub CalculatePayroll()
　　Dim hoursWorked As Single
End Sub

If you use the "private" keyword to declare the variable, then this is a module-level variable and it must be declared in the General declarations section of the module.

319

Procedure level variables should be declared at the very beginning of the procedure.

OBJECT VARIABLES

An object variable is a variable that refers to an object. It saves typing, makes code easier to read, and makes code run faster. The usual scope rules apply when creating object variables.

- **Syntax:**

[Private | Dim] variablename As [New] object

Analysis of the syntax:

• **Private** declares a module-level object variable.
• **Dim** declares a procedure-level object variable.

• **variablename is the name by which the variable object is known**
• You can use the optional **New** keyword to create new objects.
• You can use the generic object term or a specific Microsoft Excel object.

For example: **Dim ws as Worksheet** declares ws as a Worksheet
Object.

Before you can use the object variable, you must set it to point to an existing object or you must create a new instance of an object with the optional "**New**" keyword. Use the **set statement** to accomplish this task.

- **Syntax:**

Set variablename = [New] objectExpression | Nothing

Analysis of the syntax:

• The variable name is any valid object variable name.
• The optional **New** keyword creates a new instance of the object
• The optional *objectExpression* can consist of any instance of an object.

- The optional **Nothing** keyword releases the memory set aside for this variable.

For example:

Set ws = Workbooks(1).Worksheets("Sheet1")

And if a worksheet does not already exist, then we must use the **"New"** keyword as follows:

Set ws = New Workbooks(1).Worksheets("Sheet1")

Following is a code sample that demonstrates the use of Object variables.

```
'*****************************************************
'  Count the number of rows of information and cut all rows
'  below that point, handles 1,000 rows
'*****************************************************

Dim c As Range, WsRange As Range, NS As Range, cr As Range
Set WsRange = Range("D7:D1000")
i = 7
For Each c In WsRange
   If c.Value <> "" Then
      i = i + 1
   'Debug.Print i, c.Value
      End If
Next c

   i = i - 1                    'delete unformated sum of column

Range(Cells(i, 4), Cells(i, 16)).Select
Selection.ClearContents
Range(Cells(i + 1, 1), Cells(1000, 1)).Select
Selection.EntireRow.Delete
Cells(i, 4).Select
```

The Object variables "c", "WsRange", "NS", and "cr" are declared as Range Objects, then WsRange is set to point to Range ("D7:D1000"). Thereafter, when we need to refer to Range ("D7:D1000") we only have to type WsRange.

PLANNING YOUR PROGRAM

Before you write the first line of code you should think of what you want the program to accomplish. Start with the outputs (what should the program produce?). Next determine the data (inputs) needed to produce the intended output. Finally, determine how to process the data to obtain the desired output (information). By the way, information is just data processed into something meaningful and useful. A plan is a series of steps needed to accomplish a goal. The better the plan, the easier the program development process will be. Following is how I develop a program.

1. Analyze or define the problem. Determine the goal, what do you want the program to accomplish. What is the relationship between inputs, processing, and outputs. Write down what you think is the problem and get the user(s) to agree in writing. This will save you at project completion because often users will say "I know what I said I wanted, but now that I see it, it is not what I meant".

2. Design the algorithm. An algorithm is **all** of the logical sequence of steps that solve the problem. Test the algorithm by hand with representative data to make sure it works. Test with as many different conditions as you can think of.

3. Design the user interface. Determine what objects (text boxes, message boxes, input boxes, command buttons, etc.) the user will need to interact with the program to get input and display output.

4. Write the Visual Basic Code to convert the algorithm to a computer solution.

5. Run the completed program. Does it work? Test with as many variations of input data as you can think of. If the program runs it probably is free of run-time errors, but may still contain logic errors (program does not perform according to expectation). Debug the program (remove errors) and re-test until you are satisfied that the program does what was intended.

6. Finish the documentation of the program. Documentation tells another programmer the thought processes that went into the program. It also lists all of the inputs, processing steps, and outputs of the program and instructs users on how to operate the program. This is important for the maintenance of the

program. The program code should contain an appropriate amount of comments that explain what each procedure does, and lists each variable, variable type, and variable scope.

HOW TO ADD COMMENTS TO YOUR CODE

Comments in Visual Basic are preceded with a single quote mark. Anything following the single quote is considered a comment and its color is changed to green to inform the programmer that information will not be processed by the compiler.

PROGRAMMING TOOLS

Many programmers use flowcharts and pseudocode to develop algorithms. Flowcharts are a graphic representation of the steps needed to solve a problem. Pseudocode uses English-like phrases with some code to describe the steps needed to solve a problem.

FLOWCHARTS

Flowcharts make use of geometric symbols connected by arrows. Inside each symbol is an explanation of the activity taking place at that step. The type of symbol used indicates the type of processing that will occur. You can draw the symbols by free-hand, purchase a template to draw the symbols by hand, or use Microsoft Excel's built–in drawing toolbar to create the symbols. To display the drawing toolbar, select Shapes icon from the "Illustrations" group, on the Insert Tab.

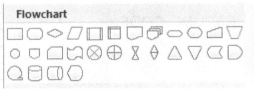

Figure 22.19

Here is a flowchart example of a program to read in seven numbers, calculate the average and print the average:

323

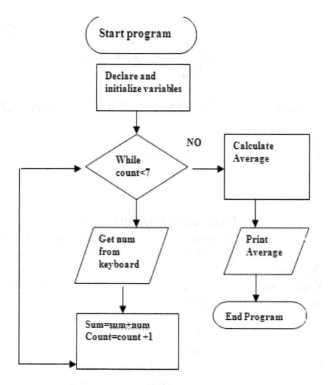

Figure 22.20

Flowcharts are useful pictures that make it easy to see program logic flow. However a flowchart of a complex problem spanning several pages may cause the picture to lose some of its clarity.

PSEUDO CODE

Now here is the same program algorithm written in pseudocode:

1. Declare and initialize variables num, count, sum, average
2. While count is less than seven (7) get a number from the keyboard, test value of count
3. If count is seven or greater calculate average and print average then end program
4. If count is less than 7 get a number from the keyboard add to sum variable, increment count variable, repeat step 2

SUMMARY

We use the Visual Basic for Applications editor and debugging tools to develop programs. The Visual Basic Editor is invoked from the Developer Tab on the Ribbon or by typing Alt+F11.

All the code we write is contained in VBA routines. Routines are also known as procedures or functions.

There are a number of tools in the Visual Basic Editor that help you write code. The Object Browser lists all the objects available to receive code and lists all of the properties, methods, and events for each object.

Controls are objects that we can place on worksheets, charts, and userforms to create an interface for the user. The most common control seen in windows products is the command button. The user clicks the command button and this causes the program to perform some action.

Most processing in Visual Basic involves numbers. We use arithmetic operators to combine numeric expressions and assign the results to variables. We can also have string variables (one or more characters).

Variables are of different types and require that different amounts of memory be set aside in storage. Although not required by Visual Basic, we should declare the variable type before we use it to make our programs more readable and more efficient.

Object variables reduce the amount of typing we have to use in coding a program and they make our programs run faster. The rules for object variables are the same as for numeric and string variables.

CHAPTER 23
SUB PROCEDURES, FUNCTIONS, AND EVENT PROCEDURES

VBA PROCEDURES

Visual Basic For Application's use of procedures has several advantages. Procedures allow modularity. Modularity means taking a big task and dividing it into smaller manageable tasks. Smaller logical tasks are easier to program and debug. Different parts of a project can be assigned to different members of a programming team for quicker development. Code can be written once and used many times in the current program and in other programs.

There are three (3) types of procedures: **General Procedures** (includes Sub procedures and Functions), **Event Procedures,** and **Property Procedures**.

General Procedures tell a program how to perform a particular task. General Procedures do not respond to events and must be specifically called into use by the program. Event Procedures, however, do respond to actions performed by the user. Some common Event Procedure actions are clicking a command button, selecting a radio button, or moving the mouse. Property Procedures are used only in class modules. Property Procedures return and assign values and set references to objects. (We will discuss Property Procedures in Chapter 30).

There are two types of General Procedures: Sub Procedures and Function Procedures. Sub Procedures do not return a value and cannot be used on the right-hand side of the equal sign in an expression. Function Procedures return a value and can be used anywhere a variable can be used. As you have seen in prior chapters, functions can be used in Worksheets as user defined functions.

The syntax for Sub Procedure:
[Public | Private | Static] SUB procedurename ([Argument list])
      [statements]
      [Exit Sub]
      [statements]
END SUB

Syntax Analysis

- Optional **Public** keyword indicates that the Sub Procedure can be used by all modules in the program.

- Optional **Private** keyword indicates that the Sub Procedure can only be used in module where declared.

- Optional **Static** keyword indicates that all variables within the Sub Procedure are preserved between calls. The Static attribute doesn't affect variables that are declared outside the Sub, even if they are used in the procedure.

- Required **SUB** keyword is beginning wrapper of the Sub Procedure.

- Required **Procedure Name** must be unique and must follow the standard rules for naming variables. It should be descriptive of the task to be performed by the Sub Procedure.

- Optional **Argument list** contains the variables and their type that are passed to the Sub Procedure for processing. A comma separates each argument.

- Optional **Statements** are lines of code to be executed within the Sub Procedure.

- Optional **Exit Sub** causes Sub Procedure to exit immediately. Processing continues at the statement following the one that called the Sub Procedure. Typically used just before error handling routines in Sub Procedures. Sub Procedure can have one or more Exit Subs that can appear anywhere in a Sub Procedure.

- Required **End Sub** the ending wrapper indicating end of the Sub Procedure.

Following is an example of a Sub Procedure:

Private Sub HelloMessage ( )
Msgbox "This is an example of a simple Sub Procedure"
End Sub
The argument list of a Sub Procedure must follow strict rules. Following is the syntax for the argument list:

[Optional] [ByVal | ByRef] [ParamArray]
variablename [( )] [As type] [= defaultvalue]

Analysis of syntax:

• **Optional** keyword indicating that an argument is not required. If used, all subsequent arguments in argument list must also be optional and declared using the **Optional** keyword. **Optional** can't be used for any argument if **ParamArray** is used.

• **ByVal** Optional keyword indicating that the argument is passed by value. Argument maintains its value after processing.

• **ByRef** Optional keyword indicating that argument is passed by reference. Passing arguments **ByRef** is the default.

• **ParamArray** Optional keyword used only as the last argument in the argument list to indicate that the final argument is an optional array of variant elements. **ParamArray** allows you to pass an arbitrary number of arguments. **ParamArray** cannot be used with **ByVal, ByRef,** or **Optional.**

• **variablename** required name of variable representing the argument; follows standard variable naming rules.

• **type** Optional data type of the argument passed to the procedure; may be **Boolean, Byte, Currency, Date, Double, integer, long, Object, Single, String, Variant.** If the argument is not **Optional,** a user-defined type, or an object type may also be specified.

- **Defaultvalue** Optional. Any constant or constant expression. Valid for **Optional** parameters only. If the type is an **Object**, an explicit default value can only be **Nothing.**

Sub Procedures by default are Public in all modules. Thus they can be called from anywhere in the application. Sometimes Sub Procedures need to be supplied with variable values in order to do their jobs. The Sub Procedure will perform some action on the supplied variables. Variable values are sent to the Sub Procedure by the calling statement. The Sub Procedure communicates with the calling statement and asks that it be sent values for the variables appearing in the Sub Procedure's argument list in the specified position and in the specified type.

WORKING WITH PROCEDURES

CREATING NEW PROCEDURES

General Procedures can be created two ways. The first way is to type the Procedure heading (use the keyword "SUB" or "Function", depending on type of general procedure wanted), follow with procedure name and a pair of parentheses, and then hit the Enter key and Visual Basic provides the end of Procedure wrapper "End Sub" or "End Function". Or the second way is to select <u>I</u>nsert, <u>P</u>rocedure from the Visual Basic Editor Menu. See Figure 23.1.

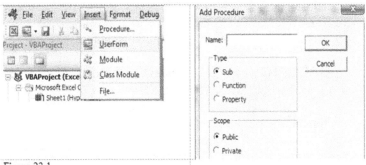

Figure 23.1

This brings up the "Add Procedure" dialog box. This dialog box allows you to visually set all of the elements of the syntax for creating a new procedure and provides the beginning and ending wrappers of the procedure.

SELECTING EXISTING PROCEDURES
To view a General Procedure in the current module, select General from the Object Box in the code window, then select the procedure in the Procedure Box.

To view an Event Procedure, select the desired Object from the Object Box in the code window, and then select the Event in the Procedure Box.

HOW DO YOU CALL A PROCEDURE?

Now that we have written procedures, how do we invoke them? The location of the calling statement (hereafter referred to as **source**) and the location of the target Procedure (the Sub Procedure that is being called) determines how you **call** a Procedure.

CALLING A PROCEDURE FROM WITHIN THE CURRENT MODULE

If both the source calling statement and the target Procedure are in the same module use one of the following syntax:

Call SubprocedureName (FirstArg, SecondArg, lastArg.)

Or
SubprocedureName FirstArg, SecondArg,lastArg

If you use the **Call** keyword, the argument list must be enclosed in parentheses. If the **Call** keyword is omitted, you must not enclose argument list in parentheses. In either approach, arguments must be separated by commas.

CALLING A PROCEDURE FROM OTHER MODULES

Remember that Public Procedures can be called from anywhere in the project. If the source calling statement and the target Procedure are not in the same module use one of the following syntax:

Call [ModuleName | FormName].SubprocedureName (Arglist)

Module Name or Form Name indicates location of the target Procedure.

Or you can call the target Procedure without using the **Call** keyword, as follows:

[ModuleName | FormName].SubprocedureName Arg1, Arg2....

The following program Procedure ExChpt04( ) calls Sub Procedure Formatyourcells ( ) to format Range "A4" on the current Worksheet. In the selected Cell, Size is set to 10 and Style is set to Bold. The Number in cell A4 is formatted with commas separating thousands and has two (2) decimal places. Finally the cell interior is painted yellow. We can call Formatyourcells ( ) whenever we need to format a Cell with the above attributes. Of course we would have to change it a little to handle general situations. Now the number "89765" is hard coded in the program.

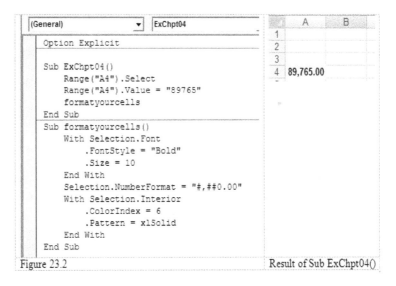

| Figure 23.2 | Result of Sub ExChpt04() |

In the sub procedure ExChpt04 ( ), when the call statement "Formatyourcells" is reached; execution jumps to the Sub Procedure Formatyourcells ( ). The statements between Sub Formatyourcells ( ) and End Sub are executed, and then execution returns to the calling procedure ExChpt04 ( ) and continues with the statement following the call statement, the End Sub statement in this example.

A new concept is introduced in the Formatyourcells ( ) Procedure; the **With / End With** construct. The With/End

331

With construct saves considerable typing strokes and your code will run faster as VBA only has to evaluate the Object once as it processes multiple properties and methods. Using the **"With / End with"** construct allows you to omit the objectname, and start the VBA statement with the dot operator followed with properties or methods. Use the following syntax:

With objectname
. Propertyname = value
. Method
End With

In the Sub Formatyourcells( ) procedure, Selection +" Font, and NumberFormat" are objects to be worked on.

The argument list of the **Call** statement must match the argument list of the Sub Procedure in type, quantity, and position order. However the variable names in the source calling statement argument list can be different than the variable names in the target Procedure argument list. Also, arguments in the target Sub Procedure can only consist of variables, while arguments in the source Call statement can be constants, variables, or expressions. This allows values obtained as input from the user to be passed to the Sub Procedure.

I try to write the target Sub Procedure or Function Procedure before I write the calling statement. After you write a Sub Procedure or Function, Visual Basic reminds you of the Sub Procedure's or Function's arguments as you type in the call statements. I wrote the Multiply Sub Procedure first (this is the target sub procedure, the one that is being called by another procedure). As soon as you type the first parentheses of a call statement or hit the space bar (if the Call keyword is omitted), Visual Basic displays a mini-message window listing in position order, the argument name and type (See Figure 23.3). Now you know that you have to supply an argument value when you call the Multiply Sub Procedure. In this example you supply a value for the variable number and it must be a data type of "Single".

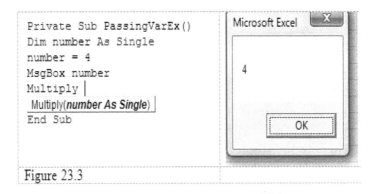

```
Private Sub PassingVarEx()
Dim number As Single
number = 4
MsgBox number
Multiply |
 Multiply(number As Single)
End Sub
```

Microsoft Excel

4

OK

Figure 23.3

Let's step through these two sub procedures line by line. See Figure 23.4. Press F5 to run this procedure. The variable "number" is declared as a "Single" data type. It is then assigned the value "4". Next line displays a message on the Worksheet and shows that the value of the "number" variable is 4. Next the procedure "Multiply" is called and supplied with the value for the variable: "number". At this point" number" is equal to 4. The first line in the "Multiply" procedure is "Msgbox number". Number is still 4 at this point. Number is multiplied by 12; number is now 48. This is displayed in the third Msgbox. Control is returned from "Multiply" procedure to the "PassingVarEx" procedure to the line immediately after the line that called the "Multiply" procedure. This next part is tricky. What do you think the value of "number" is at this point? If you guessed 48, that would be wrong. "Multiply" did not pass a value for "number" back to the "PassingVarEx" procedure. Thus the value of "number" in the "PassingVarEx" procedure is still 4 and the 4th Msgbox confirms this.

333

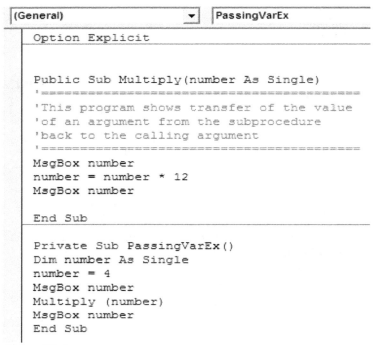

```
(General)                          ▼   PassingVarEx

    Option Explicit


    Public Sub Multiply(number As Single)
    '===============================================
    'This program shows transfer of the value
    'of an argument from the subprocedure
    'back to the calling argument
    '===============================================
    MsgBox number
    number = number * 12
    MsgBox number

    End Sub

    Private Sub PassingVarEx()
    Dim number As Single
    number = 4
    MsgBox number
    Multiply (number)
    MsgBox number
    End Sub
```

Figure 23.4

Figure 23.5 shows how the value of number changes as we
step through the two sub procedures.

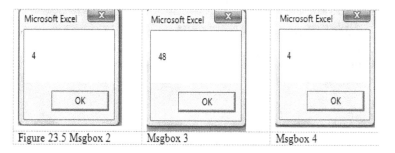

Figure 23.5 Msgbox 2   Msgbox 3   Msgbox 4

LOCAL VARIABLES VS. MODULE-LEVEL VARIABLES

Two or more variables with identical names but
located in different Sub Procedures can have different values.
A variable declared in a Sub Procedure is said to have **local
scope**. And it is only visible inside of the Sub Procedure
where it was declared. When the Sub Procedure finishes
execution, the value of the local variable is lost. Each time a
Sub Procedure is called, all declared variables that are not part

of the argument list assume their default values. The default value of a numeric variable is zero (0) and the default value of a string variable is the empty string.

Module-level variables have general scope. They are visible to every procedure in a module's code. Module-level variables must be declared in the "General Declarations Section" at the top of the Module code. When a module-level variable is assigned a value by a procedure, it retains that value when the procedure completes it execution.

FUNCTION PROCEDURES

Microsoft Excel has many built-in functions. Functions are like mini-programs. They accept input, process input, and yield output. Functions can accept many values as input, but can **only output a single value**. We can access and use built-in functions from the Microsoft Excel menu or we can manipulate all of Microsoft Excel's built-in functions with code. To manually use Microsoft Excel's built-in functions, use the Function Wizard. To invoke the Function Wizard, press SHIFT+F3 keys. We already have spent time with functions so I will be brief here. Most built-in functions use the same format. We need to know this format (syntax) so that we can use Microsoft Excel's built-in functions in our VBA programs.

Syntax for FV Function

FV(rate, nper, pmt[,pv[, type]]) As Double

Part	Analysis
"rate"	Required. Double specifying interest rate per period. For example, if you get a car loan at an annual percentage rate (APR) of 10 percent and make monthly payments, the rate per period is 0.10/12 or 0.00833.
"nper"	Required. Integer specifying total number of payment periods in the annuity. For example if you make monthly payments on a four-year car loan, your loan has a total of 4 * 12 (or 48) payment periods.
"pmt"	Required. Double specifying payment to be

335

	made each period. Payments usually contain principal and interest that do not change over the life of the annuity.
"type"	Optional. Variant specifying when payments are due. Use 0 if payments are due at the end of the payment period, or use 1 if payments are due at the beginning of the period. If omitted, 0 is assumed.

An annuity is a series of fixed cash payments made over a period of time. An annuity can be a loan (such as a home mortgage) or an investment (such as a monthly savings plan).

The **rate** and **nper** arguments must be calculated using payment periods expressed in the same units. For example, if **rate** is calculated using months, **nper** must also be calculated using months.

For all arguments, cash paid out (such as deposits to savings) is represented by negative numbers; cash received (such as dividend checks) is represented by positive numbers. [See VBA on-line help].

Suppose we have values for interest rate, number of payments, payment amount, and payment type in cells "D11:D14" on a worksheet and we want to calculate the future amount of an annuity from this information. We can write the following code:

```
Option Explicit
Sub CalculteFutureSavingsAmount()
    'The procedure calculate the future value an annuity
    Dim Fmt As String, FVal As Double
    Dim Rate As Range, pymts As Range, payAmt As
Range
    Dim paytype As Range
    Set Rate = Range("D11")
    Set pymts = Range("D12")
    Set payAmt = Range("D13")
    Set paytype = Range("D14")
    Fmt = "###,###,##0.00"  ' Define money format
    FVal = FV(Rate / 12, pymts, payAmt, paytype)
    MsgBox "Future Savings will be worth " &
Format(FVal, Fmt) & "."
End Sub
```

Running this code gives us the results shown in Figure 23.6.

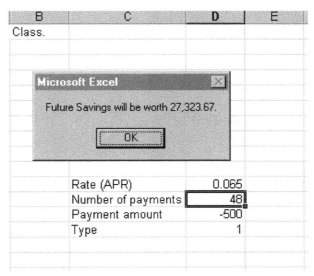

Figure 23.6

WORKSHEET FUNCTIONS

VBA provides plenty of build-in functions; enough to solve most problems. If you need more, you can use Microsoft Excel's worksheet functions. Use the following syntax:

Application.WorksheetFunction.FunctionName( )

For example: To use Microsoft Excel's built-in Pmt function type in following:
Application.WorksheetFunction.Pmt (Arguments). FYI the arguments for the PMT function in order are: (Rate, nper, pv, [fv], [type]).

USER DEFINEDFUNCTIONS

In addition to manipulating Microsoft Excel's built-in functions with code, we can also create our own functions. These user-defined functions are created the same way as Sub Procedures and can be used in the same way as built-in functions. The User Defined Functions behave as if they are constants, variables, or expressions.

337

SYNTAX FOR USER-DEFINED FUNCTION PROCEDURES

[Public | Private |Static] Function *name*
[(argumentlist)] [As type]
    [statements]
    [name = expression]
    [Exit Function]
    [statements]
    [name=expression]
End Function

There are three differences between a function procedure and a Sub Procedure:

- All function procedures begin with the Function Keyword and end with the End Function keyword.
- Function procedures can be called through formulas entered in worksheet cells.
- A function procedure can return a value to the Sub Procedure or formula expression that calls it.

You can specify the data type of each argument and of the return value. If data type of arguments or the return value is omitted, they are treated as variants by Visual Basic. Arguments are passed to Function Procedures in the same manner as they are passed to Sub Procedures.

CALLING A FUNCTION FROM A WORKSHEET CELL

You can execute a user-defined function procedure by calling it directly from a worksheet cell just as you would a built-in worksheet function. Use the following format:

- = functionName (argument list)

Suppose we have written a Function Procedure called Celsius which converts Fahrenheit temperatures to Celsius temperatures. We can call it from a Sub Procedure or we can call it from a worksheet cell. Take a look at the following code. It creates and calls the conversion function "Celsius". The "InputBox" Function is introduced here. It gets information from the user and the information can be used any number of ways. In this example we pass it as an argument to a function ("Celsius") so that it can be used to convert temperatures.

```
Option Explicit

Sub CalculateConversion()
    Dim temp As Integer
    temp = InputBox _
    (prompt:="Please enter the temperature in degrees F.")
    MsgBox "The temperature is " & Celsius(temp) & " degrees C."

End Sub
  Function Celsius(fDegrees)
     Celsius = (fDegrees - 32) * 5 / 9
  End Function
```

Figure 23.7

We call the Function Celsius ( ) as an expression in the Message Box function and pass the argument "temp" during the call. We obtain the Fahrenheit temperature from an input Box function. Running this program yields the results found in Figure 4.10.

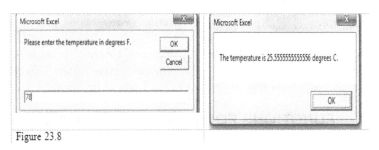

Figure 23.8

First we are prompted by an input box to enter a temperature in Fahrenheit degrees. We enter our temperature and hit the "OK" button. And our program gives us the screen shown in Figure 23.8

Alternatively we can call the function from Worksheet cell "D18" by entering the formula "= **celsius (78)**" and we see that both methods of calling a function yield the same results. We can either pass values to the function or pass range addresses to the function during the call. For example, if we had the value **78** in cell "B5" we could call the function by entering "= celsius (B5)".

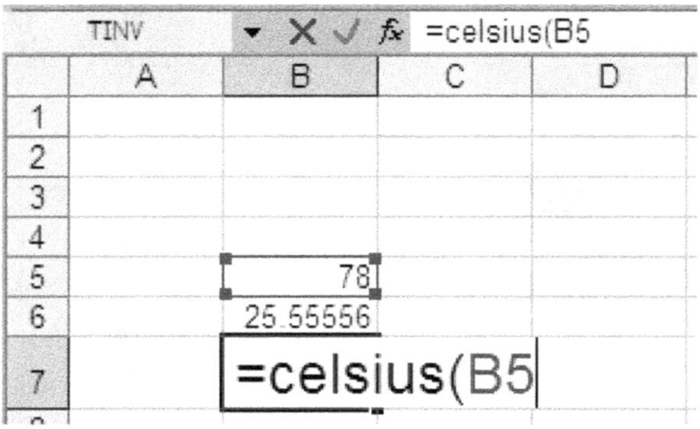

Figure 23.9

Microsoft Excel will call this function only when the values in the cells that are used as arguments change. To have our user-defined functions called whenever the value of any cell in the workbook changes (just like the behavior of built-in functions) we have to add the following as the first line of our function: **Application. Volatile True.**

"Volatile" is a method of the "Application Object". It must be called with the "True" argument to make user-defined functions behave like Microsoft Excel Built-in functions.

FUNCTIONS FOR INPUT AND OUTPUT

INPUT BOX FUNCTION

If we only want to get one piece of input data, we can use the input box function. First, we have to declare a string variable to hold the response. Then we use the following syntax:

Stringvariable= inputbox (prompt, [Title],[default]) as String

See the Celsius Function code above, for an example of the input box. After the user types a response in the text box and hits the "ok" button, the response is assigned to the string variable. If the user hits the "cancel" button, an empty string is assigned to the string variable. The **"prompt" argument** is required and it tells the user what information to type in the text box. The **"title" argument** is optional and provides the caption that appears in the Title Bar. If the "title argument" is omitted, the current file name appears in the title bar. The **"default" argument** is optional and provides the most commonly expected response. It saves typing and input time, as the user only has to hit the "ok" button if default does not have to change. The InputBox function always returns a string. If you want to get other types of data, you must use the InputBox Method. Syntax for InputBox method is:

Application.InputBox (Prompt, Title, Default, Left Top, _ Helpfile, HelpcontextId, Type)
See VBA help for details.

MESSAGE BOX

We have been using the Message box function for output. It gives a brief message to the user and only appears on the screen until user has read the message and clicks the "ok" button. The message box syntax is:

MsgBox (prompt [,Button Attributes,] [Title])

The **"prompt" argument** is required and is the string holding the message we want the user to read. The **"Attributes" argument** is optional and is an integer variable type or a "vbconstant". It determines the type of button displayed in the message box and the type of informational icon that will also appear in the message box. If the "attribute" argument is omitted, only the "ok" button appears in the box. The **"title" argument** is optional and provides the caption in the Title Bar. If omitted, Title Bar displays the name of the file from where the message box function is called. If the optional second argument is omitted, you must include double commas (, ,) as placeholder for this argument.

As was discussed in Chapter 22, you can pass arguments to the input box and to the message box by position or my name.

SOME USEFUL BUILT-IN FUNCTIONS

Visual Basic supplies useful numeric and variable functions. The numeric functions **SQR, Int, and Round** accept numeric input and yield numeric output. The SQR( ) function calculates the Square Root of a number. Int ( ) function finds the greatest integer less than or equal to a number, discarding the decimal part of positive numbers. Round (n, r), as its name indicates, rounds a number *n* to *r*

341

decimal places. If the argument **r** is omitted, then **n** is rounded to a whole number.

Arguments inside the parentheses can be numbers, numeric variables, or numeric expressions. Expressions are evaluated first to provide the input. Following are some examples of these numeric functions:

Sqr (25) is 5	Int (5.9) is 5	Round (5.9) is 6
Sqr (16) is 4	Int (6) is 6	Round (5.432,2) is 5.43
Sqr (9) is 3	Int (-7.6) is –8	Round (5.9, 2) is 6.00
Sqr (0) is 0		

To manipulate string variables, Visual Basic supplies string functions. The most common string functions are **Left ( ), Mid ( ), Right ( ), Ucase ( ), and Trim ( ).** The Left, Mid, and Right functions are used to get characters from the Left, Middle, and Right end of a string. The resulting strings are called "sub-strings" of the strings from which they were formed.

If **str** is a string and **m** and **n** are positive integers, then Left (str, n) is the string consisting of the first n characters of the string and Right (str, n) is the string consisting of the last n characters of the string. Mid (str, m, n) is the string starting at the **m**th character and continuing right for a total of **n** characters. Ucase (str) converts all characters in the string to upper case. Trim (str) removes all leading and trailing spaces from string str. Just like in numeric functions, string function arguments can be evaluated for variables and for expressions. Following are some examples of string functions:

Left ("Chicago", 4) is "Chic	Right("Chicago",2) is "go"
Mid ("Visual Basic",8 ,5) is "Basic"	Ucase("Visual") is "VISUAL"
Trim(" Visual ") is "Visual"	

Visual Basic also supplies string functions that produce numbers. The **Len (str)** function gives the number of characters in a string. The **Instr(str1, str2)** function searches the string for the first occurrence of **str2** in **str1** and gives the position at which the string is found. Following are some examples:

Len ("Chicago Bulls") is 13	Len(" ") is 1
InStr("Chicago Bulls","go") is 6	

InStr is often used to find the first space in a string.

FORMAT FUNCTIONS

Format functions are used to display numbers and dates in their expected form and to right-justify numbers.

The FormatNumber (n, r) function is the string containing the number n, rounded to r decimal places with commas every three digits to the left of the decimal point. For example FormatNumber (9878765.234,1) yields the string "9,878,765.2".

The FormatCurrency(n, r) function results in the string consisting of a dollar sign followed by the value of FormatNumber(n ,r). If the number is negative it is enclosed in parentheses. For example FormatCurrency(150831.1226, 2) yields the string $150,831.12.

The FormatPercent(n, r) function results in the string consisting of the number n displayed as a percent and rounded to r decimal places. For example FormatPercent(.0765,2) is 7.65%.

If the "r" argument is omitted, "n" in the above functions is rounded to two (2) decimal places. Numbers less than one (1) will have a zero (0) to the left of the decimal point. The "n" argument can be a number, numeric expression, or a string corresponding to a number.

If none of the above Format functions work for you, then you can design your own format as was done in the CalculateFutureSavingsAmount( ) procedure discussed earlier in this chapter. First define your format type (*user-defined format or udf*) and put it into the generic Format (n, udf) function.

EVENT PROCEDURES

VBA procedures execute whenever an event occurs. If we want to program a Workbook object or a Worksheet object to respond to an event, then we must put event-handling code in the Code Window of that object. Let's revisit the VBE that we introduced in an earlier chapter.

343

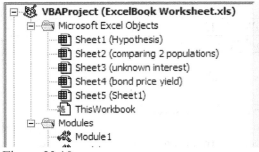
Figure 23.10

Notice the six (6) Microsoft Excel objects listed on the top left side of the VBE under VBAProject (Book1). Listed there are 5 worksheet objects and the "ThisWorkbook" object. The "ThisWorkbook" object represents the current Microsoft Excel File and is where we write event-handler code that affects the currently open Workbook.

To open the code window for any of the 6 objects, we must double-click that object. Let's write some event-handler code for "ThisWorkbook". Following are the required steps:

1.   Double-click the ThisWorkbook object to make visible its code window. Click the item "ThisWorkbook" in the object list box to get a routine wrapper.

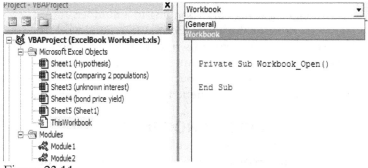
Figure 23.11

Notice the 2 items in the Object down-down list box (General and Workbook).

2.   Since we want to write code for the current Workbook, click the Workbook item. Now, all of the Procedures and Events available for the current Workbook can be accessed by clicking the desired

event or procedure in the Procedures/Events list box (Figure 23.12).

Figure 23.12

3. Click the desired procedure or event and VBA supplies the procedure wrapper and any required arguments.
4. Write the event-handling code between the wrapper. Test the code to ensure that it works and when you are finished, hit Alt+F4 keys to return to the Microsoft Excel Worksheet.

I put code in the Workbook_Open( ) event, if I want a procedure to run automatically when I open a particular Microsoft Excel file. For example, if I have a custom menu bar for an Microsoft Excel file, I put the code creating the custom menu bar in the Workbook_Open () event. The following code runs automatically whenever the workbook is opened. A message box displays "This workbook is now open" and the current time.

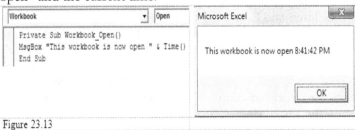

Figure 23.13

To write event-handler code for Worksheets requires the following steps:

1. Double-click one of the sheet objects and your screen now looks like Figure 23.14.

345

2.   Since we are writing code for a Worksheet, click the Worksheet item in the Object list box. Now, all of the <u>Procedures and Events</u> available for the selected Worksheet can be accessed by clicking the desired event or procedure in the Procedures/Events list box.

3.   Click the desired procedure or event and VBA supplies the procedure wrapper and any required arguments.

4.   Write the event-handling code within the wrapper. Test the code to ensure that it works and when you are finished, hit the Alt+F11 keys to return to the Microsoft Excel Worksheet.

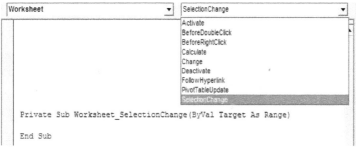

Figure 23.14

SUMMARY

All programming code must be written in Procedures or Functions. There are three types of Procedures: General Procedures (includes Sub Procedures and Functions), Event Procedures, and Property Procedures.

There are two ways to create Procedures. You can type the beginning wrapper keyword "Sub " or "Function", procedure name, a pair of parentheses, hit the enter key, and Visual Basic will supply the ending wrapper keyword "End Sub" or "End Function". Or you can select Insert, Procedure from the Visual Basic Editor menu.

Sub Procedures can be called by using the "Call" keyword or by omitting the "Call" keyword. If you use the "Call" keyword, arguments must be enclosed in parentheses. To call a Sub Procedure from outside of the module where located, precede the procedure name by the module name or form name followed by the dot operator.

The "With / End With" construct was introduced in this chapter and it saves considerable typing strokes if you have to set a lot of properties for an Object.

Arguments can be passed to Sub Procedures by reference or by value. If passed by value the variable retains its original value after the Sub Procedure ends execution.

Local variables only have a value in the Sub Procedure where declared. This value is lost after Sub Procedure finishes execution. Module-level variables have general scope and are accessible from all procedures in the Project. After a module-level procedure has been assigned a value in a Sub Procedure, it retains such value until project ceases to exist.

Functions are like Sub Procedures except that they can return a value and also can be used anywhere a variable, constant, or expression can be used. Microsoft Excel has many built-in functions and you can create your own user-defined functions. Functions can be called from Sub Procedures or can be called from cells in a worksheet.

The "input box" function is used when we only want one piece of information from the user. The "Message Box" function is used to temporarily put a message on the screen for the user to read.

Visual Basic supplies useful numeric and string functions to manipulate numeric and string variables.

Also supplied with Visual Basic are Format functions to display numbers in the expected form, to right-justify numbers, and to display dates.

CHAPTER 24
DATA VALIDATION

In this chapter we cover Data Validation, Relational and Logical Operators, the "If Statement", Select Case Blocks, and Looping.

DATA VALIDATION

Programs should be designed to inform the user when he or she has made a mistake when entering data into the program. Help should also be given to the user to correct the mistake. This is called data input validation. Many types, but not all, of input can be validated. Following are some of the more common type of data validation.

♦ For dates, any value that cannot be converted to a date is invalid.

♦ When data must be a number – for example payment amounts on loans, or interest rates – the input must be numeric or it is invalid. Sometimes the number must be greater than zero.

♦ Sometimes data must fall within some valid range. For example a birth date must not be a future date.

♦ Often data must have a particular format. For example a social security number should have the format "xxx- xx – xxxx".

♦ And in some cases strings should not exceed a maximum length.

THE BOOLEAN DATA TYPE

When making decisions we need to know if an expression or value of a variable is true or false. We can use the "Boolean" data type to handle these situations. The value of a variable declared as "Boolean" is false by default and remains false until changed by the program. When numeric values are assigned to a "Boolean" variable the value will be converted to True or False. If the value is zero (0), it is converted to False. All other values are converted to True.

CLASSIFICATION FUNCTIONS

In this chapter we introduce two new functions which will help us validate input. They are the **isDate(*expression*)** Function and the **isNumeric(*expression*)** Function. These functions tell us if a string has specific characteristics.

The isDate ( ) Function and isNumeric( ) Function tell us if a value can be successfully converted to a date or number, respectively. They do not, however, actually convert the data. They just determine whether the data can be converted. Thus they are called classification functions.

The *expression* argument is a string value that will be tested. If the expression can be converted to a date or number, the function will return a value of True; otherwise a value of False will be returned.

The following code from a database program demonstrates data input validation. We will discuss database programming in a later chapter. Here we just want to demonstrate data validation.

Option Explicit

```
'=====================================
=
'Program demonstrates data validation.   Section 1
'=====================================
=

Private Sub cmdBrowse_Click()
   datPayroll.Enabled = True
   datPayroll.Refresh
   cmdBrowse.Visible = False
   cmdUpdate.Visible = False
   txtEmployeeID.Locked = True
   txtHoursWorked.Locked = True
   txtPayRate.Locked = True
   txtPayDate.Locked = True
   cmdQuit.Visible = False
   End Sub
Private Sub cmdcancel_Click()
   Dim answer As Integer
   answer = MsgBox("Do you want to cancel?", vbYesNo +
vbQuestion, "Cancel")
   If answer = vbYes Then
   txtEmployeeID.Text = vbNullString
   txtHoursWorked.Text = vbNullString
   txtPayRate.Text = vbNullString
   txtPayDate.Text = vbNullString
   txtEmployeeID.SetFocus
   Else
```

```vb
    txtEmployeeID.SetFocus
    End If
    End Sub
Private Sub cmdQuit_Click()
'========================================
=
'Test to see if user really wants to quit or wants to return to browse 'mode.
```

Section 2

```vb
'========================================
=
    Dim response As Integer
    response = MsgBox("Do you want return to Browse?", vbYesNo +
vbQuestion, "Exit")
    If response = vbYes Then
    cmdcancel.Visible = False
    cmdUpdate.Visible = False
    cmdStartAdding.Visible = True
    datPayroll.Visible = True       'Go back to browse mode
    txtEmployeeID.Text = ""
    txtHoursWorked.Text = ""
    txtPayRate.Text = ""
    txtPayDate.Text = ""
    datPayroll.Refresh
    datPayroll.Enabled = True
    txtEmployeeID.Locked = True
    txtHoursWorked.Locked = True
    txtPayRate.Locked = True
    txtPayDate.Locked = True
    Else
    End
    End If
End Sub


'========================================
=
```

'Section 2A Add records to database copy buffer

```vb
'========================================
=
Private Sub cmdStartAdding_Click()
    datPayroll.Enabled = True
    datPayroll.Refresh
    datPayroll.Recordset.AddNew
    txtEmployeeID.Locked = False
    txtHoursWorked.Locked = False
    txtPayRate.Locked = False
```

```vb
    txtPayDate.Locked = False
    txtEmployeeID.Text = vbNullString
    txtHoursWorked.Text = vbNullString
    txtPayRate.Text = vbNullString
    txtPayDate.Text = vbNullString
    datPayroll.Visible = False
    cmdBrowse.Visible = False
    cmdStartAdding.Visible = False
    cmdcancel.Visible = True
    cmdUpdate.Visible = True
    cmdQuit.Visible = True
    txtEmployeeID.SetFocus
End Sub
'====================================
=
'Section 2B Update database
'====================================
=
Private Sub cmdUpdate_Click()
    datPayroll.Recordset.Update
    If datPayroll.Recordset.EditMode = dbEditNone Then
    datPayroll.Recordset.AddNew
    txtEmployeeID.Text = vbNullString
    txtHoursWorked.Text = vbNullString
    txtPayRate.Text = vbNullString
    txtPayDate.Text = vbNullString
    txtEmployeeID.SetFocus
    End If
End Sub

Private Sub datPayroll_Validate(Action As Integer, Save As Integer)
    Dim message As String
    If Action = vbDataActionUpdate Then

'====================================
=
    'Validate Employee ID Range between 100 and 1000 or
    'Else cancel record update.  Section 3

'====================================
=
    If (Val(txtEmployeeID.Text) < 100) Or
(Val(txtEmployeeID.Text) > 1000) Then
```

351

```
        message = "Employee ID Number must be between 100 and
1000"
        Action = vbDataActionCancel
        txtEmployeeID.SelStart = 0
        txtEmployeeID.SelLength = Len(txtEmployeeID)
        txtEmployeeID.SetFocus


'=====================================
=
        'Validate Hours worked Range greater than 0 and less than 60
        'Else cancel record update. Section 4


'=====================================
=
        ElseIf (IsNumeric(txtHoursWorked) = False) Or
(Val(txtHoursWorked.Text) > 60) Then
        message = message & Chr(vbKeyReturn) & "Hours worked must
be greater than 0 and less than 60"
        Action = vbDataActionCancel
        txtHoursWorked.SelStart = 0
        txtHoursWorked.SelLength = Len(txtEmployeeID)
        txtHoursWorked.SetFocus



'=====================================
=
        'Validate Pay Rate  Range between $4.25 and $32.50
        'Else cancel record update. Section 5


'=====================================
=
        ElseIf (Val(txtPayRate.Text) < 4.25) Or
(Val(txtPayRate.Text) > 32.5) Then
        message = message & Chr(vbKeyReturn) & "Rate of Employee
pay must be between $4.25 and $32.50"
        Action = vbDataActionCancel
        txtPayRate.SelStart = 0
        txtPayRate.SelLength = Len(txtEmployeeID)
        txtPayRate.SetFocus




'=====================================
=
        'Validate date or
```

'*Else cancel record update.* **Section 6**

```
'====================================
=
      ElseIf IsDate(txtPayDate.Text) = False Then
      message = message & Chr(vbKeyReturn) & "The Date " &
txtPayDate.Text & " is not a date."
      Action = vbDataActionCancel
      txtPayDate.SelStart = 0
      txtPayDate.SelLength = Len(txtEmployeeID)
      txtPayDate.SetFocus

      End If
'====================================
=
      ' If action is cancelled, display message box informing user with
      ' explanation. Section 7

'====================================
=
      If Action = vbDataActionCancel Then
      MsgBox message, vbOKOnly, "Input Error"
      cmdStartAdding.Visible = False
      End If
End If
End Sub
'====================================
=
'   At start-up in browse mode so text boxes should not
'   be available for input. Section 8
'====================================
=
Private Sub Form_Load()
   cmdcancel.Visible = False
   cmdUpdate.Visible = False
   txtEmployeeID.Locked = True
   txtHoursWorked.Locked = True
   txtPayRate.Locked = True
   txtPayDate.Locked = True
   datPayroll.Enabled = False
      End Sub
```

In Section 3 of the above code, the **Val ( ) Function** is used to convert a string obtained from a text box to a number. Then the number value is tested to see if it falls within a range of 100 to 1000. If the value does not fall within the range (i.e. evaluated to false), then the user is alerted by a message box that the input is invalid.

In Section 4, the isNumeric Function is used to determine if the input is a number greater than zero. The user is alerted if input is invalid. Also a range test is performed on the pay rate in Section 5 of the code.

Section 6 demonstrates the use of the isDate Function to determine if input is a valid date. And again the user is alerted if input is invalid.

To perform data validation in the above code, we used relational operators, logical operators, and the decision enabling "if – then block" construct. We discuss these new programming concepts next.

RELATIONAL AND LOGICAL OPERATORS

A condition is an expression consisting of relational operators (such as > , <, or =) that evaluates to True or to False. Conditions may also include logical operators (such as And, Or, and Not). Relational operators can be applied to numbers and to strings.

The number "a" is said to be less than the number "b" if "a" lies to the left of "b" on the number line. For example 5 < 7 and 0<1 are both True. The string "a" is said to be less than the string "b" if it precedes "b" alphabetically when using the ANSI (or ASCII) table to alphabetize their values. The order of precedence of relational operators is as follows: Digits precede uppercase letters, which precede lower case letters. Two strings are compared working from left to right, character by character, to determine which precedes the other. [Adapted from "An Introduction to Programming Using Visual Basic 6.0 by David I. Schneider, Prentice Hall Publishing Company, 1999, Page 200.]

Following is a table of relational operators, their representation in Visual Basic, and their meanings:

Visual Basic Notation	Numeric Meaning	String Meaning
=	Equal to	Identical to
< >	Unequal to	Different from
<	Less than	Precedes alphabetically

>	Greater than	Follows alphabetically
< =	Less than or equal to	Precedes alphabetically or is identical to
> =	Greater than or equal to	Follows alphabetically or is identical to [See Schneider, page 200].

Conditions can consist of variables, numeric operators, and functions. To evaluate the True or False state of a condition, first compute the numeric or string values then decide if the result is true or false.

LOGICAL OPERATORS

The three main logical operators are "**And**", "**OR**", and "**Not**". The program code example above demonstrates the use of the "Or" operator. Conditions consisting of logical operators are evaluated True or False according to the following table:

Logical Operator	True	False
Cond1 And Cond2	Both Cond1 and Cond2 are True	Otherwise false
Cond1 OR Cond2	Either Cond1 or Cond2 is True	Both Cond1 and Cond2 are False
Not Cond1	True if cond1 is false	False if cond1 is True

Parentheses used with logical operators improve program readability but are not required. If parentheses are not used, the following operator hierarchy for evaluation of logical expressions exists: "First, all arithmetic operators are carried out, and then all expressions involving >, <, and = are evaluated to true or false. The logical operators are next applied, in the following order: (1) "**Not**", then (2) "**And**", and finally (3)"**Or**."[See Schneider, page 202]

IF BLOCKS

We used the "If Block" construct in our validation routines in the data base program earlier in this chapter. The

"If-Block" construct allows a program to decide on a course of action depending on whether a condition evaluates to True or to False.

- Syntax for the IF Statement

If Condition Then
[statements]
End IF

The condition is evaluated. If it is **"True"**, then the statements in the "If Block" are executed. If the condition is **"False"**, execution jumps to the statement immediately after the End If .

Sometimes we need to execute an alternate set of statements if the condition evaluates to **"False"**. We use an **"If Then- Else"** statement if we need to make two decisions. Following is its format:

If condition Then
    [statements]
Else
    [statements]
End If

The condition is evaluated. If it is **"True"** then the statements following the **"Then"** keyword are executed. If the condition is **"False"**, then the statements following the **"Else"** keyword are executed.

There are times when we need to make three or more decisions in a block of code. We use the **"If Then- ElseIf- Then"** statement. Following is its format:

If condition Then
    [statements]
ElseIf condition2 Then
    [statements]
ElseIf condition 3 Then
    [statements]
Else
    [statements]
End If

The first condition is evaluated. If it is **"True"** the statements immediately following the beginning **"If Block"** are executed and then the program continues after the **"End If Statement"**. If the first condition is **"False"**, condition2 is evaluated. If condition2 is **"True"** the statements following the **"ElseIf statement"** are executed and then program continues after the **"End If Statement"**. If condition2 is "False", condition3 is evaluated and if **"True"** the statements in its block are executed. Execution then continues after the **"End IF Statement"**. If condition3 is **"False"**, statements following the **"Else"** keyword are executed and program continues after the **"End If statement"**.

"If statements" can be **"nested"** inside each other to handle multiple decisions.

Did you notice that the statements and the **"Else"** and **"ElseIf"** keywords were indented in the above formats? Visual Basic does not require such indentation, but it sure makes your code easier to read.

SELECT CASE BLOCKS

Nested 'If Statements" can become quite complex. A simple "Select Case Block" allows for efficient multiple decision-making and avoids complex nested if-statements. If – statements make decisions based on whether a condition evaluates True or False. Select Case Blocks make decisions depending on the value of a variable or the evaluation of an expression.

Syntax for the Select Case Block

Select Case Testexpression
Case   expressionlist-1
         Statements –block1
Case   expressionlist-2
         Statements –block 2
Case   expressionlist- n
         Statements –block n
[Case Else]
         Statements
End Select

Syntax Analysis:

When Visual Basic encounters the **Select Case** keyword, it evaluates the *"testexpression" once*. It then compares the expressionlist-1 with the testexpression. If they match, the statements in statement-block 1 are executed and then execution continues with the statement following the **End Select** statement. If testexpression does not match expressionlist-1 then expressionlist-2 is evaluated. If they match then the statements in statement-block2 are executed and execution continues after the End Select statement. Steps are repeated if testexpression does not match expressionlist-2, until all expressionlists have been tested. If none of the expressionlists match the testexpression and the Select Case contains the optional "**Case Else**", then the statements in the Case Else Block are executed and processing continues after the End Select Statement.

Each expressionlist can contain one or more of the following types of items separated by commas: (1) constant, (2) variable, (3) expression,(4) an inequality sign preceded by "**Is**" and followed by a constant, variable, or expression; and finally (5) a range expressed in the form "a" to "b", where "a" and "b" are constants, variables, or expressions and "a" is less than "b".

A FUNCTION TO CALCULATE NET PAY

LawnVan Day Care Center has a manual accounting system. LawnVan pays its employees on the 15th and 30th of each month (semi-monthly). The long-time bookkeeper has found another job and LawnVan now finds that it has to call its very expensive accountant twice a month to calculate its payroll. LawnVan has limited resources, cannot afford an outside payroll processing service, but does have Microsoft Office installed on its one computer. LawnVan asked its accountant if it was possible to use Microsoft Excel to calculate the semi-monthly payroll. Since it was the middle of tax season, the accountant agreed to provide a quick solution now, with a more comprehensive solution to follow later. This is an actual problem that I had to solve.

First I asked client for the information needed to calculate payroll: (1) Employee Name, (2) Employee Gross Pay, (3) Marital status, and (4) Number of Exemptions. And then I set up the following Worksheet for the client to use to calculate payroll.

	A	B	C	D	E	F	G	H	I
1	**Process Payroll**								
2									
3									
4	PAY PERIOD ENDING								
5									
6	LAWNVAN DAY CARE CENTER								
7	NAME	GROSS	M/STATUS	EXEMPTIONS	FED W/H	FICA	STATE W/H	TOT.DED	NET PAY
8	Employee1	$1,300.00	M	1					
9	Employee2	525.00	M	0					
10	Employee3	200.00	S	0					
11	Employee4	650.00	M	4					
12	Employee5	100.00	S	0					
13	Employee6	292.50	S	0					
14	Employee7	265.00	M	2					
15	Employee8	250.00	S	1					
16	Employee9	600.00	S	0					
17	Employee10	675.00	M	3					
18									
19									
20	Total Liability		State Tax Deposit						
21	Federal Tax W/H								
22	Social Security								
23	Federal Tax Deposit								
24									
25									

Figure 24.1

There is a command button on the Worksheet with the caption "Process Payroll". There is a cell designated for entering date of pay period ending. All the client has to do to process payroll is: (1) enter date for pay period ending and (2) click the "Process Payroll" command button.

Even though I prefer not to put controls on Worksheets, it is appropriate to use a command button in this situation. To put command button on Worksheet go to the Developer tab, Controls group and click the Design Mode icon. Next click the "Insert" icon to display available controls. Click on the ActiveX command button and draw the button on the Worksheet. Now we have to change some of the command button properties. The button does not do anything yet, later we will attach a Macro to it. So that whenever button is clicked the Macro will run.

Click the "Properties" icon in the Controls group. This is where we change the characteristics (properties) of the command button object. Change the "Name" property to something descriptive. "Name" will be used to refer to this object when we write our VBA code. Change the caption property to "Process Payroll". Make other changes as desired.

359

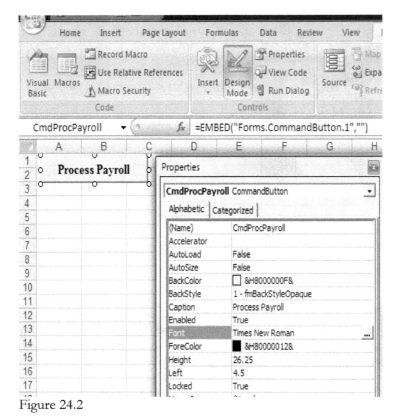

Figure 24.2

The function to calculate semi-monthly payroll uses the Year 2000 Employers Tax Guide (Circular E). None of the employees have a salary high enough to worry about the Maximum **FICA** limits. The inputs required to process the Semi-monthly payroll are: Marital status, Exemptions, and Gross Pay. The following steps are needed to design this program:

Step	Program Requirements	Function Name
1	Compute FICA Tax	FICA
2	Compute State withholding	StateTax
3	Compute Federal Tax withholding	FedTax
3.1	Adjust employee pay for exemptions	
3.2	Compute income tax for Single Employee	TaxSingle
3.3	Compute income tax for Married Employee	TaxMarried

When we finish our program we will be able to call Functions for FICA, State withholding, and Federal withholding from cells in the worksheet by using the insert function dialog box (SHIFT+F3) obtaining the functions from the User Defined category. We will also be able to call the functions by entering the = sign followed by the function name and its arguments.

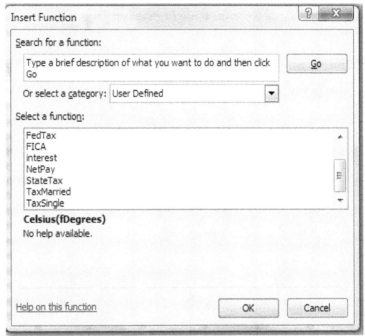

Figure 24.3

PROGRAM TO CALCULATE NET PAY

The first function we write calculates Fica withholding. Fica expense is Gross Pay x 7.65%. **Step 1.** The FICA function requires a value for grosspay to perform its calculation. Gross Pay value is supplied as an argument. We will supply as a cell reference from the Worksheet.

```
Option Explicit

'====================================
'Step 1 - Calculate FICA Tax
'Supply the single variable type "grosspay "the in argument list.
'====================================
Public Function FICA(ByVal grosspay As Single) As Single
    'Calculate FICA based on Gross Pay
    FICA = grosspay * 0.0765
End Function
```

Figure 24.5

Next we write the code to calculate State tax withheld. This function requires two arguments: Gross Pay and Number of Exemptions. The state of Illinois calculates income tax by subtracting an exemption allowance from Gross Pay and multiplying the result by 3%. Step 2. Argument values will be supplied by cell reference on the Worksheet.

```
'====================================
'Step 2 - Calculate State withholding.
'Requires grosspay and exemptions as arguments
'====================================
Public Function StateTax(ByVal grosspay As Single, _
ByVal exemptions As Integer) As Single
    'Calculate State Of Illinois Income Tax
    Dim adjpay As Single
    adjpay = grosspay - (exemptions * 68.75)
    If adjpay < 0 Then    'No tax if adjpay is less than zero
    adjpay = 0
    End If

    StateTax = 0.03 * adjpay
End Function
```

Figure 24.6

Next we calculate Federal Income Tax withheld. The FedTax Function requires three arguments: Gross Pay, Marital Status, and the number of Exemptions. First we calculate adjusted pay. Then we test to make sure it is greater than zero. This step demonstrates the use of the relational operator "less than (<)" inside a "If block." We use the "if – Then, Else "construct to calculate tax for Single persons or for Married persons. If the person is married we call the TaxMarried Function and if the person is single we call the TaxSingle Function. Step 3.

```
'=======================================
'Step 3- Calculate Federal Tax Withholdings.
'Requires grosspay, exemptions, and marital status as arguments
'=======================================
Public Function FedTax(ByVal grosspay As Single, _
ByVal exemptions As Integer, ByVal mstatus As String) As Single
    'Calculate Federal Income Tax Withheld
    Dim adjpay As Single
    adjpay = grosspay - (116.67 * exemptions) _
  '$116.67 is withholding allowance for Semi-Monthly pay

If adjpay < 0 Then           'if adjpay less than zero no tax due
        adjpay = 0
    End If

    If (mstatus = "S") Or (mstatus = "s") Then
        FedTax = TaxSingle(adjpay)
    Else
        FedTax = TaxMarried(adjpay)
    End If

End Function
```

Figure 24.7

In Steps 3.2 and 3.3 we use the Select Case Block to create a tax withholding table. Adjusted pay is compared to a range value and if it matches, tax is calculated accordingly.

Step 3.2 Calculate Federal Tax for Single Employee

```
'=======================================
'Step 3.2 - Calculate Federal tax for Single Employee
'Requires adjpay as argument
'=======================================
Public Function TaxSingle(ByVal adjpay As Single) As Single
    'Calculate Federal Tax for single person based on adjusted pay

    Select Case adjpay

    Case 0 To 110
        TaxSingle = 0
    Case 110 To 1160
        TaxSingle = 0.15 * (adjpay - 110)
    Case 1160 To 2496
        TaxSingle = 157.5 + 0.28 * (adjpay - 1160)
    Case 2496 To 5592
        TaxSingle = 531.58 + 0.31 * (adjpay - 2496)
    Case 5592 To 12081
        TaxSingle = 1491.34 + 0.36 * (adjpay - 5592)
    Case Is > 12081
        TaxSingle = 3827.38 + 0.396 * (adjpay - 12081)
    End Select

End Function
```

Figure 24.8

Step 3.3 Calculate Federal Tax for Married Employee

```
'=======================================
'Step 3.3 - Calculate Federal tax for married employee
'Requires adjpay as argument
'=======================================
Public Function TaxMarried(ByVal adjpay As Single) As Single
    'Calculate Federal Tax for married person based on adjusted pay

    Select Case adjpay

    Case 0 To 269
       TaxMarried = 0
    Case 269 To 2017
       TaxMarried = 0.15 * (adjpay - 269)
    Case 2017 To 4208
       TaxMarried = 262.2 + 0.28 * (adjpay - 2017)
    Case 4208 To 6917
       TaxMarried = 875.68 + 0.31 * (adjpay - 4208)
    Case 6917 To 12204
       TaxMarried = 1715.47 + 0.36 * (adjpay - 6917)
    Case Is > 12204
       TaxMarried = 3618.79 + 0.396 * (adjpay - 12204)
    End Select

End Function
```

Figure 24.9

Now we are ready to finish up our program with the "NetPay" Function. In this step we also demonstrate the use of the generic Format Function. Step 4.

```
End Function
'=====================================
'Step 4 - Compute take home pay
'Requires mstatus, exemptions, and grosspay as arguments
'=====================================
Public Function NetPay(ByVal mstatus As String, _
ByVal exemptions As Integer, ByVal grosspay As Single) As Single
    Application.Volatile True
    Dim statewithheld As Single
    Dim FICAwithheld As Single
    Dim Fedwithheld As Single
    Dim TotDeductions As Single
    Dim fmt As String
    fmt = "###,###,##0.00"   'design a format for data output

'Assign variables  to the functions we created above - ie. use the
'functions on the right-hand side of the equal sign

    FICAwithheld = FICA(grosspay)
    statewithheld = StateTax(grosspay, exemptions)
    Fedwithheld = FedTax(grosspay, exemptions, mstatus)
    TotDeductions = FICAwithheld + statewithheld + Fedwithheld

    NetPay = grosspay - TotDeductions
    NetPay = Format(NetPay, fmt)   ' generic format function

End Function
```

Figure 24.10

      LawnVan Day Care Center can now use an Microsoft Excel Worksheet to calculate its semi-monthly payroll. We create the worksheet, place a command button on it and write the code to automatically call the functions to calculate payroll.

CODE FOR COMMAND BUTTON

      The code attached to the command button "Process Payroll" can be found in the "Sheet1" code window. The code for the command button "Process Payroll" first calls an input box asking for the payroll period ending date. Next, functions for calculating federal tax withheld, fica withheld, state tax withheld, total deductions, and net pay are called and the results are pasted into the designated areas on the worksheet.

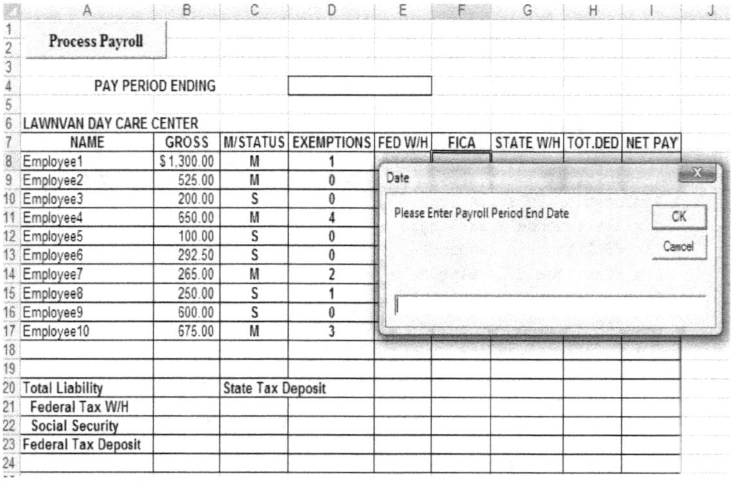

	A	B	C	D	E	F	G	H	I	J
1										
2	Process Payroll									
3										
4		PAY PERIOD ENDING								
5										
6	LAWNVAN DAY CARE CENTER									
7	NAME	GROSS	M/STATUS	EXEMPTIONS	FED W/H	FICA	STATE W/H	TOT.DED	NET PAY	
8	Employee1	$1,300.00	M	1						
9	Employee2	525.00	M	0						
10	Employee3	200.00	S	0						
11	Employee4	650.00	M	4						
12	Employee5	100.00	S	0						
13	Employee6	292.50	S	0						
14	Employee7	265.00	M	2						
15	Employee8	250.00	S	1						
16	Employee9	600.00	S	0						
17	Employee10	675.00	M	3						
18										
19										
20	Total Liability		State Tax Deposit							
21	Federal Tax W/H									
22	Social Security									
23	Federal Tax Deposit									
24										

Dialog box overlay:
Date
Please Enter Payroll Period End Date
OK
Cancel

Figure 24.11

MAIN SECTION OF COMMAND BUTTON CODE

```
Private Sub cmdPayroll_Click()
'========================================
'Main Procedure used to call Sub Procedures that calc tax
'========================================
    'Declare variables used in program

    Dim message As String
    Dim response As String
    Dim title As String

    message = "Please Enter Payroll Period End Date"
    title = "Date"
    response = InputBox(message, title)
    Range("E4").Select
    ActiveCell.FormulaR1C1 = "'" & response 'single quote means label
'Call Sub Procedures to calculate taxes

    CalcFedTax
    CalcFica
    CalcState
    CalcTotDed
    CalcNetPay
    End Sub
```

Figure 24.12

Notice the use of Sub Procedures (CalcFedTax, CalcFica, CalcState, CalcTotDed, and CalcNetPay) to call the functions needed to calculate net pay and paste the functions into the worksheet.

CALCFEDTAX PROCEDURE

Next we will look at the CalFedTax Sub Procedure to see how to reference a procedure on a worksheet that uses cells as argument inputs and how to paste the procedure to other cells on the worksheet.

Cell "E8" is the first row of our Calculate Federal Tax Withheld column. We want to paste the "FedTax" function here and copy it to the range "E9:E17". The statement "=FedTax(RC[-3], RC[-1], RC[-2])" requires some explanation. The function to calculate Federal Tax Withheld required the following arguments: Gross Pay, Exemptions, and Marital Status. On the worksheet we want to use cell references for Gross Pay, Exemptions, and Marital Status as inputs for our required arguments.

Gross Pay is in cell "B8" which is located on the same row as "E8" and three columns to the left. Thus we refer to Gross Pay as "RC[-3]". Exemptions is in the cell immediately to the left of "E8" so we refer to it as "RC[-1]". And Marital Status is 2 cells to the left of "E8", so we refer to it as "RC[-2]".

Here the column position was changing. If we wanted to change row position the reference would be R[**x**]C. Where: **x** is the relative position of the new row from the old row.

We finished up the CalcFedTax procedure with some nice number formatting.

```
'==========================================
'Procedure calculates Federal Tax withheld, calls the "FedTax( )"
'Function and pastes information in designated cells on the
'worksheet.
'==========================================
Public Sub CalcFedTax()
Dim FMT As String

    Range("E8").Value = "=FedTax(RC[-3],RC[-1],RC[-2])"
    Range("E8").Copy
    Range("E9:E17").Select
    ActiveSheet.Paste
    Application.CutCopyMode = False
    Range("E8:E17").Select
    Selection.NumberFormat = "#,##0.00"
End Sub
```

Figure 24.13

CALCFICA PROCEDURE

```
'Procedures calculates FICA and places information in designated
'cells on the worksheet.
'======================================
Public Sub CalcFica()
    Range("F8").Value = "=FICA(B8) "
    Range("F8").Copy
    Range("F9:F17").Select
    ActiveSheet.Paste
    Application.CutCopyMode = False
    Range("F9:F17").Select
    Selection.NumberFormat = "#,##0.00"

End Sub
```

Figure 24.14

CALCSTATE PROCEDURE

```
'======================================
'Procedure calculates State Tax withheld and pastes in designated
'cells on worksheet
'======================================
Public Sub CalcState()
    Range("G8").Value = "=StateTax(RC[-5],RC[-3])"
    Range("G8").Copy
    Range("G9:G17").Select
    ActiveSheet.Paste
    Application.CutCopyMode = False
    Range("G8:G17").Select
    Selection.NumberFormat = "#,##0.00"


End Sub
```

Figure 24.15

CALCTOTDED PROCEDURE

```
'========================================
'Procedure calculates Total Deductions
'and pastes in designated cells
'on the worksheet
'========================================
```

```
Public Sub CalcTotDed()
    Range("H8").Value = "=RC[-3]+RC[-2]+RC[-1]"
    Range("H8").Select
    Selection.Copy
    Range("H9:H17").Select
    ActiveSheet.Paste
    Application.CutCopyMode = False
    Range("H9:H17").Select
    Selection.NumberFormat = "#,##0.00"

End Sub
```

Figure 24.16

CALCNETPAY PROCEDDURE

After entering the payroll period ending date and hitting Process Payroll command button, our worksheet looks as follows:

	A	B	C	D	E	F	G	H	I
1									
2	Process Payroll								
3									
4					02/11/2010				
5									
6	LAWNVAN DAY CARE CENTER								
7	NAME	GROSS	M/STATUS	EXEMPTIONS	FED W/H	FICA	STATE W/H	TOT.DED	NET PAY
8	Employee1	$1,400.00	M	1	152.15	107.10	39.94	299.19	1100.81
9	Employee2	525.00	M	0	38.40	40.16	15.75	94.31	430.69
10	Employee3	200.00	S	0	13.50	15.30	6.00	34.80	165.20
11	Employee4	650.00	M	4	0.00	49.72	11.25	60.97	589.03
12	Employee5	100.00	S	0	0.00	7.65	3.00	10.65	89.35
13	Employee6	292.50	S	0	27.38	22.38	8.77	58.53	233.97
14	Employee7	265.00	M	2	0.00	20.27	3.83	24.10	240.90
15	Employee8	250.00	S	1	3.50	19.13	5.44	28.06	221.94
16	Employee9	600.00	S	0	73.50	45.90	18.00	137.40	462.60
17	Employee10	675.00	M	3	8.40	51.64	14.06	74.10	600.90
18					316.82	379.25	126.04	822.11	4,135.39
19									
20	Total Liability		State Tax Deposit		$ 822.11				
21	Federal Tax W/H	$ 316.82							
22	Social Security	$ 379.25							
23	Federal Tax Deposit	$ 696.07							
24									

Figure 24.17

LOOPING

So far we have covered two of the commonly accepted programming constructs: Sequence and Decision. Now we turn our attention to the third: Repetition or looping. Often a program will have to repeat a processing step over and over until a condition occurs. Visual Basic supplies several control structures to handle repetition.

To ensure that a loop executes properly, you must do three things:

- You must initialize the loop control variable at the beginning of the loop. Loop control variable determines how many times a loop will be repeated.
- You must test the loop control variable at either the beginning or the end of the loop.
- Loop control variable must be updated within the loop.

For - Next Control Structure

If we know exactly how many times we want to execute a block of code we can use the **For – Next** control structure. Following is its format:

For x = 1 to y [Step 1]
       Statements
Next
Analysis: | **For.** Keyword indicating the beginning of the loop.

X required loop control variable

1 Required initial value of the loop control variable

To required keyword

Y the ending value of the loop control variable.
Step optional increment value for loop control variable. If omitted, assumed to be 1.

In Figure 24.18 I used the "Debug.Print" statement to output results of the procedure to the immediate window.

```
(General)

Option Explicit

Private Sub loopex()
Dim x As Integer, y As Integer
y = 5
For x = 1 To y Step 1
Debug.Print x
Next

End Sub
```

Immediate
```
1
2
3
4
5
```

Figure 24.18

WHILE/ WEND CONTROL STRUCTURE

Another control structure is **While / Wend**

> **While condition**
>   **statements**
> **Wend**

Execution continues within the loop (processing is repeated) as long as stated condition is True. When condition becomes False, then execution continues at statement following Wend statement. The **While /Wend** is useful if we do not know the exact number of times we want to process information.

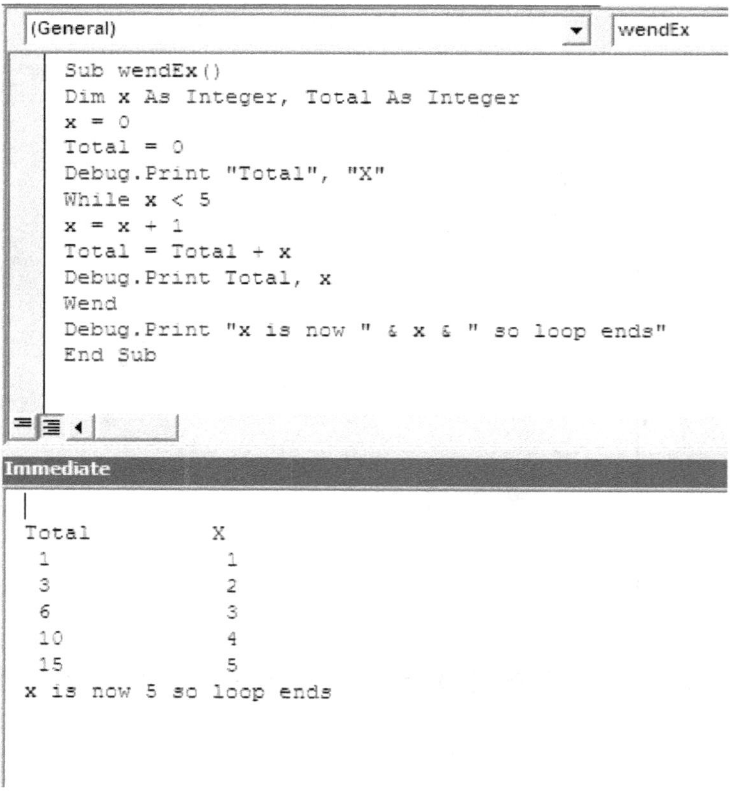

```
(General)                                          ▼   wendEx

    Sub wendEx ()
    Dim x As Integer, Total As Integer
    x = 0
    Total = 0
    Debug.Print "Total", "X"
    While x < 5
    x = x + 1
    Total = Total + x
    Debug.Print Total, x
    Wend
    Debug.Print "x is now " & x & " so loop ends"
    End Sub
```

```
Immediate

    Total             X
     1                1
     3                2
     6                3
    10                4
    15                5
    x is now 5 so loop ends
```

Figure 24.19

DO LOOPS CONTROL STRUCTURE

Do loops are useful control structures if we are uncertain as to how many times we need to process data. There are two variations of the "Do Loop".

Do While condition
Statements
Loop

Statements in the "Do While" block are executed while condition is True. When condition value changes to False, execution jumps to statement immediately after the "Loop" statement. The condition is evaluated at the top of the loop.

If we want our loop to be executed at least one time, we use the second type of "Do loop".

Do
Statements
Loop until condition

In the "Do until loop" we test the truth value of the condition at the bottom of the loop.

For Each – Next Control Structure

The most powerful looping device is the **For each – next** control structure. It allows you to loop through all of the objects in a collection or all of the elements in an array and perform the same action on each object or element. You do not have to worry about calculating how many times the loop should execute; it executes as many times as there are objects in the collection or elements in the array.

For Each [Object | Element] in [collection | array]
    Do something
Next

For example, to make each worksheet in the active workbook visible, use the following code:

For each Sheet in ActiveWorkbook.Sheets
        Sheet.Visible = True
    Next

373

PROCESSING LISTS OF DATA WITH DO LOOPS

Do loops are used to display all or selected items from lists, to search lists for specific items, and to perform calculations on numeric entries in a list. **Counters, Accumulators, and Flags** are used inside of "Do Loops" to carry out these actions. "Counters" are used to calculate the number of elements in lists. "Accumulators" are used to sum numerical values in lists. And "Flags" are Boolean data types used to record whether events have occurred. Flag information will be used after the loop terminates.

Most lists we process are read from a file. If we try to read past the end of a file we will generate an error. The **EOF (n)** function is used to tell us we have reached the end of the file and should stop trying to read it. EOF( ) is true if we have reached the end of a file and false otherwise. The argument "*n*" is the file reference number.

Here is the proper way to process a list of data contained in a file. We will discuss file manipulation in more detail in a later chapter.

- First open the file
- Test for EOF using a Do Loop
- If not EOF input data
- Process data
- Loop to second step
- Close File

For example:
Sub FileProcessingExample()
        ***Variable declarations*Open "FileName.txt" for Input As #1**
        Do while not EOF(1)
        Input #1, var1, var2,.......*var n*
Statement to process data
        Loop
Close #1
End Sub

SUMMARY

Data entered into a program should be validated and the user should be informed if he or she makes a mistake while entering data.

Classification functions **isDate( ) and isNumeric( )** are two functions Visual Basic supplies to validate user input.

Relational operators and logical operators are used in Visual Basic to make decisions on program flow. Relational operators are : less than (<), greater than (>), and Equal. Logical operators are: And, Or, and Not. The truth value of expressions created by relational and logical operators are used to control program flow.

Other **control flow constructs** are: If –then blocks, For-Next loops, Select Case blocks, For each-Next loops, and Do loops.

CHAPTER 25
WORKING WITH ARRAYS

Creating Fixed Arrays

Arrays are variables that contain multiple values. The elements of an Array (those multiple values) must be of the same data type. And just like regular variables, Arrays must be declared before they can be used. There are two types of Arrays: Fixed Arrays and Dynamic Arrays.

Following is the syntax for declaring a fixed array:

- **[Dim | Private | Public | Static] arrayname (R,C) as Data Type**

Analysis	Required. Choose among "**Dim, Private, Public, Static**" depending on desired scope and behavior as with any variable.
	Required. **Arrayname** follows the standard variable naming rules.
	Required. **(R,C)** Argument list of Rows and Columns which sets the range or size of the Array.
	Optional. **As Data Type** indicates the type of data contained in the Array. All the elements in the Array must be the same Data Type. If "As Data Type is omitted then the Array is of variant type and elements can be any VB Data Type.

Arrays can be a single dimensioned array or can be declared up to a maximum that depends on the amount of memory in your particular computer. The above syntax indicates a two-dimension Array (sometimes called a Table).

You address individual elements in an Array by index, just like referencing members of Collections. Elements in Arrays are called "Subscripts". The first index number in an Array is zero (0) by default. You can change the default index value to 1 by putting the statement **Option Base 1** in the General Declarations section of your module or form.

The lowest element in an Array is called the **Lower Bound** and the highest element in an Array is called the **Upper Bound.** There are two functions; **Lbound and Ubound,** which can be used to find the limits of an Array. Here are some examples of declaring Arrays:

Dim myArray (5) as integer	A single dimension Array with 6 elements (0 to 5), unless Option Base 1 is in use, then Array contains 5 elements.
Dim myArray (5, 6) as single	A two dimension Array with 6 rows and 7 columns unless Option Base 1 is in use, then array contains 5 rows and 6 columns.
Dim myArray (1 to 5) as integer	A single dimension Array with 5 elements with a lower bound of 1 and a upper bound of 5
Dim myArray(1 to 5, 1 to 6)	A two dimension Array with 5 rows and 6 columns whose elements are of the variant data type.

The following example demonstrates how we reference and store values in Array elements.

```
Option Base 1
Sub AnExampleofArray( )
Dim myArray (5) AS String
        MyArray(1) ="George"
        MyArray(2)="Henry"
        MyArray(3)="Susan"
        MyArray(4)="Dawn"
        MyArray(5)="Jeff"
        MsgBox MyArray(5)
End Sub
```

Figure 25.1

Multidimensional Arrays are usually used to read a table of data from a file. Nested **For....Next** statements are

377

used to process multidimensional Arrays. The following example fills a two-dimensional Array with single values:

```
Sub MultidimensionArrayExample( )
Dim j as integer, k as integer
Dim sngmultiArray ( 1 to 5, 1 to 10 ) as Single
        ' Fill array with values.
                For j= 1 to 5
' use outside loop for rows
                For K = 1 to 10
' use inside loop for columns
                    SngmultiArray ( j , k ) = j * k
                    Debug.print SngmultiArray ( j , k )
                        Next k
                        Next j
End Sub
```

DYNAMIC ARRAYS

The second type of Array, **Dynamic Array,** is used when we need to change the size of an Array during Run-time of our program. We declare a Dynamic Array in the General Procedures section of a module or form with the following syntax:

[Dim, Private, Public, or Static] arrayname ( ) As Data Type

Notice that we do not specify a range in the argument list. The "Dynamic Array" cannot be used until it is coupled with a **ReDim statement** inside a procedure. In fact you can omit the declaration in the General Declarations section of a module or form. However, be careful to spell the Array Name correctly in the procedure. "Option Explicit" does not work on "ReDim" statements and subsequent misspellings will not automatically be caught by VBA. Following is the syntax of the ReDim Statement:

ReDim [Preserve] Arrayname (subscripts) as data type

Part	Description
ReDim	Required. Keyword. Note that you can not change the type of dimension (from single to multi-dimension). Only the size (upper bound) can be changed with the required keyword ReDim.
Preserve	Optional. Keyword used to preserve the data in an existing Array when you change the size of the last dimension.
Arrayname	Required. Name of the Array; follows standard variable naming rules.
Subscripts	Required. Dimensions of an Array; up to 60 dimensions may be declared. Subscripts arguments use the following syntax: [lower to] , upper [, lower to] upper....
Type	Optional. Data type of the variable. Can be any allowed Visual Basic data type.

ReDim Statement can be used repeatedly to change the number of elements in an Array. The following example uses the "ReDim Preserve" construct to expand myArray by 10 elements while preserving existing values in the Array:

- ReDim Preserve myArray (Ubound (myArray) +10)

PASSING ARRAYS BETWEEN PROCEDURES

Array variables are subject to the same scope rules as other variables. An Array declared in a procedure is local to that procedure and is unknown to all other procedures. However, an Array, just like other variables, can be passed to another procedure. The Array name followed by an empty set of parentheses, must appear as an argument in the calling statement, and a corresponding Array name of an Array of the same data type must appear as an argument in the target procedure. We will use this concept in a sorting routine later in this chapter.

ARRAY FUNCTION

In addition to Array variables, Visual Basic supplies an Array Function which returns a variant containing an Array. This allows you to create an array during code execution without first having to declare an Array. The syntax is:

- Array (argumentlist)

The argument list is a comma-delimited list of values that are assigned to the elements of the Array contained within the Variant. If no arguments are specified, an Array of zero length is created. The <u>Array Function</u> must be assigned to a <u>variant</u> variable. For example:

Dim vVariable as variant

vVariable = Array (109)
BBKing= vVariable(79)

     The first statement above declares a variant variable "vVariable". The second statement assigns an array to the variable "vVariable" The third statement assigns the value of the 80th element of the array to variable "BBKing". The lower bound of an array created using the Array Function is always zero. Option Base statements have no effect on Array Functions.

ERASE STATEMENT

     The Erase statement reinitializes the elements of a fixed-size Array and de-allocates memory space for dynamic Arrays. The syntax follows:

Erase *arraylist*

     The required arraylist argument is one or more comma-delimited Array variables to be erased. Erase sets the elements of a fixed Array as follows:

Type of Array	Effect of Erase on Fixed Array
Fixed numeric Array	Sets each element to zero
Fixed string Array (variable length)	Sets each element to zero-length string ("")
Fixed string Array (fixed length)	Sets each element to zero
Fixed variant array	Sets each element to empty
Array of user-defined types	Sets each element as if it were a separate variable.
Array of objects	Sets each element to the special value

     Sometimes we need to know if a variable is an Array. Using the **IsArray Function** tells us if a variable is an Array. The **isArray Function** returns a Boolean value; True if variable is an Array, otherwise False. The syntax is as follows:

•   IsArray (variablename)
The required variablename argument is an identifier specifying a variable.

PARAMETER ARRAYS

Earlier we included the keyword **ParamArray** in the argument list of a Procedure. The ParamArray keyword represents a **Parameter Array.** A <u>parameter Array</u> can be used to pass an Array of arguments to a procedure. You don't have to know the number of elements in the Array when you define the procedure. The Array must be declared as a Variant data type and it must be the **last** argument in the procedure argument list.

The following example demonstrates its use:

```
Sub MultipleArguments(strName as string, ParamArray
intScores
() _
As Variant )
Dim iInteger as  Integer
For iInteger= 0 to Ubound(intScores( ))
        Debug.Print intScores( iInteger)  'Prints out the
integers only
Next iInteger
End Sub
'=====================================

'The following examples show how you can call this
procedure.
'=====================================

Sub ParamArrayExample()
MultipleArguments "Thomas", 57, 5, 21, 31, 8
End Sub
```

```
Option Explicit

Sub MultipleArguments(strName As String, ParamArray intScores() _
    As Variant)

Dim iInteger As Integer

For iInteger = 0 To UBound(intScores())
    Debug.Print intScores(iInteger)    'Prints out the integers only
Next iInteger
End Sub
'=========================================
'The following examples show how you can call this procedure.
'=========================================
Sub ParamArrayExample()

MultipleArguments "Thomas", 57, 5, 21, 31, 8
End Sub
```

nmediate
```
 57
 5
 21
 31
 8
```

Figure 25.2

SORTING ARRAYS

An Array is said to be ordered if its elements are in ascending or descending order. A **sort** is an algorithm for ordering an array. In this chapter we will discuss two of the more common sort algorithms, the **bubble sort** and the **Shell sort.** Both the bubble sort and the Shell Sort are in-place sorts: as neither method consumes extra memory while processing because they simply swap values within the array.

BUBBLE SORT

The simplest of the two sorting algorithms is the bubble sort. It is fast for Arrays with 25 or less elements. The bubble sort algorithm consists of comparing pairs of elements according to their indexes and swapping them if the element with the smaller index is greater than the element with the larger index. After one pass through the Array, the largest element should have moved to the last position in the Array. Therefore, the second pass does not have to consider it and so requires one less comparison. At the end of the second pass, the last two items will be in their proper position. Repeat these steps as you travel through the Array, each time leaving off the last element plus the number of passes through the Array. Where **n** is the number of elements in the Array, the total number of comparisons for a bubble sort is **Σn**. As the size of the Array gets bigger the number of comparisons becomes quite large and thus the sort becomes slower. For example, an Array with 10 elements requires 55 comparisons (10+9+8+7+6+5+4+3+2+1).

The pseudocode for a bubble sort of an array of n items follows. Notice that it requires the use of nested "For loops". The outer loop (For J=1 to n-1) controls the number of passes through the Array. The inner loop (For K=1 to n-J) controls the number of comparisons.

For j = 1 to n-1
    For k = 1 to n-j
        If [kth and (k+1)st items are out of order]
        then [interchange them]
    Next k
Next j

We can put this algorithm into a Sub Procedure so that it will be available whenever we need to sort small lists. For the purposes of the following example we will pass an Array of variant data type to the Sub Procedure. The following routine results in an ascending sort. To covert to a descending sort replace the greater than relational operator in the statement "If myArray(k) > myArray(k+1) Then" with the less than relational operator. So the statement becomes "If myArray(k) < myArray(k+1) Then". Also the routine can be expanded to handle two dimensional Arrays.

In the following example we first write the bubble sort routine as a function. Next we test the sort routine by passing to it an Array Function. The debug.print statement prints the sorted Array to the immediate window. We often use the immediate window to debug programs or just to help us see how the program is processing. Type in the following code and review the results.

```
Option Explicit
Option Base 1
'*****************************************************

'*  Bubble Sort Routine
'*  The outer loop controls the number of passes, Assign
'*  to variable J, the inner loop controls the number of
```

383

```
'*   comparisons, assign to variable k
'*********************************************************
Function Bubblesort(myArray As Variant)
    Dim temp As Variant, j As Integer, k As Integer, n As
Integer
    n = UBound(myArray)
    For j = 1 To n - 1
        For k = 1 To n - j
        If myArray(k) > myArray(k + 1) Then 'this yields an
ascending sort
        temp = myArray(k)
        myArray(k) = myArray(k + 1)
        myArray(k + 1) = temp
        End If
        Next k
    Next j
End Function

Sub CreateArray()
Dim myArray As Variant, i As Integer
'For example we will use the Array function to create an Array
myArray = Array(21, 10, 31, 26, 3, 5, 8)
'Sort the array and display the values in order
Bubblesort myArray
    For i = 1 To UBound(myArray)
        Debug.Print myArray(i)  'print to immediate window
    Next i
End Sub
```

Now let's look at the immediate window to see if it works.

```
Sub CreateArray()
Dim myArray As Variant, i As Integer
'For example we will use the Array function to create an Array
myArray = Array(21, 10, 31, 26, 3, 5, 8)

'Sort the array and display the values in order
Bubblesort myArray
    For i = 1 To UBound(myArray)
        Debug.Print myArray(i)   'print to immediate window
    Next i

End Sub
```

mediate

```
3
5
8
10
21
26
31
```

Figure 25.3

SHELL SORT

For sorting Arrays with 25 or more elements, it is better to use the **Shell Sort Algorithm.** The "shell sorting" algorithm was invented by Donald L. Shell. Sorting is achieved by comparing distant items first and then working down to nearby items.

The spacing of the interval separating compared items is called the **gap.** Various spacing may be used to implement the Shell Sort. The Array is first sorted with large spacing, the spacing is reduced, and the Array is sorted again. On the final sort, spacing is one.

There is general agreement on the theory behind the "Shell Sort Algorithm". However, there is considerable discussion on how to calculate the **gap.** In his book, "The Art of Computer Programming, Volume 3, Sorting and Searching, Addison Wesley, Reading Ma, 1998" Donald Knuth recommends that spacing **h** for any Array of Size **N** should be based on the following formula:

-
- Let h(1) =1, h(s+1)=3h(s)+1, and stop with h(t)

385

When h(t+2) >=N

Thus, values of h are computed as follows

h(1) = | 1
h(2) = | (3 x 1)+1 = 4
h(3) = | (3 x 4)+1 = 13
h(4) = | (3 x13)+1 = 40
h(5) = | (3 x 40)+1=121

To sort 100 items, we first find h(s) such that h(s) >= 100. For 100 items h(5) is selected. Our final value h(t) is two steps lower or h(3). Therefore our sequence of **h** values (i.e. spacing interval) will be 13-4-1 through successive passes through the Array. Once the initial **h** value has been determined, subsequent values may be calculated using the formula **h(s-1) = h(s) / 3.**

This analysis of Knuth's reasoning was borrowed from a paper written by Thomas Nieman titled **"Sorting and Searching Algorithms: A CookBook".** If you are interested you can download the paper for free from:" http://members.xoom.com/thomasn/y **man.htm" or "e-mail: Thomasn@ jps.net".**

Another approach to sorting Arrays with the "Shell Sort" algorithm, can be found in an article written by Dan Fox and published in "The Visual Basic Programmer's Journal (April 2000), Pages 76 –81, It takes All Sorts". Dan Fox calls the **gap** a **"skip count"** and he recommends an initial skip count of one-third of the distance through the Array. He then divides the skip count by three as he moves through additional iterations. Dan's version of the "Shell Sort" algorithm, with code, forms, etc. can be downloaded for free from www.vbpj.com. There is a lot of really good research material available for free on the web.

David I. Schneider has by far the easiest approach to the "Shell Sort" method.[Schneider, pages 355-358] Here is Schneider's version:

1) Begin with a gap of **g = int (N / 2)** where **N** is the **total number of elements in the Array.**
2) Compare items 1 and 1+g, 2 and 2+g ....n-g and g
   Swap any pairs that are out of order
3) Repeat step 2 until no swaps are made for gap **g**
4) Halve the value of **g**
5) Repeat steps 2, 3, and 4 until the **g** is 0.

Since, I plan to re-use over and over any clever algorithm I come across, I wrote a Function to which I can pass Arrays of any data type. First set the lower bound of Arrays to 1 by using the Option Base 1 statement. We will write the Shell Sort function and then we will write a Sub Procedure to test it. The Sub Procedure CreateNewArray() uses the Array Function to create a variant array. The Array is assigned to "myArray" and passed as an argument when we call the "ShellSort" function. See the following code:

```
Option Explicit
Option Base 1
Function ShellSort(myArray As Variant)
Dim gap As Integer, fldone As Boolean, i As Integer, k As
Integer
Dim temp As Variant, n As Integer
'======================================
=
'First find the total number of elements in the array ie.
UBound. Use
'to calculate initial gap. Make comparisons first element and
first 'element
' + gap, 2nd element to 2nd element + gap until nth element-
gap and 'gap
'Swap any pairs that are out of order. Repeat until no swaps
are made 'for gap.
'======================================
=
n = UBound(myArray)
gap = Int(n / 2)
Do While gap >= 1
   Do
      fldone = True
      For i = 1 To n - gap
      If myArray(i) > myArray(i + gap) Then
         temp = myArray(i)
         myArray(i) = myArray(i + gap)
         myArray(i + gap) = temp
         fldone = False
      End If
      Next i
   Loop Until fldone = True
'======================================
=
```

' Now that there are no more swaps for this inteval, halve the value of 'gap and
' repeat the above loop. Do until gap is 0.
'====================================

```
    gap = Int(gap / 2)
Loop
End Function

Sub CreateNewArray()
Dim myArray As Variant, i As Integer
'For example we will use the Array Function to create an Array and assign it to
'a variant variable "myArray"
myArray = Array("Jeff", "Vernice", "Vanessa", "Jennifer", "Andrew", "Markita", "Briana", "Autum", "Mark", "Emiliano")
'Sort the array and display value in order , print in immediate window
ShellSort myArray
    For i = 1 To UBound(myArray)
    Debug.Print myArray(i)
    Next i
End Sub
```

The above Sub Procedure, <u>CreateNewArray ()</u>, is used to test the above function. Below is the output to the immediate window showing that our Function works as intended.

Figure 25.4

Searching Arrays

The main reason we sort Arrays is to make it easy to search them and extract specific elements. We will discuss two search methods: the **Sequential Search method and the Binary Search method.**

Suppose we have a payroll application. We will enter employee information into a file. Later we will need to extract employee information (marital status, number of exemptions, pay rate, and misc. additional deductions) to process payroll and maybe also for reporting purposes.

On program start-up we read the file and copy it into an Array. We would then sort the Array into ascending order. Next we would ask the program (using a key), to extract the information we need to process the payroll for a specific employee. If the number of employees in our Array was 100 or less, we could start at the beginning of the Array and search sequentially until we found the employee or until we reached the end of the Array. The wait time for performing the search would not be noticeable. However, if the Array was bigger than 100 we may notice the wait.

SEQUENTIAL SEARCHES

For searches of Arrays of 100 or less you can use the following algorithm :

- **Function SequentialSearch (myArray as variant, int lb, int ub, int key)**

[lb is the lower bound of the array, ub is the upper bound of the array]
dim i as integer
For i = lb to ub
      If myArray (i) = key then
      SequentialSearch= key
      End if
Next i
MsgBox " Employee not in file"
End Function

Following is an example of the sequential search method written as a function.
Option Explicit
Option Base 1
'=====================================
=

389

```
'  Program performs sequential search
'  lb is lower bound of array, ub is upper bound of array, key
is search
'  criteria.
'=====================================
=
Function SequentialSearch(myArray As Variant, lb As Integer,
ub As Integer, _
    ByVal key As Variant)
    Dim i As Integer
    i = 0
    Do
    i = i + 1
     Loop Until (myArray(i) = key) Or i = ub
       If myArray(i) = key Then
       SequentialSearch = key
       Else
       MsgBox " item not found in file"
       ' ok item was not in the file so get out
       End If
    End Function


'=====================================
=
'  Sub Procedure to test sequential search function
'=====================================
=
Private Sub testsequentialsearch()
Dim lb As Integer, ub As Integer, key As String, i As Integer
Dim myArray(10)
myArray(1) = "Jefferson"
myArray(2) = "Vernice"
myArray(3) = "Vanessa"
myArray(4) = "Jennifer"
myArray(5) = "Andrew"
myArray(6) = "Markita"
myArray(7) = "Briana"
myArray(8) = "Autumn"
myArray(9) = "Mark"
myArray(10) = "Emiliano"
lb = LBound(myArray)
ub = UBound(myArray)
key = "Vernice"
MsgBox SequentialSearch(myArray, lb, ub, key) _
    & " was found in the file."
```

End Sub

     To make the sub procedure more flexible, I added an inputbox to get the "Key" instead of hard coding key as "Vernice". For example replace line "Key = "Vernice" with line "Key = inputbox ("Who are you looking for?")".

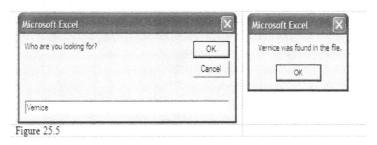

Figure 25.5

BINARY SEARCHES

     For ordered Arrays bigger than 100 elements we will want to use the powerful **binary search method.** The algorithm for a binary search follows:

```
Function BinarySearch( myArray as variant, lb as integer, ub as integer,
        Key as variant)
Do forever
        Dim M as integer
        M= int( (lb + ub) / 2 )
        If key < myArray (M) then
        Ub = M-1
        Else if key > myArray(M) then
        Lb=M +1
        Else
        Return myArray(M)
        If lb >ub then
        MsgBox "Item is not in the file" '(search was not
successful )
End Function
```

     Variables lb and ub keep track of the lower bound and upper bound of the array, respectively. Begin by examining the middle element of the array. If the key we are searching for is less than the middle element, then it must be in the top half of the array. We can discard the bottom of the

391

array and perform our search in the top half. So we set ub to (m-1) to restrict our next iteration through the loop to the top half of the array. If the key is greater than the middle element, then what we are looking for must be in the bottom half of the array. Thus we set lb to (m+1) to restrict our next iteration through the loop to the bottom half of the array. Next we calculate the middle element of the half of the array we retained and repeat the comparisons, repeating this step until we find the key or can no longer divide the Array. Each iteration requires fewer comparisons.

The binary search method is fast. Given an Array of 2,000 items we can narrow the search to 1,000 elements in one comparison, and down to 500 elements with the second comparison. Type in the following code and test it on your own.

```
Option Explicit

Option Base 1
'====================================
=
'  Program performs Binary search
'  lb is lower bound of array, ub is upper bound of array, key
is search
'  criteria.
'====================================
=
Function BinarySearch(myArray As Variant, lb As Integer, ub
As Integer, _
    ByVal key As Variant)
    Dim M As Integer, i As Integer
    M = 0
    i = 0
    Do
        M = Int((lb + ub) / 2)
        If key < myArray(M) Then
        ub = M - 1
        Do
            i = i + 1
            'perform the search on top half
            Loop Until myArray(i) = key Or i = ub
            If myArray(i) = key Then          'Found it, get out
            BinarySearch = key
            Exit Function
            Else
```

```vba
        MsgBox "Item not in file"
        Exit Function
        End If
    Else
'perform search on bottom half
    lb = M + 1
    Do
    i = i + 1
        'perform the search on bottom half
    Loop Until myArray(i) = key Or i = ub
        If myArray(i) = key Then
'Found it, get out
        BinarySearch = key
        Exit Function
        Else
        MsgBox "Item not in file"
        Exit Function
        End If
    End If
    Loop
  End Function


'=====================================
=
'  Sub Procedure to test binary search function
'=====================================
=
Private Sub testbinarysearch()
Dim lb As Integer, ub As Integer, key As String, i As Integer
Dim myArray(10)
myArray(1) = "Jefferson"
myArray(2) = "Vernice"
myArray(3) = "Vanessa"
myArray(4) = "Jennifer"
myArray(5) = "Andrew"
myArray(6) = "Markita"
myArray(7) = "Briana"
myArray(8) = "Autumn"
myArray(9) = "Mark"
myArray(10) = "Emiliano"
lb = LBound(myArray)
ub = UBound(myArray)
key = inputbox("Who are you looking for?")
```

```
BinarySearch myarray 1, 10, key
'send array to sort routine
MsgBox BinarySearch(myArray, lb, ub, key) _
& " was found in the file."
End Sub
```

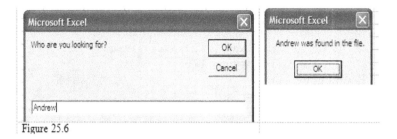

Figure 25.6

TWO-DIMENSIONAL ARRAYS

Two- Dimensional Arrays are used to hold the
contents of a table of several rows and columns. The same
rules that apply to other array variables apply to Two-
Dimensional Arrays. Two-Dimensional Arrays have two
subscripts, each with its own range. The first subscript refers
to the number of rows in the table and the second subscript
refers to the number columns in the table.

Syntax for Two-Dimensional Arrays

Dim arrayname (m1 to m2, n1 to n2) as datatype

Where m1 is the first row , m2 is the last row, and n1
is the first column and n2 is the last column.
We can read data from a file into a two-dimensional
form-level array using a pair of nested loops. The outer loop
controls input of row values and the inner loop controls input
of column values.
Here is an example of reading a file with ten records,
(each record containing an employee name and social security
number), into a two-dimensional array. Thus the array would
need to have 10 rows and 2 columns.

```
Option Base 1
Dim employee ( 10, 2 )  in general declarations section
Private sub ReadinData ( )
        Dim row as integer, col as integer
        Open "filename.txt" for input as #1
```

```
For row = 1 to 10
        For col = 1 to 2
        Input #1, employee(row, col)
        Next col
    Next row
    Close #1
End Sub
```

SUMMARY

Arrays are variables that contain multiple values of the same data type. Arrays can be fixed or dynamic. And Arrays can be single dimensional or multi-dimensional with up to 60 dimensions. Two-dimensional arrays are used to hold tables (rows and columns).

Array variables are used just like regular variables. They follow the standard variable rules for naming and data declaration. Arrays can be passed between procedures.

We sometimes need to search arrays for specific items. It is helpful if the array is an ordered array. An array is said to be ordered if it is sorted (arranged) in ascending or descending order. Two of the more common sorting algorithms are: Bubble sort algorithm and Shell sort algorithm. Use the bubble sort algorithm for small arrays and the Shell sort algorithm for arrays with 100 or more elements.

There are many methods to search for a specific item in an ordered array. Two of the more common methods are the sequential search and the binary search. Use the sequential search method on small arrays. Use the binary search method on arrays of 100 elements or more.

CHAPTER 26
CUSTOMIZING MICROSOFT EXCEL

In this chapter we discuss Workbook and Worksheet Properties and Methods, Creating Custom Dialog Boxes, Active-X Controls, and the Range Object.

MICROSOFT EXCEL INTERFACE CUSTOMIZATION RULE

Whenever you customize the Microsoft Excel interface, you must return the interface to its original state after your application finishes execution.

WORKSHEET – BASED FORMS

In Microsoft Excel we create Forms by manipulating Ranges, Worksheets, Windows, and Workbooks. Most of the time form creation is done manually. We can also use VBA code to create worksheet forms during run time.

USING THE RANGE OBJECT TO CREATE FORMS

Later in this chapter is a form created in Microsoft Excel. It is almost an exact replica of the Illinois Sales Tax Return. See Figure 26.2. In that form we manipulate several Range Objects including: cell width, font height, horizontal Alignment, interior, locked, number Format, and row height. We access the range formatting properties from the "Home" tab on the Ribbon. As an experienced Microsoft Excel user you already know how to design Worksheet based forms so what we discuss next will not be new to you. The starting point is the "Format Cells" dialog box.

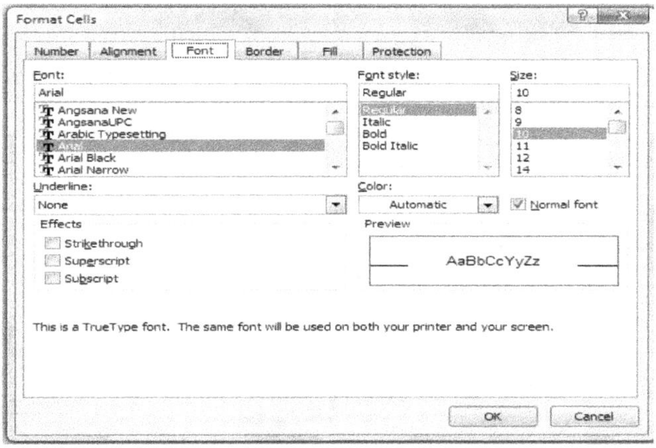

Figure 26.1

Using this dialog box, we can manually manipulate number properties, alignment properties, font properties, border properties, patterns properties, and protection properties. Clicking the tabs for any of the aforementioned properties makes the individual properties in that group accessible for change.

397

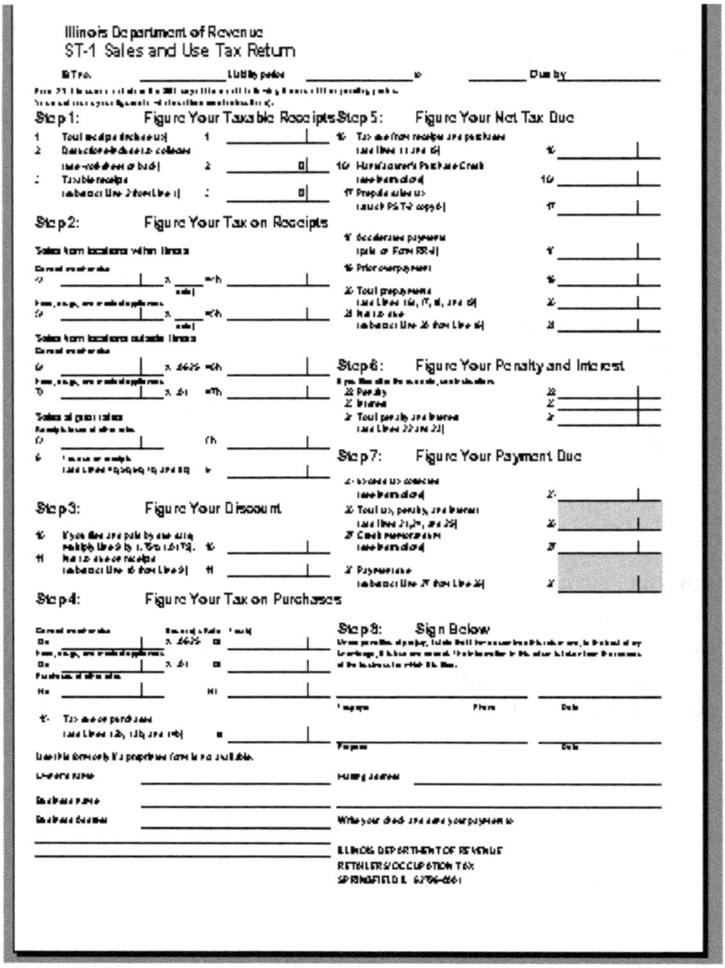

Figure 26.2

MANIPULATING THE WORKSHEET OBJECT TO DESIGN FORMS

To manipulate the worksheet object we need to know what properties, methods, and events are available. Information on any object's properties, methods, and events are available in the Object Browser. Return to the Visual Basic Editor and press the F2 key to invoke the Object Browser. Next select Worksheet in the "Classes" pane and press the F1 key. On-line help now appears with information on properties, methods, events, and examples for the selected object. After selecting the Worksheet object, the Worksheet method "Calculate" was selected. Then F1 key was pressed to display help screen for the Calculate Method.

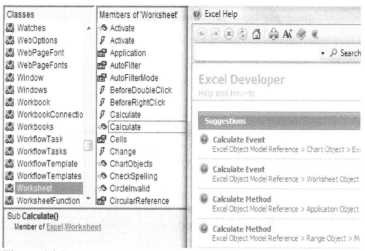

Figure 26.3

The following **Worksheet Properties** are used to design forms:

- **Name:** The name of the worksheet, is string data type
- **ProtectContents:** Boolean , if true, the cells of the worksheet are protected and are read only
- **ProtectDrawingObjects:** Boolean, if true, shapes on the worksheet are protected
- **ProtectionMode:** Boolean, if true, the worksheet is protected from changes made by user only. VBA can still be used to manipulate objects on worksheet. If false, worksheet is protected from both user and VBA manipulation.
- **ProtectScenarios:** Boolean, if true, worksheet scenarios are protected.
- **ScrollArea Property:** Returns or sets the range where scrolling is allowed. Use the A1-style range reference. Cells outside the scroll area cannot be selected. This is a Read/write property of String data type. The ScrollArea Property is useful in hiding cells from the user. For example: **Worksheets(1).ScrollArea= _ "A1:F10"** limits scroll area to "A1:F10".

399

- **Visible:** Used to display or hide the worksheet. This property has 3 possible values:

True	Worksheet is visible
False	Worksheet is not visible, but user can make it visible by choosing the sheet command from the format menu and then selecting Unhide.
XlVeryHidden	Worksheet is not visible, and user cannot make it visible. Only VBA can make visible by setting "Visible Property" to true in code

The following **Worksheet methods** are used to design forms:

- **Activate:** Activates the worksheet. Both the Activate method and the Select method (discussed below) can be used to change focus from one worksheet to another.
- **Protect:** Protects worksheet from changes made by users, accepts five arguments:

1. Password	A string used as case-sensitive password; if a password is specified, cannot unprotect worksheet without the password.
2. drawingObjects	Boolean, if true, shapes on worksheet are protected.
3. contents	Boolean, if true, contents of cells in the worksheet are protected.
4. scenarios	Boolean, if true, scenarios on worksheet are protected.
5. userInterfaceOnly	Boolean, if true, worksheet is protected from changes made by user only. If this argument is omitted, worksheet is protected from user and from VBA code.

- **Select:** Activates the worksheet. Select is used to change focus from one worksheet to another.

- **SetBackgroundPicture:** Takes one argument: "FileName", a string that points to the path of a graphic that will be used as a tiled background for the worksheet. It is a good idea to use this method on the "Home Page" of your application. For example:

   Worksheets(1).SetBackgroundPicture "C:\Filename"

- **Unprotect:** Unprotects the worksheet. Unprotect has one argument- a case sensitive string representing a password, if a password was used to protect the worksheet.

MANIPULATING THE WINDOW OBJECT TO DESIGN FORMS

The window object affects the way a worksheet appears. Most window properties can be set manually from the Ribbon.

After window properties are set, they are saved with the workbook file when the workbook file is saved.

Some window properties affect only the currently selected worksheet, while other window properties affect all worksheets in the workbook. First we will discuss **window properties that affect only the currently selected worksheet.**

DisplayGridlines	Boolean, if true gridlines are displayed on the worksheet.
DisplayHeadings	Boolean, if true, row and column headings are shown on left side and across top of worksheet.
DisplayZeros	Boolean, if true, zero values are shown. If false, zero values are not shown. True by default.
ScrollColumn	Number of worksheet column that appears at the far left of the window.
ScrollRow	Number of the worksheet row that appears at the top of the window.

401

DisplayFormulas	Boolean, if true, cell formulas are shown, if false, cell values are shown in the worksheet.

To manipulate the above properties in code, you must first make a window active. See the following code example that turns off Gridlines on the first worksheet in the first workbook:

```
Workbooks("Book1.xls").Worksheets("Sheet1").Activate
ActiveWindow.DisplayGridlines = False
```

Next we will discuss window **properties that affect an entire workbook.**

Window Caption	Displays name of active workbook in the title bar. For example to return to default caption of the window object set its caption property to **ActiveWorkbook.Name**
DisplayHorizontalScrollBar	Boolean, if true, horizontal scroll bar is shown on bottom edge of worksheet.
DisplayVerticalScrollBar	Boolean, if true, vertical scroll bar is shown on right edge or worksheet.
DisplayWorkbooktabs	Boolean, if true, sheet tabs are shown on bottom of workbook.
Height	Height of window in points (1/72 inch.)
Left	Distance of left edge of window from left edge of Microsoft Excel workspace in points.
Width	Width of the window in points.

WindowState	XlNormal = Normal window size, XlMaximized=window is maximized to fill entire workspace, XlMinimized =window is minimized and displayed as an icon in the workspace.

Examples of setting the above properties follows:
ActiveWindow.DisplayHorizontalScrollBar = True
ActiveWindow.WindowState = xlMaximized

ACTIVE-X CONTROLS

Active-X controls are pre-built objects that can be added to worksheets, userforms, and charts. They extend the functionality of Visual Basic for Application programs. Since they are objects, Active-X controls have properties, methods, and events. In chapter 24 we discussed how to add a command button to a worksheet. Here we will discuss other controls that can be added to a worksheet.

Many controls share the same properties and events. Following are common properties and events of control objects:

Common Control Properties

Name	CodeName. Name of the control you will reference in code or set manually at design time.
AutoSize	Boolean. If true, control will reduce itself to smallest possible size to display its contents.
Enabled	Boolean. If true, user can interact with the control. False, user cannot interact with control nor can control receive focus.

Font	Font name, style, size of text in the control.
Left, Top, Width, and Height	Position and size of the control expressed in points.
Locked	Boolean. If true and worksheet protection for objects is on, user cannot edit the control in design mode.
Visible	Boolean. If true, object is displayed at run-time. False, object is hidden at run-time.

<u>*Common Control Events*</u>

Click	Occurs when user clicks and releases mouse button over the control.
DblClick	Occurs when user double-clicks the mouse button over the control.
KeyPress	When control has focus, occurs whenever an ANSI key is pressed.
GotFocus, LostFocus	Occurs when the control gets and loses input focus.
MouseDown, MouseMove, and MouseUp	Indicates actions of the mouse, pressing, moving, and releasing mouse button.

For example we can change properties of a command button by clicking the "Properties" icon on the Developer tab. Resulting dialog box lists properties which can be changed.

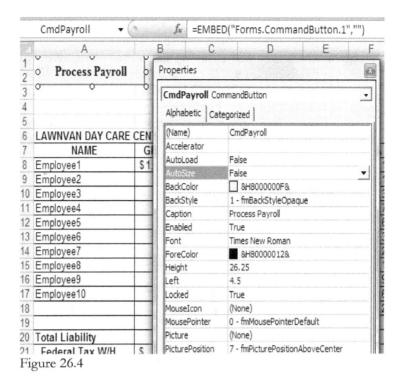

| CmdPayroll | ▼ | | f_x | =EMBED("Forms.CommandButton.1","") |

	A		B	C	D	E	F
1							
2	**Process Payroll**						
3							
4							
5							
6	LAWNVAN DAY CARE CEN						
7	NAME		G				
8	Employee1		$1				
9	Employee2						
10	Employee3						
11	Employee4						
12	Employee5						
13	Employee6						
14	Employee7						
15	Employee8						
16	Employee9						
17	Employee10						
18							
19							
20	Total Liability						
21	Federal Tax W/H	S					

Properties

CmdPayroll CommandButton ▼

Alphabetic | Categorized

(Name)	CmdPayroll
Accelerator	
AutoLoad	False
AutoSize	False
BackColor	☐ &H8000000F&
BackStyle	1 - fmBackStyleOpaque
Caption	Process Payroll
Enabled	True
Font	Times New Roman
ForeColor	■ &H80000012&
Height	26.25
Left	4.5
Locked	True
MouseIcon	(None)
MousePointer	0 - fmMousePointerDefault
Picture	(None)
PicturePosition	7 - fmPicturePositionAboveCenter

Figure 26.4

The first controls we are going to discuss are the command button control, label control, textbox control, and image control. XYZ Company needs a quick way to calculate straight-line depreciation on its fixed assets. The desired interface should look like the following:

Figure 26.5

405

This interface is from a small straight line depreciation program which was written in regular Visual Basic. We will duplicate this program inside of Microsoft Excel using Visual Basic for Applications. We will be using an Microsoft Excel worksheet as our form.

Figure 26.6 shows our Microsoft Excel worksheet formatted to appear like the form above with embedded labels, text boxes, and command buttons.

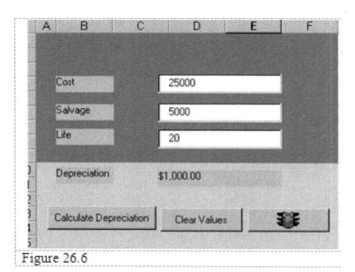

Figure 26.6

As a matter of preference, I would use a userform rather than a worksheet form for this application. We discuss userforms later in this chapter. I use worksheet forms to duplicate forms for filing with regulatory bodies, for example the Illinois Sales Tax Return (Figure 26.2). To get information from users for processing, custom dialog forms are better than Worksheet forms.

Let's analyze the creation of the form shown in Figure 26.6. From the Developer tab I selected the Design Mode icon then clicked the "Insert" icon to display available ActiveX controls. Next, the labels, textboxes, and command buttons were each selected and drawn on selected areas of the Worksheet. Then I selected each control and changed its name property. For the command buttons and labels I also changed caption properties. Remember that we need to select the Properties icon on the Developer's tab for each control. Next, I double-clicked each command button and wrote VBA code for each button's click event.

I set the TakeFocusOnClick property on all of the command buttons to false, to prevent the command buttons from receiving focus. This is a good idea for command buttons on worksheets and charts, as many properties and methods of other Microsoft Excel objects cannot be manipulated with code while a command button on a sheet has focus.

Label controls are usually used to provide a description of another control. I like to also use labels as containers for output. Labels cannot accept input from the user, therefore they are perfect for output.

Notice that all of the labels are the same size, and are aligned perfectly. I used the left and top properties of the labels to position them where I wanted on the sheet. And I used the height and width property to make them all the same size.

The command button to the farthest right has a picture. I used the red stoplight to signify stop execution and exit the program. To get a picture on the command button, select the command button picture property and enter the path to the icon location. Since I wanted the picture centered on the command button, I set the picturePosition property to "7-PicturePositionAboveCenter.

After creating the user interface it was time to write some VBA code to calculate straight line depreciation and to display the results in a label formatted as currency. So I returned to the VBE and entered the following code.

```
Option Explicit
'*****************************************************
'* Straight line depreciation program will use built-in straight line
'*depreciation function
'* SLN(cost, salvage, life ) all three variables are doubles.
'* Declare them as module level variables
'*****************************************************
Private mdblCost As Double
Private mdblSalvage As Double
Private mdblLife As Double
Private mdblDepreciation As Double
'*****************************************************
'Code for the "Clear values" command button
```

```
'*********************************************************
Private Sub cmdClear_Click()
    txtCost.Text = vbNullString
    txtSalvage.Text = vbNullString
    txtlife.Text = vbNullString
    lblAnswer.Caption = vbNullString

End Sub
'*********************************************************
'Code for "Calculates Depreciation" command button
'*********************************************************
Private Sub cmdDeprec_Click()
    mdblCost = txtCost.Value
    mdblSalvage = txtSalvage.Value
    mdblLife = txtlife.Value
    mdblDepreciation = SLN(mdblCost, mdblSalvage,
mdblLife)
    lblAnswer.Caption = Format(mdblDepreciation,
"Currency")
End Sub
'*********************************************************
'Code for Exit Program command button
'*********************************************************
Private Sub cmdExit_Click()
    ThisWorkbook.Close
End Sub
```

The caption property of lblAnswer (CodeName for the output label) was used to display the straight- line depreciation result. We changed the name of each of the controls on the worksheet because we needed to refer to the controls in code. A descriptive name helps us remember which control we need to manipulate.

We used **text boxes** to gather input from the user for the cost of the fixed asset, its salvage value, and for the life of the fixed asset. Text boxes let users type information into predefined containers. Text boxes can be used to get simple input or they can be used to create small word processors with multiple lines and word-wrap capability.

Common Textbox Properties:

Text	Text is the default property. It sets or returns the text contained in the control.

MultiLine	Boolean. If true, textbox can display multiple lines of text.
MaxLength	Integer. Used to set the maximum number of characters the textbox will accept. Set to 0 to allow any number of characters.
PasswordChar	A single character used to mask the entry of passwords. If a character is assigned to PasswordChar, this character will be displayed instead of the actual text entered into the control.

As a final touch to the user interface, I selected two different ranges of cells and set each range to a different interior color.

CREATING CUSTOM DIALOG BOXES

Custom dialog boxes are created with userforms and are often used when a limited amount of information is wanted from the user. In VBA 5.0 userforms are modal which means that they must be handled before user is allowed to take any other action. This limitation was removed in VBA 6.0. We can place all of the controls from the control toolbar on userforms.

Let's create our first userform. Fire up Microsoft Excel and invoke the Visual Basic Editor. Select **Insert Userform** and your screen should look Figure 26.7.

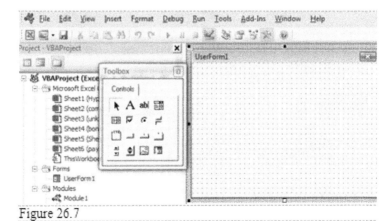

Figure 26.7

The userform appears in its own window. A toolbox containing all the controls that can be drawn on the userform is provided. There is a property window available to change the properties of the userform and the properties of any control drawn on the userform. And since the userform is an object, it is added to the project window. You can right-click anywhere in the userform to display a short-cut menu and choose properties to display the property window.

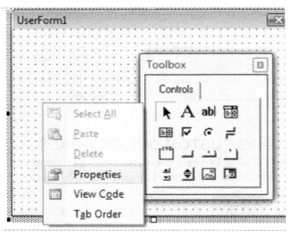

Figure 26.8

Controls are placed on userforms in the same manner as they are placed on a worksheet. You click the control on the toolbox and drag it to the userform. After the control is placed on the userform, select it to access its properties.

Userforms are objects and as such have properties, methods and events. The following six properties out of a total of 35, are the more common properties of the userform.

Userform properties

Name	CodeName property lets you refer to the userform in code. Can only be set at design time.
BackColor	Color of the userform surface
Caption	Text shown in userform's title bar
Left, Top, Height, Width	Position and size of userform in points (1/72 of an inch)
Picture	Image displayed as a backbround for the userform. Must assign **LoadPicture**

	function to picture property. Use PictureAlignment, PictureSizeMode, and PictureTiling properties to control how picture looks.
StartUpPosition	Used to center the userform. Has three values: 1-CenterOwner, centers userform in its host's window, 2-CenterScreen, centers userform on the screen, and 3 – None, no automatic entering – userform defaults to the upper left corner of the screen.

Following are three frequently used methods of userforms. Remember that all of the properties, methods, and events of an object can be found by invoking the object browser from the VBE.

UserForm methods

Show	Displays the userform
Hide	Closes the userform
PrintForm	Prints an image of the userform

Following are three frequently used userform events:

UserForm events

QueryClose	Fires just before userform closes. Put code here asking user if he/she really wants to close the form.
Initialize	Fires when the userform is about to be displayed.
Terminate	Fires after the userform is closed.

We still have a few additional controls to discuss, so let's use the userform to demonstrate those controls.

Our next program will use the built-in RGB Function to display different colors in an image control as we change argument values in the RGB Function. We will use the ScrollBar control to change RGB Function arguments. The RGB Function accepts three arguments: one argument for the red color, one argument for the green color, and one argument

411

for the blue color. We can combine Red, Green, and Blue to create other colors. Each of the arguments has a value of 0 – 255. For example RGB(0,0,0) would represent the color black, RGB(255,255,255) is white, RGB(255,0,0) is red, RGB(0,255,0) is green, and RGB(0,0,255) is blue. Other combinations of argument values result in other colors. Red and green makes yellow so RGB(255,255,0) should be yellow. The finished program interface looks as follows:

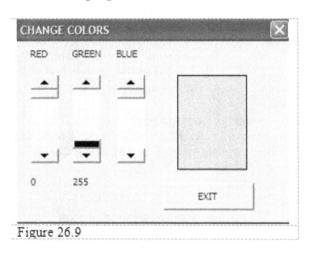

Figure 26.9

Our program has three scroll bar controls which will be used to change the value of the arguments in the RGB Function. There are six labels. Three are at the top of the scroll bar controls to identify the argument being changed. And three labels are at the bottom of the scroll bar controls to show the value of each argument. An image control is used to display the changing colors. And finally, a command button is provided to exit the program.

Open a new Workbook, Hit Alt+F11 to invoke the Visual Basic Editor, and insert a userform. In the Property window change the name property to something descriptive and change the caption property to "Exercise in Changing Colors". Notice that the title bar changes to reflect the new caption.

Next, draw the six label controls on the userform. Use the top, left, height, and width properties to place and size the labels on the userform. The three labels at the top of the userform will be used only to identify the scroll bar controls and will not be referred to in code. Thus we can accept their default names: label1, label2, and label3.

Next, draw the three scroll bar controls on the userform and change their name properties respectively to vsbRed, vsbGreen, and vsbBlue. We will be referring to these controls in code thus we need descriptive names.

Microsoft Excel also has another control called the SpinButton which is similar to the scroll bar. Both the ScrollBar control and the SpinButton control provide a graphical interface for adjusting numeric values. The values of ScrollBars can be changed in three different ways. You can click inside the body of the scrollbar control to change its value property, you can use the mouse and move the scrollbar slider, or you can click either of the arrows at the beginning of the control or the end of the control. The SpinButton can be changed only by clicking its spinner arrows.

Common ScrollBar and SpinButton Properties

Max	Maximum value of the scrollbar or spinner. Must be a positive integer or zero.
Min	Minimum value of the scrollbar or spinner. Must be a positive integer or zero. Must also be less than the value assigned to the Max property.
SmallChange	Negative or positive integer representing the change in value when user clicks one of the arrows.
LargeChange	Negative or positive integer representing change in value when user clicks in the body of the scroll bar. This property is not available for the SpinButton control.
Value	Indicates the current value of the Scrollbar or SpinButton.
LinkedCell	A range on the worksheet to which the Value

413

property of the control is linked.

Commonly used ScrollBar and SpinButton events

Change   Default event. Occurs after the value of the control changes.

Scroll   Occurs as scroll box is repositioned, thus resulting in a smoother appearing transition.

Ok back to our problem. Set the min property of each scrollbar to zero and the max property to 255. This represents the possible range value of the RGB function arguments. To make the colors change faster, I set the LargeChange property on each scrollbar to 5. I accepted the default SmallChange property of 1 for each scrollbar. The scrollbar control will be used later in an enhanced payroll program to navigate through an employee list.

Next draw the image control on the userform. The image control is used to display a graphic (bitmap, metafile, icon, etc). However, in this program we will be manipulating the backcolor of the image control to show the change in colors by changing the values of the RGB Function arguments. An important image control property is the picture property. This is where we use the LoadPicture Function to get the graphic into the image control.

Now draw the command button on the form, change its caption to "Exit" and its name to cmdExit.

We are almost ready to write VBA code to make our userform work. First let's change the name and caption of the three labels appearing at the bottom of the scrollbar controls. Name the labels lblBcount, lblGcount, and lblRcount and leave the caption blank for each label. We will be referring to these labels in code. Each time the scrollbar is moved, we change the value of the RGB argument attached to that scrollbar. We will use the caption property of these labels to display the new value of the scrollbar.

The finished program code follows:

```
'****************************************************************
' Program demonstrates the use of scroll bars and the RGB
function
```

'**

```
Private Sub cmdExit_Click()
'Code for the Exit command button
    Dim response As Integer
    response = MsgBox("Do you want to Exit?", vbYesNo +
vbQuestion, "Quit?")
    If response = vbYes Then
    Unload Me
    End If
End Sub
'*******************************************************
'Code responds to event of moving Blue ScrollBar
'*******************************************************
Private Sub vsbBlue_Change()
    imgColor.BackColor = RGB(vsbRed.Value,
vsbGreen.Value, vsbBlue.Value)
    lblBcount.Caption = vsbBlue.Value
End Sub

Private Sub vsbBlue_Scroll()
 imgColor.BackColor = RGB(vsbRed.Value, vsbGreen.Value,
vsbBlue.Value)
    lblBcount.Caption = vsbBlue.Value
End Sub
'*******************************************************
'Code responds to event of moving Green ScrollBar
'*******************************************************
Private Sub vsbGreen_Change()
 imgColor.BackColor = RGB(vsbRed.Value, vsbGreen.Value,
vsbBlue.Value)
    lblGcount.Caption = vsbGreen.Value
End Sub

Private Sub vsbGreen_Scroll()
 imgColor.BackColor = RGB(vsbRed.Value, vsbGreen.Value,
vsbBlue.Value)
    lblBcount.Caption = vsbBlue.Value
End Sub
'*******************************************************
'Code responds to event of moving Red ScrollBar
'*******************************************************
```

```
Private Sub vsbRed_Change()
 imgColor.BackColor = RGB(vsbRed.Value, vsbGreen.Value,
vsbBlue.Value)
   lblRcount.Caption = vsbRed.Value
End Sub

Private Sub vsbRed_Scroll()
 imgColor.BackColor = RGB(vsbRed.Value, vsbGreen.Value,
vsbBlue.Value)
   lblBcount.Caption = vsbBlue.Value
End Sub
```

And the program in action after selecting the exit button
appears as follows:

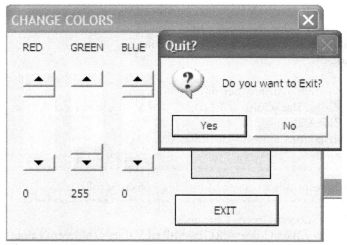

Figure 26.10

CHECKBOX CONTROL

The recommended prefix for the CheckBox control is
"chk". The CheckBox control is used to let the user indicate a
choice. The choice is stored in the value property of the
CheckBox. If checked, the value is true. If unchecked its value
is false.

Common CheckBox
properties

Caption   Shows text displayed next to
                               CheckBox.
Value   Boolean. If true it's checked, false it is

	unchecked.
LinkedCell	String that points to cell reference on worksheet. Where you can store the value property of the CheckBox. **Did I mention that the LinkedCell property only relates to controls that are placed on worksheets and not to controls that are placed on user forms?**

Common CheckBox Event

Click is the default event of the CheckBox. It is used by VBA to respond to the user clicking the CheckBox. You can write event handling code here or you can, when appropriate, just check the CheckBox value.

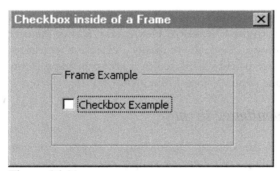

Figure 26.11

417

OPTION BUTTON CONTROL

Common OptionButton properties

Caption	Text displayed next to the OptionButton
GroupName	String that identifies Group to which OptionButton belongs
Value	Boolean. Returns state of the OptionButton. True – Button is checked, False – Button is unchecked.
LinkedCell	For control placed on worksheet only. String cell reference where you can automatically store the value of the OptionButton.

The recommended prefix is "opt". The OptionButton control is similar to the CheckBox. However, it allows the user to choose among several mutually exclusive options. OptionButtons are usually displayed in a group inside a frame control. Only one OptionButton in a group can be selected at a time.

Common OptionButton Event

Click is the default OptionButton Event. You can write event handling code here or simply check the value of the OptionButton.

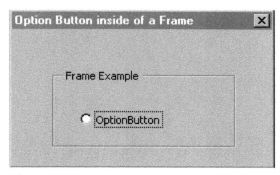

Figure 26.12

LISTBOX CONTROL

The recommended prefix for naming this control is "lst". That is a little L, not a one (1). The ListBox control allows a user to select one or more items from a list. You can size the ListBox on the worksheet or on the userform to control how many items can be seen by the user at one time. There are two types of ListBoxes. The "Single-Select ListBox" allows the user to select only one item at a time. And the "Multi-Select ListBox" allows the user to select multiple items. Use the MultiSelect property to choose ListBox type.

Common ListBox Properties:

List	Array of strings that represents the list
ListCount	Total number of items in the list
ListFillRange	If control is on a worksheet, it is the range on the worksheet to which the ListBox is linked. Contents of ListBox can be housed here rather then in the control.
LinkedCell	Range on worksheet to which the value property (text of the currently selected item in the list) is linked.
ListIndex	Index of currently selected item in the ListBox. Just like the default Array variable, lowerbound is 0.
MultiSelect	Governs number of items that can be selected at one time.
Selected	Array of Boolean values. If it is true for an item in the array then that item is currently selected. False, item is not selected.
Value	Text of currently selected item in the ListBox

Common ListBox Methods

AddItem	Adds items to ListBox one at a time
Clear	Removes all items from the ListBox, resulting in an empty ListBox.

RemoveItem	Removes items one at a time. Takes one argument which is the index of the item to be removed.

Common ListBox Events

Click is the default ListBox event. It responds to the selection of an item in the ListBox by a click of the mouse.

Three ways to populate a ListBox

Setting the List property	Assign Array of values to the List property. This adds a group of items to the ListBox all at once.
Call the AddItem method	Adds items to the ListBox one item at a time.
Setting the ListFillRange property	Assign a worksheet range to this property.

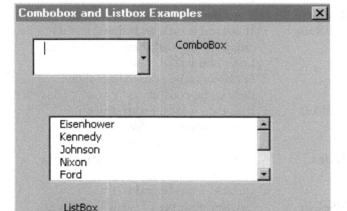

Figure 26.13

COMBOBOX CONTROL

The recommended prefix is cbo. The ComboBox control is similar to the ListBox control. User can select an item from a list. ComboBox control displays only one list item at a time – the selected item.

There are two types of ComboBox controls: Drop-down List Style (behaves like a ListBox) and the Drop-down Combo Style. The Drop-down Combo Style ComboBox lets the user type in a new entry item that is not required to be already in the list. The typed entry does not become part of the list, but is assigned to the value property of the ComboBox.

Use the <u>Style</u> property of the ComboBox to select the desired type. The ComboBox control has most of the properties, methods, and events of the ListBox. It has additionally, a <u>"ListRows" property</u> which accepts an integer which indicates the number of items that are displayed in the Drop-down list after the user clicks the down arrow. Also different from the ListBox is how you determine the selected item. For a ComboBox use the value property to indicate the selected item. ComboBoxes are populated in the same manner as are ListBoxes.

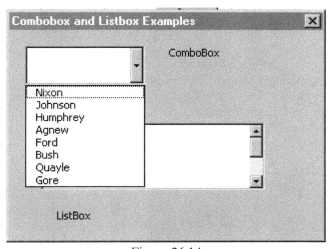

Figure 26.14

Following code demonstrates one way to populate a ListBox and a combobox using the "AddItem" method.

`****************************************************`

'Code to populate a list box

`****************************************************`

```
Private Sub UserForm_Initialize()
    ListBox1.AddItem "Eisenhower"
    ListBox1.AddItem "Kennedy"
    ListBox1.AddItem "Johnson"
    ListBox1.AddItem "Nixon"
    ListBox1.AddItem "Ford"
    ListBox1.AddItem "Carter"
    ListBox1.AddItem "Regan"
```

421

```
ListBox1.AddItem "Bush"
ListBox1.AddItem "Clinton"

'*******************************************************
'Code to populate a combo box
'*******************************************************
    ComboBox1.AddItem "Nixon"
    ComboBox1.AddItem "Johnson"
    ComboBox1.AddItem "Humphrey"
    ComboBox1.AddItem "Agnew"
    ComboBox1.AddItem "Ford"
    ComboBox1.AddItem "Bush"
    ComboBox1.AddItem "Quayle"
  ComboBox1.AddItem "Gore"
End Sub
```

MULTIPAGE CONTROL

MultiPage Controls can only be used on userforms. They are used to create tabbed dialog boxes. Separate controls can be placed on each tab. Clicking the tab grants access to the controls associated with that tab.

Figure 26.15 is an example of the MultiPage control.

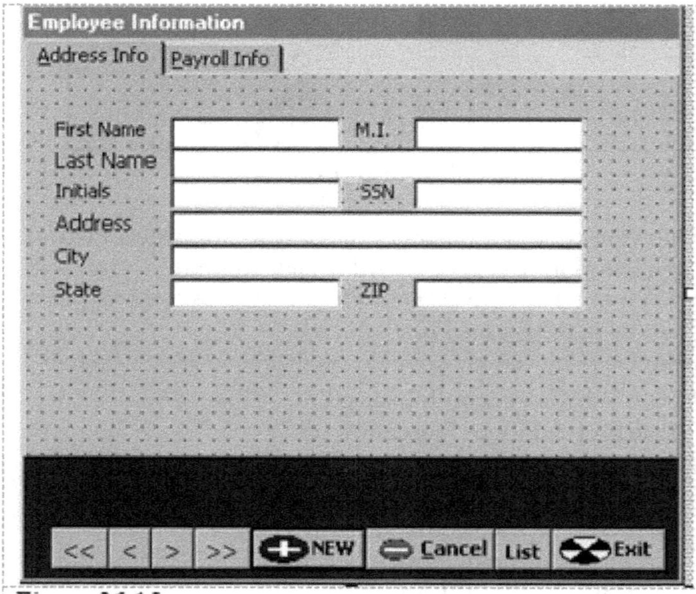

Figure 26.15

Compare the controls on the Address Info tab to the controls on the Payroll Info tab shown in Figure 26.16.

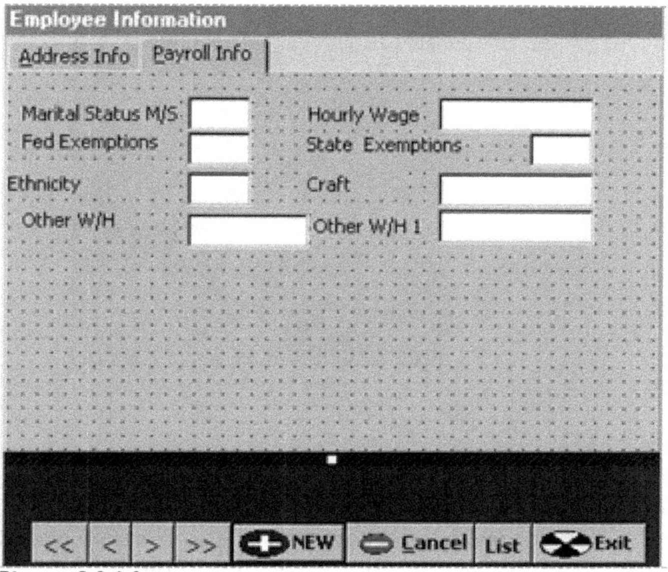

Figure 26.16

At design time you can insert, delete, reorder, and rename the tabs by right – clicking the tab control, and then selecting a command from the resulting menu. To add controls to the MultiPage container select a tab and drag the control on to it.

REFEDIT CONTROL

Like the MultiPage control, the Refedit control can only be used on a userform. The Refedit control points to cells behind a dialog box for the purpose of selecting a range. It also has a small button on its right side that when clicked, temporarily hides the dialog box to let the user see the entire worksheet. With a little work, you could create your own data form with this control. A data form speeds up data input .

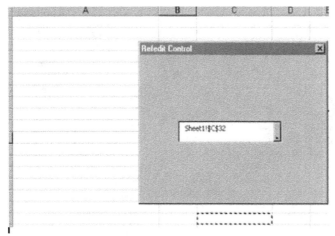

Figure 26.17

Linking Controls on userforms to worksheets

The **ControlSource** property of the controls placed on userforms (applies only to controls that allow the user to enter or set values) can be set to an Microsoft Excel reference or single-cell range name. It works like the LinkedCell property of controls that are placed on worksheets. You cannot cancel changes made to the dialog box as all changes link as they occur.

Setting Tab Order

Tab order regulates which control will become active **(i.e. receive focus)** as you press the tab key. The order should be logical. You can set the tab order of each individual control by accessing its Tabindex property in the Property Window. Or you can select **View, Taborder** from the VBE menu. Then select the control you want to use and click the appropriate button to move it.

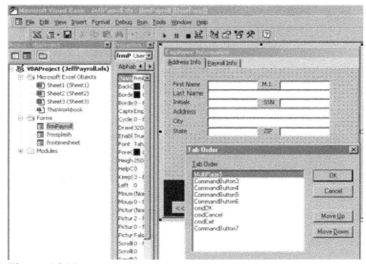

Figure 26.18

DISPLAYING BUILT-IN MICROSOFT EXCEL DIALOG BOXES

Use the **"Dialogs Collection"** and its associated constant as an index to display a built-in dialog box. Note that we have to go up the object hierarchy to the **Application Object** to reference the "Dialogs Collection. To open the "Print Dialog Box" use the following code.

Sub DisplayPrintDialog ( )
   Application.Dialogs (xlDialogPrint).show
End Sub

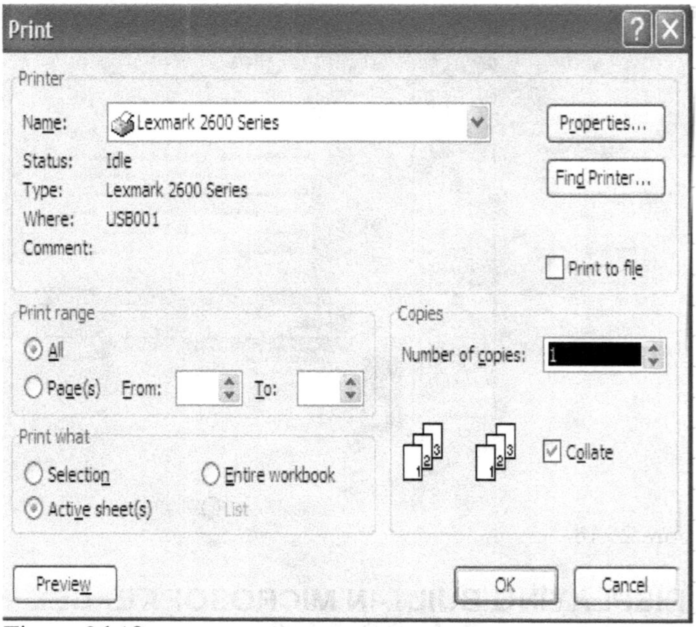

Figure 26.19

We have to use the plural because Dialogs is a collection. We call the "Show" method to display the dialog box . When you use the "Show" method of the Dialog object, you can pass arguments that affect how the built-in dialog box appears. For example, to see all files in the current directory when invoking the "Open Dialog Box", pass the string filter "*.*" as the first argument.

Sub DisplayOpenDialog( )
      Application.Dialogs(xlDialogOpen).show "*.*"
End Sub

- This code presents you with all files that are available to be opened.

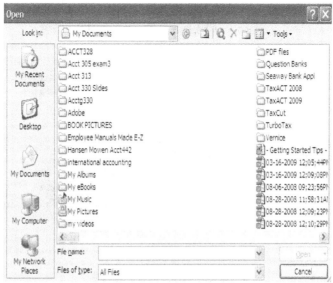

Figure 26.20

USING THE APPLICATION OBJECT TO CHANGE MICROSOFT EXCEL

The changes we make to the Microsoft Excel interface using the Application Object are temporary. They must be reset every time you run Microsoft Excel. Changes to the Application Object are usually made in a routine housed in the **WorkBook_Open event of the ThisWorkBook Object**. This event occurs whenever you open a WorkBook.

Application Object properties

Calculation	Microsoft Excel's calculation mode. XlCalculationAutomatic, xlCalculationManual, and xlCalculationSemiAutomatic.
Caption	String. Text shown in Microsoft Excel title bar.
Cursor	Sets the cursor type: xlNormal, xlDefault, xlWait (Hourglass pointer), xlNorthwestArrow, xlIBeam (I-Beam pointer)
DisplayAlerts	Boolean. If true, Microsoft Excel's built-in alerts are displayed during

427

	routine execution. False, not displayed. **Warning: <u>if you set DisplayAlerts to false and issue a quit command, program will cease operation without asking if you want to save the changes made.</u>**
DisplayFormulaBar	Boolean. If False, the formula bar at the top of the Microsoft Excel workspace is not displayed.
DisplayStatusBar	Boolean. If False, status bar at bottom of Microsoft Excel workspace will not be displayed.
Height	Height of the Application Window in points (1/72 inch).
Left	Distance in points from the left edge of the Application window to the left edge of the screen.
OperatingSystem	String that returns information about the underlying operating system. Windows 3.1, 95, 98 , NT
ScreenUpdating	Boolean. If False, screen display is not updated during routine execution.
StatusBar	Text that is displayed in the status bar at bottom of the screen. Useful in communicating messages to user.
Top	Distance in points from top edge of Application Window to the top edge of the screen.
Version	Version number of Microsoft Excel that is running.
Width	Width of the Application window in points.
WindowState	State of the Application window: xlNormal, xlMaximized, xlMinimized.

Application Methods

Quit	Closes down the Microsoft Excel application. If changes have been made and DisplayAlerts is not False then asks if you want to make changes to the file.

WORKBOOK AND WORKSHEET EVENTS

Use WorkBook and Worksheet events to automatically manipulate the Application Object properties when you run Microsoft Excel.

WORKSHEET EVENTS

Worksheet events are found in the code modules of a workbook. To view them go to the VBE and double-click a worksheet. This brings up the code window and you can view event routines by selecting worksheet in the object box and then clicking the procedures listbox.

Activate	Occurs when the worksheet is activated.
Change	Occurs when data changes on the sheet. The target argument is a Range object representing the cell that have changed.
Deactivate	Occurs when the sheet is deactivated.
SelectionChange	Occurs when the selection changes. The target argument is a Range object representing the new selection.

WorkBook Events
WorkBook Specific Events

BeforeClose	Occurs before the workbook closes. Can set cancel argument to true to prevent workbook from closing.
BeforePrint	Occurs before the workbook prints (or the print preview is displayed). Pass the cancel argument to prevent printing.
BeforeSave	Occurs before the workbook saves. Pass the cancel argument to prevent saving.
NewSheet	Occurs when a new sheet is inserted into the workbook. The argument Sh is a sheet object representing a new sheet.

429

Open   Occurs when workbook opens.

WORKING WITH WORKSHEET EVENTS

Worksheet events can be manipulated to have your application perform seemingly impossible feats. The event I find most useful is the Worksheet "Change" Event. It is triggered when any cell in the Worksheet is changed by the user or is manipulated by a VBA procedure. However, not all changes trigger an event. Event is not triggered when a recalculation occurs. You have to play around with the Worksheet and monitor which actions trigger the "Change" event. Following is the syntax of the change event:

Private Sub Worksheet_Change (ByVal Target As Microsoft Excel.Range)
 Statements
End Sub

Target can be a cell or a group of cells. Usually you are interested in the change of a specific cell.

USING THE RANGE OBJECT

We briefly discussed the Range Object in Chapter 21. Now we will take a closer look at this important object because much of the programming work done in VBA involves the manipulation of Range Objects.

SOME USEFUL RANGE OBJECT PROPERTIES

Cells Property

As was mentioned in Chapter 21, the Cells property can be used to refer to a range. The Cells property requires two arguments: row and column in the following format:

Cells(r, c) :where **r** is the row and **c** is the column.

The following example sets the font size for cell C5 on Sheet1 to 12 points.
Worksheets("Sheet1").Cells(5,3).Font.Size =12

The Cells property is more flexible than the regular range object as variables rather than actual numbers can be used as Cells arguments. The following example demonstrates the use of variables as Cells arguments in an algorithm that sums multiple columns.

```
'*****************************************************
'Calculate the sum of columns
'*****************************************************
y=3
total=0
Dim x as integer: x=4
Dim NS as Range, CR as Range
For x = 4 to 12
Set NS = Range(Cells(7,x),Cells(y, x))
For Each Cr in NS
Total = total + Cr.Value
Next Cr
Cells(y, x).value = total
Total = 0
Next x
```

Hidden Property

Sometimes we need to hide columns from the user. The Hidden Property of the Range Object handles this task. The following example hides column D on Sheet1.

Worksheets("Sheet1").Columns("D").Hidden = True

Locked Property

On worksheet based forms we want the user to be able to enter input but we also want to prevent the user from changing the worksheet format. Using the Locked property of the Range Object with the Protection property of the worksheets object can accomplish the above task. The following example unlocks cells A1:G37 on Sheet1 so that they can be modified when the sheet is protected.

Worksheets("Sheet1").Range("A1:G37").Locked=False
Worksheets("Sheet1").Protect

Offset Property

The Offset Property is another useful way to refer to ranges. It lets you refer to a cell that is a particular number of rows and columns away from another cell. The Offset property takes two arguments which can be actual numbers or variables.

Syntax
Range.Offset(RowOffset, ColumnOffset)

431

RowOffset is an optional variant. It is the number of rows (positive, negative, or zero) by which the range is to be offset. The default value is 0 (zero).

ColumnOffset is an optional variant. It is the number of columns (positive, negative, or zero) by which the range is to be offset. The default value is 0 (zero).

The following example activates the cell three columns to the right of and three rows down from the active cell on sheet1.

```
Worksheets("Sheet1").Activate
ActiveCell.Offset(rowOffset:=3, columnOffset:=3).Activate
```

REFERRING TO ENTIRE COLUMNS AND ROWS

To refer to a range that consists of one or more entire columns use the following format:
```
Columns("A:C")
```
And to refer to a range of one or more entire rows use the following format:
```
Rows("1:5")
```

Value Property

Use the Value property to read or set the value in a cell. If the cell is empty, value returns the value Empty (use the isEmpty function to test for this case). If the Range object contains more than one cell, it returns an array of values (use the isArray function to test for this case). The following example loops on cells A1:D20 on Sheet1. If one of the cells has a value of less than 0.001, the code replaces the value with 0 (zero).

```
For Each c in Worksheets("Sheet1").Range("A1:D20")
        If c.Value < .001 Then
                c.Value=0
        End if
Next c
```

SOME USEFUL RANGE OBJECT METHODS
Clear Method

The Clear Method clears the entire Range Object. The following example clears the formulas and formatting in cells A1:J50 on Sheet1.
```
Worksheets("Sheet1").Range("A1:J50").Clear
```

Copy Method and Paste Method

These two methods are usually used together. The Copy method can be used in three different ways.

Syntax 1	**Copies the object to the Clipboard.**
Syntax 2	**Copies the Range to the specified range to the Clipboard.**
Syntax 3	**Copies the sheet to another location in the workbook.**

Syntax 1

Object. Copy

Syntax 2

Range. Copy (Destination)

Destination **is an optional variant. It specifies the new range to which the specified range will be copied. If omitted, the range value is copied to the Clipboard.**
Syntax 3
Worksheets.Copy(Before, After)

Before **is an optional variant. It specifies the sheet before which the copied sheet will be placed. You cannot specify** Before **if you specify** After.

After **is an optional variant. It specifies the sheet after which the copied sheet will be placed. You cannot specify** After **is you specify** Before.

If you don't specify either Before or After, **Microsoft Excel creates a new workbook that contains the copied sheet.**

The following example copies sheet1, placing the copy after sheet3.
Worksheets("Sheet1").Copy after:= Worksheets("Sheet3")
The following example copies the formulas in cells A1:D4 on sheet1 into cells E5:H8 on sheet2.
Worksheets("Sheet1").Range("A1:D4").Copy _
        Destination:=Worksheets("Sheet2").Range("E5")

Cut Method

This method cuts the object to the clipboard or pastes it into a specified destination using the following format:

Object.Cut (Destination)

The following example cuts the Range B4 and pastes it to Range B2.

Range("B4").Cut Range("B2")

Delete Method

The Delete method appears the same as the Clear method but it is different. When you delete a range, Microsoft Excel shifts the remaining cells to fill up the range you deleted. Use the following format:

Range. Delete(shift)

Shift specifies how to shift cells to replace deleted cells. Can be one of the following xlDeleteShiftDirection constants: xlShiftToLeft or xlShiftUp. If Shift argument is omitted, Microsoft Excel decides based on the shape of the Range.

The following example deletes cells A1:D10 on Sheet1 and shifts the remaining cells to the left.

Worksheets("Sheet1").Range("A1:D10").Delete
Shift:=xlShiftToLeft

GoalSeek Method

The GoalSeek method calculates the values necessary to achieve a specific goal. If the goal is an amount returned by a formula, this calculates a value that, when supplied to your formula, causes the formula to return the number you want. It returns True if the goal seek is successful.

Syntax

Range.GoalSeek(Goal, ChangingCell)

Range	**Range must be a single cell in this method.**
Goal	**Required variant. It is the value you want returned in this cell.**
ChangingCell	**Required Range that specifies which cell should be changed to achieve the target value.**

The following example assumes that Sheet1 has a cell named "SomeFormula" that contains the formula $=(x^{35})+(3*x^2)+65$ and another cell named "x" that's empty. The example finds a value for x so that SomeFormula contains the value 115.

Worksheets("Sheet1").Range("SomeFormula").GoalSeek _
    Goal:=115, _
    ChangingCell:=Worksheets("Sheet1").Range("x")

PrintOut Method

The PrintOut method applies to several Microsoft Excel Objects including the Range Object. It prints the object.
Syntax:
Object. PrintOut(From , To, Copies, Preview, ActivePrinter, PrintToFile, Collate)

From	**Optional variant that indicates the number of the page at which to start printing. If this argument is omitted, printing starts at the beginning.**
To	**Optional variant that indicate the number of the last page to print. If omitted, printing ends with the last page.**
Copies	**Optional variant that indicated the number of copies to print. If omitted, one copy is printed.**
Preview	**Optional variant. If True, print preview is invoked before printing. If False (or if omitted), object is printed immediately.**
ActivePrinter	**Optional variant that sets the name of the Active Printer.**
PrintToFile	**Optional variant that if** True **prints to a file. User is prompted to enter the name of the output file.**
Collate	**Optional variant that if** True **causes Microsoft Excel to collate multiple copies.**

The following example prints the active sheet.

ActiveSheet.PrintOut
<u>Select Method</u>

Method selects the specified Range Object. Before using you must first activate the Worksheet where the Range is contained or you will generate an error.

Syntax:

Range.Select

Note: To select a cell or a range of cells, use the Select method. To make a single cell the active cell, use the <u>Activate</u> method.

The following example selects cell A1:B5 on Sheet1.

Worksheets("Sheet1").Activate

Range("A1:B5").Select

Sort Method

This method sorts a PivotTable, a range, or the current region (if the specified range contains only one cell).

During our discussion of Arrays in chapter 25, we discussed methods to sort arrays. If you have a range of data on a worksheet, it is more efficient to use the <u>Range Object Sort method</u> than the methods we introduced in Chapter 25. The Sort method takes 15 arguments, most of which can be left in their default value most of the time. Therefore, I recommend that you pass the arguments by name rather than by position.

Syntax:

Range.Sort (Key1, Order1, Key2, Type, Order2, Key3, Order3, Header, OrderCustom, MatchCase, Orientation, SortMethod, DataOption1, DataOption2, DataOption3)

Key1	**Optional variant indicating the first sort field, as either text (a pivot field or range name) or a Range Object ("Dept" or cells(1,1) for example).**
Order1	**Optional variant. Can be one of the following xlSortOrder constants: xlAscending or xlDescending. Default is xlAscending.**
Key2	**Optional variant indicating the second sort field as either text (a pivot field or range name) or a Range object. If this argument is omitted, there is no second sort field. Not used when sorting PivotTables.**
Type	**Optional variant. Specifies which elements are sorted. Can be one of the following xlSortType constants:**

	xlSortValues, xlSortLables. Used only when sorting PivotTables.
Order2	Optional variant. Can be one of the following xlSortOrder constants: xlAscending or xlDescending. Default value is xlAscending. Not used when sorting PivotTables.
Key3	Optional variant. The third sort field as either text (a range name) or a Range Object. If omitted, there is no third sort field. Not used when sorting PivotTables.
Order3	Optional variant. Can be one of the following xlSortOrder constants: xlAscending or xlDescending. Default is xlAscending. Not used when sorting PivotTables.
Header	Optional variant. Specifies whether the first row contains headers. Can be one of the following xlYesNoGuess constants: xlYes, xlNo, or xlGuess. Use xlYes is the first row contains headers (it should not be sorted). Use xlNo if there are no headers (the entire range should be sorted). Use xlGuess to let Microsoft Excel determine whether there is a header, and to determine where it is, if there is one. The default value is xlNo. Not used when sorting PivotTables.
OrderCustom	Optional variant. A one (1) based integer offset to the list of custom sort orders. If omitted, 1 (Normal) is used.
MatchCase	Optional variant. If True do a case-sensitive sort; if False do a sort that is not case sensitive. Not used when sorting PivotTables.
Orientation	Optional variant. If xlTopToBottom is used, the sort is done from top to bottom (by row). If xlLeftToRight is used, the sort is done from left to right (by column).
SortMethod	Optional variant. The type of sort can

437

be one of the following xlSortMethod constants: xlSyllabary (to sort phonetically) or xlcodePage (to sort by code page). The default is xlSyllabary.

DataOption 1, DataOption 2, DataOption 3	**Optional XlSortDataOption: Specifies how to sort text in key1, key2, or key3. Not used when sorting PivotTable reports.**

The following example sorts the range A1:C20 on Sheet1, using cell A1 as the first sort key and cell B1 as the second sort key. The sort is done in ascending order by row, and there are no headers.

```
Worksheets("Sheet1").Range("A1:C20").Sort _
 Key1:=Worksheets("Sheet1").Range("A"), _
      Key2:= Worksheets("Sheet1").Range("B")
```

SUMMARY

Worksheets can be used to create forms by manipulating Range, Font, Interior, Border, Style, WorkSheet, and Window objects.

Active-x controls can be placed on worksheets and on userforms to extend the functionality of Microsoft Excel.

You can manipulate the Application Object to control Microsoft Excel's environment. Application Object properties must be reset every time you run Microsoft Excel. Use the Workbook_Open event to store routines that affect the Application Object.

CHAPTER 27
USING SEQUENTIAL FILES

In this chapter we discuss sequential Files. Topics covered are: (1) Creating sequential files, (2) writing records to sequential files, (3) reading sequential files, (4) deleting records from sequential files, and (5) error trapping.

USING SEQUENTIAL FILES

Sequential files are text files. To gain access to a record in a sequential file requires beginning at the first record of the file and reading each record in order, until the desired record is located. Sequential files can be created and read in the Windows' program "NotePad". In this chapter we use VBA to create and use sequential files. Sequential file records are of variable length. The syntax for using sequential files follows:

Open "FileName" for [Output | Append | Input] As #n

Statements to process the file

Close #n

Analysis:

FileName	**String. Contains the full path and name to where file is presently located or name and path if file is presently being created. For flexibility I still use the DOS convention of Eight Characters followed by the dot operator and then followed by the three characters "txt" extension. However, the maximum file name is now 255 characters.**
For	**Required keyword.**
Output | Append | Input	**Specifies the mode for opening the file. Output mode creates a new file. If file with same FileName already exists, then the contents of this file will be overwritten with**

439

	new file records. <u>Append</u> mode opens file and allows writing new records to the end of the file. If FileName does not exist, Append will create a new file. <u>Input</u> opens a file for reading.
As	Required Keyword.
#n	#n is the reference number for the file. Must be an integer from 1 to 511.
Close #n	Required Keyword. After you open a file and finish processing its records, close the file. <u>Close #n</u> closes the specified file. <u>Close</u> without the #n closes all open files. <u>Close #1, #2</u> closes files #1 and #2.

Writing records to Sequential Files

The <u>Write #</u> statement is used to write records to sequential files. If Str is a string then the statement:

Write #n, str

Writes the string "str" to the file surrounded by quotation marks. If Num is a numeric variable then the statement:

Write #n, num

Writes num to the file. (No quotes for numbers). And the following statement:

Write #n str, num

 Writes the str and numeric value to the file separated by commas. After each Write# statement the "Carriage return" and "Line Feed" are added to the end of the line to indicate the end of the record.

A file can be open in only one mode at a time. If you open a file for input (reading) and later want to write records to that file; the file must be closed and then reopened in the <u>Append</u> mode.

Opening Sequential Files for Reading

Follow the steps below to open a sequential file for reading:

- **Declare (DIM) variables to hold input values read in** from the file. Variables must be the same type as the items in the file.

- Test for file's existence using <u>Dir ("FileName")</u> Function.

- Use the <u>Do Loop</u> construct and <u>EOF( )</u> Function to prevent reading past end of file.

- Use the <u>"Input #n,"</u> statement to retrieve each record.

- Close the file with the <u>"Close #n"</u> statement.

If you try to open a file for input that does not exist a <u>"File Not Found"</u> Error message will be generated. Visual Basic provides the <u>Dir("FileName")</u> Function to tell us if a file already exists. It returns the FileName if the file exists and it returns the empty "" string if the file does not exist. Use the following code to avoid errors when opening sequential files for input:

If Dir("FileName") < > "" Then

    Open "FileName" for Input As #1

Else

    Msgbox " File Not Found"

End if

DELETING RECORDS FROM SEQUENTIAL FILES

You cannot directly delete or change a record in a sequential file. To change or delete a record, create a new file. Next read each item from the original file and then write to a new file all the items including the single item changed and omit the item that was deleted. Next, erase the original file with the <u>Kill "FileName"</u> command and rename the new file with the name of the original file.

Use the following statement :

Name "oldfileName" As "NewFileName".

Kill "OldFileName"

The "Kill" statement and the "Name" statement can only be used on closed files. If you try to use these statements on open files, a "File Already Open" error message will be generated.

NotePad can be used to read a sequential text file. Look at the following example:

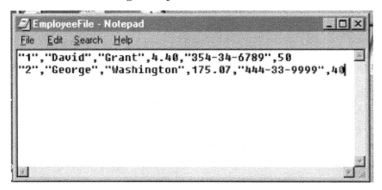

Figure 27.1

The above sequential file has two records. Each record contains items for employee number, employee first name, employee last name, hourly pay rate, social security number, and hours worked. Note that strings are enclosed in quotation marks while numbers are not.

ERROR TRAPPING

When reading to and writing from files or when opening and quitting applications it is important to handle errors that may occur. If an error occurs while error trapping is active, execution jumps to an error handling routine and the user is informed of the error. The Number property of the <u>Err Object</u> displays the error number and the Description property displays a description of the error. The error handler will take corrective action based on the value of <u>Err.Number</u>. Following are some common errors and the number value they generate:

Type	Error Number
Subscript out of Range	9
Division by Zero	11
File Not Found	53
File Already Open	55
Disk Full	61
Disk Not Ready	71

The Error Handler must be located inside a procedure. Following are the steps to creating an error handler:

- Enter as first line in the procedure the following statement.

On Error GoTo ErrorHandler

- Enter the statements to carry out the purpose of the procedure.

- Enter Exit Sub statement – this prevents the program reaching the Error Handling routine if no error has occurred. Execution would then jump to the End Sub statement.

- Enter the <u>line label</u> (40 characters maximum length, must start in the first column, and end with a colon). In our example we are calling the line label <u>ErrorHandler:</u>

- Enter the statements to handle the error and display the message to user.

- Enter Resume statement

- End Sub

If you want the program to continue processing and ignore the error, place the statement "<u>On Error Resume Next</u>" as the first line in the procedure. Program will then continue execution at the line immediately following the line that generated the error.

443

Enhanced Payroll Example

Tax season is dying down and LawnVan Day Care Center's accountant has time to work on the payroll problem. The program uses a sequential file to hold information about employees. The interface consists of a userform upon which is placed a multipage control. Page one (1) of the multipage control contains textboxes to get and display the employee's name and address (Figure 27.2).

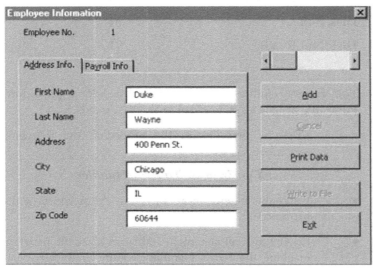

Figure 27.2

Page two (2) of the multipage control (caption "Payroll Info") contains a checkbox control to designate employee marital status, and textboxes to get and display social security number, federal and state exemptions, other exemptions, and wages. A combobox is used to designate employee ethnicity.

On the userform is a label to display the currently selected employee. A scrollbar control is used to navigate the employee file. There are command buttons to add records to the file, to cancel add actions, to print data to paper, to write a new record to the file, and to end the program. As with other window programs, the buttons are programmed to be enabled and available to the user depending on the present state of the program. For example when the program first starts, the cancel button and write to file button are visible but are not available to the user. This is accomplished by setting their enable property to false. Buttons are enabled and disabled based on what makes sense. The cancel and write to file buttons only make sense when the user is adding records to the file. So after pressing the add button, cancel and write to file buttons become available to the user (i.e. we set their enabled property to true).

See Figure 27.3 for Page two(2) of the multipage control.

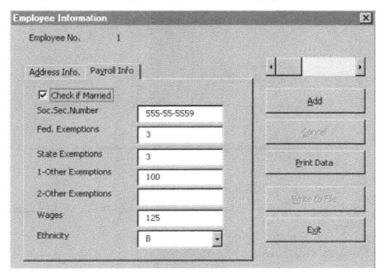

Figure 27.3

The following steps are needed to design this program:

Step	Program Requirements	Procedure Name
1	Initialize the userform, open file for reading, populate a two-dimensional array, keep track of the number of records read using irow variable, assign total number of records to the Max property of scroll bar to limit scroll slide to last record, and close the file after all records are read. Also a error handling routine is created to handle possible file activity errors. Finally, display the first record in the file.	Userform_in itialize, calls the displayempl oyee procedure

2	Navigate the file displaying successive employees from beginning of the file to end of file.	ScrollEmply_Change
3	Add new records to the buffer.	CmdAdd_Click and AddingRecords
4	Cancel add activity	CmdCancel
5	Write new record to the file.	WriteData

```
'********************************************************
' Enhanced Payroll Program
'********************************************************

Option Explicit
Option Base 1
Dim Employees(50, 15) As String  'Dim as Form level
Dim irow As Integer      'Dim as Form level

Private Sub UserForm_Initialize()
'********************************************************
'   Open file for reading, and populate two-dimensional
array.
'   Keep track of number of records read using irow
variable, Assign
'   total number of records read to Max property of scroll
bar to limit
'   scroll slide to last record. Close file after input is
complete. Step 1
'********************************************************
On Error GoTo Errorhandler
irow = 1
Dim employeenum As String, firstname As String,
lastname As String
Dim address As String, city As String, state As String
Dim zipcode As String, mstatus As String
Dim ssn As String, fed As String, stwheld As String
```

```
Dim exemptone As String, exempttwo As String
Dim wages As String, ethnicity As String
If Dir("C:\my documents\employee.txt") <> "" Then
Open "C:\my documents\employee.txt" For Input As
#1
Else
MsgBox "Employee File not found"
End If
    Do Until EOF(1) = True
    Input #1, employeenum, firstname, lastname, address,
city, state, zipcode, mstatus, ssn, fed, stwheld,
exemptone, exempttwo, _wages, ethnicity
    Employees(irow, 1) = employeenum
    Employees(irow, 2) = firstname
    Employees(irow, 3) = lastname
    Employees(irow, 4) = address
    Employees(irow, 5) = city
    Employees(irow, 6) = state

    Employees(irow, 7) = zipcode

    Employees(irow, 8) = mstatus

    Employees(irow, 9) = ssn

    Employees(irow, 10) = fed

    Employees(irow, 11) = stwheld

    Employees(irow, 12) = exemptone

    Employees(irow, 13) = exempttwo

    Employees(irow, 14) = wages

    Employees(irow, 15) = ethnicity

    irow = irow + 1

      Loop

    Close #1

    ScrollEmply.Max = irow

    cmdWrite.Enabled = False

    cmdCancel.Enabled = False

    DisplayEmployee

Exit Sub
```

Errorhandler:

MsgBox "Opening & Reading file Procedure failed", , "Error"

MsgBox Err.Number & " " & Err.Description, , "Error"

End Sub

'**

'Event fires whenever we move the scrollBar control Step 2

'**

Private Sub ScrollEmply_Change()

    DisplayEmployee

End Sub

'**

'Display employee information in text boxes, information is from array

'Step 2A

'**

Public Sub DisplayEmployee()

Dim pagename1 As String, pagename2 As String

Dim emplNo As Integer

emplNo = ScrollEmply.Value

ScrollEmply.Max = irow - 1

lblNum.Caption = Employees(emplNo, 1)

 txtFirstName.Text = Employees(emplNo, 2)

 txtLastName.Text = Employees(emplNo, 3)

 txtAddress.Text = Employees(emplNo, 4)

 txtCity.Text = Employees(emplNo, 5)

 txtState.Text = Employees(emplNo, 6)

 txtZipCode.Text = Employees(emplNo, 7)

```
chkMStatus.Value = Employees(emplNo, 8)
txtSSN.Text = Employees(emplNo, 9)
txtFed.Text = Employees(emplNo, 10)
txtStexp.Text = Employees(emplNo, 11)
txtExp1.Text = Employees(emplNo, 12)
txtExp2.Text = Employees(emplNo, 13)
txtwages.Text = Employees(emplNo, 14)
cboEthnic.Value = Employees(emplNo, 15)
End Sub
'************************************************
****

'Step 3.   Add Records to the File
'************************************************
****

Private Sub cmdAdd_Click()
 AddingRecords
End Sub
'************************************************
****

'Step 3A. Routine called when Add Command button is
clicked
'************************************************
****

Public Sub AddingRecords()
lblNum.Caption = vbNullString
  txtFirstName = vbNullString
  txtLastName = vbNullString
  txtAddress = vbNullString
  txtCity = vbNullString
  txtState = vbNullString
  txtZipCode = vbNullString
```

449

```vb
    chkMStatus.Value = False
    txtSSN = vbNullString
    txtFed = vbNullString
    txtStexp = vbNullString
    txtExp1 = vbNullString
    txtExp2 = vbNullString
    txtwages = vbNullString
    cboEthnic.Value = ""
    cmdAdd.Enabled = False
    cmdWrite.Enabled = True
    cmdCancel.Enabled = True
    txtFirstName.SetFocus
End Sub
'********************************************************
'Step 4. Cancel Add Activity
'********************************************************
Private Sub cmdCancel_Click()
    cmdCancel.Enabled = False
    cmdWrite.Enabled = False
    cmdAdd.Enabled = True
    irow = irow - 1          'Get last employee
    lblNum.Caption = irow
    txtFirstName.Text = Employees(irow, 2)
    txtLastName.Text = Employees(irow, 3)
    txtAddress.Text = Employees(irow, 4)
    txtCity.Text = Employees(irow, 5)
    txtState.Text = Employees(irow, 6)
    txtZipCode.Text = Employees(irow, 7)
    chkMStatus.Value = Employees(irow, 8)
```

```
    txtSSN.Text = Employees(irow, 9)

    txtFed.Text = Employees(irow, 10)

    txtStexp.Text = Employees(irow, 11)

    txtExp1.Text = Employees(irow, 12)

    txtExp2.Text = Employees(irow, 13)

    txtwages.Text = Employees(irow, 14)

    cboEthnic.Value = Employees(irow, 15)

End Sub
```

'***
****

'Step 5. **Write new record to the file**

'***
****

```
Private Sub cmdWrite_Click()

    WriteData

End Sub
```

'***
****

'Step 5A. **Add new employ to the end of the employees file, and also 'add to employees array, and update max property of scrollbar.**

'***
****

```
Private Sub WriteData()

On Error GoTo Errorhandler

cmdWrite.Enabled = False

cmdCancel.Enabled = False


Open "C:\my documents\employee.txt" For Append As #1

lblNum = irow
```

451

```
Write #1, lblNum, txtFirstName, txtLastName,
txtAddress, txtCity, _

txtState, txtZipCode, chkMStatus, txtSSN, txtFed,
txtStexp, txtExp1, _

txtExp2, txtwages, cboEthnic

Close #1

Employees(irow, 1) = lblNum

Employees(irow, 2) = txtFirstName

Employees(irow, 3) = txtLastName

Employees(irow, 4) = txtAddress

Employees(irow, 5) = txtCity

Employees(irow, 6) = txtState

Employees(irow, 7) = txtZipCode

Employees(irow, 8) = chkMStatus

Employees(irow, 9) = txtSSN

Employees(irow, 10) = txtFed

Employees(irow, 11) = txtStexp

Employees(irow, 12) = txtExp1

Employees(irow, 13) = txtExp2

Employees(irow, 14) = txtwages

Employees(irow, 15) = cboEthnic

irow = irow + 1

ScrollEmply.Max = irow

cmdAdd.Enabled = True

Exit Sub

Errorhandler:

MsgBox Err.Number & " " & Err.Description

Resume

End Sub

'**************************************************
****
```

'**Step 6. Exit the Program**

'***

Private Sub cmdExit_Click()

  End

End Sub

Code Explanation – Step 1.

We use a two dimensional array to hold the variables read in from the file. Array elements will be assigned to textboxes, checkboxes, and combo boxes to display employee information. First we declare a form level array to hold 50 employees with 15 pieces of information per employee. And we declare a form level integer variable to be used to count the number of records in the file.

In the general declarations section of the form module place the following statement:
Dim Employees (50,15) as string, irow as integer

Next we write the code that fires as the userform initializes (for the Visual Basic programmers – this is the same as the Form_load event).

In part 1 of the userform_Initialize() event we document the purpose of the procedure with comments. Next we turn on the error handling procedure and dimension all of the local variables we will be using. Then we test to see if the employee file exists (using the Dir (filename) function) and if it exists we open the file for reading.

We then use a "Do Loop" to read all of the records in the file; and for each record we assign its fields to the aforementioned dimensioned variables. The file is closed and the maximum value of the scrollbar is set equal to the total number of records in the file. The "Cancel" command button and the "Write to file" command button are disabled. And we display the first record in the file.

Next, we write our error handling routine. An error that occurs is identified by number and description and this information is communicated to the user by message box.

Code Explanation – Step 2.

453

The userform is on the screen and the user has a choice of four (4) actions. User can navigate through the file using the scroll bar, can add a new record to the write buffer, can print the file to paper, or user can exit the program.

Let's navigate through the file. When we move the scrollbar slider, or click the left or right arrow, or click inside of the scroll area; the <u>Change event</u> of the scrollbar fires. So this is where we will put the code to display employees. Since we must handle the displaying of employees more than one time, we wrote a sub procedure to handle this action. From the Scrollbar change event, we call the "DisplayEmployee" procedure. Remember that in the userform_initialize()_ event we set the scrollbar max property equal to the total number of records read in from the file. This was done so that the scrollbar slider reaches the right end of the scrollbar and moves no farther when the last record of the file is displayed.

The employee number that is displayed in the label at the top of the user form is the value property of the scrollbar (emplNo=ScrollEmply.value). The information in the textboxes, checkbox, and combobox used to display employee information comes from the array elements holding field information of each record. Each time the <u>scrollbar change event</u> fires, a new record is displayed (i.e. each time the scroll bar value changes).

<u>Code Explanation – Step 3.</u>

After we have inspected all of the records in the file, let's add a new record. In the click event of the "Add" command button we will call the "<u>AddingRecords</u>" subprocedure. The "AddingRecords()" procedure clears the information on the screen and prepares the write buffer to receive new information. Since it now makes sense for the user to have access to the "Cancel" button and to the "Write to File" button, each button's enabled property is set to true. And since it no longer makes sense for the "Add" button to be available to the user, its enabled property is set to false. Finally the cursor is set to the first textbox that will receive information (txtFirstName.SetFocus).

<u>Code Explanation – Step 5.</u>

Now that we have new information in the write buffer, we can either cancel the add action or write a new record to the file. Let's first write a new record to the file. We press the "Write to File" button and the <u>WriteData procedure</u> is called. In the "WriteData" procedure, we turn on an error handling procedure, and we disable the "Cancel" and "Write to File" buttons; as access to these two buttons no longer makes sense.

Next, we open the employee file in the <u>append mode</u>, and using the next record number we write the new record to the file. The file is immediately closed so that if a power interruption occurs no data will be lost. We then add the new record to our two dimensional array so that it may be displayed. Then our record count is updated and assigned to the max property of the scrollbar. Finally the "Add" button is made available to the user.

<u>Code Explanation – Step 4.</u>

Remember, that after adding information for a new record to the write buffer and before writing that information to the file; the user can cancel the add action by pressing the "Cancel" button. The cmdCancel procedure first disables the "Cancel" button, and then enables the "Write to File" button and "Add" button. The number of the last record is ascertained so as to determine the last employee in the file. The last employee in the file is displayed on the screen.

<u>Code Explanation – Step 6.</u>

The program's last possible action is to end the program. The cmdExit procedure handles the end of the program action.

SUMMARY

For those times when information must be maintained between sessions, use a sequential file. Opening sequential files requires specifying in advance how the files will be used. For reading, open the file for <u>input</u>. To create a new sequential file, open the file for <u>output</u>. And to add records to an existing file or to create a new file, open the file for <u>Append</u>. Files must be closed after use to avoid losing data and when we need to change modes.

CHAPTER 28
USER DEFINED TYPES AND RANDOM ACCESS FILES

In this chapter we will discuss user defined types, records, creating random access files, writing to and reading from random access files.

USER DEFINED TYPES

In Chapter 22 we discussed the twelve data types available in Visual Basic, here we go into detail about the characteristics of the <u>user defined</u> data type. First we introduce a new string type (Fixed-length) which will be used with user defined data types.

Fixed – length strings:

Fixed – length string variables follow standard variable naming rules. Fixed - length strings are created by using the following format.

Dim var as string *n

n is a positive integer. This declares var **to have a length of n characters.**

Records

A record is a user-defined data type consisting of related variables of different types. The individual variables are called fields and the length of a field is the number of bytes allocated to it. A field of type string *n requires n bytes of memory. An integer field requires 2 bytes. And a field of type single requires 4 bytes. The length of a record is the sum of the bytes of all fields contained in the record.

User – defined data types are created using the following syntax:

[Public | Private] Type VarName

      elementname [([subscripts])] As Type

      [elementName [([subscripts])] As Type]

      End Type

Public	Optional. Used to declare <u>user-defined types</u> that are available to all

	procedures in all modules in all projects.
Private	Optional. Used to declare user-defined types that are available only within the module where the declaration is made.
VarName	Required. Name of the user-defined type; follows standard variable naming conventions.
Elementname	Required. Name of an element of the user-defined type. Element names also follow standard variable naming conventions, except that <u>keywords</u> can be used.
Subscripts	Optional. Dimensions of an array element. Use only parentheses when declaring an array whose size can change. The subscripts argument uses the following syntax:
	[lower To] upper[,lower To] upper]...
	When not explicitly stated in lower, the lower bound of any array is controlled by the Option Base statement. The lower bound is zero if no Option Base statement is present.
Type	Required. Data type of the element may be Byte, Boolean, Integer, Long, Currency, Single, Double, Date, String, String* length (for fixed-length strings), Object, variant, another user-defined type, or an object type.

The Type statement can be used only at module level. In standard modules, user-defined types are public by default. In class modules, user-defined types can only be private. Before a user-defined type can be used it must be declared using the following format:

457

Dim recordvar as user-defined type

For example let's put employee information into a user - defined data type.

```
Type employee
        Fname As String * 25
        Lname As String * 25
        Address As String *45
        City As String *20
        State As String * 2
        Zipcode As String *5
        SSN As String * 9
        Wages As single
        FedExemptions As integer
        StateExemptions As integer
        OtherExemptions As integer
End Type
Dim unionEmployee as employee
```

Just like other variables, records can be passed to and from Sub procedures and Functions. The arguments therein must be declared as follows:

[Function | Sub Procedure] (Argument as user-definedtype)

If a fixed – length string is passed to and from Sub Procedures or Functions, the corresponding argument in the Sub Procedure or Function statement must be an ordinary (variable – length) string.

RANDOM ACCESS FILES

A random access file is like an array of records stored on a disk. The records are numbered 1, 2, 3, ... n and are referenced by their numbers. Recall that to access a record in a sequential file, you start at the beginning of the file and read (in sequence) all records until the desired record is reached. With a random access file you can jump directly to the desired record by using its number.

Remember that with sequential files you must specify the mode when opening (i.e. Input, output, or append). With random access files one statement is used for opening the file in any mode. Also you do not have to close the file to change modes. Open random access files using the following format:

Open "FileName" for Random As # n Len =Len(recvar)

To write to a random access file, first assign a value to each field of a record variable and then write the data into record r of file #n with the statement:

Put #n, r, recvar

Fields are referenced by the following format:

Recordvar.FieldName

The following example writes a unionEmployee record to a random access file.

Private Sub SaveRecords ( )

> **UnionEmployee.Fname=txtFirstName**

> **UnionEmployee.Lname=txtLastName**

> **UnionEmployee.Address=txtAddress**

> **UnionEmployee.City=txtCity**

> **UnionEmployee.State=txtState**

> **UnionEmployee.ZipCode=txtZipCode**

> **UnionEmployee.SSN=txtSSN**

> **UnionEmployee.Wages=txtWages**

> **UnionEmployee.Exemptions=txtExemptions**

> **UnionEmployee.StateExemptions=txtStateExem**
ptions

> **UnionEmployee.OtherExemptions=txtOtherExe**
mptions

> **Put #n, currentrecord, UnionEmployee**

> **Currentrecord=currentrecord+1**

' make ready for next record

> txtFirstName=""

459

txtLastName=""""

txtAddress=""""

txtCity=""""

txtState=""""

txtZipcode=""""

txtSSN=""""

txtWages=""""

txtExemptions=""""

txtStateExemptions=""""

txtOtherExemptions=""""

txtFName.Setfocus

End Sub

As shown above, after writing a record to the random access file, textboxes should be cleared out to make ready for the next record. And focus should be set to the first textbox that will receive data.

To read from a random access file, first execute the following statement:

Get #n , r , recvar

This assigns record r of file #n to the record variable recvar. Next, use the field variables of the record variable to display the record in textboxes or transfer values to other variables with assignment statements. For example:

Sub DisplayEmployee( )

Get #1,4, UnionEmployee   'read record #4

txtFirstName=UnionEmployee.FName

txtLastName= UnionEmployee.LName

txtAddress= UnionEmployee.Address

txtCity= UnionEmployee.City

txtState= UnionEmployee.State

txtZipcode= UnionEmployee.ZipCode

txtSSN= UnionEmployee.SSN

txtWages= UnionEmployee.Wages

txtExemptions= UnionEmployee.Exemptions

txtStateExemptions=
UnionEmployee.StateExemptions

txtOtherExemptions=
UnionEmployee.OtherExemptions

End Sub

Appending Records to the End of the File

To append records to the end of a random file, first use the LOF(n) function to get the total number of bytes in a file with reference n. Since all records in a random access file have the same length (from 1 to 32,767), the number of the last record in the file can be calculated by dividing LOF(n) by the record length. For example to add records to the end of the file, use the following statements.

LastRecord = LOF(n) / Len (recvar)

Put #n, LastRecord + 1, recvar

Another useful function is LOC(n). This function returns the number of the record most recently written to a file or read from a file with a Put or Get statement.

SUMMARY

For faster access of records in a file, use the random access file rather than the sequential file type. Random access files consist of a number of user – defined data type variables called records. Use the Type / End Type construct to create user – defined data types.

Random access files require one statement for opening in all modes. And random access files can change modes without first closing in one mode and opening in another mode.

CREATING DATABASES

In this chapter we will learn how to create a database and how to add, change, and delete records in a database. Microsoft Excel lets you retrieve data from or write data to any database that supports the ODBC standard (Microsoft Access, Microsoft FoxPro, SQL Server, Dbase, Paradox, Oracle, and many more). Microsoft Excel also supports Microsoft's Messaging Application Programming Interface (MAPI). So you can exchange data between Microsoft Excel and any MAPI-compliant e-Mail system.

DATA ACCESS OBJECTS

Data Access Objects (DAO) are manipulated to accomplish the above database tasks. Before you can use DAO in Visual Basic for Applications, you must make the DAO Object library available to the project. From the VBE, click Tools, References, Microsoft DAO 3.6 Object Library. And your screen looks like Figure 29.1.

Office Products 2000 and later versions and VBA 6.0 use a different scheme for Database manipulation, Active-X Data Objects (ADO). Microsoft pushes ADO as the now preferred method of Database programming. DAO is still available and in my opinion is better. If you want to learn ADO refer to VBA on-line help.

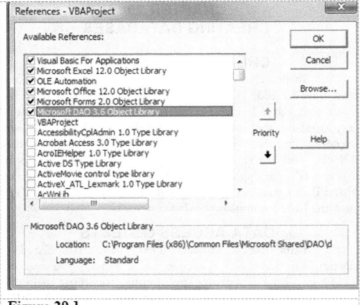

Figure 29.1

Data Access Objects are organized into a hierarchy. (See Figure 29.2) The DBEngine occupies the top rung of the hierarchy. Unlike other objects used in Visual Basic for Applications, you do not have to declare the DBEngine Object in your project. In fact, doing so will generate an error. The DBEngine Object is predefined by Visual Basic. When you connect to the Microsoft Jet Engine (Visual Basic's default database manager), a default workspace (called a session) is created.

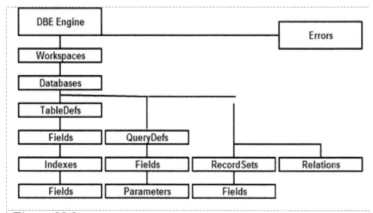

Figure 29.2

All of the Data Access Objects, except for the DBEngine, are collections or members of collections. If you remember from earlier chapters, when referencing objects in a hierarchy, (depending on context), you sometimes have to include objects up the ladder to make the object expression make sense. You separate the objects in the hierarchy with the (.) dot operator. Also, note that DAO collections are zero based, so when using For-Next loops remember to start indexing from Zero (0).

Since Microsoft Access Jet DataBase Engine ships with Office 2003 and 2007, we will spend the remainder of this chapter discussing the features of the Jet DataBase Engine. You can find information on other ODBC DataBases in VBA's online help.

Microsoft Access DataBases have a .MDB extension. It is commonly believed that .MDB stands for Microsoft DataBase. The MDB file can contain Tables (TableDef Objects), Queries (QueryDef Objects), and Relations (Relation Objects). We can create a MDB file using VBA, but why brother when Access is available and much easier to use. We will instead use VBA to manipulate the database after it is created.

HOW TO OPEN A DATABASE

When you open a data base, the default workspaces(0) is created. Workspaces is where we handle security concerns and make provisions for multiple users, groups, or connections. If we only need one session then we can start our object reference at the Database object and open a database by placing the following statements in the General Declarations section of a form or in a standard module:

Public dB as DATABASE

(Dim db as DATABASE, placed inside of a procedure also works)

And in a procedure, initialize the database object with the following:

Set dB = OpenDataBase(dbName[,Options][,Read-Only])

OpenDataBase	**Required method of DataBase Object.**
DBName	**Complete path to location on disk where database can be found**
Options	**Boolean. If True, Database is open in Exclusive mode. False (Default), Database is open in shared mode, allowing multiple users at the same time.**
Read-Only	**Optional. User not allowed to make changes to database**

RecordSet Object

The RecordSet Object is probably the most important DAO Object. The RecordSet lets you retrieve, add, update, and delete records from tables. To open a RecordSet place the following statements in the General Declaration Section of a form:

Private rsRecordSet As RecordSet

(Dim rs as Recordset placed inside a procedure also works)

And in a procedure initialize the RecordSet Object with the following:

Set rsRecordSet = dB.OpenRecordSet(Source [,Type][,Options] _[, lockedits])

dB.OpenRecordSet	**"dB" refers to the name of the currently open database.**
Source	**Required. Table or SQL select statement.**
Type	**Optional. Refers to the type of RecordSet to create.**

dBOpenTable, dBOpenDynaset
, dBOpenSnapshot. Table and
Dynaset types lets you read and
change database records.
Snapshot is read-only.

Options	**Optional. Additional options that control the creation of the RecordSet. See VBA's on-line help.**
Lockedits	**Optional. Used in multi-user environments where users must access the database at the same time.**

For example:

Set rsRecordSet = dB.OpenRecordSet ("TblEmployee")

where dB is the previously declared database Object.

A RecordSet has characteristics similar to a two-dimensional Array. Each column of a RecordSet Object is a table field (or a Query field), and each row represents a record. Only one record, called the CurrentRecord, can be active at a time. When you first open a RecordSet, the cursor points to the first record in the database.

RecordSet Navigation Methods

There are four (4) methods available to navigate through a RecordSet. (1). MoveFirst takes you to the first record in the RecordSet. (2) MoveLast takes you to the last record in the RecordSet. (3). MoveNext takes you to the next subsequent record in the RecordSet. And (4) MovePrevious moves the cursor to the immediate preceding record in the RecordSet.

Be careful with these navigation methods. If you call the MovePrevious method and you are already at the first record in the RecordSet, the cursor will move to an area called the BOF (Beginning of File) and the BOF property of the RecordSet will be set to True. If the MovePrevious method is called again (while the BOF property is True) a DAO Error will be generated. Likewise, if the cursor is on the last record in the RecordSet and you call the MoveNext method; the cursor will move to an area called the EOF (End of File) and the EOF property of the RecordSet will be set to True. Calling the MoveNext method again, (while the EOF property is True) will generate a DAO Error. Your code should be written so as to prevent the generation of DAO Errors. It is a good idea to check the cursor position before calling any of the navigation methods.

Referring to Fields in a RecordSet

To refer to a Field Object in a RecordSet use one of the following syntax forms:

Fields(0)

Fields("Name")

Fields![Name]

Must use the third syntax if field name has a space in it.

To reference fields in a RecordSet you must explicitly copy data from RecordSet to textboxes, and from textboxes back to the RecordSet.

For example:

TxtEmployeeID.value=rsRecordSet ! [FieldName]

reads a field in the RecordSet and stores it in textbox TxtEmployeeID.

Remember that upon program start-up, the RecordSet's current record pointer references the first record in the RecordSet. This record should be loaded into textboxes on the Userform. Since displaying records happens frequently in a program, a Sub procedure should be written to handle this task.

Common RecordSet Tasks

The three most common RecordSet tasks are: Editing, Adding, and Deleting records of the DataBase. Dynaset

RecordSets and Table RecordSets can be modified. A Snapshot RecordSet is Read-Only and cannot be modified.

Editing Records

To Edit a record of the DataBase, call the Edit method of the RecordSet, reference the record you want to change, and then call the Update method of the RecordSet. For Example:

rsRecordSet.Edit

rsRecordSet![fldEmployeeID]=txtEmployeeID.Value

rsRecordSet.Update

Adding Records

To Add a new record to the DataBase, call the AddNew method of the RecordSet, move the information from the textbox to the RecordSet with an assignment statement, and then call the Update method of the RecordSet. For Example:

rsRecordSet.AddNew

rsRecordSet![fieldname] = textbox.value

rsRecordSet.Update

Deleting Records

To delete a record from the DataBase, navigate to the record you want to delete and call the delete method of the RecordSet. Then call the Update method of the RecordSet. Finally call the movenext method of the RecordSet so user does not see a blank record. For Example:

rsRecordSet.Delete

rsRecordSet.Update

rsRecordSet.MoveNext

469

Searching for Specific Records

To find a specific record in a Table-type RecordSet, first set the current index with the index property and then use the Seek Method.

The Seek Method locates the record in an indexed table-type RecordSet Object that satisfies the specified criteria for the current index and makes that record the current record (works in   Microsoft Jet Workspaces only). See following syntax:

recordset.Seek comparsion, key1, key2,.....key13

Recordset	**An object variable referencing an existing RecordSet Object that has a defined index as specified by the RecordSet Object's index property.**
Comparsion	**One of the following string expressions: <,<=,=,>=, or >.**
Key1, key2,...key13	**One or more values corresponding to fields in the RecordSet Objects current index, as specified by its index property setting. You may use up to 13 key arguments.**

If the search fails, then the recordset's nomatch property is set to true and the current record is undefined. Use the bookmark property to return to the record that was current before the search was initiated.

To locate a record in a Dynaset or snapshot type recordset that satisfies a specific condition that is not covered by existing indexes, use one of the find methods (findfirst, findnext, findprevious, findlast).

Writing SQL (Structured Query Language) Statements

In the late 1970's IBM developed a powerful database manipulation language called SQL. It was standardized by the ANSI in 1986. The 1986 version of SQL ships with Visual Basic. SQL consists of two parts: Data Definition Language (DDL) and Data Manipulation Language.

The Data Definition Language consists of statements that change the structure of a DataBase. The Data Manipulation Language consists of statements that Add, Change, and delete records in a DataBase table or query. Data Definition Language activities are beyond the scope of this book.

Data Manipulation Language

The Data Manipulation Language can be grouped into two types of Queries:

♦ Select Query – returns records from a DataBase and stores them in a RecordSet Object as a result of a Select statement.

♦ Action Query – performs an action on a DabaBase table or query but does not return any records (e.g. Add, Update, Delete).

DML Statements

SELECT	**Retrieves one or more rows from a database table or query.**
INSERT	**Inserts rows (i.e. records) into a database table.**
UPDATE	**Changes (edits) contents of one or more existing columns (fields).**
DELETE	**Removes one or more rows (records) from a database table.**

By convention DML statements are written in capital letters.

Insert database records

Use the following syntax to insert a record into a database table:

INSERT into Target (field1 [, field2][, fieldn])

Values (Value1 [, value2][,value n])

Target	**Name of the table or query where records will be added.**
Field	**Each field in the record where information will be added.**
Value	**Value for each field to be added. Number of fields and values must be the same. Commas separate each field and each value. Text data are enclosed by single quotation marks. Numbers are not.**

For example:

INSERT INTO tblPayroll (fldEmployeeID, fldHrsWorked, fldDatepaid)

Values ('A32148', 40, #2/29/00#)

The above statement is not a valid VBA statement. It is incomplete. We will fix this problem later in the chapter.

If you do not specify a field and corresponding value for a field, a Null value is inserted for the missing field. If the number of fields does not match the number of values, a run-time error is generated.

To complete the above INSERT statement and all other action queries, you must call the Execute Method. See the following syntax.

Object.Execute Source [, Options]

Execute Method:

Object	Object is currently defined Database Object.
Source	String containing the SQL statement or the name property of a

QueryDef Object.

Options   Optional. Argument contains
                           constants to determine
                           characteristics of the statement. See
                           VBA on-line help.

For Example:

**dB.Execute "INSERT INTO tblPayroll" &
"(fldEmployeeID)**

     Values ('A123467')"

Store <u>INSERT</u> statement in a string (Concatenate
each part of the INSERT statement together). Text should be
enclosed in single quotation marks, dates should be enclosed
in pound (#) signs, and numbers stand alone. See the
following:

Dim strSQL as String

StrSQL = "INSERT INTO tblPayroll "

    **& "(fldEmployeeID,fldHrsWorked,fldDatePaid)
"**

    **& " Values "&"(" ' "& strEmployeeID &" ' "& ",
"& " sngHoursworked & "," & "#" & datepaid &"#"
&")"**

Or you can use multiple assignment statements.
Because the expression shown above can easily be coded
incorrectly, I usually use the intermediate window to test the
correctness of the string expression.

To complete the above operation, use the EXECUTE
statement, as follows:

dB.Execute strSQL

<u>Update database records</u>

The UPDATE statement is used to change the contents of one or more rows (records) from one or more fields in a table or query.

Syntax for UPDATE Statement:

UPDATE tableName

Set FieldName = NewValue , [FieldName = NewValue]

TableName	**Name of existing table or query**
FieldName	**Field from the table or query specified by the tableName.**
NewValue	**Can be a literal value or expression.**

For Example:

StrSQL = "UPDATE tblPayroll " & "Set fldLastName = ' Smith' " & _

"WHERE fldEmployeeID = 'A23456' "

dB.Execute StrSQL

The above statements update the field named "fldLastName" in the table named "tblPayroll". The value is set to "Smith". The "WHERE" clause ensures that the program updates only the record having an EmployeeID of A23456.

Unlike the INSERT statement, the UPDATE statement operates on many rows (records) rather than on a single row (record).

Using the Where Clause

WHERE conditionList

Condition list has the following syntax:

FieldName Operator Value

FieldName	**Field from the table or query used in the select statement**
Operator	**Works like an operator in an If-statement condition, eg. >,<, =,<>,>=, <=**
Value	**Can be variable, a property, or a literal value. If it is a date, you must enclose in pound signs (#), if it is a string, enclose in single quotation marks. Multiple conditions can be concatenated using the "AND" and "OR" operators.**

Removing database records with the DELETE statement:

With the DELETE statement you can remove one or more records from a table. Syntax follows:

DELETE *

>**FROM tableExpression**

>**WHERE criteria**

 For Example:

DELETE * FROM tblPayroll WHERE fldDatePaid = #3/26/99#

Or a more complete example:

Dim StrSQL AS String

Dim StrDatePaid AS String

StrDatePaid = inputbox ("Enter date paid","PayRoll", Date)

StrSQL = "DELETE * FROM tblPayroll" & "WHERE fldDatePaid = _ "& "#" & "strDatePaid " &"#"

dB.Execute strSQL

Selecting records from the database with the SELECT statement

The SELECT statement is used to retrieve a set of records from a database. Its syntax follows:

SELECT * FROM tableExpession

The asterisk (*) indicates that every field in the table should be selected. "TableExpression" is an existing table or query name preceded by the Keyword "FROM". For Example:

*SELECT * FROM QryEmployeesPayroll*

You must enclose the SELECT statement in a string variable just like the format for other SQL statements. Don't use the Execute method with SELECT statement. The SELECT statement string is used as an argument in the OpenRecordSet method.

Write the SELECT statement so that it stores each individual clause in a separate string variable then concatenate them into one string variable containing the entire SELECT statement. You will need a variable to store the entire SELECT statement, another to store the FROM clause, and another to hold the individual Fields selected by the user. Additionally, you will need a local Object variable to store the recordSet that will be opened when the program calls the OpenRecordSet method. Use the string variable containing the SELECT statement as the argument for the OpenRecordSet method. For Example:

Sub cmdSelect( )

Dim strSQL as String

Dim strFROM as String

Dim strFields as String

Dim rsRecordSet as RecordSet

StrFields =" * "

StrFROM = "FROM QryEmployeePayroll"

StrSQL= "SELECT" & strFields & strFROM

Set rsRecordSet = dB.OpenRecordSet (strSQL)

End Sub

Order SELECT statement syntax

SELECT * FROM tableExpression

WHERE [conditionlist]

[ORDER BY] field1 [ASC|DESC], field2 [ASC|DESC]

The above SELECT statement retrieves all records from a table that meets a criteria and sorts on field1 in either ascending order or descending order, then further sorts on field2 in either ascending order or descending order. Sort order default is ascending.

Select individual fields from a table or query

SELECT table.field1 [AS Alias1], table.field2 [As Alias2]

FROM tableExpression

WHERE conditionlist

Use keyword Alias if you want column headers to be different from original field names.

JOIN statements

With JOIN statements you can establish relationships between two tables within a query. There are three types of JOIN statements that can be used in a query.

♦ **INNER JOIN:** Used to join records from two tables whenever there are matching values in the specified field in each table. For Example:

Select Field1,Field2 FROM Table1

> INNER JOIN Table2 On
> Table1.field1=Table2.field2

♦ **LEFT JOIN:** Includes all of the records from the first table (to the left of the JOIN statement) and all of the matching records from the second table. (Records match when they have equal values in the specified fields). For Example:

The following query selects all records from the paytransactions table and from the employee table all records that have a matching value in the employeeID field of both tables.

SELECT paytransactions.*, employee.* FROM paytransactions

> LEFT JOIN employee on
> paytransactions.employeeID = employee.employeeID

♦ **RIGHT JOIN:** Includes all of the records from the second table (to the right of the JOIN statement) and all of the matching records from the first table. (Records match when they have equal values in the specified fields.)

The following query selects from the employee table all fields for all records and from the paytransactions table all fields of records that have a matching value in the employeeID field of both tables.

SELECT paytransactions.* ,employee.* FROM paytransactions

> RIGHT JOIN employee on
> paytransactions.employeeID = employee.employeeID

OK that's enough. Entire books are written on the SQL language and more information is available in VBA on-line help. In fact, entire books have been written on using VB with databases. This chapter should be considered a brief overview of the subject.

Let's demonstrate some simple data base concepts in an actual program. I had to tackle this program in a VB programming class. [Programming with Visual Basic 6.0, An Object-Oriented Approach, Michael Ekedahl and William Newman, Course Technology, Cambridge MA, 1999, Page 433.] It shows you how to open a database and how to edit the database using the Data Manipulation Language statement "UPDATE". Also demonstrated is how to use frames and option button controls. The program consists of two forms. One form is used to collect the changes in price of steel for a country, and one form is used to display the prices of steel for a country.

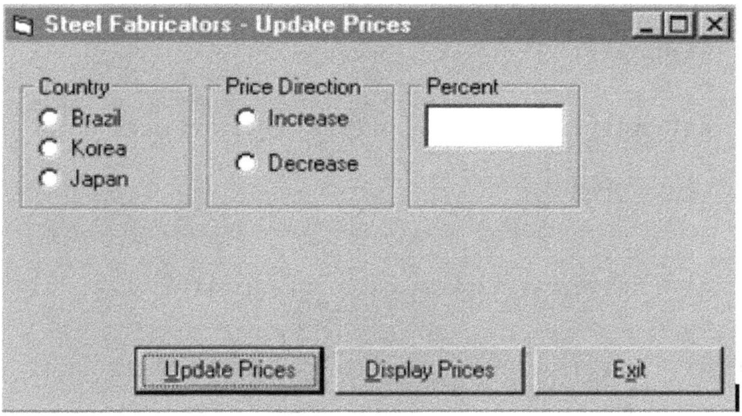

Figure 29.3

A country is selected, then the price direction is selected; both activities are handled by selecting option buttons contained in a frame. Next the percentage change is entered into a text box. The command button "Update Prices" is clicked to execute the price change and the command button "Display Prices" is clicked to show prices of steel for each of the three countries shown above.

Clicking the "Display Prices" command button causes your screen to appear as follows:

479

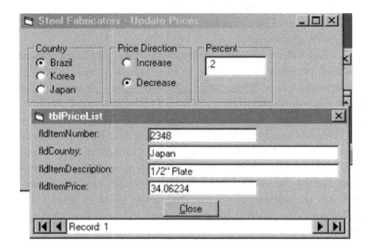

Figure 29.4

Following is the code behind the "Update Prices" form:

Option Explicit

'***

'Steel Fabricators Program. Declare public variables

'***

Public dbCurrent As Database   'Declare database object

Public CountryIndex As Integer   'use in option button
country

Public DirectionIndex As Integer   'use in option button
direction

Public strSQL As String

'***'Co
de for the "Display Prices" command button

'***

Private Sub cmdDisplay_Click()

   frmtblPriceList.Show vbModal

End Sub

'***

```
'Code for the "Exit" command button
'*****************************************************
Private Sub cmdExit_Click()
    End
End Sub
'*****************************************************
'Code for the "UpDate Prices" command button
'*****************************************************
Private Sub cmdUpdate_Click()
    Dim strCountry As String, sngPriceChange As Single
'Determine which option button is selected and store in variable
    'strCountry.
If optCountry(0).Value = True Then
        strCountry = optCountry(0).Caption
        ElseIf optCountry(1) = True Then
        strCountry = optCountry(1).Caption
        Else
        strCountry = optCountry(2).Caption
        End If
    'Store price change in variable sngPriceChange. If option button
    'increase is selected, then number is positive. If option button
    'decrease is selected, then number is negative (multiply by -1 to make number negative. )
If optDirection(0).Value = True Then
            'increase option button selected
        sngPriceChange = Val(txtPercent.Text)
    Else
    'decrease option button selected
```

481

```
        sngPriceChange = Val(txtPercent.Text) * -1
```

End If

'Update field fldItemPrice in table tblPriceList, Criteria-
"Where field named is the same as the selected Country. Price
stored in fldItemPrice should be increased or decreased by
amount specified by user.

```
strSQL = "UPDATE tblPriceList " _

    & "SET fldItemPrice = flditemprice + (flditemprice * '
& sngPriceChange & ")" _

    & " WHERE fldCountry = " & """" & strCountry & """"



    dbCurrent.Execute strSQL


End Sub
```

'***

'Open database as form loads

'***

```
Private Sub Form_Load()

    Set dbCurrent =
OpenDatabase("A:\homework\steel.mdb")

    End Sub
```

SUMMARY

In this chapter we discussed how to retrieve records
from a database and how to add, update, and delete records in
a database. We mentioned that Microsoft Excel supports the
Open Database Connectivity Standard (ODBC) and that it can
manipulate any ODBC - compliant database.

Data Access Objects are used to manipulate databases
and a reference to Microsoft Jet DAO 3.6 must be established
to include databases in your projects. The DAO hierarchy was
discussed and we examined many of the DAO objects and
collections contained therein.

We introduced the powerful database language
created by IBM (SQL) and gave a few examples of its use.
Database programming is a difficult subject and you are not
expected to understand it with this brief overview. I

recommend that you make use of the VBA on-line help and read a couple of books on database design.

CHAPTER 30
OBJECT ORIENTED PROGRAMMING

CREATING CLASSES

As we have said before, Visual Basic for Applications is an object oriented programming language. In earlier chapters, we manipulated objects to accomplish programming tasks. In this chapter we will show you how to create custom objects with their own properties, events, and methods.

An Object is just another word for Class. Encapsulation is a requirement of an object oriented programming language. Encapsulation means that an object's data, events, and methods are all grouped together. A class module encapsulates related functions into a portable, self-contained object. You should think of a class module as a template for objects you create.

To create a class module select from the Visual Basic Editor: Insert, Class Module. Notice that the class module looks like a standard module. (See Figure 30.1)

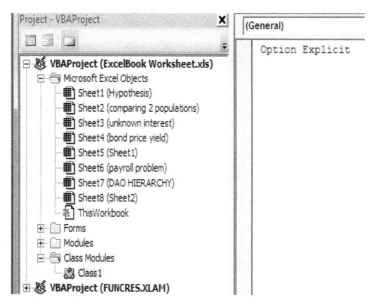

Figure 30.1

The class module has only one property ("Name "). The name is used in code to refer to the custom object. Change this property to something that describes the nature of the object. For example, the text box class is called textbox and the first instance of the textbox drawn on a userform has the name textbox1.

You can call the custom object's properties, events, and methods from the rest of your code, just like you would any other standard Visual Basic object.

ADDING PROPERTIES AND METHODS TO THE CUSTOM CLASS

The easiest way to add a property to a custom object is to declare a public variable in the General Declarations section of a class module. The naming convention for Properties and Methods in a class module is a little different than the naming convention for standard variables. Following are the rules for naming Properties and Methods in a class module:

♦ Use whole words, first letter of each word should be capitalized.

♦ If the name of a property or method seems too long, use first syllable of the word rather than other abbreviations.

♦ Use plural names for collections.

♦ When creating properties, use nouns such as CarMake.

♦ When creating methods, create the method's name using a verb for the first word, followed by a noun, such as CalculateFica.

♦ The following are reserved Keywords and cannot be used as property or method names: QueryInterface, AddRef, GetTypeInfoCount, GetTypeInfo, GetIDsOfNames, or Invoke.[Ekedahl and Newman, page 619]

For example, the code in Figure 30.2 creates properties for an employee class:

485

```
(General)                                                      ▼

    Option Explicit

    Public FirstName As String
    Public LastName As String
    Public SocSecNo As String
    Public Address As String
    Public wages As Single
    Public hiredate As Date
    Public exemptions As Integer
```

Figure 30.2

To create methods for a class, place Public
Procedures in the class module. If you want a method to
return a value, use a Function Procedure rather than a Sub
Procedure. The code to create a method for the employee
class that calculates FICA tax follows.

```
Public Function FICA()
    FICA = (wages - (84 * exemptions)) * 0.0765
End Function
```

Figure 30.3

Remember that you have to instantiate an object
before you can use it. First declare an object based on the
class, then instantiate the object using a Set statement. For
example:

In the General Declarations section of a form put the
following statement:

Dim hourlyemployee as Employee

then in a procedure put the following statement:

Set hourlyemployee = New Employee

Let's use our newly created class in a userform to
calculate FICA tax for an employee.

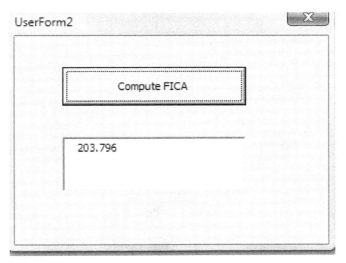

UserForm2

Compute FICA

203.796

Figure 30.4

The code to calculate FICA is attached to a command button "Compute FICA".

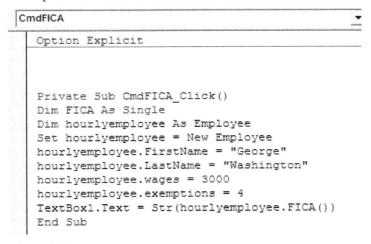

CmdFICA

```
Option Explicit


Private Sub CmdFICA_Click()
Dim FICA As Single
Dim hourlyemployee As Employee
Set hourlyemployee = New Employee
hourlyemployee.FirstName = "George"
hourlyemployee.LastName = "Washington"
hourlyemployee.wages = 3000
hourlyemployee.exemptions = 4
TextBox1.Text = Str(hourlyemployee.FICA())
End Sub
```

Figure 30.5

After a class is created, it is added to the Object Browser of your project and VBA will remind you how to use the class. Typing the object name followed by the dot operator (.) invokes a window containing all the properties and methods for the custom object. (See Figure 30.6)

487

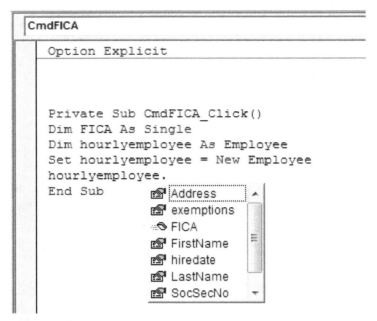

```
CmdFICA

Option Explicit


Private Sub CmdFICA_Click()
Dim FICA As Single
Dim hourlyemployee As Employee
Set hourlyemployee = New Employee
hourlyemployee.
End Sub
```

Figure 30.6

Property Procedures

Using Public variables to implement properties for a custom object is easy but this technique has some disadvantages:

♦ You can't create properties that are read-only or write-only. Public variables are always accessible.

♦ You can't track changes to public variables.

♦ You can't manipulate the value when the public variable is set (such as hiding an object when its visible property is set to False).

♦ You can't validate what goes into public variables.

Visual Basic for Applications provides a way to overcome the disadvantages listed above. We will use Property Procedures in the class module to create publicly accessible properties of a custom object. The dialog box we used to insert a procedure into a standard module can also be used to insert a property procedure into a class module. Or you can type in the header of the Property Procedure and VBA will add the ending wrapper.

When you use the "Add Procedure" dialog box, VBA will give you a pair of matched procedures (Property Let and Property Get). [See Figure 30.7] If you want a property to be read-only, use only the Property Get Procedure. If you want the property to be write-only, use only the Property Let Procedure. And if you want the property to be both read-write, use both Procedures.

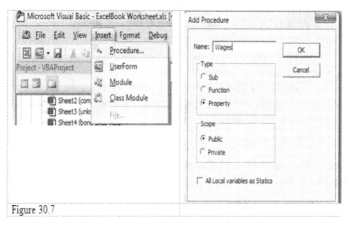

Figure 30.7

Notice that the Property procedure's Scope is Public by default. The data type of the variables in the procedures is variant by default. Change the data type to reflect the type of variable to be used in your Procedure or Function.

```
Public Property Get Wages() As Variant

End Property


Public Property Let Wages(ByVal vNewValue As Variant)

End Property
```

Figure 30.8

Hiding Data in a Class Module

To control how other programmers manipulate the class interface (class interface is the properties and methods of a class), we declare the member variables (variables used to hold data) of the class as Private. Then we can use Property Get and Property Let Procedures to control object

489

manipulation. This is called <u>Data Hiding</u>. By convention member variables should begin with the prefix "m_".

Creating Property Procedures in Code

While Property Procedures look like Sub Procedures and Function Procedures declared in a Standard Module, you do not explicitly call them as you do Sub and Function Procedures. Property Procedures execute when you write or read the property. Also the name of the Property Procedure becomes the name of the Object Property. For example, in our Property Procedure template wrapper above, "Property Get Wages ()", the property defined here for our "Employee" class is "Wages". If the Property is used to set a reference to an Object variable, use a <u>"Property Set "</u> Procedure instead of a Property Let Procedure.

Following is the syntax for the Property Get Procedure:

[Public | Private | Static] Property Get Name [(Argument list)] [As type]

> **[statements]**
>
> **[Name = Expression]**
>
> **[Exit Property]**
>
> **[statements]**
>
> **[Name = Expression]**

Exit Property

Private | Private | Static	Determines the scope of the Property Procedure. <u>Public</u>- visible to all other Procedures in all other modules. <u>Private</u>- visible only to the Procedures in the module where it was declared. <u>Static</u>- value of the local variables declared in the Property Procedure will be preserved between calls to the procedure.
Name	Defines the name of the property and follows standard naming convention for variable names.

Argument list	Allows arguments to be passed to the Procedure, when necessary, to set the Procedure.
Type	Data type returned by the Property Procedure.
Statements	Any number of statements may be executed when the property is set.
Name = Expression	Expression is the name of the Private variable declared in the General Declarations section of the Class Module to hold the value of the property.
Exit Property	Allows exit from Property Procedure before the last statement in the procedure executes.
End Property	Designates the end of the Property Procedure.

The Property Get Procedure automatically executes whenever code is used to retrieve (read) the value of the property. Since it returns a value, the Property Get Procedure behaves like a Function Procedure. Following is an example of a Property Get Procedure.

Public Property Get name ( ) AS Data Type

Name = m_variableName

End Property

To make a property read-only, you could omit any code in the Property Let Procedure. Then if the programmer tried to set the property, nothing would happen. But the programmer would not know that nothing happened. A better solution is to eliminate the Property Let Procedure from the class module. Then when a programmer tries to set the value of a property (a write function), and a Property Let Procedure does not exist, an error will be generated and Visual Basic will send a Error Message to the programmer with notification that you cannot write to a read-only property.

491

The Property Let Procedure syntax is similar to the Property Get Procedure, except that the Property Let Procedure takes one more argument than the corresponding Property Get Procedure. And the final argument in the Property Let Procedure must be of the same data type as the return value of the Property Get Procedure. Both the Property Let procedure and the Property Get procedure must be of the same data type. An example of a Property Let Procedure follows:

Public Property Let Name (ByVal vNewvalue as Data type)

    m_variableName = vNewValue

    [statements]

End Property

The argument "vNewvalue" holds the data that is written to (stored in) the property. This value is assigned to our private member variable and will be used when a read activity occurs.

Initialize And Terminate Events

Class modules have two built-in events. The Initialize event executes as the class is instantiated, and the Terminate event executes just before the class goes out of scope or is destroyed explicitly with the "set objectname = nothing" statement. Use the Initialize event to establish a connection to a database and to initialize variables used in the class. Use the Terminate event to perform the class's cleanup tasks, for example closing a recordSet used by the class.

For example:

Private Sub Class_Initialize( )

    Dim db as database

    Set db = OpenDataBase ("A:\ Payroll.mdb")

End Sub

Private Sub Class_Terminate( )

    rstEmployee.Close

    Set rstEmployee = Nothing

End Sub

User – Defined Events

In addition to creating custom properties and methods for a custom Object, you can also define custom events to communicate changes of properties, errors, and the progress of lengthy operations. Statements for triggering user-defined events are placed in the class module and the event is dealt with in the form code. For example if we have an event named UDE which has arguments arg1, arg2, arg3, we would place the following statement in the General Declarations section of a class module:

Public Event UDE (arg1,arg2,arg3)

and in the locations in the class module where the event should be triggered, we would place the following code:

RaiseEvent UDE (arg1,arg2, arg3)

For example, in the form module, create an instance of the class (call it firstObject) with the following statement:

Private WithEvents firstObject As CclassName

The above statement enables the program to respond to the user-defined event.

The template of an event procedure for firstObject will be:

Private Sub firstObject_UDE (arg1, arg2, arg3)

    statements

End Sub

Using Run-Time Errors to Validate Property Input

One of the reasons we use Property Procedures rather than Public variables to create properties for our custom Object, is our ability to write code within Property Procedures to communicate to the user the receipt of invalid data by the Object. We use the <u>Err Object</u> with the <u>Raise Method</u> to generate custom run – time errors. When a run – time error occurs, the properties of the Err Object provide information that uniquely identifies the error and also provides information that can be used to handle it. See the following syntax:

Err.Raise number [,source][, description][, helpfile][, helpcontext]

Number	Required. Long integer that identifies the error. Both Visual Basic Errors and user-defined errors are in the range of 0 - 65,535. When setting the Number property to your own error code in a class module, add your error code number to the vbObjectError constant. For example to generate the error number 1158, assign vbObjectError + 1158 to the Number property.
Source	Optional. String expression naming the object or application that generated the error. When setting this property, for an object, use the form *project. class*. If source is not specified, the programmatic ID of the current Visual Basic project is used.
Description	Optional. String expression describing the error. If unspecified, the value in Number is examined. If error can be mapped to a Visual Basic run-time error code, then the string that would be returned by the Error Function is used as Description. If there is no Visual Basic error corresponding to Number, then the "Application-defined or object-defined error" message is used.
Helpfile	Optional. The fully qualified path to the Microsoft Windows Help file in which help on this error can be found. If unspecified, Visual Basic uses the fully qualified drive, path, and file name of the Visual Basic Help file.
Helpcontext	Optional. The context ID identifying a topic within helpfile that provides help for the error. If omitted, the Visual Basic Help file context ID for the error corresponding to the Number property is used, if it exists.

In the following example we use the Err object and the Raise method to validate data stored in our CarType property. We only want to allow specific GM cars to be written into our CarType.

Public Property Let CarType (ByVal vNewvalue as String)

Select Case vNewValue

Case Corvette, Impala, Seville, Olds98, Catera, _

GrandAM, Bonneville

Case Else

Err.Raise vbObjectError+27,,"Invalid Car Type"

End Select

m_CarModel=vNewValue

End Property

Creating a Collection

In earlier chapters we used arrays to store Object references and we showed you how to manage the size of an array with the ReDim Preserve statement. We had to specifically keep track of the number of elements in the array and we had to increase the array size each time we added an element to it. A more efficient way to store Object references is to use a collection Object. Well, that's not completely correct. While a collection requires less code to manage, it does use more memory resources. Collections use variant data types to store Object references. Remember that a variant consumes 16 bytes of memory at a minimum for each Object reference in the collection.

A collection name should always be plural and should match the name of the Object it references. For example a collection of car objects should be named "Cars". Remember that some earlier collections we discussed were zero based and some were one based. All collections you create will be one based (i.e. the index starts at one (1)). The following statement is used to create a collection:

Public collectionName As New Collection

The collection Object supports one (1) property and three methods.

<u>Collection Object Attributes</u>

Count Property:	Read-Only. Returns a <u>long integer</u> containing the total number of Objects referenced in the collection.
Add method:	Adds an item (Object reference) to the collection.
Item method:	Returns a specific item (Object reference) from a collection Object through either a string <u>Key</u> or a numeric index.
Remove method:	Removes an item (Object reference) from a collection Object.

The process of adding and deleting Object references from a collection is very similar to adding and removing items from a list box at run – time.

Add items to a collection

Use the following syntax to add an item to a collection:

Object. Add item [, key] [, before | after]

Object	Required. Name of a Collection Object.
Item	Required. Argument is the name of the object reference to be added to the collection.
Key	Optional. Argument must be a unique string <u>key</u> that can be used instead of a positional numeric index to reference an item in the collection.
Before | After	Optional. Argument before or after is an <u>integer or string</u> specifying the relative position of the new item in the collection. You can specify a before position or an after position, but not both. The item to be added is placed in the collection before or after the item identified by the argument. If an integer, the before or after

argument must be a number from one (1) to the value of the collection's Count property. If a String, the before or after argument must correspond to the string key specified when the relevant item was added to the collection. To specify which argument you are using, use the following syntax:

before: = *value*

or

after: = *value*

Following example demonstrates how to add an object to a collection with a string key identified.

Dim CurrentCar as New Car

Cars.Add CurrentCar "Corvette"

We assume here that CurrentCar is a valid instance of a Car Object. A reference to this object is added to the Cars Collection having a string key of "Corvette". Before you can add a Car object to the collection, you must create an instance of the object and store a reference to the object inside an object variable. After the Object and reference to it exist, you must set the Object's properties. Only then can the object be added to the collection.

Since the string key for each object in the collection must be unique, you must ensure that the user does not enter duplicate strings in the collection for an object. Visual Basic will generate a run-time error if user tries to enter a duplicate key. You can write an error handler to trap this error and communicate the error status to the user. For example in a click event of a command button used to add objects to the collection, you could enter the following code:

Private Sub cmdAdd_( )

On Error GoTo ErrorHandler

Statements

Exit Sub

ErrorHandler:

MsgBox "Cannot add. Object KeyString already _

    exists. ", vbOKOnly, "Error"

End Sub

    If a duplicate string key is detected, the error handler executes and displays a message box advising the user that the Object cannot be added because it already exists.

Remove items from a collection

Use the following syntax to remove an item from a collection:

Object. Remove index

Object	Required. Name of a Collection Object.
Remove	Required. Keyword indicating the method operation for the collection object which deletes an item from the collection..
Index	Required. Argument is an expression that specifies the position of an item in the collection. Index can consist of a number from one (1) to the value of the collection's Count property (numeric index) or a string expression (string key). If the value provided for the index does not match an existing member of the collection, a run-time error will occur.

For example the following statement:

Cars.Remove "Corvette"

removes the object having a string key of "Corvette" from the Cars collection.

Finding items in a Collection

    Use the <u>item method</u> to locate an item in a collection. Search is made using a numeric index or a string key. See the following syntax:

Object. item(index)

Item	Returns a reference to a specific member in the collection.
Object	Must be a valid instance of a collection object.
Index	Numeric index or string key

For example:

Dim CurrentCar as Car

Set CurrentCar = Cars . Item(1)

Or

Set CurrentCar= Cars. Item ("Corvette")

Cars is assumed to be a collection containing references to Car objects. First statement above declares the object variable "CurrentCar" so that it can reference a Car object. The second and third statement following the declaration statement shows the numeric method of access and the string method of access. After item in collection is retrieved, it can be assigned to a label, textbox, or other output object.

SUMMARY

Programming class objects is advanced programming. You will probably have to consult VBA on-line help to get a good understanding of this subject. However in this chapter, we did show you the basics of creating a class (Object) with its own custom properties and methods.

Objects are created in the Class Module. From the Visual Basic Editor, select Insert, Class Module to invoke the class module. A class has only one property, Name. Change the Name property to something descriptive of the Object's function. Create properties for the Object by declaring Public variables in the General Declarations section of the Class Module or by using Property Procedures. Methods of an Object are created by placing Public Sub Procedures and or Public Functions in a class module.

Using Property procedures to implement Object properties has advantages over implementing Object properties with Public variables.

You can create user-defined collections to hold references to multiple objects. Collections are easier to

499

program than dynamic arrays but they use more memory resources. Collection Objects have one property (count) and three methods: Add, Item, and Remove. The Add and Remove methods are similar to the listbox object's Additem, and Removeitem methods.

CHAPTER 31
DISTRIBUTING VBA APPLICATION

DISTRIBUTING VBA APPLICATIONS

After creating a VBA application, sometimes you have to pass it to other users. I recommend a combination of an Microsoft Excel Add-in and other workbooks as a complete application. Add-ins have special attributes that make them ideal for distributing applications.

Add-in code is fully compiled so it runs faster than normal workbooks. Password protected Code modules and Userforms can not be changed by the user. The workbook window is hidden so you can hide lists and calculations from the user. And the user cannot bypass automatic events (i.e. Workbook_Open ()) by holding down the Shift key. Add-ins have .XLA extensions to distinguish them from normal workbook files.

FOLLOWING IS HOW WE CREATE AND DISTRIBUTE AN ADD-IN

♦ Compile the project. Select Compile VBA project from the Debug menu in the Visual Basic Editor.

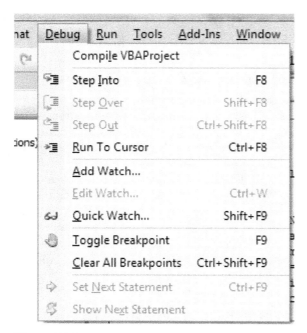

Figure 31.1

♦ Protect the project from viewing by using the lock project for viewing checkbox on the protection tab of the VBA Project Properties dialog box. Select Tools, VBAProject Properties....

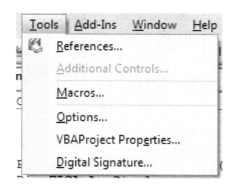

Figure 31.2

and then enter a case-sensitive password in the indicated text box.

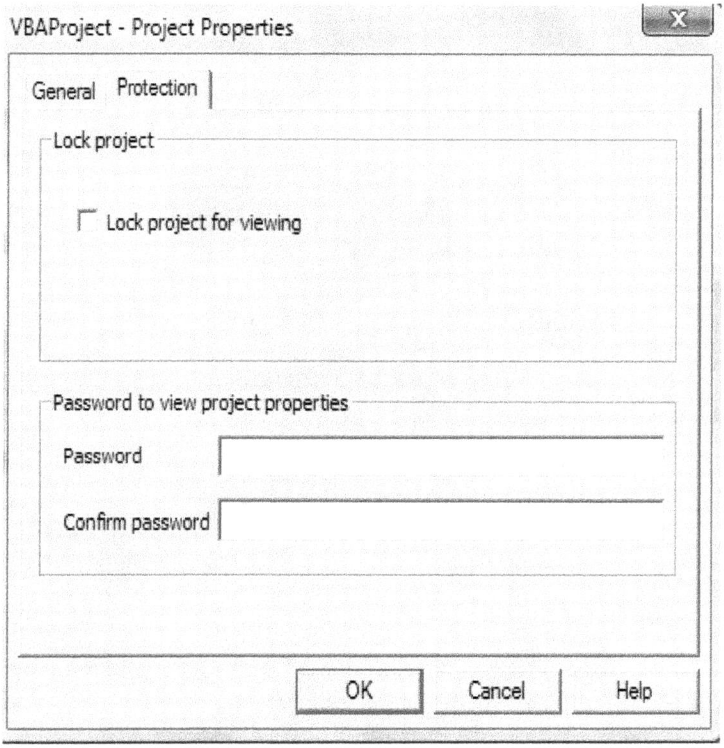

Figure 31.3

After supplying a password, user will not be able to view the objects in the project without entering the password. Return to main Excel screen (Alt+F4)

♦ Select File, <u>Save As,</u> and "Save As dialog box" appears. Choose "Excel Add-In" and hit "Save".

Figure 31.4

It is better to distribute VBA applications in multiple files rather than in a single file. However, the files and references to the Add-in should be saved in the same folder on the intended user's hard drive.

The End

505

507

509

513

www.ingramcontent.com/pod-product-compliance
Lightning Source LLC
Chambersburg PA
CBHW071354050326
40689CB00010B/1645